INVENTING BENJY

INVENTING BENJY

William Faulkner's Most Splendid Creative Leap

Frédérique Spill

Translated from French by Arby Gharibian

Foreword by Taylor Hagood

University Press of Mississippi / Jackson

www.upress.state.ms.us

The University Press of Mississippi is a member
of the Association of University Presses.

Any discriminatory or derogatory language or hate speech
regarding race, ethnicity, religion, sex, gender, class, national origin,
age, or disability that has been retained or appears in elided form
is in no way an endorsement of the use of such language
outside a scholarly context.

Original publication in French. *L'Idiotie dans l'oeuvre de William Faulkner*
(Presses Universitaires de la Sorbonne Nouvelle, 2009)

Translation copyright © 2024 by Frédérique Spill
All rights reserved

∞

Library of Congress Cataloging-in-Publication Data

Names: Spill, Frédérique, author. | Gharibian, Arby, translator. |
Hagood, Taylor, 1975– writer of foreword.
Title: Inventing Benjy : William Faulkner's most splendid creative leap /
Frédérique Spill, Arby Gharibian, Taylor Hagood.
Other titles: L'Idiotie dans l'œuvre de Faulkner. English
Description: Jackson : University Press of Mississippi, 2024. |
"Originally published in 2009 by Presses de la Sorbonne
Nouvelle as 'L'Idiotie dans l'œuvre de Faulkner,' this translation brings the book to
English-language readers for the first time" : University Press of Mississippi website. |
Includes bibliographical references and index.
Identifiers: LCCN 2023048024 (print) | LCCN 2023048025 (ebook) |
ISBN 9781496849007 (hardback) | ISBN 9781496849014 (trade paperback) |
ISBN 9781496849021 (epub) | ISBN 9781496849038 (epub) |
ISBN 9781496849045 (pdf) | ISBN 9781496849052 (pdf)
Subjects: LCSH: Faulkner, William, 1897–1962—Criticism and interpretation. |
Faulkner, William, 1897–1962. Sound and the fury. |
Faulkner, William, 1897–1962—Characters—People with mental disabilities. |
Stupidity in literature. | Intellectual disability in literature.
Classification: LCC PS3511.A86 Z9727313 2024 (print) |
LCC PS3511.A86 (ebook) | DDC 813/.52—dc23/eng/20231024
LC record available at https://lccn.loc.gov/2023048024
LC ebook record available at https://lccn.loc.gov/2023048025

British Library Cataloging-in-Publication Data available

For Romain

To André Bleikasten, thank you

CONTENTS

Foreword by Taylor Hagood ix
Introduction to the Translated Edition xiii
Abbreviations xvii
Introduction 3

Part I: Idiosyncrasies of an Idiocy: Disarticulation of Bodies, Disconnecting of Narratives

Chapter 1. Is the Idiot a Monster? 17
Chapter 2. The Flabby Flesh and Flaccid Bodies of Idiots 20
Chapter 3. Inarticulate Voice and Story 31
Chapter 4. Faulknerian Idiotisms: The Mechanisms of Repetition 51
Chapter 5. States of a World in Disintegration 74

Part II: To the Roots of the World: Idiocy and Its Objects

Chapter 6. Idiots Have Blue Eyes 83
Chapter 7. The Idiot Gaze and Its Representations 86
Chapter 8. Idiocy's Fetish Objects: Substitutive Fixations and Logic . . . 109
Chapter 9. The Exacerbation of Sensation 128
Chapter 10. Idiocy, Alcohol, and Other Illicit Substances:
    "A Derangement of All the Senses" 146

Part III: "Trying to Say"

Chapter 11. The Fury of Origins, the Ringing of Sound 155
Chapter 12. The Aesthetics of Idiocy: Writing and Aphasia 160
Chapter 13. The Disorders of Predication
    and the Order of a World: The Idiot Idiom 188
Chapter 14. Trying to Read Faulkner 205

Conclusion: Fiction of Origin and the Origin of Fiction 219

Notes 223
Bibliography 263
Index 273

FOREWORD

In the autumn of 2009, when not teaching or playing soccer in Munich's Englischergarten, I was hard at work writing my book, *Faulkner, Writer of Disability*. The field of disability studies had existed for nearly three decades but only since the turn of the century had it begun to pick up serious traction. I had had the pleasure of attending a plenary lecture by Rosemarie Garland-Thomson in Atlanta in 2005, and she opened massive doors for me, raising multitudes of questions I had never considered before about embodiment, policy, invisible constructs, and literature. As far as Faulkner was concerned, scholars had wrestled with Benjy Compson's disability since the publication of *The Sound and the Fury*, but disability studies raised new ways of approaching him as well as other disabled characters and disabling situations in Faulkner's writing. In my excitement about the field, I had set out on a book-length examination of disability woven in the very fabric of Faulkner's writing.

I was also taking advantage of my time in Europe to take trips on weekends, and one of my first destinations was Paris. On one morning there, after a visit to Jardin du Luxembourg in the golden colors and soft air of the season, I found myself passing the display window of the Presses Sorbonne Nouvelle bookstore. A familiar face on one of the covers caught my eye, and the title drove me inside, pulling euros out of my wallet to make the purchase. The book was *L'Idiotie dans l'oeuvre de Faulkner*, by Frédérique Spill. I hurried out the door excited with my new acquisition, for just the most cursory reading showed me that the author was delving into *l'idiotie* in far deeper ways than had ever been done before. As I read the book on the train back to Munich, I reveled in the deft ways Spill teased out myriad dimensions of the tag applied to Benjy, showing how *l'idiotie* functioned as an actuating factor in Faulkner's imagination.

Spill's study could succeed because of the curious pocket of simultaneous similarity and difference between present-day French and English connotations of "idiocy." An entire book exploring the term and concept would be unthinkable to English or American disability scholars without heavy contextualizing, historicizing, and distancing. Certainly, the unblushing use of the term could only be carried out by a scholar working with it from a distinctly different angle, situation, and language. That said, it had been long established that Faulkner was evoking the specificities of "idiot" as a descriptor of Benjy that were as plugged into the moment of his writing as were ideas of "feeble-mindedness" he applied to Popeye. "Idiot," in the late 1920s, retained its quasi-clinical valence, and even in the early 2000s some older scholars tended to use the term. One of the more memorable moments from graduate school for me was a prominent Faulkner scholar innocently stating, "Benjy's not a moralist, he's an idiot." By the end of the first decade of the twenty-first century, however, the term was embarrassing and uncomfortable for most scholars, and there was impetus to try to identify Benjy's disability as "cognitive" while still acknowledging Faulkner's use of "idiot" and the context of his doing so.

The power of Spill's book lies in its capturing the moment of transition from problematic modes of discussing Benjy to approaches thoroughly grounded in the precepts and cautions of disability studies. Spill's is a kind of pre–disability studies disability studies book. As such, both then and now in translation it accomplishes something Anglophone scholars would have struggled with, which is to bring "idiocy" in its historical cross-cultural and cross-national signifying into deep overt consideration as a topic in itself. That was work that needed to be done, but circumstance had caused the time of doing so to pass in the Anglophone world. In 2009, Spill's book served as a link from the past to the present and future, and in its own way it was confirming the Faulknerian precept of the past not being dead.

And now it is not even past, for here it is translated into English and with a new title, *Inventing Benjy: William Faulkner's Most Splendid Creative Leap*. That title works well, helping to position this book as the unique and absolutely *relevant* creature it is. The question might be raised whether publishing the book in English now makes sense, with disability studies having grown tremendously and significant studies of disability in Faulkner having been published in the intervening years. The answer is "yes" because Spill's book has value beyond its being a representative of prior development in the field. Subsequent work in disability studies and on disability in Faulkner provides context and apparatus that can enable a fresh look at the concept of "idiocy." Now, with the contours of Benjy's disability far more elucidated, returning to that vexed "idiot" concept works in new ways that can navigate the sweating-browed problematics of this term that Faulkner employed and which there is no getting around.

I was immeasurably happy, then, to learn that Spill's book had been translated into English and that the University Press of Mississippi would be publishing it. The richness of Spill's scholarship in this and other works well complements that of Faulkner's writing, and the perspective this volume brings to bear on the subject will enrich the field in entirely new contexts.

Taylor Hagood
West Palm Beach, Florida

INTRODUCTION TO THE TRANSLATED EDITION

The PhD thesis that is behind this book was conducted under the supervision of Professor Christine Savinel at the Sorbonne-Nouvelle University in Paris; it started at the very end of the 1990s as I was teaching French as a teaching assistant at Louisiana State University, while taking classes in American literature and roaming the air-conditioned alleys of the Troy H. Middleton Library. It started as Professor John Law made me read most, if not all, of Faulkner in a single semester as part of the requirements of one of the classes I was then taking. This intense spell of reading, most of which I did on the front porch of a shotgun house on Pericles Street in Baton Rouge, sitting in a battered red leather chair, confirmed my earlier intuition, after reading *Light in August* as part of my undergraduate curriculum at the Sorbonne, that only Faulkner's writing could possibly bring me to muster the time, energy, and determination necessary to complete a PhD program. This is when I began to explore a particular corner of the Middleton Library and to hire friends to help me Xerox one article from the *Faulkner Journal* and from the *Mississippi Quarterly* after the next, as well innumerable chapters from monographs on Faulkner, marveling at all the material available with nothing yet definite in mind beyond a strong partiality for Benjy Compson. I started reading some of these pages then and there, slowly delineating my topic; but most of them were shipped across the Atlantic and were of great help in the following years, while I actually started working on the project that was to become *L'Idiotie dans l'oeuvre de Faulkner*, from 2000 to 2006.

This personal preamble imposed itself to me in order to account for some of the many loopholes in this book, which was recently translated from the original French into English, thanks to the financial help of the University of Picardy–Jules Verne in Amiens, France. Indeed, this book was written at a time when scientific journals were not digitized, books not available through the internet, and interlibrary loans much more complicated and costly than they are now. Hence sources are lacking, all the more so as my research phase roughly ended by 2005. As a result, more than a decade and a half of Faulkner criticism is not represented in the following pages, though I would doubtless have found treasures in books, chapters, and papers published since by Faulkner scholars around the world, some of whom have since welcomed me in the wondrous circle of the Faulkner community. Let this be the occasion for me to acknowledge some of them, who have since become regular companions and sometimes dear friends: Peter Lurie, John T. Matthews, Aurélie Guillain, Jay Watson, Randall Wilhelm, Taylor Hagood, Susan Scott Parrish, Mary Knighton, Michael Zeitlin, Ahmed Honeini, Michał Choiński, and Bernard T. Joy have definitely contributed to developing not only my perception of Faulkner but also my work on him in new directions. Yet, as, partly under their impulsion, I undertook to have *L'Idiotie dans l'oeuvre de Faulkner* translated, I decided to leave it as it was written then. Updating it would have made it an entirely different book, which I neither wanted nor would have been capable of.

Moreover, the project behind the book started at a time when the Modern Language Association did not yet consider disability studies an academic field (this became the case in 2005). Working within French academia, I had still to hear about them when I defended my PhD in the fall of 2006. The approach adopted in this book would not fit in that category anyway since it mainly is poetic, making words, narration, and the writing of sensations its main objects and close reading its leading method, in keeping with the French Faulkner critical tradition. The concept of idiocy as it is developed in this book designates, beyond its ordinary restrictive description of a physical and mental disability, a very singular way of being in the world. The time and attention Faulkner devoted to this condition, which he must have perceived as a way for him to "make it new," resulted in a radical creative gesture. In this context, idiocy refers to the specific condition of they who sense and feel with the utmost intensity without being able to name or voice their sensations and feelings; of they who are irremediably anchored in a timeless present that, to their minds, keeps repeating itself. In this respect, the aim of this book is to examine how Faulkner decided to penetrate the consciousness of individuals who are totally unaware of the mechanisms of their consciousness; how, in the process, he gave a voice to the voiceless, inventing a language some aspects of which would soon merge with his own unmistakable writing style.

As I moved along with the publication process, with the most graceful help of Mary Heath at the University Press of Mississippi, I was forced to admit that my initial French title would need to be amended, which was further confirmed when I first presented a few pages adapted from that book at the annual Faulkner and Yoknapatawpha Conference in Oxford, Mississippi, in July 2022, devoted to Faulkner's modernism. While my paper on Benjy Compson's sensational modernism was received warmly, I was made aware that there are certain words that cannot be used without second thoughts in today's United

States, and "idiot" and "idiocy" appear to be two of them. Hence, out of concern for political correctness, I gave a twist to the English title of the book, placing its focus on Benjy Compson, though he is certainly not its only topic. I hope the new title, which both winks at Faulkner's perception of *The Sound and the Fury* as "his most splendid failure" and at the 1976 English translation of André Bleikasten's groundbreaking study of the novel, keeps some of the original provocativeness without hurting any feelings.

However, I must insist that the reception of that word in the French language is extremely different: it is considered an objective, descriptive word that possibly encompasses several forms of mental disability while precluding the need to identify them in medical terms, which was exactly my initial purpose. In French, though often pejorative when used in everyday life, that word is by no means offensive; its purport and impact have certainly not evolved in the same direction as in the United States. The way the notion of idiocy has been taken up by a number of significant French thinkers in humanities, giving it a singularizing value in keeping with the etymology of the word, will be illustrated through the following pages. From the very beginning of this project, I have never meant to associate Benjy with any determined form of disability or autism, which other critics have found relevant to do, though Faulkner himself simply called Benjy "an idiot" and never suggested any more accurate prognosis regarding his condition. My aim has always been to consider Benjy's singular condition and the perceptive, aesthetic, stylistic, and narrative constraints engendered by his condition as Faulkner's perhaps most fruitful self-imposed creative constraint. Along this line, I have always perceived Benjy Compson's radical otherness as most valuable and Faulkner's immersion within his consciousness as one of his most radical, most beautiful, poetic decisions.

It is a great honor and an immense pleasure for me to experience that book's second birth. I am extremely grateful to the warm welcome of the University Press of Mississippi and, again, to Mary Heath's kindest help. I want to thank my two anonymous reviewers for their precious suggestions and advice. I want to address my warmest thanks to Arby Gharibian for being such a sharp and attentive translator and to the University of Picardy for its unfailing support of my Faulkner projects. A thousand thanks to Taylor Hagood for showing an interest in this book long ago and for accepting to write a foreword to the new translated edition; I could not have hoped for a more consistent, more perfect, tutelage in the United States. Last but not least, I want to thank Solveig Dunkel and Astrid Maes for encouraging me, consciously or not, to go on with this book through their own young and stimulating work on Faulkner in France. Keep the spark alive.

Amiens, December 2022

ABBREVIATIONS

SP	*Soldiers' Pay*
FD	*Flags in the Dust*
SF	*The Sound and the Fury*
AILD	*As I Lay Dying*
S	*Sanctuary*
LA	*Light in August*
AA	*Absalom, Absalom!*
U	*The Unvanquished*
H	*The Hamlet*
T	*The Town*
M	*The Mansion*
EPP	*Early Prose and Poetry*
ŒI	*Œuvres romanesques I*
ŒII	*Œuvres romanesques II*
ŒIII	*Œuvres romanesques III*
FU	*Faulkner in the University* (Gwynn and Blotner, 1959)
LIG	*Lion in the Garden* (Meriwether and Millgate, 1980)
PF	*The Portable Faulkner* (Cowley, 1984 [1946])
"Intro SF, I"	"An Introduction for *The Sound and the Fury*" (Meriwether, Autumn 1972)
"Intro SF, II"	"An Introduction to *The Sound and the Fury*" (Meriwether, Summer 1973)
"Hill"	"The Hill" (from *Early Prose and Poetry*)
"Kingdom"	"The Kingdom of God" (from *New Orleans Sketches*)
"Sun"	"That Evening Sun" (from *Collected Stories*)
"Wash"	"Wash" (from *Collected Stories*)
"Monk"	"Monk" (from *Knight's Gambit*)
"Barn"	"Barn Burning" (from *Collected Stories*)
"Hand"	"Hand upon the Waters" (from *Knight's Gambit*)

"Afternoon"   "Afternoon of a Cow" (from *Uncollected Stories*)
"Appendix"   "Appendix/Compson, 1699–1945" (from *The Portable Faulkner*)

INVENTING BENJY

INTRODUCTION

> I became interested in the relationship of the idiot to the world.
> —WILLIAM FAULKNER, *LION IN THE GARDEN*

William Faulkner's first novel that sparked interest and recognition among critics and readers, and began the author's meteoric rise all the way to Stockholm in 1950, where he was awarded the Nobel Prize in Literature for his body of work, is entitled *The Sound and the Fury*. Marked by a radically singular form of writing bursting with innovation and built on an architecture of extraordinary complexity, *The Sound and the Fury* is undoubtedly among those novels that provoked, disrupted, and ultimately influenced twentieth-century literature the most. It was published on October 7, 1929, by Jonathan Cape and Harrison Smith, and opens with the chaos and confusion of a story that resists understanding or any clear categorization, for its first narrator is an idiot. Yet Benjy Compson is not the first Faulknerian idiot. "The Kingdom of God," one of the short stories published in 1925 that Faulkner wrote in and dedicated to New Orleans, focuses on a first idiot who remains unnamed. The idiot from the short story is simply one type of character among others, although he immediately stands out due to his imperviousness to the logic of his surrounding world, in contrast to the crowd of small-time criminals, police officers, and onlookers bustling about him. Beginning with this youthful text, the figure of the idiot takes the form of a failing and imperfect double of a normal human being, characterized by his deficiencies, shortcomings, and deprivation. Normal humans are ideally endowed with abilities (acting, choosing, expressing oneself) that leave the idiot confused; normal humans are beings in the making, whereas powerless idiots are already everything they can be, their idiocy akin to a static and irreparable state. The idiot's world coincides with that of ordinary humans but remains distinct, as if suspended within a singular temporality and spatiality shared by no one. Paradoxically, while he is not quite of the world, at least in the world that is ours, the idiot nevertheless inhabits the world, is rooted within it and present in a relation of absolute proximity. The idiot adheres to the world's surface in a relation of immanence, where normal humans, always seeking what they do not yet have, frenetically engage in the transcendent pursuit of an unattainable object, of a direction or meaning. The idiot simply *is*: being represents his only dimension. A normal human, on the other hand, is continually preoccupied with time, and never ceases becoming.

Idiocy is thus rooted in the very beginnings of Faulknerian fiction, although its treatment radically transformed between "The Kingdom of God" and *The Sound and the Fury*. The narrator of the first text approaches it from an extradiegetic standpoint, relating and describing what he sees in panoramic fashion by clearly establishing his omniscience and superiority over the story. In the characterization of the first idiot character in Faulkner's work, idiocy resembles an anomaly, an object of curiosity approached with a certain distance and circumspection. Section 1 of *The Sound and the Fury* represents a major revolution, as the external narrator's control is sacrificed for what can be called a mimetic approach. Idiocy is no longer represented but is rather presented without mediation: it is shown and gradually takes shape through a voice that shows all of the symptoms of the most radical alterity. In the first monologue of *The Sound and the Fury*, the discourse of reason recedes and fades away, making way for a thoroughly disconcerting discourse—the impossible discourse of idiocy in action. The Faulknerian project that emerges when the idiot Benjy speaks involves an "inner experience"[1] that leads to nonsense, depersonalization, destructuring, and immoderation. This project is based on a dual challenge to both the rational logic that governs apprehension of the world, and the expectations and constraints that govern literary creation. It is built on immense sacrifice and renunciation—in the name of the radical liberty offered by unbridled writing—as well as a discourse that frees itself from the authoritarian requirements of reason and instead exclusively obeys the disorganized accumulation of raw perceptions and sensations. It does not seek to demonstrate anything, or to arbitrarily justify preestablished answers: it does not know where it is going—"When I began it I had no plan at all" ("Intro *SF*, I": 227)[2]—just as an idiot never knows where his random steps will take him. The aimless idiot paradoxically becomes the aim of writing.

The essential role played by idiocy at the beginning of *The Sound and the Fury* coincides with the precise moment when Faulkner decided to deliberately abandon the restrictive constraints of professional writing and the publishing world. After suffering a number of failures with the publication of his first novels—*Soldiers' Pay* (1926) and *Mosquitoes* (1927) enjoyed very modest success, while *Flags in the Dust* was a publishing disaster[3]—Faulkner decided to renounce his dreams of fame[4] and to instead follow his imagination and sense of pleasure: "that anticipation and that joy which alone ever made writing pleasure to me" ("Intro *SF*, I": 226). On that day when he "could" write and give free rein to this solipsistic exaltation, he did so in the consciousness of an idiot. One could say that it was Faulkner's immersion in the idiocy of Benjy Compson that marked his entry into literature, with idiocy in a way representing the unlikely source of creative power.

In trying to grasp the centrality of idiocy and the importance given to idiot characters in the work of Faulkner, a quick stroll through Faulkner's biography may prove helpful, albeit without providing clear and satisfactory answers. If the creating subject and the worldly man must be completely distinguished from one another, as Proust suggested in his *Contre Sainte-Beuve*,[5] certain coincidences and influences can nevertheless prove illuminating. With this in mind, it is worth noting that Faulkner worshiped "difference" quite early on, even before he thought of writing: "I read and employed verse, firstly, for the purpose of furthering various philanderings in which I was engaged, secondly, to complete a youthful gesture I was then making, of being 'different' in a small town" (*EPP*: 115). Faulkner, who was from an old family of Oxford, Mississippi, was not an ordinary member of the community. He long made it a point of honor to distinguish himself from the values shared by the majority of the community and in doing so assumed a series of postures—the dandy, the bashful lover, the *poète maudit*, the war hero—in an effort to display his uniqueness. Such demonstrations were fairly uncommon in the general tranquility of the countryside in the Deep South, and helped attract attention. His fellow men, who gave him the mocking nickname "Count No Count," often held him in supreme contempt. Admittedly, his arrogant stances did not project a particularly sympathetic image of the young man that he was, as demonstrated by this partially fictitious autobiographical note he drafted himself in 1924, when he hoped to publish his poetry collection *The Marble Faun* (which was indeed published that year):

> Born in Mississippi in 1897. Great-grandson of Col. W. C. Faulkner, C.S.A., author of "The White Rose of Memphis," "Rapid Ramblings in Europe," etc. Boyhood and youth were spent in Mississippi, since then has been (1) undergraduate (2) house painter (3) tramp, day laborer, dishwasher in various New England cities (4) Clerk in Lord and Taylor's book shop in New York City (5) bank- and postal clerk. Served during the war in the British Royal Air Force. A member of Sigma Alpha Epsilon Fraternity. Present temporary address, Oxford, Miss. "The Marble Faun" was written in the spring of 1919. (Blotner, 1974: 117)[6]

The tone of this sketch, simultaneously impudent and deprecatory, is no more than a poorly disguised attempt to highlight the eccentricity of his background, the scope of his ambitions, and his very high opinion of himself. In the wake of his illustrious forebear, Faulkner wanted to be somebody rather than just anybody. Paradoxically, Faulkner felt lasting unease toward his late and sudden fame, which he never really knew what to do with. From the moment his acceptance of the Nobel Prize, and the famous speech associated with it, put him in the limelight, earned him international and national recognition (he was strangely idolized abroad, especially in France, before even being recognized in his own country), and set him on the turbulent life of a public figure, Faulkner insistently repeated that he was no more than a peasant from the South, asserting values opposed to those that his admirers (and detractors) hoped to find in one of the greatest writers produced by America during the first half of the twentieth century. He was reluctant throughout his life to stay away too long from Oxford, Mississippi, the nerve center for creating Yoknapatawpha County, where he rests today accompanied by a bottle of bourbon perched atop his tomb in lieu of a floral arrangement. Faulkner was so successful at passing for a halfwit that disconcerted literary critics wondered what miracle enabled this same man to write novels manifestly inspired by genius. What to make of his notorious alcoholism, which John Maxwell Coetzee suggested, in an article in the *New York Review of Books*, was an integral part of "becoming William Faulkner" (Coetzee, April 7, 2005: 24)? Was Faulkner's chronic alcoholism not one way, among others, to gain access to idiocy, as was the case for the aptly named Uncle Bud,[7] the young boy who at the end of the twenty-fifth chapter of *Sanctuary* drinks beer and develops a taste for it while the ladies make conversation in the parlor of Miss Reba's brothel: "Limp-knees he dangled, his face fixed in an expression of glassy idiocy. 'Miss Reba,' Minnie said, 'this boy done broke in the icebox and drunk a whole bottle of beer. You, boy!' she said, shaking him, 'stand up!' Limply he dangled, his face rigid in a slobbering grin" (*S*: 259)? Alcoholism and idiocy present similar symptoms and distortions. The "glassy" look of idiocy brings to mind the bottom of a glass, or perhaps it is the other way around.

Two categories of idiots marked the childhood and formative years of Faulkner the writer. The first was a young boy he knew named Edwin, who was the younger idiot brother of Miss Annie Chandler, his first primary school teacher at Oxford Graded School, which he started attending on his eighth birthday.[8] The second idiot of importance in the genesis of Faulknerian idiocy was a literary idiot, the central character from the collection of poems entitled *A Shropshire Lad*, which was published in 1896 by Alfred Edward Housman and met with considerable late success. This lad and his many avatars—young soldiers, shepherds, and athletes—is obviously not an idiot in the literal sense.

Yet it was probably in this collection that Faulkner found the archetype of the fallen, dispossessed, and desperate hero, the model for the singular individual marked by deficiencies and defeats, who would play a central role in most of his novels, with the idiot representing the most accomplished version. The double of Narcissus fatuously contemplating his reflection—"But in the golden-sanded brooks / And azure meres I spy / A silly lad that longs and looks / And wishes he were I" ("A Shropshire Lad," pt. XX)—and the innocent and even simple-minded shepherd with his blissful smile that nothing can wipe away—"Oh whence, I asked, and whither? / He smiled and would not say, / And looked at me and beckoned / And laughed and led the way" ("The Merry Guide") (Housman, 1994: 34, 61)—are the collections' two most striking figures in this regard.[9] In addition to his boundless admiration for Housman, it is tempting to believe that during his exploration of English poets, Faulkner also had the opportunity to read "The Idiot Boy" (1798) from William Wordsworth's *Lyrical Ballads*. The poem retraces the special relation between Betty Foy and her idiot son Johnny, who hunts the moon: "Consider, Johnny's but half-wise." The poem seems to directly address this mother, who alone understands the idiot's unintelligible language, and gives direction to his days: "And Betty o'er and o'er has told / The boy, who is her best delight, / Both what to follow, what to shun, / What to do, and what to leave undone, / How turn to left, and how to right." These two figures evoke, and one could even say announce, the relation between Caddy Compson and her younger idiot brother in *The Sound and the Fury*, even though their "travel"—"And that was all his travel's story" (Wordsworth, 1965: 67–80)—does not end as well as that of Betty and Johnny.

A moon hunter? A half-wit? What precisely is an idiot in the general sense of the term? And what is an idiot in literature? How to define the characteristics and aspects relating to the literary idiocy specific to Faulkner? At this point it is important to try to define idiocy, as well as the values that are ascribed to it and that will be given to it in this book. The most common meaning for the notion of idiocy is medical in nature. According to dictionary *Le Grand Robert de la language française*, idiocy was defined from 1836 onward as the "most serious form of mental retardation, of congenital origin, usually associated with various deformities and sensory-motor impairments."[10] Idiocy originally referred to a series of impairments or dysfunctions affecting both the body and the mind, with its causes invariably being described as uncertain. The late nineteenth century saw an increasing number of medical treatises on idiocy: Jules Voisin, a doctor at Salpêtrière Hospital in Paris, distinguished between four kinds of idiocy based on their seriousness. The two most serious forms were, in his words, "complete, absolute, congenital, or acquired idiocy," deemed to be incurable, and "incomplete, congenital, or acquired idiocy, potentially improvable."[11] It is therefore necessary to distinguish idiocy from imbecility and debility, which are defined in a more nuanced manner in terms of deficiency, feebleness, or impairment. It is also important to distinguish it from cretinism as it appears among the sickly and tormented patients of Doctor Benassis in Honoré de Balzac's *Le Médecin de campagne* (1833; *The Country Doctor*).[12] Faced with his inability to "paint a single picture" of idiocy, Paul Sollier built his definition on the absence of "moral pain":

> With respect to moral pain, it can clearly appear only in relation to the development of the affective sensibility. It is nonexistent among complete idiots, but can occur in less intense degrees, albeit without ever attaining a high level of development. It is also rare to see idiots cry. To do so they must be affected in their physical sensitivity or the immediate satisfaction of their tendencies. It must happen abruptly in order for them to feel the impressions rather intensely. They are concerned neither by worries for the future nor by memories of the past, with only the present existing for them. In such conditions, moral sensibility is necessarily quite dampened. (Sollier, 1891: 116–17)

What is surprising, to say the least, is that while it claims to be medical, this definition of idiocy is absolutely not scientific. Sollier strives to describe some of the symptoms of idiocy in a highly factual manner. For him, the idiot is an individual marked by radical apathy, which can be disrupted only by a violent event that triggers a strong physical reaction within that person—such are, Sollier believes, the limits of the idiot's "moral sensibility," hermetically sealed off from the effects of time. It was from a similar perspective that Édouard Séguin, one of the founders of child psychiatry, defined an idiot as a succession of negations:

> What exactly is idiocy? Idiocy is a disability of the nervous system, which has the radical effect of shielding some or all of the child's organs and faculties from the regular activity of their will, thereby abandoning them to their instincts and cutting them off from the normal world. [. . .] The typical idiot is an individual who knows nothing, can do nothing, and wants nothing, and every idiot comes more or less near to this height of incapacity. (Séguin, 1997 [1846]: 79)[13]

Idiots are therefore beings deprived of knowledge, power, and volition, with the accumulation of these "incapacities" cutting them off from the logic of "the normal world." An idiot is consequently an *ab*normal being, one who is not normal, and develops outside the bounds of normality. The idiosyncrasies of idiocy continue to unfold against a backdrop of a fantasized normality, one that is defined, by contrast, in terms of intelligence, harmony, and plenitude. The combined effects of his amorality and abnormality are such that the idiot often causes shame and disgust. This is notably how Gustave Flaubert, who also had his moments of idiocy[14]—if one is to believe *The Family Idiot*, Jean-Paul Sartre's philosophical and biographical essay on the writer—evoked a particularly frightening encounter in his correspondence: "A few days ago I met three poor idiot women who asked me for alms. They were horrible, disgusting in their ugliness and cretinism; they could not speak, they could scarcely walk" (Flaubert, 1980: 32). From the viewpoint of normality, idiocy often presents all the signs of the most shameful degradation. By extension of its medical meaning, in the late nineteenth century idiocy came to designate a lack of intelligence and mental alertness. Its definition began to resemble those for foolishness (*bêtise*), silliness (*sottise*), and stupidity (*stupidité*), immersing us—while we remain in a Flaubertian universe—in the world of *Bouvard et Pécuchet* (1881). Beginning in the twentieth century, the term "idiocy" was used to refer to an action reflecting a lack of intelligence or common sense. An individual's gestures and acts can thus be called idiotic without the person in question actually suffering from idiocy. Similarly, in common parlance the term "idiot" refers to someone whose level of intellect is abnormally low, someone who is backward, naïve, or simple(-minded)—the village idiot.

A Faulknerian idiot can in no way be considered a clinical case for a number of reasons: an idiot is not, strictly speaking, someone who is sick, as the definition of idiocy eludes a clear medical typology, and developing a phenomenon's symptomatology is not the objective of literary criticism. In the end it matters little whether Benjy Compson and his companions in Faulkner's work are credible idiots from a pathological point of view. There is no doubt that the Faulknerian idiot is a "production," which is to say a necessarily artificial and fake character. Yet it is precisely through the production of idiocy, through a new and unexpected discourse and manner of apprehension, that Faulkner successfully mastered a thoroughly singular writing. The accuracy of Faulknerian idiocy is therefore not a central concern—what matters are its accomplishments. This is why the goal of literary criticism is not to establish a list of the clinical and scientific symptoms of idiocy in connection with explanatory categories, as the neurosciences, psychiatry, psychology, and the behavioral sciences do. Literary criticism is antipsychiatric: it adheres to the notion that idiots do not fall within any accurate codification, and that the word and person likewise resist medical classification. In the absence of pinning down and explaining its behavior, literary analysis must therefore aim to describe, understand, and assess the literary aspects involved.

The Faulknerian idiot is not a sick, autistic, or crazy person, although madness does have a number of points in common with idiocy. As with idiocy, madness is a multifaceted term that raises suspicion and tends to be used as a kind of insult. From a normative perspective, madness and idiocy both designate disgraceful flaws; they are two forms taken by transgression. Furthermore, both manifest themselves through errors of judgment and are defined in opposition to reason, indicating that which escapes its control: madness is the loss of reason (unreason), while idiocy marks its failure (irrationality). Moreover, idiots and madmen are subject to similar treatment, locked away behind the same walls, which for Faulkner were those of the mental asylum of Jackson, Mississippi. In both cases, the madman and the idiot are iniquitously excluded by a society whose "conformism they disturb" (Castel, 2003: 436). On a fundamental level, madness is radically different from idiocy, for it can take the form of an intrusive pathology that secretly spreads, taking root in a body that, unlike the idiot's body, has all the appearances of being normal and healthy. This is why it can be difficult to distinguish madness from perfect lucidity. It is with this in mind that Cash Bundren meditates, in the final pages of *As I Lay Dying*, on the blurred dividing line between sanity and insanity, as well as the arbitrary nature of the judgments that stigmatize madness: "Sometimes I aint so sho who's got ere a right to say when a man is crazy and when he aint. Sometimes I thing it aint none of us pure crazy and aint none of us pure sane until the balance of us talks him that-a-way" (*AILD*: 233). It is notable that idiocy rarely lends itself to such hesitation. Ordinarily, if one thing is for sure, it is that an idiot is an idiot. Madness is commonly defined as a more or less serious alteration of psychological health, causing behavioral disorders ranging from neurosis to psychosis, and taking forms as varied as hysteria, persecutory delirium, schizophrenia, and the like.[15] In the end, madness takes numerous forms, although they all bear the names of detectable illnesses (formerly said to be of the soul), which in the best-case scenario can be cured by psychiatry, psychotherapy, or chemistry. Consequently, unlike the idiot, whose health resides in an involuntary ataraxia, the madman suffers and is aware of his state. In an oversimplification, one could say that madness is a kind of illness that creeps into a healthy body, whereas idiocy is a form of health rooted in a body that appears sick. Finally, while idiocy is defined by its obviousness and permanence, madness is characterized by the suddenness with which its manifestations alter—and even interrupt—a situation that is nevertheless part of an appearance of normality. As a result, sudden bursts of madness are often seen as a threat, while idiocy is deemed relatively inoffensive because it is foreseeable and can usually be channeled. In Faulkner, madness is present in Darl Bundren's visions and irrational laugh in *As I Lay Dying*, and also reveals itself in Joanna Burden's body fetishism and subsequent idolatry of God in *Light in August*.

While an idiot shows a propensity to be ridiculous and provoke laughter, he is not a fool. If he invites mockery, it is always in spite of himself and at his expense. As such, the Faulknerian idiot is manifestly different from the Shakespearean fool or jester, who enjoys a rare immunity allowing him to say anything, and is characterized by his *bons mots*, witticisms, and art of repartee. Faulknerian idiots have few words at their disposal, which are arranged in combinations that entail no ambiguity and whose meaning is necessarily univocal—he is both *un faible d'esprit* (a dimwit) and *faible en esprit* (witless). Nor are they like the fools of commedia dell'arte, the famous *zanni* who, like Harlequin and Brighella, entertain through the spectacle of their blundering and naïveté. These characters, who always resemble one another in the costumes and masks that help identify them, come down to a few fixed types whose repetition is indispensable to the produced effect. The originality of commedia dell'arte, which presents itself as comedy and uses all of the means at its disposal to provoke laughter, is based on the actors' improvisation within these conventions. However, in the diverse reactions it creates, even when it occasionally veers into comedy, Faulkner's writing rarely generates roaring laughter, at best a smile. The recurrence of idiots changes little in this regard, as they do not have the means to be humorous.

While they are different from the figures discussed above, idiots are readily caught up in a myth and form of mysticism, both based on similar foundations. The idiot often appears as an avatar of the mystifying myth of *l'homme naturel* (the natural human) or *le bon sauvage* (the noble savage), as it was constituted following the arrival of Europeans in America in travel narratives, and was notably discussed by Rousseau in his *Discourse on the Origin and Basis of Inequality among Men* (1755). Rousseau believed that the primitive state of humans spontaneously inclined them toward virtue and happiness, in the sense that ignorance of evil prevented them from spreading evil.[16] Driven by the raw forces of nature before its conquest by civilization, the noble savage personifies an idealized natural life (giving rise to symbolic and figurative narratives fulfilling a revelatory function), far from the debauchery that corrupted Sodom and Gomorrah. The primitive and backward manner of noble savages as compared to the incessant progress of civilization is not considered inferior; on the contrary, they are seen as living in a natural golden age. Despite being rooted in the modern world, Faulknerian idiots stand out through their similar attachment to nature and its objects. For instance, Benjy Compson's speech is full of references to the plant and animal kingdoms, while the senses of Ike Snopes are awakened by the breaking dawn. A natural man par excellence, the idiot can be seen as a spirit of nature of sorts. This closeness between the mythical noble savage and the idiot was present in the unusual character that

Henry David Thoreau counted among the "visitors" to the woods where he chose to live at Walden Pond. He was a robust lumberjack with a child's soul: "[T]he intellectual and what is called spiritual man in him were slumbering as in an infant" (Thoreau, 1982 [1854]: 396–98). This man, with his steady and joyful mood, had a silent but effective affinity for the trees and small birds of the woods: "[T]he chickadees would sometimes come round and alight on his arm." Thoreau readily described this idiot (he specifically refers to his "stupidity") as being in perfect harmony with his environment like a true son of Nature, which conceived him as an eternal child: "When Nature made him, she gave him a strong body and contentment for his portion, and propped him on every side with reverence and reliance, that he might live out his threescore years and ten a child."[17] With this in mind, the use of the adverb *naturally* in the description of the idiot's acts and gestures reconnects with the natural roots of its etymology: "he was so simply and naturally humble." This is fully expressed only in the English language, as the substantive "natural" sometimes replaces terms explicitly referring to idiocy.[18] Due to the preeminence of the natural instincts that govern it, from a psychoanalytical perspective idiocy can be interpreted as a manifestation of what Freud called "id," as the representation of an unbridled (literally: without a bridle), instinctive life, beyond the defense mechanisms of the ego and the censorship activity of the superego. The dynamics of life circulate freely through idiots; no influence can corrupt the direction of their instincts. The motifs of nature and childhood are thus closely connected; they contribute to the myth of an original purity and liberty built around individuals who, like the noble savage and the idiot, are characterized by their convergence. Moreover, they are behind another myth with mystical accents, namely the great closeness of such innocents to a God whose benevolent presence is revealed by nature—an idea that is an essential thread of American transcendentalism. Idiots are often seen as children of God because they are emblematic of a kind of ideal innocence, and analyses of idiocy often fall prey to a temptation to mystify as a result.[19] *Infans* in the literal sense of the word, idiots are not endowed with speech and are therefore unable to impede divine will, to which they are necessarily subject. It is because they are pure, gentle, and disciplined that idiots enjoy a place of great importance in "the kingdom of God," which is promised to the simpleminded in both the New Testament and Faulkner's first short story depicting an idiot ("The Kingdom of God"):[20] "Except ye be converted, and become as little children, ye shall not enter into the kingdom of heaven" (Matthew 18:3); "Suffer the little children to come unto me, and forbid them not: for such is the kingdom of God" (Mark 10:14). Some critics consider idiocy as one of the major pillars of Faulknerian idealism. Yet with Faulkner, the innocence of idiots is no doubt less of an ethical project than a crucible, a source of impetus for an aesthetics.

Faulknerian idiots are therefore far removed from Prince Myshkin, widely considered as the archetypal literary idiot, who was explicitly conceived by Dostoevsky as a modern Christ, an avatar of God. "Candor," "sincerity," "simplicity," and "goodwill" are some of the expressions that give a positive overtone to Myshkin's behavior,[21] whose idiocy is one of the manifestations of an incurable epilepsy: "Everybody also considers me an idiot for some reason, and in fact I was once so ill that I was like an idiot" (Dostoevsky, 2003: 75). Alternately idealized and ridiculed by the Petersburgian aristocracy surrounding him, Dostoevsky's idiot is explicitly described at the end of the novel as an individual to whom the divine meaning of things is "revealed": "Hidden from the wise and clever, and revealed unto babes" (Dostoevsky, 2003: 596). Wisdom and reason, intelligence and intellect are thus reduced to vain abilities when compared to the penetrating possibilities offered by idiocy.

Faulknerian idiots thus play an unprecedented aesthetic role through their unique relation to the world. This world in which Faulkner was "interested" when he began writing the first monologue of *The Sound and the Fury* is a raw world, one that is in keeping with nature in its generic and first sense (the world as it was created by God), as well as with the nature of things, which is to say the series of sensitive coordinates that make them things. It is also a world freed from the predefined models of civilization, a world unburdened of the expectations and limits of normative perception. In his essay entitled *Le Réel: Traité de l'idiotie* (The Real: Treatise on Idiocy), Clément Rosset makes idiocy the figurehead for the notion of singularity. He defines the adjective "idiot" by exploring its etymological meaning:

> *Idiôtès*, idiot, means simple, particular, unique; then through a semantic extension with a far-reaching philosophical meaning, a person devoid of intelligence, lacking reason. A thing or a person is thus idiotic when it exists only in itself, which is to say is unable to appear differently than where it is or how it is: hence incapable, first and foremost, to *reflect* itself, to appear in the mirror's double. (Rosset, 1986: 42)

With this in mind, beyond its definition as a serious congenital deficiency, idiocy designates the unique and unequivocal character—entirely singular and devoid of reflection—of that which exists only in itself. Rosset's definition incidentally justifies the use of "idiot" as an adjective in these pages, as an attributive adjective in connection with objects that spontaneously call for a noun complement built on the genitive "of the idiot." Through a kind of contamination, the characteristics of idiocy differentiate the objects connected to it such that they appear to be idiot objects, as if struck by idiocy, beyond the characterization of idiot characters. The idiot's world thus unfolds like an idiot world, and the idiot's perception makes way for idiot writing, which is to say a radically singular writing that unfolds, unlike any other, both within and beyond the limits of the subjectivity of idiots, creating the great Faulknerian work.

Part 1 of this book defines the idiosyncrasies that give bodily substance—and paradoxically a voice—to the Faulknerian idiot. Part 2, which analyzes the idiot's stance toward objects, closely connected to the roots of the world, focuses on the idiot's mechanisms of perception. Finally, part 3 considers the Faulknerian idiot as the transcendental character in Faulkner's work, as both its paradigm and the focal point from which Faulknerian writing is organized.

Part I

Idiosyncrasies of an Idiocy: Disarticulation of Bodies, Disconnecting of Narratives

The small white-haired boy shambled into the back of the hall and stood peering forward at the stranger. He had on the bottoms of a pair of blue pajamas drawn up as high as they could go, the string tied over his chest and then again, harness-like, around his neck to keep them on. His eyes were slightly sunken beneath his forehead and his cheekbones were lower than they should have been. He stood there, dim and ancient, like a child who had been a child for centuries.
—FLANNERY O'CONNOR, *THE VIOLENT BEAR IT AWAY*

Chapter 1

IS THE IDIOT A MONSTER?

> Let us record the atoms as they fall upon the mind in the order in which they fall, let us trace the pattern, however disconnected and incoherent in appearance, which each sight or incident scores upon the consciousness. Let us not take it for granted that life exists more in what is commonly thought big than in what is commonly thought small.
> —VIRGINIA WOOLF, "MODERN NOVELS"

The body plays a fundamental role in the characterization of Faulknerian idiots. It is in the peculiar texture of the bodies of idiots, which are as limp as Dalí's clocks—and hence different from the general and customary perception of normative bodies—that the central aspects of Faulkner's idiocy are woven. It is in bodies, in the extreme flabbiness of the flesh—the singular (*idios*) combination (*sugkrasis*) that makes up idiot matter—that the idiosyncrasies of Faulkner's idiocy connect (and more precisely disconnect). In general, the idiot's idiosyncrasies are defined as an antithesis and counterpoint to a fantasized normal human. The opposition between idiots and normal humans, with the latter entailing the existence of a norm for which they are the most developed result, reiterates the conflict (which is also a commonplace) opposing illness and health. The "great Valentin Knox," the philosopher of the literary evenings organized by Angèle in André Gide's *Paludes* (1895), adopts the words of another philosopher, Nietzsche, and reformulates this opposition in the following manner:

> Health does not strike me as a good that is so desirable. It is only a balance, a mediocrity of everything: the absence of hypertrophy. Our value lies only in that which distinguishes us from others; idiosyncrasy is our valuable illness; in other words, what is important in us is what we only possess, what cannot be found in any other, what your *normal human* does not have—hence what you call illness. (Gide, 2003 [1895]: 81–82)

As in Nietzsche, for whom normality goes hand in hand with the stifling of the individual,[1] what is valued here is illness, physiological anomaly: while normality is likened to a soothing balance that abolishes any distinction among beings, plunging all of them into the same "mediocrity," illness is considered to be a distinctive character, as that which distinguishes individuals and consequently gives them "value," their own value. While normality can be seen as repetition of the same, illness is the domain of singularity and difference. This is also what the Greek *idiotés* means: simple, particular, in other words unique. The literally extraordinary value of idiots is therefore superior to that of the normal human, for at least there is something to say about them.

The idiot is related to the monster, from the Latin *monstrum*, which is etymologically defined as a prodigy, as something unbelievable or worthy of being made into a spectacle (*monstrare*). A living being or organism with an abnormal anatomical composition (due to excess, impairment, or the abnormal position of some of the organism's parts), the monster, like the idiot, does not radiate health. In his 1962 essay entitled "La monstruosité et le monstrueux" (Monstrosity and the Monstrous), Georges Canguilhem defined the monster as an "appearance of specific equivocity" and a "morphological failure" (Canguilhem, 1980: 171). The monster's specificity and singularity reside in the particularity of its shape, which is a consequence of its hybridization. The monster is traditionally the result of a strange collage, which brings to mind the exquisite corpses and sundry bricolages of surrealism. The body of the monster from Paul Verlaine's eponymous poem "The Monster,"[2] which was contemporaneous with *Fêtes galantes* (Gallant Festivals), was patched together from dismembered parts from miscellaneous sources: the monstrous body, whose evocation combines images and comparisons, includes "a mammoth's muzzle," a lobster's whiskers, the "long hair [...] of a giant goat," and teeth like "levers" (Verlaine, 1962: 129–30). The ambivalence of reactions to monsters is obvious enough, ranging from fear and panic to curiosity and even fascination. As an assembly of disparate elements, the monster—always unique—is a "hodgepodge" (Guillain, 2003: 122).[3]

With their poorly defined and flabby bodies, a trickling jumble of flabbiness, idiots are neither one thing nor another; like the half-human, half-animal monsters that abound in traditional iconography, they are simply "quasis." Idiots are defined by the simultaneously radical and constitutive disharmony of their physiological and psychological development, and therein lies their most striking anomaly: their adult bodies, naturally marked by the stigma of their between-two-ages, contain a child's intelligence. Idiots are clearly a variation on the theme of the monster: young victims of a malformed cell or organ in the early stages, they are an uncertain collage of adult parts, infantile functions, and animal instincts whose absolute singularity both frightens and fascinates.

It is therefore important to determine the distinctive characteristics that give idiots their value: is there a physiognomy of Faulknerian idiots? Do the singular bodies of Faulkner's idiots speak? Do they mirror souls that are no less singular? Do idiots bear on their bodies or unique faces "a *mark* that can simultaneously be the sign of good and bad fortune, a feature of character, a symptom of illness, and a social stigma" (Courtine, 2005: 306)?

Chapter 2

THE FLABBY FLESH AND FLACCID BODIES OF IDIOTS

> He remembered how he looked back and she was still sitting as he had left her, and that now (and he had not heard him enter) there stood in the hall below a hulking young light-colored negro man in clean faded overalls and shirt, his arms dangling, no surprise, no nothing in the saddle-colored and slacked-mouthed idiot face.
> —WILLIAM FAULKNER, *ABSALOM, ABSALOM!*

The collection entitled *New Orleans Sketches*, published in 1958 as a belated record of Faulkner's formative years, includes short stories and sketches composed when Faulkner was part of the artistic world revolving around Sherwood Anderson in New Orleans. Most of these short stories were published around 1925 in the local press, especially the New Orleans *Times Picayune*. One of them, "The Kingdom of God," depicts a first idiot figure, a kind of preparatory sketch of Benjy Compson, the challenging character-narrator who opens the narration of *The Sound and the Fury*, published in 1929. While the characterization of the short story's idiot is considerably more succinct, lapidary, and traditional than Benjy's, the short story's creation of the unnamed idiot marked the beginning of a long series of singular bodies whose most complete development would be the flabby and limp appearance of idiots to come.

"The Kingdom of God" is a third-person narrative whose narrator, omniscient but discreet, makes prominent use of direct speech. The short story begins in medias res, and the time in which the action takes place coincides with that of the narration, with no lapses between the two. The plot unsurprisingly takes place in New Orleans, which is identifiable thanks to the evocation of Decatur Street, a bustling street running along the Mississippi. The time in which the action takes place is revealed gradually and indirectly through clues given here and there: at question is a delivery of bags whose contents, we are given to understand, remain undefined due to their unmentionable nature.[1] The back-and-forth movements of the characters involved in this activity take place quickly. Their gestures are hasty because they apparently have good reason to be afraid, and they are especially concerned about being noticed by the police, whose intervention is the short story's sole incident: "They've got liquor in here" ("Kingdom": 86), one of the officers cries out. The gray areas are clarified as we discover that the man and his friend are bootleggers. "The Kingdom of God" can therefore be read as a short contemporary account of the crimes and misdemeanors prompted by the prohibition of alcohol. The short story's structure emphasizes the shift from crime to the prospect of its punishment, from liberty to captivity. When the story begins, the two associates enter the scene in their car; at the end, they exit escorted by two police officers—"with an officer on each fender" (86)—headed to the police station. The reader is left behind at the scene of the crime as the narrator ends the story, lost in a thinning crowd that watches the characters disappear into the distance: "the car drew away from the curb and on down the street, and so from sight" (86). The unusual, disruptive element that, central to the structure of "The Kingdom of God," attracts our attention and dramatically alters the story's very simple plot (a failed delivery of illegal goods) is the appearance of an idiot.

Paradoxically, the idiot, the younger brother of one of the bootleggers, is not part of the action despite occupying a central role. He stubbornly refuses to take part in the event, not out of a sense of idealism but because he simply does not understand a thing about what is happening around him: "'Listen!' the man was near screaming, 'do you wanta go to jail? Catch hold here, for God's sake!' But the idiot only stared at him in solemn detachment" (82). His angelic calm contrasts with the hysteria of the two other characters. What's more, he is the unintentional source of the downfall of his companions, the final link in an inescapable logical chain, for if there is one thing that the short story's idiot is not indifferent to, it is the narcissus that he carries everywhere and cares for with fetishistic adoration. This fragile narcissus breaks amid the frenzy, triggering the idiot's pathetic yelling and sparking the curiosity of an officer, who does not suspect that it will break up a small-scale trafficking ring. This is how the story ends, with the bootleggers being caught in the act and quiet returning to Decatur Street, the reader walking away with the notion that justice will be served.

Despite being an unusual and incongruous presence in this story about bootlegging, the idiot's characterization is the most developed of the three central figures. From the short story's opening lines, the idiot is distinguished from the two other characters, who are described as an entity that acts rather than as distinct individuals: "Two men alighted, but the other remained in his seat" (78). The separation between the idiot and the others exists first on the spatial level; but it can also be seen in bodily movement, as the two men step out of the car and busy themselves, while the idiot stays where he is, motionless and apathetic. This separation is also economic, as the idiot does not take part in this little exchange: etymologically derived from the Greek *idiôtès*, the idiot is literally he who knows no trade and is thus ignorant of the working world.[2] In "The Kingdom of God," the idiot is involuntarily protected from the surrounding corruption. The only distinctive sign that helps identify the two bootleggers comes in the words prompted by the idiot's presence, namely his brother's surprising sense of family and concern for his simpleminded younger brother—"Listen. He's my brother, see?" ("Kingdom": 80); "I just want to fix his flower for him" (86)—which prefigures Caddy's thousand kindnesses toward Benjy. His associate gives vent to superstitious and ultimately prophetic aphorisms regarding idiots as birds of ill omen, all of which touch on the topic of bad luck: "there ain't no luck in making a delivery with a loony along" (78); "I been taking no squirrel chasers for luck pieces" (78); "What luck, what rotten luck!" (82). The passive and apathetic idiot thus finds himself at the center of attention.

The comparison of the sketch of the idiot from "The Kingdom of God" with the full-length portrait found in *The Sound and the Fury* shows how their primary shared characteristic is inscribed in their bodies; the resemblance is one of flesh and blood, rooted in the relation between the idiot body and its underlying flesh. The distinction between body and flesh involves a difference of matter, texture, and substance. The body takes shape in the hardness of bones and firmness of muscle; it constitutes the architecture of animals and humans. The flesh is all of the mucosities contained in the body, its viscera and guts, the effusion of liquid humors. The body's organic firmness is opposed by the flaccidity of the flesh. The bodily architecture of Faulknerian idiots creates unusual compositions in the interplay between shape and shapelessness: in Faulkner, the specificity of the idiot's outer appearance or shape is precisely not to have a neat and clearly definable shape. The bodies of idiots seem to consist solely of their flabby parts, with an overabundance of flaccid flesh, such that the skeletal structure disappears beneath the excess of flabby matter. It is this disproportion of flesh—its very enormity (the Latin *enormis* meaning "that which is outside the rule," *norma*)—that prevents the idiot's body from being identified as "normal" or normative. The idiot body is enormous, its excess flesh signifying its anomaly.

Side-by-side analysis of the physical descriptions of the idiots from "The Kingdom of God" and *The Sound and the Fury*, the first at the beginning of the short story and the second at the end of the novel, underscores the shared distinctive characteristics that determine the appearance of idiocy as well as how it literally takes shape in writing. The first passage cited below shows how the minimalist plot of "The Kingdom of God" is quickly relegated to the background, compared to the importance given to the mute and passive character of the idiot. The second extract is in keeping with the logic at work in the final section of *The Sound and the Fury*, which, in contrast to the successive interior monologues of the three Compson brothers, reveals an intention to "clarify." This detailed physical description of Benjy—the only one, and coming late in the work—grows out of "a final distillation" ("Intro *SF*, II": 231) that is as surprising as it is unexpected. The two passages can be compared term for term, insofar as they derive from a similar narrative strategy: an omniscient narrator relates in the third person from the exterior; in both cases, distance from the scene is strengthened by use of the past tense.

> The face of the sitting man was vague and dull and loose-lipped and his eyes were clear and blue as cornflowers, and utterly vacant of thought; he sat a shapeless, dirty lump, life without mind, an organism without intellect. ("Kingdom": 55)

> Luster entered, followed by a big man who appeared to have been shaped of some substance whose particles would not or did not cohere to one another or to the frame which supported it. His skin was dead looking and hairless; dropsical too, he moved with a shambling gait like a trained bear. His hair was pale and fine. It had been brushed smoothly down upon his brow like that of children in daguerrotypes, his eyes were clear, of the pale sweet blue of cornflowers, his thick mouth hung open, drooling a little. (*SF*: 274)

In addition to their eyes, which are the blue of cornflowers, the primary resemblance between the two idiots is their deformity and the very absence of shape: the adjective "shapeless" used in connection with the noun "lump" evokes a shapeless mass, a counterpart to the slack and indescribable "substance" that does not adhere to its underlying skeletal structure. It is as if flesh and flabby matter cover the structure of the idiot body in an approximate and ill-adjusted manner, overflowing a frame to which they are poorly suited. The excess of flesh that characterizes the idiot body is also mentioned in the short story "Monk," whose eponymous character is also an idiot.[3] "Monk" is a first-person story narrated by the young Charles Mallison (called Chick) on the basis of revelations made by his uncle, Gavin Stevens. In addition to numerous details regarding his clothing, Monk's physical appearance is mentioned twice: "a youth not tall and already a little pudgy, as though he were thirty-eight instead of eighteen, with the ugly shrewdly foolish, innocent face whose features rather than expression must have gained him his nickname"

("Monk": 42); "his warped, pudgy, foolish face" (46). Repetition of the adjective "pudgy" situates Monk within the tradition of chubby idiots who are so abnormally fleshy that they seem shapeless in all senses of the word. Their lack of shape goes together with an unfinished and crude appearance: their bodies are simply the beginnings of bodies. Idiot bodies ultimately have an unaesthetic appearance; because they resemble nothing and are far removed from normative canons, idiots can rarely be considered beautiful.

Distinguished by flesh that is too flabby or abundant to be effectively held together by the skeletal structure, the idiot body also gives the impression of being enervated in the first and privative sense of the word, which is to say lacking nerves, thereby giving idiots their deeply apathetic air. This is expressed through the repetition of the adjectives "dull" and "empty," which are often used together, signaling an extreme dim-wittedness, a dull gaze, and a radical absence of expressivity—in a word, a void. It is incidentally in these terms that the narrator of *The Hamlet* lingers for the first time over the face of another idiot, Ike Snopes: "the mowing and bobbing head, the eyes which at some instant, some second once, had opened upon, been vouchsafed a glimpse of, the Gorgon-face of that primal injustice which man was not intended to look at face to face and had been blasted empty and clean forever of any thought" (*H*: 95). The idiot's congenital apathy is described here as the result of a cataclysm: the irreversible petrification of the Medusa annihilated within the idiot face the very possibility of thought and its emotional manifestation; ignorance is displayed there like a kind of absolute virginity, whose corollary is an almost infallible constancy. The idiot is a vacuum. That is how Faulkner evoked the idiot Benjy in the famous interview he granted Jean Stein in the *Paris Review* in 1956: "He knew only that something was wrong, which left a vacuum in which he grieved. He tried to fill that vacuum" (Stein, Spring 1956: 74). The idiot's face looks like a mask; frozen, enervated in the sense of having undergone nerve removal, it experiences no passion. Even in the grip of intense pain, the idiot's swollen face remains faithful to his unshakeable apathy, for he expresses nothing. We will see how his pain is expressed through other channels (gestures, the voice). To repeat one of Faulkner's favorite adjectives, which often characterizes the harshness and even indifference of female characters, the idiot is "impervious," which is to say impermeable, sealed off from the enticements of the world around him; he lives, practically imperturbable, within a protected sphere.

The empty faces of idiots sit atop languid bodies. Soft and apathetic idiot bodies are held together—agglomerated ("to cohere")—solely through the miracle of an uncertain assembly subject to malfunctioning ligaments. It is as though idiocy performs a strange ablation of all tension in the body, drowning the hardness of the skeletal structure in a soft and shapeless mass. Bodies appear to lose their contours, with the notion of silhouette giving way to that of "shape," which through the extension of the semantic field designates a being or an object that is vaguely perceived, whose nature cannot be assessed. In their shapeless swelling, idiot bodies are reduced to a heap of matter, to masses. In the penultimate scene from the short story "Hand upon the Waters,"[4] which was published in the *Saturday Evening Post* on November 4, 1939, before being included in *Knight's Gambit*, one of the two idiots in the story, named Joe, appears for the last time as follows: "the creature, the shape which had no tongue and needed none, which had been waiting nine days now for Lonnie Grinnup to come home, dropped toward the murderer's back with its hands already extended and its body curved and rigid with silent and deadly purpose" ("Hand": 79). In this description, the indeterminate notion of "creature" is paradoxically sharpened by the use of the even more indeterminate word "shape." The creature's shapelessness is confirmed by the use of the personal pronoun and the possessive adjective "it" and "its," which complete the denial of any human appearance for the idiot. The first appearance of Ike Snopes in *The Hamlet* is in the same vein: when the attention of Ratliff (and the reader) focuses on the new village idiot for the first time, his appearance is so little human that it brings an objectifying interrogative pronoun to Ratliff's lips, showing the extent of his surprise. "What's that?" (*H*: 90), he cries out before the spectacle of a man in overalls dragging two metal boxes behind him on a bit a string. The narrator, whose voice tends to be confused with that of the hawker of sewing machines and tales, assumes the latter's surprise for himself, hesitating over what terminology to use in referring to this thing that resembles nothing. The narration is consequently interspersed with expressions such as "the figure," "the creature," and "the hulking shape," which show the narrator's reluctance to recognize a human being in this body. It is only a few pages later that he comes upon, almost with relief, the adequate noun, which explains everything: "the idiot" (*H*: 90, 95). Faulkner himself described Benjy as a shapeless mass, and overcame the difficulty of clearly referring to his idiot by resorting to a variety of privative attributive adjectives: "Without thought or comprehension; shape*less*, neuter, like something eye*less* and voice*less* which might have lived, existed merely because of its ability to suffer, in the beginning of life; half fluid, groping: a pallid and help*less* mass of all mind*less* agony under sun" ("Intro *SF*, II": 231; emphasis mine). Through the accumulation of these adjectives, Faulkner retrospectively establishes an almost complete inventory (the two opening texts of *The Sound and the Fury* were composed in 1931) of his idiot's idiosyncrasies. An absence of intellect and shape,[5] a deficient voice and gaze, an embryonic mass, both fluid and indistinct: the idiot is almost nothing, and yet all misfortunes seem to converge within him. Characters, narrators, and the author all use the same depersonalizing and neutralizing vocabulary, as well as the same lexical delaying to signify the difficulty that language faces in giving shape to that which has none.

In a 1929 article from *Documents*, Georges Bataille wrote that the adjective "formless" is "not only an adjective having a given meaning, but a term that serves to bring things down in the world" (Bataille, 1985: 31). The notion of formlessness "brings down" idiots and helps to blur identities, just as the notion of form enables the classification of individuals deemed to be normal.[6] Diametrically opposed to the flabbiness of idiot bodies, "normal" bodies are readily described as rigid and inflexible; they neither bend nor sag, and bring to mind small tin soldiers. For example, Jewel in *As I Lay Dying* is described as "a flat figure cut leanly from tin" (*AILD*: 218), while his first name evokes the hardness of a diamond, although the firmness of his body is more often expressed through the choice of another material, wood. This is especially true of Darl, who describes Jewel as a wooden man. Many of Darl's monologues focus on this brother, who both obsesses and fascinates him, with Jewel almost always appearing to be carved from hard wood.[7] Jewel's face is revealed for the first time in the following manner: "his pale eyes like wood set into his wooden face" (4). His wooden body quickly becomes the subject of creative semantics, with the adjectives "wooden-faced" and "woodenbacked" (with varying spellings) appearing nearly every time Darl mentions his brother.[8] This rigidity even affects his gaze, which, depending on the narrator, resembles wood ("Jewel's eyes look like pale wood," Darl: 17), marbles ("Jewel's eyes look like marbles," Vardaman: 101), and broken dishes ("His eyes look like pieces of a broken plate," Tull: 126). In the symbolism of the characters, the man-of-wood—Jewel's solidity—stands in sharp contrast to the elusive contours of Darl—sometimes seen as crazy ("the one that folks say is queer," 24) and sometimes as an idiot ("the one that aint bright," 152)—who continues his inevitable disintegration and provides small folk with ample opportunity for comment.

Against all expectations, Jewel's rigidity, as it is inscribed in his body and expressed in his gaze, is threatened during a small anecdote recounted during the story. Taking the form of an analepsis, this comic interlude narrated by Darl[9] comes shortly after the Bundrens embark on their long odyssey toward the Jefferson cemetery. Beginning with the narcoleptic attacks that Jewel suffered for a few weeks around his fifteenth birthday, this story evokes—backward, with the consequences leading to the cause—the circumstances in which Jewel acquired his horse. Jewel began to suffer from sudden fatigue and grew so emaciated—"He was losing flesh" (130)—that he looked "gaunt as a bean-pole" (128-31). Jewel's exhaustion came from his running away at night, with his older brothers Darl and Cash showing the same taste for clownish comedy, offering comical guesses as to why. After concluding in less than flattering terms that there is a woman involved—"rutting" (131)—they wonder about the identity and endurance of the lady who put their brother in such a state: "'She's sure a stayer,' I told Cash. 'I used to admire her, but I downright respect her now'" (133). Jewel imagines that his nocturnal escapades go unnoticed, but he betrays them through his changed appearance and bearing: the wooden man is suddenly saddled with a soft body, his gait looks like that of a drunk—"stumbling along like he was drunk" (128)—and his hard gaze gives way to a dazed stupor, which soon evokes that of the idiot: "that first state of semi-idiocy" (133). Cash, a man of few words, secretly follows his brother and discovers the truth: "It aint a woman." It is indeed true that Jewel is being dragged from his bed by something other than a woman, for the object of his desire and the cause of his sleeplessness is a horse—his horse—won through long hours of nocturnal labor: "'It's all right,' Cash said. 'He earned the money. He cleaned up that forty acres of new ground Quick laid out last spring. He did it single handed, working at night by lantern. I saw him. So I dont reckon that horse cost anybody anything except Jewel. I dont reckon we need worry'" (135). During his next monologue a few pages later, when Darl returns to the story of the Bundrens' slow advance, Jewel is characterized by the same adverbs and affect ("trembling") as the horse he is riding. During the dangerous river crossing, man and horse are one, made of the same muscle and vertebrae: "The horse slips, goes under to the saddle, surges to its feet again, the current building up against Jewel's thighs" (47). The centaur's body has regained the hardness of wood; he is the favorite son, rigid, proud, and imperturbable, with an independence of which the others have been deprived,[10] the real man who leads the funeral procession.

Faulkner worked with living matter for his idiot characters, as the inert appearance of tin plate, rubber, wood, or glass is replaced by the mucosity of flesh. At the heart of the physical description of Benjy cited above is the adjective "dropsical" (*SF*: 274), which specifically refers to the condition of one suffering from hydropsy—an inflammation of serosity, organic fluids or watery parts in a natural body cavity or between two connective tissues—and is behind the impression of excess water. The use of this adjective suggests that Benjy's body owes its distended appearance to an abnormal inflow of liquids, which disturbs its continuity, conjunction, and assembly. The body of the second idiot in "Hand upon the Waters," Lonnie, who drowned, is displayed covered in a quilt in the room where the witnesses are questioned. The furtive gesture made by Gavin Stevens, who has just looked at Lonnie's familiar face for the last time, reflects the monstrousness of the deformed corpse, whose lengthy stay at the bottom of the river has engorged it with water: "The body lay under a quilt on the low platform to which the silent mill was bolted. He crossed to it and raised the corner of the quilt and turned, already on his way back to town" ("Hand": 68). Lonnie's corpse represents the acme of the Faulknerian idiot's hydropical body: the glut of water has irreversibly disfigured this body, which is no more than a vague amalgamation of decaying matter.

The verbs "to drop," "to dangle," "to drool," "to bob," and "to hang," combined with the adjectives "pendulous," "muscle-bound," and "loose," designate the essentially shapeless nature of idiot bodies through a semantics of dangling or flapping things, things that are loose or slack. The face of the idiot from "The Kingdom of God" seems precariously attached to the rest of the body: "his vacant, pendulous face hung over the back seat" ("Kingdom": 57). As the tension in his neck cannot hold his head upright, it constantly sways back and forth, with its little movements bringing to mind those of a pendulum. Benjy's hands hang motionless, struggling with the emptiness, as though no longer connected to his body: "But Ben sat in the chair, his soft hands dangling between his knees, moaning faintly" (*SF*: 285). This apparent autonomy of body parts reflects the failure of an organizing organ, in this case the brain, that can harmonize and unify the body's various functions. The singular dismemberment that is characteristic of the bodies of Faulknerian idiots finds a literal illustration in the episode of Benjy's castration, one that is as sordid as it is extreme. The disintegration of the idiot body also occurs through leaking bodily fluids. The constant repetition of the word "to drool," sometimes replaced by "to slobber," marks the outpouring of the surplus water characteristic of the idiot body through the incessant flow of drool. The idiot drools incessantly, his jaws never keeping his limp, half-open mouth closed. He stands gaping. This almost uninterrupted flow of viscous saliva becomes, in the case of Ike Snopes, the literal and prosaic expression of noble aspirations, for Ike is agape with admiration before his heart's desire, drooling for love of his cow. Here, drool becomes an unusual metaphor for the idiot's desire: "he stopped the alarmed and urgent moaning and followed her into the shed, speaking to her again, murmurous, drooling, and touched her with his hand" (*H*: 185). In similar fashion, Benjy's continual drooling marks the slackening of any form of bodily tension as well as his rootedness in a prolonged childish state, all the while metaphorically signaling the essential void presiding over his existence. The idiot always seems to be lacking something; he drools from a longing for the uncertain memory of the object either desired (the intimacy of a cow) or lost (an older sister's tenderness).

Since he cannot keep his jaws closed, Benjy needs constant help with his most basic needs. Dilsey, the Compson family's old Black servant who endeavors to compensate for the failure of motherly love, patiently wipes Benjy's mouth with the hem of her skirt: "Dilsey led Ben to the bed and drew him down beside her and she held him, rocking back and forth, wiping his drooling mouth upon the hem of her skirt. 'Hush, now,' she said, stroking his head. 'Hush. Dilsey got you'" (*SF*: 316). She is tender and nurturing, and gives the thirty-three-year-old idiot her full maternal attention. Luster, Dilsey's grandson and Benjy's keeper like his father before him, feeds Benjy with a spoon, as if he were having a baby try out solid food.[11] The idiot can indeed be pathologically considered an eternal child. With a three-year-old mind in an adult body,[12] one that bears the stigma of its anomaly—whose flabbiness and lack of muscle recall a baby's body, but one that it has largely exceeded in size with no subsequent hardening of matter—there is something incomplete about Benjy. This approximate character is reflected in his gait, which resembles that of a shambling bear. The disarticulate appearance of the idiot body gives it a singular appearance. When the idiot, who is not inclined to movement,[13] decides to walk, his step is marked by extreme clumsiness and awkwardness. He systematically drags his feet while passively following the trajectory that someone has generally set for him. In *The Sound and the Fury*, the passages relating to the narrative present repeatedly show Benjy struggling to follow the movement initiated by Luster.[14] His feeble, limp, and clumsy gait is notably depicted through use of the verb "shamble"[15]—"Ben shambled along beside Dilsey, watching Luster who anticked along ahead" (*SF*: 297)—thereby indicating his physiological inability to imprint, within his own body, the minimum of agility and flexibility needed for brisk movement.

In his book entitled (in its French translation) *Du Sens des sens: Contribution à l'étude des fondements de la psychologie* (The Sense of the Senses: Contribution to the Study of the Fundamentals of Psychology), Erwin Straus emphasizes how the human gait is radically different from that of animals: "By achieving the ability to stand and move while upright, men freed themselves from the direct contact with the ground that characterizes animals in all of their forms" (Straus, 1989: 323). By virtue of his stooping stance and lurching locomotion, the idiot occupies an intermediate position between an animal and a human. The animal nature of the idiot Joe, whose gestures are similar to those of a wild animal, is highlighted in "Hand upon the Waters": "suddenly a man rushed out of the undergrowth"; "he turned and scuttled past him" ("Hand": 64). The "undergrowth" can be interpreted as a local version of the jungle from which beasts and primitive creatures emerged. Joe could thus be seen as a Southern avatar of Tarzan, whose large stature he incidentally shares. This impression is confirmed in the short story's penultimate scene, in which Joe saves the life of Gavin Stevens by jumping from the tree where he was secretly perched onto the back of the criminal threatening Stevens with his weapon: "*He was in the tree*, Stevens thought" (79). Benjy's "shambling trot" (*SF*: 315) is the gangling appearance, to use the word's etymology, of one who moves in a dislocated manner. Repetition of the verb "shamble" also evokes, through extension of the semantic field, the disorder of a chaotic step. The gait signifies the step and is also a way of acting; the step thus becomes the preferred image for a way of being in the world: "Ben went on vaguely and purposelessly" (314). Vague and undefined, Benjy's step takes him nowhere, as the idiot is unable to move toward any particular goal. His step is feeble and indecisive because it is indeterminate and subject to the contingencies of recollection and feeling. In similar fashion, Ike Snopes's step is marked by a lack of coordination, "the thick reluctant hips working with a sort of abject and hopeless unco-ordination" (*H*: 186), "that paradoxical unco-ordinated skill and haste" (187), and "that thick, reluctant unco-ordination of thigh and knee" (203). The lack of coordination in movement is echoed by the spelling Faulkner uses for the word, which he systematically dismantles. This detail offers a clue for how the idiot's walk determines the approach taken by Faulknerian writing. The idiot's relaxed step is in keeping with a consciousness freed of all tension: "Ben ceased whimpering. He watched the spoon as it rose to his mouth. It was as if even eagerness were muscle-bound in him too, and hunger itself inarticulate, not knowing it is hunger" (*SF*: 276). The idiot's emotions and sensations are as limp as the body they inhabit. The psychological corollary of the body's flaccidity is expressed in the same terms as the lymphatic temperament (one of the four temperaments of ancient humoral medicine), characterized by slowness and apathy in addition to heavy and fatty forms. Eagerness, appetite, and any form of enthusiasm are distended, made slack, in a word diverted from their primary definition connected to the notion of tension. Benjy's impatience is "paralyzed" (according to the translation of "muscle-bound" proposed by Maurice-Edgar Coindreau [1971]), with excess flabbiness combining with a fundamental incapacity to express intention. This is why the idiot is often described in a relaxed and inevitably idle position—"Ben sat, tranquil and empty" (*SF*: 284)—whereas nothing, or almost nothing, can disturb his inner void "utterly vacant of thought." Nothing in Benjy's everyday gestures is motivated by a signification—he sees nothing but emptiness. Just as the particles of his body are precariously assembled, the events of his existence do not logically follow one another, nor do they "cohere." Limp body and lymphatic spirit contribute to the essentially "inarticulate" appearance of the idiot's reality: his perception of the world lacks articulation and is expressed in a language with no clarity, steeped in a strange confusion.

Chapter 3

INARTICULATE VOICE AND STORY

> Charlie came and put his hands on Caddy and I cried more. I cried loud.
> "No, no." Caddy said. "No. No."
> "He cant talk." Charlie said. "Caddy."
> "Are you crazy." Caddy said. She began to breathe
> fast. "He can see. Don't. Don't."
> —WILLIAM FAULKNER, *THE SOUND AND THE FURY*

Joints or articulations, which in a normally constituted body refer to the soft and hard parts that connect two or more adjoining bones, are under threat in the idiot's body, which is built on a precarious architecture in which flesh engulfs the bone structure so much that the connection between them no longer seems to exist. The idiot's body is a dislocated body, as if amputated in articulation. In a spillover effect, the idiot's time is disconnected and dislocated, with no form of unity. The notion of "inarticulation" is based on a neologism created from the English word *inarticulate*, which as a synonym for "incoherent" or "unintelligible" refers to speech lacking any quality of expression. It obviously includes the word "articulation" in its phonetic and phonological sense: to articulate also means to produce an element of language through movements of the lips and tongue. On the contrary, in the adjective "inarticulate," the negative prefix "in" introduces the impossibility and even inability to produce intelligible vocal sounds. The notion of an inarticulate story will be defined as an exercise in failing speech, replaced instead by cries that reveal the idiot's rootedness in the world of feeling, beyond the realm of knowledge. In line with this reflection, the possible existence of an idiot narrator raises questions regarding the essence of narration. Ultimately it will become clear that an inarticulate story develops like a discourse entirely bereft of articulations, which is to say connections, as opposed to a normative discourse whose comprehension is notably guaranteed by the logical links that ensure its coherence.

CHAPTER 3

THE MONOTONOUS DRONE OF FAILING SPEECH

When in a moment of irritation Luster describes Benjy Compson as a deaf-and-dumb person—"He deef and dumb" (*SF*: 49)—he draws on popular beliefs that denied idiots any possible form of communication whatsoever. Yet do Faulknerian idiots actually suffer from deafness and muteness? Is this dual pathology a commonplace that irremediably reduces them to an unfathomable silence, or is it simply an image that depicts the narrow world in which they live? The first description of Joe, the idiot from "Hand upon the Waters," highlights the strange cohabitation of adult and childlike characteristics in a body whose intense gaze compensates for the silence to which Joe is condemned for eternity: "an adult, yet with something childlike about him, about the way he moved, barefoot, in battered overalls and with the urgent eyes of the deaf and dumb" ("Hand": 64). Joe is therefore an authentic deaf-mute. There is no doubt that Benjy is also deprived of speech: "He cant talk" (*SF*: 47). However, the first lines of *The Sound and the Fury* immediately demonstrate his keen sense of hearing. The oft-repeated qualifier "inarticulate"—"Ben squatted before it, moaning, a slow, inarticulate sound" (315)—signals both an unintelligible sound and a congenital inability to express oneself clearly; it refers to the means of expression available to the idiot, which never surpassed the level of early childhood. As perpetual *infans*, Faulknerian idiots literally have no tongue, as they lack the organ of speech. Joe is described as "the shape which had *no tongue* and needed none" ("Hand": 79; emphasis mine here and in the following examples). Ike, whose peculiar love is condemned to fuel the voyeuristic appetites of the community from Frenchman's Bend (with Lump Snopes converting the scandal into a lucrative peep show), appears at the center of the gazing crowd like "the blasted *tongueless* face" (*H*: 217). However, not all Faulknerian idiots lack a tongue, as there is one notable exception. Monk, the idiot from the short story of the same name, is described on multiple occasions as a chronic chatterbox, as long as he has an audience: "pleasant, impervious to affront, *talkative* when anyone would listen, with that shrewd, foolish face, that face at once cunning and dreamy" ("Monk": 43). The approximate mastery of language that distinguishes Monk from other Faulknerian idiots—despite his undeniable consanguineous origins—results from the fact that Monk is not formally identified as an idiot: the word "idiot" is never actually used in the story. The narrator prefers circumlocutions such as "He was a moron, perhaps even a cretin" (39), "a mere flesh-and-blood imbecile" (50), or "that half-wit they hanged" (53). Yet this dithering ("moron," "cretin," "half-wit") over the term "idiot" is not the mark of a genuine difference in nature between Monk and other Faulknerian idiots. While Monk may be simpleminded, the victim of unfavorable family and social circumstances, Faulkner is not interested in the causes, origins, or specific symptomatology of his idiocy. In fact, while Monk does speak, the narrator does not reveal the content of his words and insists on their unintelligibility instead.

With the Faulknerian idiot, the physiological anomaly represented by the absence of language can, via metonymy, be seen as the literal image of the failure of language. Upon further analysis, it can also be interpreted as reflecting a special relation with the sensible world, one of indivisible and alinguistic proximity.[1] Claude Romano has shown how Benjy (and this is the case for all of his literary fellows) is rooted in the world of feeling, beyond concepts and words: "The world of feeling unfolds [. . .] wholly on the level of nascent, preverbal significations, inseparably sensitive and emotive" (Romano, 2005: 44). He adds that "feeling is the locus for the significations that adhere to things, which are known before they are recognized, the seat of an indivisible and global 'knowledge,' one that is nonanalytical and nonthematic, but nevertheless consistent" (46). That he cannot speak in no way detracts from the fact that the idiot experiences a certain number of things. Idiocy is actually a locus for a singular adhesion to the sensible world, in which the distinctions between the feeling subject and the felt object, between the name given to a thing and the thing itself, are abolished. For the idiot, there is no articulation between the subject and the object, between language and the thing: the very notion of a link dissolves in a relation of absolute immanence. The idiot exists on the same level as things, he is a thing among others, for whom a word has meaning only if it *is* the thing it designates. The very possibility of a conceptual language is also completely frustrated. If a word has meaning for an idiot only through its absolute adhesion to the thing it designates, and if the idiot is likely to identify a word solely with a single object, we can understand his fundamental resistance to the notion of polysemy, which according to Ferdinand de Saussure's terminology attributes multiple signifieds to the same signifier. This explains the drama that opens *The Sound and the Fury*, as the word "caddie" only has one possible meaning for Benjy—it can only be his sister's name. In addition, the use of this same word—or more specifically the acoustic image of the word—in a different context (that of golf) necessarily takes him back to the absent figure of Caddy, whose absence is precisely materialized by the fact that, in this specific case, the only thing (person) that can be designated by the word no longer adheres to the word, is no longer summoned by it. If it is divorced from the thing it designates, and does not coincide with the presence of the designated thing, then the word is invariably a source of pain for the idiot, who is cruelly deprived of the few rare markers he possesses.

The idiot exists in the domain of action, of immediate presence. In his limited understanding that is impervious to multiple meanings, words have little value in comparison to the sensible reality of experience. The idiot's experience can do without the mediation of words, which, all things considered, are for him no more than conventional designations that he somehow integrates within the extreme limits of his comprehension, for the individuals he mixes with use them with such insistence that he cannot escape them entirely. However, on a fundamental level, the words that Benjy makes out do not stand out from the visual or olfactory sensations that he records. As Stephen Ross notes in *Fiction's Inexhaustible Voice*, for Benjy words are akin to sound sensations: "For Benjy the speech of others is just another sensation to be recorded, like sights and smells" (Ross, 1989: 178). Benjy reacts to a small number of words that essentially correspond to the endlessly repeated names that ultimately refer, even in his mind, to his kin. In *The Hamlet*, Ratliff, the stunned and fascinated viewer who serves as a filter of perception in the example below, speculates about the idiot's relation to words. Faced with the tribe's males, who satisfy their baser instincts and frustrated desires in the pathetic spectacle of Ike imprisoned in a pen with his cow, he notes that the idiot is alone and debased by the circumstances but no less rich in the authentic passions he has experienced: "him who had been given the *wordless* passions but not the specious words" (*H*: 217). In identifying with the idiot, Ratliff appears to suggest that sincere passions can willingly forego language, whose words are forever "specious" and illusory. For him, the humiliation suffered by the idiot is transcended by what he implicitly interprets as a gift, which further distinguishes the idiot from the community's men and raises him above them: the singular ability to be one with reality, to have a privileged relation to life, even if primitive and preverbal. Romano remarks regarding Benjy that "he is the one through whom the world reveals itself in its radical injustification, in its pure and naked donation" (Romano, 2005: 37); this is also true of Ike Snopes. The idiot, who cannot speak, thus emerges as the prominent locus for genuine emotions, because these emotions remain irreversibly inexpressible, which is to say protected from the corrupting power of words, forever condemned to fail at grasping reality. As suggested by Erwin Straus, "All that is previously structured and thought by language masks that which is experienced on the nonlinguistic level the moment we try to understand our experience, or to even simply express its content" (Straus, 1989: 325). Language acts like a mask with respect to experience, necessarily altering its authenticity.

At the center of *As I Lay Dying*, in the only monologue for which she is the disembodied source, Addie Bundren, the dead mother whose body is being laboriously conveyed to the cemetery in Jefferson, despite the storm and flooding that has swept away all of the bridges and indefinitely extended the terrible odyssey she has imposed on her kin, forcefully rejects language by saying "words are no good" (*AILD*: 171). The voice that comes from the coffin, emanating from a body that, after suffering many curses, is in an advanced state of putrefaction—as demonstrated by the concentric circling of the buzzards around an odor that attracts more and more of them—denounces the fundamental inability of words to say things. The position of this unique monologue in crafting the story helps to intensify its aim, for at the very moment when she retraces her journey as a spouse and mother, and denies the power of words, "Addie"—the source of the speech as indicated by the heading for the novel's fortieth chapter—is hardly identifiable by this name, for at best she is the remains of a life and at worst an unrecognizable heap of putrid flesh. Indeed, Addie is no longer; her name no longer refers to a tangible reality. Yet, she considers words to be labels that can be interchanged indiscriminately: "Anse or love; love or Anse: it didn't matter" (172); "It doesn't matter. It doesn't matter what they call them" (173). The only power she concedes to language is that of laying traps, with the verb "to trick" interspersed throughout her discourse. The choices and decisions that defined her life were so many lures: "It was as though he had tricked me, hidden within a word like within a paper screen and struck me in the back through it. But then I realised that I had been tricked by words older than Anse or love, and that the same word had tricked Anse too" (172). According to Addie, Anse (her husband) and herself were both victims of an immemorial machination: the transitory blindness of words that speak powerful emotions. Yet the word "love" and the words of love are, like other words, simply containers without contents—pods without seeds, vague "shapes" filling a dizzying emptiness: "I knew that that word was like the others: just a shape to fill a lack" (172). The content of these shapes is irremediably destined to disappear, to vanish: "liquefying," "flowing," "fading away." The text increasingly uses images of dissolution. Experience is rooted in a here and now that words—invented to fill in for its immediate disappearance, to mask the absence of life—are condemned to *mis*speak. Ultimately, words are needed only by those who do not have access to the things they designate: "I knew that motherhood was invented by someone who had to have a word for it because the ones that had the children didn't care whether there was a word for it or not" (171). For her, life does not need wording. On a fundamental level, what Addie is calling into question in this monologue (paradoxically characterized by her superb eloquence) is the relation between reality and words, between the signifier and the signified: "words dont ever fit even what they are trying to say at" (171). More generally, she denounces the chasm separating reality from its representations. In the body of the text, when Addie tries to recall the memory or the "shape" of her own virgin body, the inadequacy of the word for the thing is represented by a blank space, the only acceptable sign, resonantly materializing the failure of language: "The shape of my body where I used to be a virgin is in the shape of a   " (173).

What is irremediably lost for Addie is lost all the more so for language. In his *Le Réel: Traité de l'idiotie*, Clément Rosset's examination of Addie Bundren's monologue distinguishes between "two kinds of realities," "verbal reality and material reality":

> The reality that, on the one hand, sticks to the word and disappears with it, consisting of words that Addie compares to "spiders dangling by their mouths from a beam, swinging and twisting and never touching"; the reality that, on the other hand, lies dormant behind the word and reveals itself through the gap between itself and the word, which at best is able to suggest it. All that language can do, again in the best of cases, is to show how impotent it is to say what it seeks to say. Addie links this impotence of the word to an evaporation effect in which any reference to reality dissipates in the air like butter melting in an overheated pan, and opposes it to the rootedness of reality, destined to crawl, destined to the forced attachment of things. "I would think how words go straight up in a thin line, quick and harmless, and how terribly doing goes along the earth, clinging to it." (Rosset, 1986: 117)[2]

Rosset's analysis of Addie Bundren's only monologue in his essay devoted to the idiocy of the real is not fortuitous: taking up the traditional distinction between words and deeds, the opposition between the evaporation (dissolution) of words and the rootedness of things brings to mind the singular being-in-the-world of idiots. Faulknerian idiots offer an ideal alternative to the visceral frustration underpinning Addie's monologue: beyond a language that they in no way control, one that remains fundamentally foreign to them, idiots nevertheless have a privileged connection with things. Unable to "go straight up" to the abstraction of language, they "cling" to things, maintaining an intense and unequivocal relation with them, one that is impervious to the arbitrariness of language. Accordingly, Addie's dismay from inside her coffin toward the fallacious mechanisms of words can be read as regret for not being an idiot, irremediably plunged in "the dark voicelessness in which the words are the deeds" (*AILD*: 174).[3] Addie Bundren's melancholy can be interpreted through its connection to the frustration of not being able, like animals and idiots, "to absorb oneself in the nonlinguistic world": "[M]en are banished from paradise, with only artificial paradises being open to them. It is impossible for us to fully reach the nonlinguistic world, which we will succeed in doing only as we turn our back to the authentic human world" (Straus, 1989: 323–24). Addie's speech fades away at the end of her monologue as she gains access to the nonlinguistic ideal only through the silence of her own death.

While he may not be able to speak, the idiot nevertheless has a voice, for the absence of speech does not exclude the existence of a voice. In his treatise *On the Soul*, Aristotle distinguishes the voice (*phônè*), which is shared by humans and animals, from speech (*logos*), which is particular to humans: "[Voice] is a particular sound made by an animate thing" (Aristotle, 2018: 38). Benjy, Ike, Joe, the idiot from "The Kingdom of God," and Jim Bond, the last survivor of the Sutpen lineage in *Absalom, Absalom!*, use their voice simply to moan or yell, modulating the notes of their voices across a broad range of sounds, often at a high decibel level. Throughout *The Sound and the Fury*, only one thing is regularly asked of Benjy: that he keep quiet, that he be silent. The first such request comes on the opening page of the novel: "Hush up that moaning" (*SF*: 3); the novel incidentally concludes, some three hundred pages later, in the frenetic, intertwined voices of Luster and Jason, his keeper and his brother, both of whom are powerless to stop Benjy's booming voice, which does not articulate an intelligible language—the adjective "tongueless" (320) is used—but nevertheless expresses a tremendous sense of distress. Impervious to imploring or authoritarian requests to "Hush!" and "Shut up!" (320), the inhuman voice that surges forth in the last lines of *The Sound and the Fury*, before recovering its precarious calm, is the voice of horrible pain,[4] all the more intense as it is conveyed through an unfathomable furor, one that could only be uttered by this sound. Yelling and moaning, inarticulate sounds that by definition deliver no clear message, emerge as the only way for idiots to show themselves and attract attention, to try to express something: "Ben recalled him by whimpering again" (*SF*: 277). As it were, idiots truly exist for others solely on the condition that they make noise, which is why yells and moans are steadily present at all ages of the idiot's life, a sign that neither salvation nor evolution are possible. Idiocy can be seen as a state without remission, in which the cry has definitively replaced speech.[5] The horrifying continuity of Benjy's screams is emphasized by his three successive keepers, all members of the Gibson family, specifically Versh, T. P., and Luster. Serving as temporal milestones of sorts that provide vague points of reference within the confusion of the narrative, their very function is proof of the idiot's stagnation in an inexorable state of dependence. Each has a different vocabulary to refer to the same racket they find unbearable yet cannot appease, for the idiot's cry never stops, except to give way to a moan: "He had ceased crying, but now he began to whimper again" (317).

Through their rootedness in the world of feeling and inability to articulate a clear language in which the voice becomes speech, idiots exist on a level that is close to that of animals. In his interview with Jean Stein, Faulkner confirmed this notion of similarity between idiots and animals in connection with Benjy: "He was an animal. He recognized tenderness and love though he could not have named them, and it was the threat to tenderness and love that caused him to bellow when he felt the change in Caddy" (Stein, Spring 1956: 74). Faulkner defined the animality of his idiot by opposing feeling with an inability to say: for an idiot, it is not words but cries that signal change, which he invariably perceives as a threat to his order, habits, and adaptation to the world. The terms used by Erwin Straus to define "the symbiotic understanding" of animals could apply to the idiot, who like an animal "does not understand language as such, which is to say as a series of words that carry general meanings." If animals, and let us include idiots, react to a word, "only the acoustic structure acts, and precisely does so as a signal" (Straus, 1989: 319). Hermetically isolated from the noise of the world surrounding him, Joe wails like a beast; a single verb, repeated incessantly, attests to his presence: "whimper."[6] He emits what the narrator considers "an actual sound"—"the deaf-and-dumb man began to make an actual sound" ("Hand": 65)—one that strikes him as conveying a meaning, only when he instinctively feels that his guardian and master, Lonnie, is under threat. It is from this same master, to whom he is as loyal as a dog, that came the only sound to which the idiot could respond: "the deaf-and-dumb youth lay on the porch or the ground just outside, where he could hear him who was brother and father both, breathing. It was his one sound out of all the voiceless earth. He was infallibly aware of it" (67). Joe functions according to an animal logic in which a stimulus invariably leads to the same reaction: he lies near his master to hear him breathe and, reassured by the permanence of this sound, falls asleep. However, after Lonnie's death, the "voiceless earth" grows even more silent: depriving Joe of the only sound he could understand, it plunges him into absolute silence, in which his own cry rings hollow.

"Whimper," "moan," "wail," "cry," "roar," and "bellow" make their mark through juxtaposition, alternation, and repetition, all of the possible variations of the idiot's cry, from yells of pain to the mewling of a newborn, from the plaintive yelping of a puppy to the wailing of a siren, the lowing of a cow to the bellowing of a bull, the roaring of a storm to the rumbling of the sea, from vociferation to clamor. When he appears for the first time in *The Hamlet*, Ike Snopes is silent, entirely absorbed in contemplating the cloud of dust kicked up by the toy he is dragging on a string. The men of Frenchman's Bend, who seem to have taken up permanent residence on the porch of Varner's store, offer the stunned Ratliff a few brief explanations regarding the odd customer that is Ike Snopes.[7] One of them straightaway suggests that the idiot, who lives under the guardianship of the innkeeper Mrs. Littlejohn, does not speak their language: "He sleeps in her barn. [. . .] She feeds him. He does some work. She can talk to him some how" (*H*: 90). Yet even the hamlet's oafs acknowledge that the idiot has, in a manner of speaking, his own form of communication, which only a few rare individuals seem capable of decoding. The scene continues with Ike entering the store, his toy getting stuck against the base of the counter. Disturbed by this obstacle that he is entirely unable to overcome, the idiot gives free rein to his immense sorrow, "beginning a wet whimpering moaning at once pettish and concerned and terrified and amazed until Snopes kicked the block free with his toe" (*H*: 95). This appalling cry over a trifle (a little kick of the toe ends the drama) is represented here by the accumulation of modifiers: here "moaning" is used as a noun, accompanied by the adjectival and redundant "whimpering," itself preceded by a "wet" filled with drooling and tears. In the continuity of the phrase, the adjectives that qualify the content of the idiot's grievance, including bad mood ("pettish"), worry ("concerned"), terror ("terrified"), and stupor ("amazed"), form a muddle of affects in which the narrator struggles to find bearings. The accumulation of redundant and sometimes contradictory terms intensifies the cry, all the while signaling the mystery of this cry, which says nothing and everything at once, resisting any label. In section 2 of chapter 1 from "The Long Summer" (the third book of *The Hamlet*), devoted to the adventure of Ike Snopes and his cow, the narrator seems to similarly hesitate over the right word for the idiot's cry: the repetition of "moaning," which appears up to eight times on a single page (*H*: 195), increases with the appearance of Houston, who tries to take the cow and put it back in the pen; the alternation of long moans and brief silences is marked by the duality between "moaning" and "not moaning," with silence being no more than a nascent moan. Moaning is also sometimes described as "whimpering" (187) and culminates with the repetition of "bellowing," which seems to express the idiot's frustrated desire, and is answered by "the bellowing cow" (192). Faced with the indeterminacy of the nature and signification of the idiot's cry, the narrator is sometimes content with using the word "sound," which generally refers to noise. A long chain of adjectives and nouns follows in an attempt to describe this sound, which refuses any clear qualification: "the faint, hoarse sound" (186); "the hoarse sound of bafflement and incredulous grieving" (186). Through the interplay of articles transforming into possessive adjectives—"his faint hoarse sound" (194)—this indefinable cry in the end becomes Ike's sound, the specific manifestation of his unique presence in the world: "the one sound which he knew, or at least was ever known to make, and that infallibly when anyone spoke to him" (197). In the chain of communication, the idiot's cry occupies a space left vacant by words; the cry is ultimately the language of what the idiot senses and feels.

The idiot's expressiveness is therefore limited to the range and possible modulations of his vocal chords, in what Gilles Deleuze defined in *Francis Bacon: The Logic of Sensation* as a "*zone of indiscernibility or undecidability between man and animal*" (Deleuze, 2003: 16). In Benjy's case, the consistency and regularity of his cry are expressed through repetition of the adverb "steadily," which brings color to its various nuances: "he wailed steadily" (*SF*: 317). The cry, which is both gradual and uninterrupted, mixes with the rough and hoarse tones characteristic of Benjy's breaking voice, similar to the croaking of a toad:[8] "Ben clung to the fence, wailing steadily and hoarsely" (316).

Rarely silent, the idiot untiringly sings his painful melody, sometimes very quietly when he is alone: "Ben was still moaning a little, as to himself" (301); "Ben was still whimpering, though not loud" (298). At the other end of the sound spectrum, the idiot's voice can assume a terrifying scope: "He screamed a hoarse, inarticulate bellow. [...] The idiot howled unceasingly, filling the street with dreadful sound" ("Kingdom": 58). The voice of the character from "The Kingdom of God" fills both the space of the short story and the street it takes place in with his howling, which becomes all the more terrifying as it grows louder all while remaining inarticulate, doomed by the failure of his desire to say. This accentuation and intensification of the cry leading to its climax in an "unbelievable crescendo"[9] is conveyed by the recurrence of verb-"and"-verb or noun-"on"-noun syntactical structures, which signify a process in which sound accumulates on sound: "Ben's voice roared and roared" (*SF*: 319); "Bellow on bellow, his voice mounted, with scarce interval for breath" (320). The accumulation of sounds and the filling of the narrative space by the cry evoke no more than sound and its opposite, namely the emptiness and silence that characterize the beyond. However, for individuals whose ears are endowed with speech, this tumult, this "fury," signifies nothing. This brings to mind the excerpt from Shakespeare's tragedy that gave the book its title:

> Life's but a walking shadow, a poor player
> That struts and frets his hour upon the stage,
> And then is heard no more: it is a tale
> Told by an idiot, full of sound and fury,
> Signifying nothing. (*Macbeth* 5.5.24–28)

The idiot is like the poor player that is life, whose vain gesticulations and senseless droning last a moment before the great silence; his fundamentally abstruse language gathers fury into a chaos of sound "signifying" nothing, a chaos that nevertheless clears the way for a logic of infra-language meaning. The idiot's cry is pure sound, "just sound," in which agony can gather; or perhaps it is a superimposition of vibrations in the air, stirred about ridiculously, ephemerally: "Then Ben wailed again, *hopeless* and prolonged. It was nothing. Just sound. It might have been all time and injustice and sorrow become vocal for an instant by a conjunction of planets" (*SF*: 288). It is because Benjy says nothing that his cry can contain both what is infinitely great and what is insignificant, everything and almost nothing;[10] as suggested by the form "might have been," it is simply a question of interpretation. The return of adjectives containing privative suffixes describes the cry through absence and emptiness: "the grave *hopeless* sound of all *voiceless* misery under the sun" (316); "There was more than astonishment in it, it was horror; shock; agony *eyeless, tongueless*; just sound" (320; emphasis mine). This cry without an origin, which says nothing but can nevertheless express everything from astonishment to the most intense horror, is the voice of that which has no words.

Deleuze's analysis of Francis Bacon's painting in *The Logic of Sensation* makes it possible to establish a link between the painter's pictorial aesthetics and Faulkner's stylistic choices, in the sense that both seem to prefer the isolated figure of the cry to the "figuration" of what looms within the hollowness of this cry: "Bacon has always tried to eliminate the 'sensational,' that is, the primary figuration of that which provokes a violent sensation. This is the meaning of the formula, 'I wanted to paint the scream more than the horror'" (Deleuze, 2003: 27). This also brings to mind Edvard Munch's famous painting *The Scream*, in which, as noted by Christine Savinel in her article "L'Informe dans *Sanctuaire*" (The Shapeless in *Sanctuary*), "the linguistic inability of the pictorial medium mirrors, through its silence, the terror portrayed on the face" (Savinel, October 1995: 297). Faulkner similarly favors the scream to the horror, which paradoxically takes nothing away from the intensity of the horror contained in the scream. The miserable story of Benjy thus unfolds beyond words, in "the slow intervals of Ben's voice" (*SF*: 316).

THE IDIOT *I*

A singular irony and "tour de force" in the gallery of Faulknerian idiots, Benjy enjoys a special status, for he is not only a character but also a narrator. What's more, he is the novel's first narrator. In his book entitled *Jusqu'à Faulkner* (Until Faulkner), Pierre Bergounioux remarks: "It is Benjy who opens the ball. What will emerge in the stories of Quentin and Jason is first submerged in the brain of an idiot" (Bergounioux, 2002: 131). Section 1 of *The Sound and the Fury* is therefore based on a fundamental paradox, as Faulkner makes Benjy an idiot endowed with a voice, but one who is unable to articulate words, hence making the idiot a being of language. With this in mind, the *I* with which the narrative opens can be considered an impossibility, even an imposture. Numerous critics have evoked the radical way in which the novel's opening frees itself of novelistic conventions. While I cannot cite all of them, below are a few of their observations. In his *William Faulkner: The Yoknapatawpha Country*, Cleanth Brooks describes Benjy's monologue as a tale that is not told: "Benjy's section, a tale told by an idiot, is not a tale told at all, but a kind of fuguelike arrangement and rearrangement of sights, smells, sounds, and actions, many of them meaningless in themselves, but tied together by some crisscross of association" (Brooks, 1963: 347). More recently, Martin Kreiswirth has emphasized that none of the specifications that accompany the notion of exposition are present: "Instead of beginning with a traditional introductory apparatus—the setting of the scene, the description of the major characters, the initiation of the action, and so forth—Faulkner eschews conventional exposition and offers a technical tour de force, directly presenting the curiously formal idiolect of an abnormally limited mind" (Kreiswirth, Summer 1981: 288).[11] From its very first words, *The Sound and the Fury* is a small revolution. Phillip Novak foregoes the umpteenth detailed analysis of the novel's opening paragraph but nevertheless provides a complete list of its various aspects:

> So much has been said about this particular bit of modernist "defamiliarization" during the course of the past fifty years that there is little need here for yet another catalog of the qualities that have made it one of literature's most notorious opening gambits. It is, however, worth noting that the most apparent of its stylistic idiosyncrasies—the extreme simplicity of the sentence structure; the odd, dream-like vacuity which marks the text's attempts at identifying its objects and actions; the absence of the kind of causality that would allow us to see the relation between the golfer's "Here, caddie" (which seems in fact to emanate from nowhere) and Benjy's moaning [...]—all of these work toward the impoverishment of the narrative voice. (Novak, Fall 1996: 67)

The Sound and the Fury opens with a feeling of radical strangeness, a direct consequence of the narrator's eccentricity, for the voice that rises in the novel's first lines is decentered and disembodied. The question of its source immediately emerges as a problem or a rupture, or as Noel Polk has suggested in his *Children of the Dark House*, a "violation"[12] of the reader's legitimate expectations. In *The Sound and the Fury* Faulkner thus finds himself in an awkward position with regard to narrative conventions and the subsequent expectations of the listener. Through the character of Benjy, the idiot narrator, he puts in place an idiolect, a particular language that is used by only one person, thereby distorting the notion of idiom: the language that imposes itself in these first pages does not coincide with a community's means of expression or match a particular form of thought; this is the essential surprise of this novel's opening and its negation of any sense of familiarity. The idiolect is the expression of the specificity of a unique being and narrator; in this instance it is the language of an individual who fundamentally does not know how to speak or think. Faulkner pretends to be the faithful transcriber of this language. Since Benjy is mute in the sense that his vocal production is limited to moaning and yelling, the interior monologue emerged for the author as the only technical subterfuge that could transmute an idiot deprived of language into a narrator, a literary convention whose function is to be in charge of the story. In a narrative, the narrator is usually the one that speaks, as opposed to the author, who is the one that wrote. The narrative method of the "stream of consciousness"[13] can avoid the obstacle presented by the idiot's muteness in that it reflects a thought that has not risen to the status of speech. Polk reminds us that "it is useful to keep in mind that Benjy does not use words; he does not *tell* us things, but experiences them directly" (Polk, 1996: 105). Since it is not a narrative in the traditional sense of the term, Benjy's section unfolds like a tangle of scenes experienced beyond words. Yet it is indeed a book of language that readers of *The Sound and the Fury* hold in their hands. With regard to the narrator Benjy, the circumvention of the spoken word is actually based on a multifaceted illusion: consisting of written representations of vocal sounds, which the reader apprehends as silent traces on the page, the stream of consciousness presents itself as the establishment of a direct and therefore privileged communication with the consciousness of the idiot character. At the same time, the stream of consciousness technique indirectly brings about a return to the source of the written word, for if Benjy the narrator is nonlinguistic, the language of section 1 of *The Sound and the Fury* can only be that of Faulkner the writer. The first paradox surrounding Benjy's monologue, placing an idiot suffering from muteness in the position of narrator, indirectly emphasizes the crucial importance of he who, in distributing the roles, assigned him this one—namely the author, the self-proclaimed stage director who also acts as a prompter. This first interior monologue, a name that Gérard Genette preferred to replace with that of "discours immédiat" (immediate speech),[14] is despite appearances not at all immediate, as the author's mediation with respect to "narrative patronage" precisely plays both a central and decisive role.

Benjy the narrator thus assumes a dual value, both paradigmatic and demystifying: his muteness as an idiot narrator indirectly draws attention to the illusion entailed by the invention of any narrator, whose discourse consists simply of the words that an author has placed within him. By creating an idiot narrator, Faulkner implicitly denounces the artifice that generally presides over the art of the novel: he unmasks the many complexities that narrative strategies have tirelessly worked to conceal over the ages. Any literary work is the act of an author, even if he or she strives to disappear behind the narrator. As a result, there is an author behind every narrator, a demiurge on a human scale, with the narrator being no more than one of the many artifices of literary creation. Faulkner's narrator idiot can subsequently be seen as the manifestation of a voluntary regression, as the desire for a return to primitive forms of apprehending the world and narrative art. In the interview with Jean Stein, Faulkner justified his decision to open *The Sound and the Fury* from the point of view of an idiot narrator in the following way: "I had already begun to tell the story through the eyes of the idiot child, since I felt that it would be more effective as told by someone capable only of knowing what happened, but not why" (Stein, Spring 1956: 73). The effectiveness of his choice resides in the fact that the idiot narrator does not ask why, that he exists outside the causal chain. Yet what Faulkner artfully does not reveal—for it would undermine the ruse on which the first monologue of *The Sound and the Fury* is based—is that its narrator not only is deprived of speech but also and especially exists outside of language, thereby representing, term for term, the exact opposite of what a narrator is. If we return to Faulkner's words mentioned above, the paradox of a story that is not recounted is implicitly contained in the intentional vagueness of the passive "told by someone." The idiot narrator can claim to fulfill his function as a narrator only because the author first invented a language that resembles him: "The only thing I can feel about him personally," Faulkner added, "is concern as to whether he is believable as I created him" (Stein, Spring 1956: 74). We understand why Benjy's credibility is such a central concern for his creator, for beyond the characterization of his idiocy, it takes place through the invention of a language that is literally unprecedented (for a nonlinguistic idiot never had the opportunity to ascribe words to his feelings) as well as unique (because it necessarily has no model).[15] The second paradox of the novel's opening is that by being positioned first, the idiot's impossible discourse is nevertheless plausible, for while readers could revolt against the impossibility of the idiot character's discourse, they have already deferred to the *I* raised by the idiot's voice.[16] Such is the trap that Faulkner ultimately laid for us: he wins readers over to his cause through literary convention and then shamelessly refers them back to their own credulity. In other words, at the very moment when the impossibility of Benjy the narrator appears, this voice, whose source is dubious to say the least, has already gripped the reader in its twists and turns: it is too late to backtrack, too late to no longer believe it.

One could say that in order to create Benjy, and to invent his language in particular, Faulkner set out in search of "his inner idiot."[17] For Faulkner, Benjy's consciousness (we will discuss this later) was a pretext for creating new and unique forms, in a dual rupture with both centuries of literary tradition and the expectations of his readers. Pierre Bergounioux has emphasized the latter point:

> When Faulkner returns to origins—which is to say what those who live on the other side of the thin boarded wall do, feel, and say—when he returns to the essential and shall we say prehistoric confusion that the narration and the story have denied and forgotten in order to establish themselves, he directly clashes with the expectations of cultured minds, the only ones likely to read it. (Bergounioux, 2002: 121)

The invention of an idiot language could be nothing but iconoclastic. In inventing a language for his idiot narrator, Faulkner had no choice but to summon his talent and intelligence to act the idiot, and to immerse himself in a process of identifying with the idiot, an imaginative high-wire act whose singularity has no doubt shaken or shocked more than one reader.

DISCONNECTIONS

What are the constituent elements of this idiot language, whose source is not—and cannot be—the idiot narrator but rather the author, who verbally represents what characters see, feel, and in a word experience, as they are experiencing it? What are the idiosyncrasies of idiot syntax, a fiction of a nonexistent language? To begin with, two levels of language can be distinguished in Benjy's monologue: the ebb and flow of his own impressions, expressed in rudimentary language; and snippets of dialogue and conversations overheard and memorized over the years, which tend to belong to a much more developed register of language. In his essay "A Rhetoric for Benjy," L. Moffitt Cecil suggests that "when, in the telling, [Benjy's] own few words are quickly exhausted, the remembered speech of others filters conveniently through his consciousness, carrying the burden of his narrative" (Cecil, Fall 1970: 37). Yet such a division of section 1 of *The Sound and the Fury* hardly accounts for the confusion that is its heart and soul. Benjy's discourse[18] is a jumble of raw and immediate impressions whose incessant emergence is experienced as a constantly renewed present. Recollection is cut off from bygone days and is instead condemned to present events. As suggested by André Bleikasten, Benjy's discourse is like the tape in a recording device,[19] for it neither sorts nor imposes a hierarchy on the information it communicates, nor does it clearly label the source of the voices of which it consists. The way in which direct speech is reported is symptomatic of an unusual connection between the speech and the source of the enunciation, and bears witness to how Benjy juxtaposes information he has perceived without establishing the least hierarchy for its content. All of Benjy's perceptions are raw perceptions that differ from knowledge in that the idiot, like an animal, "does not face his world like a thinking being, he is on the contrary oriented toward it in the act of union and separation. Feeling contains no element of judgment and can therefore only be controlled through propositions and judgments" (Straus, 1989: 324). Benjy identifies the presence of voices, with neither control nor judgment, within the continuum of their emergence; sensitive to acoustic changes, he signals with unfailing regularity the transition from one voice to another through the repetition of elementary structures that combine a first name (the source of the enunciation) with the verb "to say."

In the episodes corresponding to the narrative present, which recount the day of Benjy's thirty-third birthday (which he unsurprisingly spends with his keeper), "Luster said" is obviously the expression that appears the most often. It is repeated identically up to ten times on the same page (*SF*: 55) because the pronominalization of "Luster" into "he" is an impossible abstraction for Benjy. Benjy's syntax reflects an elementary and highly limited level of discernment, albeit one that is coherent, for the words heard do not come from a hypothetical and impersonal he but from an individual (Luster) identifiable as such. However, when Benjy is unable to identify the source of enunciation for the words he hears, the voices are deprived of origin, and the words float in the air as they do on the page. In a scene in which Benjy does not know who Luster is speaking to, Luster appears to be speaking to a ghost: " 'Is you all seen anything of a quarter down here.' Luster said. 'What quarter' " (*SF*: 14). In such cases, with Benjy being entirely unable to grasp the source of the speech, even the use of the personal pronoun, with neither antecedent nor clear referent, appears as an overtranslation of what he perceives.[20] The punctuation of passages in direct speech contributes to this appearance of neutrality by masking the significant inflections and accentuations of voices, another type of convention that is intentionally flouted. English-language punctuation requires words related in direct speech to be marked off by quotation marks, with a comma preceding the closing quotation mark, followed by an introduction of the source of the speech. But in Benjy's monologue, Faulkner opts to systematically replace the conventional comma with a period. Moreover, his speech contains no question marks or exclamation points. We know of the problems relating to punctuation that Faulkner had with his publisher, who was keen to reestablish the norm.[21] This flattening of vocal intonation represents Benjy's inability to grasp the significant elements contained in the tone of voice: he is also impervious to questioning, to the expression of an emotion or an order. Regardless of their content, all words are monotonously perceived (as effectively represented by the ubiquitous period) as affirmations, containing neither logic nor expressiveness. The punctuation that is characteristic of Benjy's discourse unifies and standardizes the tone of the words that are related. The way in which Benjy records the Black dialect of the Gibsons further distinguishes his relation to the voice. As demonstrated by Mark Lencho in his article on the dialectical variations in *The Sound and the Fury*, the novel's first section stands out from the others because it exclusively presents the syntactic components of Black dialectical grammar, keeping quiet the phonological components highlighted in the other sections:

> In section 1 of *The Sound and the Fury*, Faulkner attempts to communicate the syntactic component of black grammar, while in the remaining

chapters, he includes the phonological component as well, a pattern which seems to indicate that Faulkner's intentions for his novel as he embarked on its composition were in a state of flux, clarifying themselves as the novel progressed. (Lencho, Summer 1988: 410)

What Lencho sees as an incoherence and even a failure in Faulkner's writing can be more readily interpreted as a deliberate approach. Benjy's deafness to the phonological idiosyncrasies of Black dialect stems from Faulkner's choice of punctuation for direct speech. It appears again in the perception of voices on a single level, as though they were contiguous: white voices and Black voices stand next to one another without being sorted, almost without distinction. At the same time, Benjy's deafness to the acoustic characteristics of Black speech erase any residual trace of racial or class sentiment, which is highly present in the monologues of his two brothers. In Benjy's discourse, the notion of similarity replaces that of difference. With this in mind, in his elementary naïveté, Benjy's generosity of heart and spirit have nothing to envy compared to the behavior of his brothers. Yet, it is important to remember that he has nothing to do with it, for unlike his brothers, he is simply incapable of the least prejudice.

The preferred mode in Benjy's discourse is juxtaposition, the unconnected and unrelated assembly of apparently distinct elements, coordination within disorder. Since it presents syntactical and semantic issues that are markedly more complicated and abstract than the simple mode of coordination, subordination is subsequently reduced to minimal use. It is in these terms that Jacqueline Guillemin-Flescher, in her book chapter "The Linguistic Representation of Perception in Benjy's Monologue"—a catalog of sorts of the grammatical particularities of Benjy's language—broaches the question of subordination: "Since Benjy can account only for what is immediately accessible, subordination is reduced in his monologue to clauses expressing either spatial or temporal location, or qualification of the activity expressed in the main clause" (Guillemin-Flescher, 1996: 49). The few subordinate clauses, spatial and temporal, interspersed in Benjy's monologue are loosely linked to their main clause, without ever identifying the object precisely: "I went around the kitchen, where the moon was" (*SF*: 46). In this example, the subordination is ultimately only one of the forms taken by the contiguity of reality in Benjy's perception; it is simply a somewhat different way of expressing coordination, as for Benjy the moon truly appears in the continuity of the kitchen. Through the indiscriminate use of coordinating conjunctions and the particle "and" in particular, Benjy's discourse connects independent propositions to unsteadily form long compound utterances that, like the bodies of idiots, are characterized by their loose and distended appearance. These phrases, which unfold by fits and starts and consecutive additions, reproduce the different phases of Benjy's reaction to an event or series of events in their chronological order, without interpretation or accentuation of any kind:

> We finished eating. T. P. took Quentin up and we went down to T. P.'s house. Luster was playing in the dirt. T. P. put Quentin down and she played in the dirt too. Luster had some spools and he and Quentin fought and Quentin had the spools. Luster cried and Frony came and gave Luster a tin can to play with, and then I had the spools and Quentin fought me and I cried. (*SF*: 30)

This short paragraph, which includes the conjunction "and" no less than ten times, illustrates the coordinating process at work in Benjy's narration. The actions are described according to a precise chronological order from the end of breakfast to Benjy crying due to Quentin's response (Caddy's daughter, who is still very young). Yet it is remarkable that changes of location and movements in space—from the kitchen to T. P.'s house, from Quentin's elevated position to a sitting position—are evoked in the same manner as a temporal succession. For Benjy, time and space are not two distinct categories but objects within an edge-to-edge and term-by-term juxtaposition. The "spools" change hands twice as Quentin fights to get them, and then fights because she no longer has them, while Benjy, who has taken them in the meantime, describes Quentin's anger at him without understanding why, and then begins to cry. The juxtaposition follows the journey of the spools, which attract the children's attention. Repetition contributes to the chaotic nature of the continuity, as though the constant return of the same words marked out—in the gaps between the connectors—the boundaries of a rather stunted reality. Asyndeton, the absence of conjunction between two closely related terms or groups of terms, offers a variation to the conjunction without the intermediary of a particle: in Benjy's rhetoric, the comma or the period can fulfill this role. However, the resulting effect is essentially the same. If we turn to the definition given by Pierre Fontanier in *Les Figures du discours* (Figures of Discourse), conjunctions multiply objects all while emphasizing their singularity:[22] "This figure in a way increases objects by emphasizing each one in particular, making them more present and distinct, than if they had been offered as a group, as though they were one" (Fontanier, 1993: 339). When Benjy signals a change in state, he describes the transformation as a succession of two distinct but contiguous states: "Caddie took her dress off and threw it on the bank. Then she didn't have on anything but her bodice and drawer" (*SF*: 18). Being unable to grasp the transitional phase, which from one state to another cannot be perceived in a single act of perception, Benjy insists on each of the two states in particular, on the before and the after. In this example, he dislocates the single gesture consisting of undressing by replacing it with two separate vignettes: Caddy takes off her dress, Caddy is wearing only her underwear. However, the link that logically explains the transition from the first to the second state is erased by Benjy's syntax. It has not materialized because it has not been understood.[23] Through his perception of reality as something contiguous, Benjy shows more than he says. Lacking the abstract and generic term that signifies undressing and an increase in speed, he offers a step-by-step description of what he sees. He initiates a return to the source of language, to the thing preceding the invention of the word. It is with this in mind that Claude Romano, in his *Le Chant de la vie* (The Song of Life), anchored Benjy within the myth of the "roots of the world":

> He is a pure witness of appearance casting a primitive gaze onto the world. He is the one through whom the world manifests itself in its radical injustification, in its pure and naked donation, in that virgin appearance to which the novel's title seems to make reference. [. . .] In Benjy's gaze the world returns to the original state of pure manifestation without cause or reason. It is no more than the primordial chaos of dialogues initiated and interrupted, of dawning movements and partial situations, over which reason or the intellect have no hold. It is a series of appearances and disappearances, in which the only remaining logical link is the elementary one of a series of conjunctions. (Romano, 2005: 37)

Coordination circumscribes Benjy's world; it establishes its limits and can simultaneously be interpreted as the emblematic mark of his perception. Benjy perceives reality in a contiguous manner, beyond any form of idealization, as a necessarily disordered juxtaposition of objects and situations. The notion of totality is sacrificed in the succession of particular occurrences, each one grasped in its own specificity or in its idiot singularity, to use the etymological sense of the word. The mechanisms of a normative, encompassing, and generalizing perception are dislocated by the systematic nature of the juxtaposition. Paradoxically, the rendering of reality is disarticulated by the excess of articulations, by the overload of conjunctions that flatten it until it becomes unrecognizable. The notion of hierarchy (ideological, grammatical) is replaced by the image of a line on which all of the elements and gaps that make up Benjy's little world succeed one another as distinct and contiguous points within the minuscule enclosure of his perception. Benjy approaches reality as a succession of vignettes that are abruptly linked to one another, with the logical links that signify the result and dependence—in a word the causality—fundamentally lacking in his speech, which consists solely of states without reasons, effects without origins, affects without causes. Benjy's perception coordinates reality while precariously plugging up the system of ruptures that necessarily underpin it, the transformations and disturbances that threaten the permanence of things, the breaches into which the impalpable logic governing the world rushes headlong. The very principles of juxtaposition and rupture both evoke and ensue from the process of modernist writing, which emerges from heterogeneous forms and fragments. Meanwhile, the traditional definition of the novel as a finished artifact is discredited. The instability of forms is the indisputable mark of Benjy's tale, which consists of uncertain elements flowing within the continuity of space and the moment. For all that, in Benjy's discourse modernity is brought to a fever pitch, for even the ultimate requirement of meaning is sacrificed. Fragments succeed one another to form a kind of everything, which lays claim to disarticulation rather than its transcendence following a dialectical process. Yet on a fundamental level, that which is everything to the idiot persists in signifying nothing.

Benjy's monologue unfolds like a chain of images that are never the subject of commentary, and do not lead to any form of organization. They are raw images whose grain has not been refined, through which a story is sketched out—a story that, strictly speaking, is not recounted. Benjy's monologue resembles his "spools": it consists of strings that are distinct but slack and overstretched; the motifs appear only after a painstaking effort of weaving, which is left to the reader and the analyst, its result condemned to randomness. Yet Faulkner deliberately made Benjy into a very poor weaver, who in the end provides us with strings that are loose and undone. Benjy is both an impossible narrator and a poor creator in that he does not have the intelligence to forge and manipulate reality and, in the final analysis, to make it lie. His authenticity is necessary and is never subjected to any calculation. The challenge assumed by Faulkner in writing Benjy's perception as an idiot is perfectly paradoxical as a result, for if Benjy the idiot narrator can only tell the truth, Faulkner, who is not an idiot, can be the transcriber of this truth only through what is invented and artificial. In its privileged relation to a reality that is not corrupted by language, Benjy's perception as an idiot is nevertheless a creation, a necessarily fictitious act.

Chapter 4

FAULKNERIAN IDIOTISMS

The Mechanisms of Repetition

> The dark was filled with the voices, myriad, out of all time that he had known, as though all the past was a flat pattern. And going on: tomorrow night, all the tomorrows, to be a part of the flat pattern, going on. He thought of that with quiet astonishment: going on, myriad, familiar, since all that had ever been was the same as all that was to be, since tomorrow to-be and had-been would be the same.
> —WILLIAM FAULKNER, *LIGHT IN AUGUST*

TEMPORAL TWITCHING: THE ETERNAL PRESENT OF BENJY COMPSON'S DISCOURSE

In the short story "The Idiots" (1898), Joseph Conrad depicts idiots as being forgotten by time: "Such creatures are forgotten by time, and live untouched by years till death gathers them up into its compassionate bosom" (Conrad, 1974 [1898]: 94). Their imperviousness to time spares idiots the misery of humans. Idiots have no awareness of the irreversibility of time; they are ignorant of what Northrop Frye defined in his *Fools of Time* as the tragic dimension of existence:

> The basis of the tragic vision is the being in time, the sense of the one-directional quality of life whereas everything happens once and for all, where every act brings unavoidable and fateful consequences, and where all experience vanishes, not simply into the past, but into nothingness, annihilation. (Frye, 1967: 3)

The fools of time hardly have the sense of tragedy. As emphasized by Faulkner, Benjy is not aware of Caddy's disappearance, her absence from the present moment, or the unavoidable nature of this situation: "[B]eing an idiot he was not even aware that Caddy was missing." Benjy's present is so saturated with episodes from the past, which are grasped as vividly as the minor events of his everyday life, that in a certain sense Caddy is still there. When Caddy appears in flesh and blood in the present, as an adult who has changed after her long absence, Benjy does not know what to make of this appearance: "If Caddy had reappeared he probably would not have known her" (Stein, Spring 1956: 74).[1] He is unable to integrate her within the little system in which he exists cut off from the world, in that singular place where past and present constantly infringe upon one another.

While Benjy may be seen as being "untouched" by the passing years, he is nevertheless a being of time (even if he is unaware of it); in fact, his monologue can actually be seen as a web of time. It is characterized by the alternation of recollections and scenes that take place in the narrative present. This pattern, which as it happens is also present in the monologues of Quentin and Jason, accelerates rapidly as Benjy's discourse advances. The tumult caused by the constant juxtaposition of moments from different temporal strata underscores the intensity of the decisive absences that Benjy does not mention, since the past being for him indistinct from the present, he does not grasp them as patent realities. While he senses departures and death, for Benjy neither of them takes on the clear form of defined, locatable, and surpassable events. Death and departures atemporally refract in the form of sensations that can emerge at any moment. The reading proposed by Stephen Ross and Noel Polk in *Reading Faulkner: "The Sound and the Fury"* (1996) distinguishes fourteen different temporal phases in Benjy's monologue. The one that takes up the most space in the section corresponds to the present, marked by the date of April 7, 1928, which serves as a title to section 1. If we arbitrarily reestablish the chronology of events referenced, we notice that the images that reappear in Benjy's mind stretch back to his early childhood and the death of Damuddy, which is closely associated with the image of Caddy hoisting herself, in her muddy underwear, onto the branches of the pear tree to observe the strange vigil of adults gathered around the grandmother's body. Then follow episodes, always in the greatest appearance of disorder, connected to his name change, the letters carried to Uncle Maury's mistress, and a series of images relating to Caddy's first romantic experiences, with scenes including perfume, the swing, the loss of her virginity, and ultimately her marriage. Finally, there comes the accumulation of catastrophes: Benjy's castration, Quentin's suicide, the father's death, the visits to the cemetery, and finally the death of Roskus. These moments from the past stretch from 1900 to approximately 1915, leaving a gap of thirteen years between the most recent past and the present. This gap inscribes a total absence of notable events within the framework of the text. Nothing occurs between 1915 and 1928, and one may suppose beyond that as well: "[N]othing happens, everything happened" (Sartre, 1987: 267). Benjy was deserted by all those whose presence brought a little light and movement to his dark and narrow world. As a result, these years and all those that remain for him are thoroughly lacking and empty, as demonstrated by the barren desert that underpins his discourse. On the morning of his tale, Benjy has for a long time had no other prospect than the few images that serve as recollections for him.

Section 1 opens in the present, on Benjy's thirty-third birthday—"Aint you something, thirty three years old, going on that way" (*SF*: 3)—and ends at night with a childhood memory developed indirectly starting on page 17, the day of the grandmother's death. Benjy is five years old at the time and falls asleep next to Caddy, in a moment of infinite comfort and calm that nothing could ever disturb. A detailed analysis of the end of Benjy's monologue reveals how the temporal layers are entangled and how the triggers operate. The final scene is preceded by a last vignette, corresponding to the narrative present and set off by italics, indistinctly evoking Benjy's castration and the nocturnal escapades of Quentin, who flouts the family's rules by receiving young men in her room, within the very sanctuary for which Jason is the intransigent guardian. These two images are both indicated by personal pronouns shorn of their referents, in accordance with the logic specific to the idiot, who names only that which he grasps directly and is capable of naming. In both cases, the personal pronouns refer both literally—"*Looking for them aint going to do no good. They're gone*" (73)—and metaphorically—"*It came out of Quentin's window and climbed across into the tree. We watched the tree shaking. The shaking went down the tree, then it came out and we watched it go away across the grass*" (74)—to the sexual organ that has on a number of occasions violated the precarious order of the family. Benjy's monologue ends by reiterating the image of the tree, whose roots underpin the entire structure of the tale as well as the framework of this past that refuses to completely be the past. A thinly disguised phallic symbol, the shaking tree that the impetuous Caddy climbs on the verge of childhood is the same one through which her daughter Quentin gives free reign to her teenage passions. The motif of the tree and the superimposed images of Caddy and Quentin, undifferentiated within a generic "she" ("Here she come"), coincide with bedtime and, in connection with Caddy, with a final evocation of the past on the night of the novel's key episode, as demonstrated by the little girl's soiled underwear: "'Just look at your drawers.' Dilsey said. 'You better be glad your maw aint seen you'" (74). This final episode unfolds like a summary of section 1 of the novel, with each character playing the role, in an almost caricatured manner, for which they are destined. The older brother Quentin is already distant, as though detached from the contingencies of everyday life; his already fleeting presence is captured in the space of a few words as he disappears into the bed he shares with Jason: "Quentin got in the other one" (74). Jason is once again stigmatized in his role as an informer, the self-proclaimed traitor of Caddy's trust: "'I already told on her.' Jason said" (74).[2] Through her attention and care, Dilsey stands in for the absent mother, who is either sick—"'Mother's sick.' Caddy said"—or simply imagines being so—"'Is Mother very sick.' Caddy said. 'No.' Father said" (75). The affection Mr. Compson shows his children is too rare for him to garner much attention. Critics have repeatedly seen him as incapable, as someone who outsources and delegates his responsibilities. Caddy, whose luminous presence is materialized in the incessant repetition of the syllables of her first name, embodies the insolence, drive, and life that each of her brothers so cruelly lacks. She is the one who watches over them with authority ("So we still have to mind me," 74) and tenderness ("'Are you going to take good care of Maury.' 'Yes.' Caddy said," 75). It is she who reassures Benjy—who is still called by his given name—with her words and gestures ("Caddy said, 'Hush, Maury' putting her hand on me. So I stayed hushed"), and who holds him close ("Caddy held me," 75) in the dark sleep with its bright shapes. Benjy's day and tale withdraw into childhood: the unhappy childhood in which, unbeknown to him, he is congenitally kept prisoner; the happy childhood in which he falls asleep in Caddy's arms forever. The idiot's monologue closes with the "smooth, bright shapes" (75) that evoke the indeterminacy of the images that flow between the present and the past through his consciousness, reflecting his monologue's dissolved temporal mechanisms and signifying Caddy's intangibility in the darkness of the present.

According to the count established by Ross and Polk (1996), the narrative present, which serves as the foundation of Benjy's tale on which all of the elements of the past are built, can be subdivided into thirty distinct moments. From the perspective of the plot, however minimal the preoccupations of an idiot may be, section 1 of *The Sound and the Fury* could be entitled: "In Search of a Quarter." Luster's quarter is an effective temporal marker for identifying different moments in the text, and his search for it is the only notable activity on that April day, just barely interrupted by Benjy's birthday snack. References to Luster's quarter increase from the first page of the novel—"Aint you going to help me find that quarter so that I can go to the show tonight" (3)—to the final appearance of the present time a few pages before the end of the section: "*Here you is*, Luster said. *Look what I got. He showed it to me. You know where I got it. Miss Quentin give it to me. I knowed they couldn't keep me out*" (72). At this point in the tale, the indefinite nature of the pronoun "it" no longer leaves any doubt regarding its meaning, as Luster can go to the show with his replacement coin, and the story of that day, which is probably not very different from those that preceded or followed it, can come to a close. Yet everything does not stop at this little stunted day, which Benjy devotes with blind zeal to all the rituals of his idiocy: pacing up and down in his miserable pasture waiting for a Caddy who disappeared years ago, "Miss Caddy done gone long ways away. Done got married and left you" (51); hoping for golfers to approach the fence; or impatiently awaiting his drive to the cemetery. For such is the extent of Benjy's possibilities. Inside the fence, the present shows the extent of the idiot's extreme confinement, but it also represents the crucible of recollection, the place from which different moments from the past reappear. While in the present moment the fence prevents Benjy from moving beyond it, it is symbolically crossed through the recurrence of these trips back in time. It is no coincidence that this liminal space is where the incessant flow of past images begins:

> We went along the fence and came to the garden fence, where our shadows were. [. . .] We came to the broken place and went through it.
> "Wait a minute." Luster said. "You snagged on that nail again. Cant you never crawl through here without snagging on that nail."
> *Caddy uncaught me and we crawled through. Uncle Maury said to not let anybody see us, so we better stoop over, Caddy said. Stoop over, Benjy. Like this, see. We stooped over and crossed the garden, where the flowers rasped and rattled against us.* (SF: 4)

The first recollection is literally "snagged" on the fence. A symbol of the impassable and the forbidden, the nail is also that which opens the way for ghosts from the past, which are looming in the cast "shadows." The nail firmly maintains Benjy in the isolation of his narrow world but also signals the freeing of recollection, for when Caddy "uncatches" Benjy, they can proceed with crossing the fence and into the past ("crawled through"). The novel's second temporal episode then unfolds, revolving around the anecdote of the letter delivered to Mrs. Patterson for Uncle Maury. In the end, the transition from one time to another occurs surreptitiously through the image of being caught and uncaught, through which Caddy becomes an avatar for Luster, or the other way around. In both episodes, Benjy is ordered to pass through the fence, and in both cases he is caught against it. The temporal gap is masked by the continuity of the gesture but is nevertheless signaled by the use of italics, which are deliberately provided to enlighten the reader in their deciphering of the scene.[3] In a letter to his editor Ben Wasson, Faulkner justified the typographical changes that characterize the text of *The Sound and the Fury*:

> A break indicates an objective change in tempo, while the objective picture here should be a continuous whole, since the thought transference is subjective; i.e., in Ben's mind and not in the reader's eye. I think italics are necessary to establish for the reader Benjy's confusion; that

unbroken-surfaced confusion of an idiot which is outwardly a dynamic and logical coherence. (Blotner, 1974: 243–44)

The italics stand as the mark of "continuity" in Benjy's psychological functioning. They highlight the absence of breaks in his perception of the present and the past, as part of a logic that ignores any form of temporal distinction. The italics mark this active "confusion," while for the reader they signify the entry into a new temporal layer. For all that, they do not represent systematic markers, and their reliability is put to the test on a number of occasions. While the pace and regularities of the passages relating to the narrative present receive increasing emphasis, the italics of the first sentences tend to very quickly transform back into a normal font, thereby rendering the temporal identification of the passages in question much more difficult. In these examples, italics only appear a little later and initiate the following temporal layer. What was provided as a tool for reading can therefore become a trap. In the end, italics simply act as a signal for a transition. This is suggested by Polk, who in his efforts at preparing new editions of Faulkner's works had his hands full with the author's unusual choices in punctuation: "They represent images buried in Benjy's unconscious which then work their way into the front of his conscious life, his own narrative present, elbowing April 7 out of the way, until it, too, pushes its way back into what registers, also in italics" (Polk, 1996: 107). Italics signal Benjy's congenital inability to associate the images flowing through his mind with a specific moment. Moreover, they contribute to the confusion of the reader, whose journey through an idiot consciousness lacks a truly stable point of reference. Finally, italics, which are visually marked by a rightward slant that bends the word's appearance, can be seen as the preferred typographical image of idiocy in contrast to that of normalcy, which is straight.

Benjy is inevitably transported from the present to a past episode, or from one past situation to another, by an element from the temporal situation in which he is temporarily present. However, as stressed by Olga Vickery, this transposition never results in a considered association of ideas, a notion that is based on the principles of analogy and synthesis to which the idiot is in essence resistant:

With consummate skill the repetitions and identifying sensations which are used to guide the reader are also used as the basis of Benjy's own ordering of experience. Benjy's mind works not by association which is dependent, to some extent, on an ability to discriminate as well as compare but by mechanical identification. Thus, being caught on the fence while walking with Luster does not recall an associated feeling or fact but the exact replica of the incident. More important is the fact that the three deaths in the family, which Benjy senses as repetitions of each other, provoke an identical response. What he reacts to is the fact of death or the fact of being caught on the fence. To differentiate in terms of time and circumstance is a logical matter and therefore beyond Benjy's range of apprehension. (Vickery, 1964: 34)

The juxtaposition of similar sensations, which appear to the idiot as the exact replicas of one another, is a more suitable concept than the association of ideas. On page 9, the sight of the new wheel on the Compsons' carriage is enough to immerse Benjy in a scene from fifteen years earlier, when Dilsey mentioned the piteous state of the wheels as they set out to visit the cemetery: "*We passed the carriage house, where the carriage was. It had a new wheel.* 'Git in, now, and set still until your maw come.' Dilsey said. [. . .] 'This thing going to fall to pieces under you all some day. Look at them wheels.'" On page 17, playing in the water transports Benjy from the present back to a childhood memory that has a central role in his monologue, and that is crystallized in the image of Caddy's wet dress; there is a mischievous joy and a bond that cannot be found anywhere else in the novel. On page 40, it is the sensation of Caddy's arms embracing him that transports Benjy from his sister's marriage scene to the earlier episode in which she is wearing perfume for the first time: "Caddy put her arms around me, and her shining veil, and I couldn't smell trees anymore and I began to cry. *Benjy, Caddy said, Benjy.* She put her arms around me again, but I went away. 'What is it, Benjy.' she said." These last two scenes instill a similar feeling of strangeness in Benjy, with Caddy's smell being lost under the artifice of the veil and the perfume, both of which signify the end of innocence and prefigure the loss to come. In both cases Caddy does not understand Benjy's reaction and has distanced herself from him in spite of herself. Incidentally, why can't her "what is it," which is no longer in italics, apply equally to both episodes? In their extreme diversity, all of these triggering elements confirm the same idea, namely that for Benjy time unfolds like a succession of instants that appear in his consciousness according to the impressions that trigger them. Past or current, dreamed or real, they are all experienced with the intensity of the present. The intensity of a recollection therefore has nothing to do with its proximity in time. As Sartre emphasized once again, what is true for the idiot is confirmed in the everyday experience of us all: "It would be wrong to think that when the present is past it becomes our closest memory. Its metamorphosis can cause it to sink to the bottom of our memory, just as it can leave it floating on the surface. Only its own density and the dramatic meaning of our life can determine at what level it will remain" (Sartre, 1987: 268).

Benjy's present can subsequently be interpreted as a long and uninterrupted chain of presences. For Benjy, everything plays out in the moment. There is only "now" that can make sense to the perception of an idiot, whose future is forever hindered by his enclosure and his inability to formulate the abstraction of a forward projection of himself. An exclusively sensitive being, Benjy can only live in the instant, in the realm of palpable things. All of the scenes from his life are concentrated into a tide of inarticulate emotions and sensations, couched within a disarticulate time: representations of the past offer themselves to him as heretofore unseen presentations, revivals that have the value of "vivals." Benjy's tale is characterized by the inalterable vivaciousness of his present. The very process of memory is invalidated in the idiot, for remembering entails experiencing the transposition of a past event into his present sphere. Memory is defined by its grounding within hierarchical time, which clearly distinguishes past events from the order of the present and the possible. Yet for an idiot, time has no more meaning than death or rain, and the uniqueness of his perception is characterized by his radical emancipation from all forms of temporal convention. Despite being blocked by the impossibility of conceiving the future, the idiot's temporality is one that is fundamentally free of its movements and representations. His reality is contained in the instant, is erased with the instant, and can reappear at any moment, in a form that is confined to the bright and lively colors of the present.

THE WORKINGS OF REPETITION

With its complex structure of multiple narrators and listeners in interchangeable roles, *Absalom, Absalom!* recalls the informal methods for transmitting tales by word of mouth, as the same story is repeated and extended through different voices. The fact that the story is in the form of a novel, a story set down in writing, does not eliminate the hesitations and delays, emphatic peaks and silences, and slowing and acceleration that are the soul of oral storytelling. The tradition of word-of-mouth stories, from one narrator to another and from one listener to another, is based on continuous transformations and evolutions, with repetition distancing each new version of the story a little further from the mythical original, by and large conserving only vague similarities. Similarly, the true story of *Absalom, Absalom!* (supposing there is one, a palimpsest concealed behind a heap of conjectures)—revolving around the core fascination sparked by the character of Thomas Sutpen, whose peculiar story will be difficult for the reader to approach—indefinitely repeats the same events through changing viewpoints and different versions, which present themselves as so many reconstructions or re-creations.[4] The child's pleasure, as noted by Freud in his 1920 essay "Beyond the Pleasure Principle," peremptorily requires the exact repetition of the same story:

And once anyone has told him a nice story, he [the child] wants to hear the same story again and again rather than a new one; he implacably insists that every repetition be exactly the same; and he corrects every least change that the story-teller misguidedly incorporates, perhaps fondly imagining it will gain him extra kudos. (Freud, 2006: 164)

Conversely, it is precisely the "kudos" of successive and systematic modifications that *Absalom, Absalom!* builds up, and on which the uneasy pleasure of its reading is based. The structure and difficulty specific to *Absalom, Absalom!*, with its repetition of the same story (that of Sutpen and his dynasty), directly echoes *The Sound and the Fury* (which repeats four different versions of Caddy's story) in an obvious relation of formal similarity. *Absalom, Absalom!* contains numerous and varied allusions to the effort of narrative (re)construction, as the plot is interspersed with structural nodes—why did old Mr. Coldfield accept to marry his daughter Ellen with Thomas Sutpen? Why did Henry Sutpen, in such untimely manner, leave the family domain with Charles Bon in the middle of Christmas celebrations, swearing to never return?—that tend toward a kind of explanation or resolution, without ever achieving it. To do so, Quentin and his friend Shreve present themselves as investigators gathering clues and building hypotheses (the expression "I can imagine" punctuates the fourth chapter, in which the story is transmitted from Mr. Compson to Quentin, from father to son);[5] they try to ultimately establish a coherent story from often contradictory snippets of information, suppositions, and intuitions. At times, their language is similar to that of Sherlock Holmes, who is perplexed by the incoherence of an investigation: "They are there, yet something is missing" (*AA*: 80), with the exception that the veracity of the version of events on which Shreve and Quentin ultimately agree is not of great importance to them. The test of truth even seems, to a certain extent, the least of their preoccupations:

> The two of them creating between them, out of the rag-tag and bob-ends of old tales and talking, people who perhaps had never existed at all anywhere, who, shadows, were shadows not of flesh and blood which had lived and died but shadows in turn of what were (to one of them at least, to Shreve) shades too. (*AA*: 243)

In many regards, *Absalom, Absalom!* can be read metafictionally as a novel on the art of the novel, in which story and reinvention are synonymous and fully accepted as such, far from the fantasy of novelistic truth. For nothing is true in *Absalom, Absalom!*: "Perhaps Quentin himself had not been listening when Mr. Compson related (recreated?) it that evening at home; perhaps at that moment on the gallery in the hot September twilight Quentin took that in stride without even hearing it just as Shreve would have" (268). *Absalom, Absalom!* is a twilit realm of intangible "shadows" and uncertain conjectures ("creating," "recreated," "perhaps") founded on hearsay ("old tales and talking," "listening [. . .] without even hearing").

Absalom, Absalom! ultimately unfolds as a creation that bears the traces of its perpetual re-creation. Its composition, which is inscribed in the convolution of stories that equally resemble and differ from one another, resists any sense of completion: it is governed by the principle of repetition (with variation), as the same situation of narration and listening are repeated. In each chapter, the story narrated by one of the four character-narrators is intended for a recipient who, with the exception of the two chapters for which he is himself the narrator, is invariably Quentin Compson. It includes the repetition of the same snippets of stories about a few central events, such as the construction of the Sutpen estate, Sutpen's unhappy marriage with Ellen Coldfield, Henry's comings and goings with his friend Charles Bon, the men's departure for war, and so on; and the same obsessions, including the temptation of incest as well as the father's interracial love affairs and illegitimate children, which are later mirrored by the disowned son—repetition can thus be seen as a manifestation of fate. Finally, the same themes repeat (the theme of the slight as a driver of destiny), as do the same images (portraits of Ellen Coldfield as a moth and Judith as a wax statue) and the same words (Sutpen's "design" and later his "mistake").[6] What immediately jumps out is how the repetition occurs on two distinct but inextricably connected levels, that of the event or act that repeats, and that of the word repeated in order to indicate the repetition of the thing. Repetition emphasizes the obvious *indissociability* of the phenomenon and language.

In the genealogy of great Faulknerian novels, from *The Sound and the Fury* to *Absalom, Absalom!*, there is the repetition, transmission, and hereditary transfer of a certain number of characteristics that can be defined as idiotisms or "Faulknerisms," which is to say a series of singular locutions specific to a language (and hence often impossible to translate literally into another language of similar structure). Many critics have shown how certain scenes and motifs, couched in markedly similar expressions, become Faulknerian commonplaces through their reappearance from one novel to another. Polk provided a list of these commonplaces in his introduction to *Children of the Dark House*:

> For all its astonishing variety, Faulkner's work returns constantly, compulsively, to certain powerful images that form a sort of ground zero in Yoknapatawpha, images based in family pathologies and the terror that is childhood in Faulkner: seductive mothers, weak fathers; ironhaired bespectacled repressive grandmothers; dark houses from which children must escape through windows instead of doors; windows that

separate characters from a fecund world that beckons and terrifies. (Polk, 1996: xiv)

It is indeed possible to identify certain themes (mirrors and the arson that engulfs humans and dwellings in a violent conflagration) in Faulkner's work, as well as certain character types; we would add to the previous list the "tieless casual" originating from "The Hill" (92), antiheroes such as the excluded and marginalized, and of course idiots. It is tempting to see them as the repetitive traces of obsessions, or the literary manifestations of compulsive repetition, as defined by André Green in *Time in Psychoanalysis*:

Compulsion is above all the repetition of a force which sometimes compels one to act out, and sometimes to dream, to put oneself in similar or identical conditions, to reproduce affectively, and to act out in accordance with an unconscious organisation pushing towards the uncontrollable recurrence of the same or of what is identical. (Green, 2002: 83)

My intention is not to establish an exhaustive list of the canonical scenes and configurations that compulsively repeat in Faulkner's work, but to show how repetition can be seen as one of the manifestations of idiocy in Faulkner, as well as a consequence of the Faulknerian aesthetics of idiocy. Born in the stagnant and ratiocinating consciousness of Benjy Compson, who due to his limitations tirelessly trots out the same images and impressions in the same words, the principle of repetition can be interpreted as one of the most prominent Faulknerisms. Repetition, which etymologically refers to the act of striving after (*petere*) once again, is a (multifaceted) event that can be located in space (that of a life, an image, or page), and that is reiterated in time. Two occurrences of a repetition are separated by a certain amount of time, which is entirely variable. The complexity of the notion of repetition lies in the fact that it is simultaneously a concept, a percept, and an effect at the intersection of philosophical, artistic, and psychological critical discourses.[7] With repetition being a figure of the discourse that gives shape to the discourse, its mechanisms must be defined in their relation to resemblance and the muddle of its thematic, structural, and stylistic aspects, in their relation to the multifarious question of time, memory, and fate. How did repetition, setting out from the compulsive repetition specific to the idiot consciousness, become the Faulknerian idiotism par excellence?

Repetition is usually defined as the fact of being said or expressed multiple times, thereby often being negatively likened to a rambling of sorts; the same old song and story told in families, old saws, and rehashed and worn-out phrases are based on a similar art of repetition. In *As I Lay Dying*, Anse obstinately reiterates, droning on about the promise he made to Addie to ward off the bad luck that has befallen the odyssey on which he led his kin, especially to justify the affront he is inflicting on his wife's corpse: "'It's Addie I give the promise to,' he said. 'Her mind is set on it.'" (*AILD*: 115); "'I give her my promised word in the presence of the Lord,' Anse says" (125); "'I give my promise,' he says. 'She is counting on it'" (140). When he mentions the deceased, Anse expresses himself in an unfailing present that accepts no compromise: he can speak of her in the past (definitively dismissing her by replacing her) and bring an end to his litany once he puts her in the ground next to her kin in Jefferson. The turning over of the same phrases and saws coincides, on the level of syntax, with the systematic return of the same words. For instance, the repetition of the word "saw" in a different context, at present considered in its primary and literal sense as a hand tool, effectively represents, via its regular movement, this abstract sense of rehashing. The seventeenth monologue of *As I Lay Dying* comes a few pages after the mother's death, as her kin keep vigil over her body throughout the rainy night and Cash finishes building her coffin. It is constructed around a series of repetitions, like the movements of the carpenter son's saw. Cash picks up the saw that was placed on the ground in between the sawing of two planks. The saw, whose back-and-forth is minutely described, is the instrument that gives the section a certain rhythm; its repeated rasping fills the silence and stupor that follow death.

> Cash labors at the trestles, moving back and forth, lifting and placing the planks with long clattering *reverberations* in the dead air as though he were lifting and dropping them at the bottom of an invisible well, the sounds ceasing without departing, as if any movement might dislodge them from the immediate air *in reverberant repetition*. He saws again, his elbows flashing slowly, a thin thread of fire running along the edge of the saw, lost and recovered at the top and bottom of each stroke in unbroken elongation. (*AILD*: 75–76; emphasis mine)

The air is "dead" because the mother no longer breathes, while the planks of the unfinished coffin seem to split into two, forever repeating the clattering of wood against wood, already invoking the depth of the deep sleep that they will enclose. If the wood is a sound, that is because silence engulfs any other form of discourse, scarcely interrupted by snippets of purely functional dialogue: "'Give me that plank,' Cash says. 'No; the other one'" (*AILD*: 76). This impoverished speech is imbued with references to sawing planks. Nothing hinders the sound of the planks "ceasing without departing" or their precarious echo, not even the renewed sound of sawing new planks. This short passage unfolds like a dance of sound and visual (the word is repeated as a noun and adjective, just as the word "saw" is sometimes a noun and sometimes a verb) "reverberations," a dance of shadows, of quick sparks and quiet sounds, which highlight the misery of this long scene where nothing happens, where all is repetition of the same gestures and words. Repetition also seals off the misery brought by a death that they lack the words to speak, let alone utter: it stops up the gaps of the unspoken. These lines offer an initial definition of sorts for the mechanism of repetition in Faulkner:[8] the reverberation of the same words, of the gestures they refer to and of the emotions they stifle, underpins the framework of the text as a delayed shattering. Yet when it does occur, repetition is hardly a self-evident fact on the formal level;[9] it is notably the bottomless well ("at the bottom of an invisible well," "at the top and bottom," "in unbroken elongation") in which the most unbearable pain is drowned to prevent it from emerging on the surface of language. Hence, repetition is the return of both the same act (sawing) and the same words (vocabulary associated with working with a saw): the same words refer to the same acts and define the outlines of the event, as if by saturation. However, with Faulkner, the saturation of language through the repetition of the same words often takes the form of a heavy lid that covers a lack, a void, a deficiency—"content more complex" and "unique" that precisely unfolds in what has been kept quiet, beyond words.

IDIOT CYCLES: *THE SOUND AND THE FURY*, *THE HAMLET*

In its relation to enunciation, repetition is defined as the return of the same words, or as the act of repeating the words of another. According to this rule, the psittacism characteristic of (Faulknerian) idiots reveals,[10] through its burdensome automatic reflexes, a destitution whose full extent cannot be shown by any single concept.[11] Hence, repetition indirectly (it shows and generates feeling rather than says) reveals truths that are kept quiet. Etymologically derived from the Latin *psittacus* and the Greek *psittakos*, the notion of psittacism evokes the parrot, a bird that can imitate human speech, and whose name derives from the same root. Psittacism refers to the act of repeating or reciting like a parrot, in other words without understanding, without a clear awareness of the ideas that the words express. This phenomenon is normal among children, whose gradual acquisition of speech is precisely based on the systematic but approximate repetition of the words pronounced by the language-speaking beings surrounding them. It is frequently present among mentally disabled persons and idiots, for whom repetition occupies the vacancy left by the impossibility of autonomous, intelligible, and varied language. In his perpetual rehashing of the same events in a language that is congenitally resistant to any kind of alteration, Benjy's discourse is at the confluence of two tendencies toward repetition: repetition of a few words and simple syntactical structures is, indeed, combined with the faithful repetition of other people's words. In Benjy's discourse (I pointed out earlier how this term is problematic), repetition is an act: as it is produced, it leaves traces within the framework of the text that can be seen as clues regarding its functioning. On a fundamental level, if idiots repeat others and themselves, it is because they cannot make reality abstract, as stressed by Jacqueline Guillemin-Flescher: "The constant repetitions in Benjy's monologue can also be explained by his inability to view events in relation to each other, and to refer to them anaphorically" (Guillemin-Flescher, 1996: 52). For the idiot, evocation necessarily occurs by designating the exact thing, with each evocation coinciding with the exact repetition of the word or words referring to the thing. In the discourse of the idiot Benjy, repetition goes hand in hand with an extremely limited vocabulary. Benjy incessantly repeats the same words because he obviously knows few of them; he has no choice but to constantly repeat the same words because the notion of a synonym is entirely foreign to him. In *The Structure of the Artistic Text*, Jurij Lotman points out that no text can escape repetition: "Since any text is formed through the positional combination of a limited number of elements, the presence of repetitions is inevitable" (Lotman, 1977: 105).[12] Mathematically, this rule is all the more inevitable in Benjy's discourse, for the more limited the constituent elements of a text, the greater the repetition. Benjy's lexicon is limited to approximately five hundred words, most of which are verbs and nouns, along with a hundred adjectival and adverbial modifiers. The first page of *The Sound and the Fury* marks out a certain number of key words of Benjy's operational vocabulary: "fence," "gate," "flag," "cold," "smell," and "Caddy" are repeated over and over. All of them, even the words referring to sensations ("cold," "smell"), are imbued with a thick concreteness. Instruments of separation ("fence," "gate," "door") represent the confinement of language within ratiocination and mark the unsurpassable univocity of meaning (let us recall the confusion between "caddie" and "Caddy" presented on the very first page). These few words can be seen as Benjy's "flags," the rallying sign of his idiocy. These words are repeated in a simplistic and often deficient syntax: Benjy's failed syntax stems precisely from the limitations of his language. When the idiot does not have the word to say the thing, the syntax increases the unsound subordinate clauses whose function is to compensate for his lexical deficiencies. In the example "They were coming toward where the flag was" (*SF*: 3), the noun called for by the preposition "toward" is replaced periphrastically by a circumstantial subordinate of place, which is given the value of an object.[13] It is once again the repetition of known words (in this case, "flag") that by default refers, in the muddle of the syntax, to the things that do not have a specific name for Benjy. The periphrastic circumlocutions that enable him to evoke things that he cannot name, or does not know, do not escape repetition, as they still use the same words to refer to a difference.[14]

Benjy's psittacism also manifests itself through surface-level expressions in his discourse that particularly contrast with the extreme simplicity characteristic of his language. The flow of words that he reports in the form of direct speech includes idiotisms specific to Black dialect—"'I dont ricklick seing you around here before.' Luster said" (*SF*: 49)—as well as snatches of Latin reflecting the cynical erudition of Mr. Compson: "'*Et ego in arcadia* I have forgotten the Latin for hay.' Father said" (44). It is fairly clear that in either case, Benjy is completely unable to understand the meaning of the words he robotically repeats, much like Loulou, Félicité's parrot in Flaubert's "A Simple Heart": "Almost as if he were deliberately trying to entertain her, he would imitate the clicking of the turnspit, the shrill cry of the fishmonger, or the sound of sawing from the joiner's shop on the other side of the street. Whenever the front doorbell rang, he would imitate Madame Aubain: 'Félicité! The door! The door!'" (Flaubert, 2005: 31). Like Loulou, who indiscriminately reproduces sounds and words, in the end Benjy does no more than imitate the human voice. His idiot repetition of the speech of others reveals, behind his infallible mechanics, a fundamental incomprehension of the world around him.

Be that as it may, Benjy's essentially repetitive discourse is in perfect harmony with the small, routine gestures he has been repeating for thirty-three years: there is no need for a profusion of words to describe the insignificant actions to which he devotes his daily activity, no need for a highly diversified language to invariably rehash the same past events. Similarly, it is hardly surprising that people and things undergo very little change in Benjy's perception. Repetition is actually central to the characterization of the Faulknerian idiot and his perception of the world: the idiot is impervious to any form of development, and condemned to endlessly recommence and reiterate the same processes. However, with his congenitally failing memory, he does not perceive repetition as such, for he is not aware of his repetitions, or that his reality is captive to the workings of repetition. From Benjy's viewpoint, there is nothing morbid about repetition; he is unaware that the actions and images that define his everyday life are simply the stuttering of past actions and images. His memory is not a coprophagous memory feeding on its own disjecta, for it preserves no clear trace of the preceding occurrences of the same actions and images. His amnesia toward repetition, or more precisely the event that repeats itself, highlights how repetition is intimately connected to memory.

The memory lapses that Benjy suffers from link him with some of the patients Oliver Sacks discusses in *The Man Who Mistook His Wife for a Hat*, especially the lost mariner, for whom one of the book's essays is named. Benjy's short-term memory displays a capacity to forget similar to the phenomenon described by Sacks in his neurological interviews with the lost mariner, a forty-nine-year-old former navy officer who had no memory of what had happened to him over the previous thirty years. Life for the man stopped, as it were, in 1945, when he was twenty-five years old: "Homing in on his memory, I found an extreme and extraordinary loss of recent memory—so that whatever was said or shown or done to him was apt to be forgotten in a few seconds' time" (Sacks, 1986: 25). After stepping out for a few minutes, when Sacks returned to his medical office, where the patient was waiting, the latter showed him "no sign of recognition" (24). Unlike the lost mariner, Benjy does not entirely obliterate the recent past, instead integrating it within his unusual temporality that indiscriminately combines all periods of his life. Repetition thus functions within a system of "faint memories, some dim echo or sense of familiarity" (Sacks, 1986: 26).[15] Memory resists being labeled as such because both the mariner and the idiot are equally incapable of situating the event in a dated and bygone past; on the contrary, the past event is endlessly reiterated with the sparkling intensity of a present moment. Keeping this in mind sheds light on Green's statement that "acting out repetitively is a manner of recollecting that takes the place of memory" (Green, 2002: 75). The mariner discusses his navy experience in "the actual present tense of immediate experience" (Sacks, 1986: 23). Despite the three decades separating him from this professional experience, he behaves as though he had never stopped serving. With respect to Benjy, despite the years and his sister's departure, he never stops being Caddy's little pet. As impervious to time as they are incredulous to its signs, neither the lost mariner nor the idiot corresponds to his body's age. The lost mariner panics before the mirror held out to him by the doctor (since he is forever twenty-five years old, his white hair is frightening). Similarly, it has been thirty years since Benjy was three years old: "You mean, he been three years old thirty years" (*SF*: 17). The idiot and the lost mariner are hostages of an eternal youth and childhood, of a time that is hostile to change and aging, one that repeats and stagnates with repetition. This crystallization occurred for both of them at a precise—and disastrous—moment: "'He [the lost mariner] is, as it were,' I wrote in my notes, 'isolated in a single moment of being, with a moat or lacuna of forgetting all around him. . . . He is a man without a past (or future), stuck in a constantly changing, meaningless moment'" (Sacks, 1986: 28).[16] For the two men (which neither is fully capable of being, for different reasons), repetition is the result of an interruption, a rupture that dramatically changes the order of things by irremediably compromising the continuity of time. Time is lost in the crack, in the "hiatus"[17] caused by the catastrophe. For Benjy this precise moment converges, as Faulkner has often said, with Caddy's soiled underwear; for the lost mariner, it is precisely the indeterminacy of this moment that makes healing impossible.[18]

The connection between the notions of repetition and fate is a vast topic in and of itself, one that goes far beyond the framework of this book; it is nevertheless tempting to see an idiot irrevocability in *fatum* and its rigid outlines, as well as how it determines everything that happens in advance, without the least flexibility. Idiocy in Faulkner can moreover be interpreted as a manifestation of fate, as a curse that befalls great families as if to punish them for unbridled hubris, according to a logic that repeats itself from one novel to another. For instance, in her endless lamentations, Mrs. Compson likens her son's idiocy to divine punishment: "I thought that Benjamin was punishment enough for any sins I have committed" (*SF*: 103). Finally, idiocy is a congenital fate in the sense that—as in the case of the lost mariner's amnesia—the idiot's condition is final, irreversible, and definitive. For John Irwin, destiny in Faulkner takes the form of cycles that repeat unfailingly. In this respect, he notes how the Compson dynasty is condemned to the same misguided ways simply due to their origins and history (it is in a way overseen by destiny):

> This sense of a cyclic repetition within whose grip individual free will is helpless presents itself in Faulkner's novels as the image of the fate or doom that lies upon a family. [. . .] In the genealogy that Faulkner appended to *The Sound and the Fury*, he begins with the Indian chief Ikkemotube from whom the first Compson got his land—Ikkemotube, whose name was translated into English as "Doom." (Irwin, 1975: 60)

Quentin, the eldest son of the most recent generation, will not rest until he has broken the cycle of repetition. To do so, he takes destiny into his own hands by choosing death, thereby refusing to become a father himself and one day resembling his own father. It is paradoxically in the youngest son, the last-born idiot, that the transgenerational repetition of the same familial patterns is definitively broken.[19] Irwin continues his reflections on the fate that strikes great Faulknerian families through repetition of the same, by pondering the names of Faulknerian characters:

> We might note as an aside that in the decaying, aristocratic families like the Sartorises and Compsons, the given names of the male descendants tend to alternate between two possibilities from generation to generation—between John and Bayard in the Sartoris family and between Quentin and Jason in the Compson family. This alternation is one mark of the inbred character of these families and of the way that the locked in repetition of traditional patterns has made them unable to cope with changing times. One sign of the mongrel vigor and adaptability of the family that supplants the Compsons and Sartorises is that no member

of the Snopes family has a given name that is the same as any other member of that family. (Irwin, 1975: 64)

The Sartorises and Compsons deliberately choose to embody the family's fate by reincarnating themselves in one another, with the name of the son binding him to the paternal destiny. On the other end of the spectrum, the vigor of the Snopeses stems from the fact that they each have their own name, virginal and unique, the little stamp of soil on which, freed from any models, they can find individual fulfillment. The liberty of the Snopeses (whether they are despicable merchants, miserable sharecroppers, or simpletons) is contained in the originality of their name, and one Snopes never repeats another.

The change of name suffered by Benjamin Compson when his idiocy was confirmed around the age of five is obviously full of symbols. The three brothers of the most recent generation each duly bear the name of a more or less illustrious ancestor. The addendum to *The Sound and the Fury* entitled "Appendix/Compson, 1699–1945" reveals that Quentin is the third of his name, and Jason the fourth; regardless of what their mother thinks,[20] they are full-fledged Compsons. On the other hand, they had to borrow from the maternal family in order to name the youngest son, who has the same first name as his maternal uncle, Maury Bascomb, and bears this name until his mother, ashamed of his idiocy, begs that he be renamed.[21] It is Quentin, the well-read intellectual, who uses his knowledge of the Bible to choose a new first name for his younger idiot brother: "Who, when at last even his mother realised what he was and insisted weeping that his name must be changed, was rechristened Benjamin by his brother Quentin (Benjamin, our lastborn, sold in Egypt)" ("Appendix": 213).[22] Eventually, the idiot's name undergoes a final modification that prefigures the mutilation that he will suffer, for it is a truncated version of Benjamin that becomes his definitive name as an idiot. Caddy rebaptizes Benjamin "Benjy," to the great displeasure of Mrs. Compson, who is offended by the attribution of nicknames.[23] Finally, the omniscient narrator from section 4 of *The Sound and the Fury* shortens his nickname even further by calling him Ben. In Faulkner's world one must therefore be a Snopes[24] or an idiot to have a chance of escaping the compulsion to repeat destiny, and to move forward in the everyday dance of suns and moons, rather than the great cycles of fateful repetition.

The temporality of Faulknerian idiots unfolds in the tirelessly repetitive succession of days and nights, beyond any form of instrumentation of time, as moments of brightness and darkness in which all the occurrences of the same event merge sometimes in light, and sometimes in shadow, in the abstract form of the same. The repetition that is characteristic of the temporality of the idiot in *The Hamlet* is inscribed in the text's grammar by the iterative return of the modal *would*. Instead of differentiating the actions of Ike Snopes, or adhering to the particularities of each occurrence of an event, the modal *would* situates actions and events in a perspective of periodic return of the same, blurring their specific qualities under the effect of similarity. In *Narrative Discourse*, Gérard Genette precisely defines repetition in its relation to resemblance:

> The "repetition" is in fact a mental construction, which eliminates from each occurrence everything belonging to it that is peculiar to itself, in order to preserve only what it shares with all the others of the same class, which is an abstraction: "the sun" that "rises" every morning is not exactly the same from one day to another. . . . This is well known, and I recall it only to specify once and for all that what we will name here "identical events" or "the recurrence of the same event" is a series of several similar events considered only in terms of their resemblance. (Genette, 1980: 113)

The *would* that opens the story revolving around Ike Snopes combines with circumstantial complements in the plural to infinitely reflect the idiot's gestures, as if through a mirroring effect: "that morning and all the other mornings" (*H*: 184). That morning unfolds, without distinction, as the repetition of all the mornings of a world that has been repeating for three months—"the place where he had lain at each dawn for three months now, waiting for her" (196)—in an expectation resembling a ceremony, one that shows the extent of Ike's deep desire for his inaccessible beloved. This ritual of amorous expectation brings to mind the favorite posture of Benjy, who grips the fence—"I held to the fence" (*SF*: 4)—every afternoon of his life, waiting with absurd loyalty for she who will never return.[25] From the beginning of the section devoted to the peculiar love of the most innocent of Snopes, the iterative *would* generically reveals the successive stages of the rite of veneration to which the idiot devotes his early morning hours, as his senses awake: "and then he would begin to hurry" (*H*: 182); "Then he would hear her" (182); "He would smell her" (183); "He would lie amid the waking instant of earth's teeming minute life. [. . .] Then he would see her" (183). It is significant that in order to better arrange the coming surprise (which is already announced in the somewhat odd use of the verb *to smell* in referring to the beloved), the object of such adoration is still hidden behind the undefined objective personal pronoun *her*, referring to the immemorial woman whose identity is shrouded in mysterious morning mist. Finally, it is another modal, *can*, that in the same manner as an absolute present, offers a summary of sorts for the repetitive ritual of the amorous idiot, whose extreme simplicity is highlighted by the exclusive use of monosyllables: "He can lie in the grass and wait for her and hear her and then see her when the mist parts, and that is all" (186). The transition from *would* to *can*, whose use here is not particularly conventional, inscribes this silent and secret love in a system of possibilities and impossibilities, which implicitly paints the portrait of an extraordinary lover who is still satisfied with the quasi-religious repetition of the same gestures.

Faulknerian idiots move through a fundamentally iterative mode; they advance by retracing their steps, by unconsciously repeating the gestures they have already experienced so many times. Their blocked future is thus inscribed within their journey, which in their essential naïveté condemns them to return to the same places. That is why their destiny never takes the shape of a straight line: repetitive and concentric, it could nevertheless take material form as a system of spirals, such as the title sequences created by Saul Bass for Alfred Hitchcock's film *Vertigo*, in which the convulsions and repetitions of memory are depicted by dizzying circumvolutions.[26] Despite being unaware of it, Faulknerian idiots are caught in the coiling of a spiral as it were: but instead of following its flat curve, which, as it is portrayed geometrically, traces out revolutions around a pole that moves farther and farther out, they come and they go, moving away and toward this pole indiscriminately, which can be interpreted as the abstract representation of their here and now, their spatial and temporal present. Faulknerian idiots go in circles through space and time. In a slow whirlwind, space and time tend to mix indistinctly: as a result, the outlines of categories for space and time ultimately become blurred. In *The Hamlet*, the notion of destination, which by definition is spatial, is replaced by the image of a temporal destination for Ike Snopes:

> [T]here is no distance in either space or geography, no prolongation of time for distance to exist in, no muscular fatigue to establish its accomplishment. They are moving not toward a destination in space but a destination in time, toward the pinnacle-keep of evening where morning and afternoon become one. (*H*: 198)

In the blurring of spatiotemporal categories, the star-crossed lovers move not toward a place where their love can be consummated but toward an ideal moment that can welcome the intense union of their two beings separated by everything. This moment is presented as the culmination of the day, and its constant struggle to join with night: "they will advance only as the day itself advances, no faster. They have the same destination: sunset" (*H*: 203). The lovers patiently advance toward the sunset, a prelude to the darkness of night in which the distinctions between beings are abolished, in which the dissension of the world ends in a truce. It is the dark cradle in which obstacles and hurdles disappear, in which an idiot can freely love a cow, a Montague a Capulet. This theme of union in the shadows is a commonplace in Western literature. Romeo and Juliet meet in the darkness of the vault, where they fall, one after the other, into an even darker sleep: "I still will stay with thee: / And never from this palace of dim night / Depart again" (*Romeo and Juliet* 5.3.106–8). Similarly, for the mythical couple of *The Hamlet*, darkness ensures unity: the extinguishing of the light of day makes the lovers disappear, erasing their silhouettes and making them indiscernible from one another, one and the same. For them, light plays the role of a kindly matchmaker: "At the same moment all three of them cross the crest and descend into the bowl of evening and are *extinguished*. The rapid twilight *effaces* them from the day's tedious recording" (*H*: 205; emphasis mine). The world grows dim, finally allowing intimacy for the lovers. On the same page, images of effacement are replaced by three adjectives that imperceptibly slip toward one another through their graphic and phonic similarity: "indivisible," "invisible," and "invincible," materializing through their succession the power that the night provides for the lovers. During the night, the lovers' "invisibility" combines them "indivisibly," as if into a single entity; their union makes them "invincible" to the malice of the world around them. In this section from book 3 of *The Hamlet*, Faulkner increasingly uses semantic slips of this kind, in a way that parodies his own tendency toward repetition. He links words whose sounds are similar but whose meanings are different, for instance in the expression "one intact inconstant instant" (*H*: 201), in which the same syllables are refracted in vaguely different combinations. To better appreciate the effect of this slippage, here is the aforementioned passage reproduced in its entirety:

> She nuzzles into it, blowing the sweet breath-reek into the sweetish reek of feed until they become indistinguishable with that of the urgent and impatient milk as it flows among and about his fingers, hands, wrists, warm and *indivisible* as the strong inexhaustible life ichor itself, inherently, of itself, renewing. Then he leaves the *invisible* basket where he can find it again at dawn, and goes to the spring. Now he can see again. Again his head interrupts, then replaces as once more he breaks with drinking the reversed drinking of his drowned and fading image. It is the well of days, the still and insatiable aperture of earth. It holds, in tranquil paradox of suspended precipitation dawn, noon, and sunset; yesterday, today, and tomorrow—star-spawn and hieroglyph, the fierce white dying rose, then gradual and *invincible* speeding up to and into slack-flood's coronal of nympholept noon. (*H*: 205; emphasis mine)

These three adjectives, which pretend to repeat even though they are entirely unrelated semantically, describe within a single movement the lovers and the primordial nature sheltering them, and ensure the fluidity of images and words.

An abundance of liquid images evokes the union of the lovers, as the section slowly builds toward its grand finale before ending on a feeling of plenitude: the essential beverage that is milk, which flows from the cow's teats, the vital ichor flowing through the veins of Greek gods, and finally springwater, an elemental symbol of life. It is no surprise that this superlative night, which appears to bring an end to repetition[27]—into which all of the tributaries of abundance flow—is characterized by emphatic adjectives ("inexhaustible," "renewing," "insatiable") that highlight the vitality and regenerative power of nature. In the darkness that disrupts all human categories, the original Earth Mother also seems to contain the roots of time: it houses the "well of days," the matrix of repetition in which all of the dawns, noons, and dusks will break and vanish, the alternation of yesterdays, todays, and tomorrows in an uninterrupted dance of appearances and disappearances.

Faulknerian idiots experience the repetition of days and the natural alternation of day and night as a succession of births and deaths. Benjy's world unfolds in the half-open doors, which in their hushed sound allow a sliver of light to penetrate, or on the contrary seal in great darkness. Doors open to let the world burst forth in pools of light, then close and carry them into the shadows:

> "You a big boy." Dilsey said. "Caddy tired sleeping with you. Hush now, so you can go to sleep." The room went away, but I didn't hush, and the room came back and Dilsey came and sat on the bed, looking at me.
>
> "Aint you going to be a good boy and hush." Dilsey said. "You aint, is you. See can you wait a minute, then."
>
> She went away. There wasn't anything in the door. Then Caddy was in it.
>
> "Hush." Caddy said. "I'm coming." (*SF*: 44)

In this scene where Benjy, who is too old to share his sister's bed, refuses to sleep alone, his distress is choreographed through a singular sound and light. Dilsey's coming and going, along with the comforting appearance of Caddy, are experienced in the incessant racket of the idiot's pain (which represents the only permanent element: "I didn't hush"), like complete appearances and disappearances. For Benjy, the darkness coincides with a literal annihilation of the world, and similarly an appearance is like a religious epiphany or even magic for him (Caddy suddenly appears in visible form), with objects seemingly endowed with autonomy and supernatural powers.[28] For Benjy, each new occurrence of repetition seems like a radical novelty. Faulkner's dialectic of repetition is not very different in this regard from the one defined by Søren Kierkegaard in his unusual little essay entitled "Repetition," in which philosophical meditation is lost amid a kind of user's manual for lovesick heroes (is it truly a coincidence that Ike Snopes and Benjy Compson belong to this latter category?): "The dialectic of repetition is easy, because that which is repeated has been, otherwise it could not be repeated; but precisely this, that it has been, makes repetition something new" (Kierkegaard, 2009: 19). While it appears to the eyes of normative humans as being rooted and bogged down in stagnation, idiot repetition is, on the contrary, experienced by the idiots directly concerned as an opening or a blossoming; unlike (re)collection, which by essence is deleterious, repetition is a bearer of lively passions, as emphasized by Kierkegaard once again:

> Repetition and recollection are the same movement, just in opposite directions, because what is recollected has already been and is thus repeated backwards, whereas genuine repetition is recollected forwards. Repetition, if it is possible, thus makes a person happy, while recollection makes him unhappy. (Kierkegaard, 2009: 4)

The idiot apprehends each occurrence of repetition as a world that is beginning, as an absolutely new day bringing with it new events and impressions that delight or afflict him with the intensity of the first time. For him, every recommencement is a commencement, every reiteration equivalent to a first appearance, a kind of birth that is approached with that entirely naïve and virginal wonder characteristic of the inalterable childhood of idiots. His perception of the world can be qualified as palingenetic, in the sense that the Stoics defined palingenesis (from the Greek *palin*, "again," and *genesis*, "birth") as the periodic and eternal return of the same events. When the idiot indefatigably repeats the same gestures and tirelessly summons up the same images and words, with each occurrence of repetition the gestures, images, and words are reborn, rising to the surface of life with an intensity that can in no way be tarnished by the constant return of the same. For the same does not exist for idiots, as their world only consists of singular objects. Each repeated event appears religiously in their consciousness in the form of a resurrection. In fact, there is repetition only in the gaze that observers direct at the doings of Faulknerian idiots. In that respect, repetition is no more than a tool of analytical discourse. Even though idiocy seems to manifest itself through repetition, and Faulkner intentionally chose repetition as one of the literary figures for idiocy, it does not have a real existence for the idiot characters. Repetition is no more than an artifice of normality, a deception of normative discourse that can check elusive or disturbing logic.

Chapter 5

STATES OF A WORLD IN DISINTEGRATION

> What seems beautiful to me, what I should like to write, is a book about nothing, a book dependent on nothing external, which would be held together by the internal strength of its style, just as the earth, suspended in the void, depends on nothing external for its support; a book which would have almost no subject, or at least in which the subject would be almost invisible, if such a thing is possible.
> —GUSTAVE FLAUBERT, LETTER TO LOUISE COLET, JANUARY 16, 1852

Flaubert's iconoclastic and avant-gardist dream was also that of modernism: replacing the rigid subject matter of literature with little insignificant things; replacing the weighty framework of the classical novel with weak and open structures that could include an infinitely varied reality; and admitting that the "stuff of fiction" is perhaps entirely different from what habit and the tradition have led us to believe. In her essays, Virginia Woolf led a determined struggle for the modern novel—"the proper stuff for fiction is a little other than custom would have us believe it" (Woolf, 1988: 33)—whose radical singularity takes shape through litotes ("little other"). Its purpose can be formulated only by default, or through formal oppositions of disarming simplicity, namely replacing the old with the new, converting the center into the margin, the essential into the accessory, the large into the small. It is with this in mind that she made the death of a moth the subject of an exemplary text:

> To have only a moth's part in life, and a day moth's at that, appeared a hard fate, and his zest in enjoying his meagre opportunities to the full, pathetic. He flew vigorously to one corner of his compartment, and, after waiting there a second, flew across to the other. What remained for him but fly to a third corner and then to a fourth? That was all he could do, in spite of the size of the downs, the width of the sky, the far-off smoke of houses, and the romantic voice, now and then, of a steamer

out at sea. What he could do he did. Watching him, it seemed as if a fibre, very thin but pure, of the enormous energy of the world had been thrust into his frail and diminutive body. As often as he crossed the pane, I could fancy that a thread of vital light became visible. He was little or nothing but life. (Woolf, 1970 [1942]: 4)

A fragile and ephemeral creature, the day moth leads its short life between the four corners of a window that is little compared to the hills and skies just beyond the frame. For all that, it is the lexical fields of vigor and intense enthusiasm that depict the moth's pathetic dance against the glass: "zest," "vigorously," "enormous energy," "vital." Despite its frail capacities, the moth lives at the height of its potential, and its energy is such that it has no reason to envy the giants of literature. It is the pure incarnation of a life lived fully and absolutely. In the wake of James Joyce, modernist literature opened its doors—previously reserved all too often for noble subjects—to shapeless or insignificant things widely considered to be "incoherent inanity" (Woolf, 1988: 34). The revolution in literary subject matter was accompanied by the upheaval of fictional material. It was the beginning of the momentary but decisive reign of the fragmentary—"we must reconcile ourselves to a season of failures and fragments" (Woolf, 1988: 435) wrote Woolf in "Character in Fiction"—and of disarticulation. There was the emergence of shapeless shapes, in the great destructive roar that annihilated old Europe: "Thus it is what we hear all around us, in poems and novels and biographies, even in newspaper articles and essays, the sound of breaking and falling, crashing and destruction" (Woolf, 1988: 434). Letters were abruptly freed of conventions and models, and began to imitate the world struggling to emerge from the disaster of the First World War, a shattered world dominated by fragments and doubt. It was on the shifting foundations of this great project that the world and modern letters began to rebuild. However, as Jean-Yves Jouannais remarked in his "L'Idiotie en art, l'anti-Biathanatos" (n.d.; Idiocy in Art, the Anti-Biathanatos), in order to exist as modern, "the work is in effect condemned to idiocy. [...] It must never have existed before itself." These new forms and figures of literature were intended to be absolutely singular, with this singularity initially emanating from the imitation of the postwar chaos that Joyce transposed in his treatment of the consciousness, which he described "before it becomes aware and sets things in order" (Bergounioux, 2002: 118).

On the other side of the Atlantic, in a Mississippi stagnating in its rural nature and age-old prejudices, Faulkner took up the watchword of Flaubert (whom he had read) and inscribed his budding work in the direct line of descent of T. S. Eliot's *The Waste Land* (1922), to which his first novel, *Soldiers' Pay* (1926), pays discreet tribute.[1] Yet nothing seemed to predispose the young

Faulkner, who had just added a vowel to his name,[2] to the revolution he was about to initiate, alone and far from the frenetic agitation of the Old World:

> Then, we would seek in vain someone who considers writing in such a rural setting, and who moreover wonders how to have so-called reality pierce the imperfect and outdated image that it had heretofore received on the page, in the order of writing. Of course, it is not solely beneath the reservoir of a dusty hamlet that such a question is asked. It also torments a few minds in major metropolises on the Atlantic coast. But what is new, the heresy, is that someone considers doing it in a community numbering a few hundred souls, half of whom, without speaking of the Blacks, are illiterate, while the others find in the Bible the light and consolations that less busy and more refined people seek out in great libraries. (Bergounioux, 2002: 76)

Against all expectation, the genius of Faulkner was born from the languid dynamics of his native Oxford, where he decided to be thoroughly idiotic (in the previously established sense of *idios anthropos*, a singular man with a particular character standing in contrast to the public and the commonplace) in the kingdom of the simpletons. It was also in this region devastated by its history and defeat (where a war had changed everything a few decades earlier)—a "world of dust," in which the legendary figures of heroes worthy of the name had become outdated—that Faulkner became a writer. His first novel was about a vegetative, deaf, and dying veteran. His third novel, *Flags in the Dust*, offers his first depiction of the antihero par excellence, an average, passive, and meditative lawyer who is in love with his sister and expresses his frustration on glass vases whose feminine forms he cherishes. In *Sanctuary*, it is the same Horace Benbow who satisfies, with ridiculous and degrading zeal, his wife's insatiable appetite (whom he took in horror) for the shrimp he brings home for her in dripping packages every Friday night. The inanity of his existence materializes in the little pools he leaves behind on the sidewalk, and the smell of shrimp becomes the pathetic symbol for monotonous repetition, his inertia and his impotence:

> Just Friday. But I have done it for ten years, since we were married. And still dont like to smell shrimp. But I wouldn't mind the carrying it home so much. I could stand that. It's because the package drips and drips, until after a while I follow myself to the station and stand aside and watch Horace Benbow take that box off the train and start home with it, changing hands every hundred steps, and I following him, thinking

Here lies Horace Benbow in a fading series of small stinking spots on a Mississippi sidewalk. (S: 17)

The stink of the shrimp juice reflects, in a succession of little mirrors, the grotesque situation of former notables and heroes, whose prestigious past evaporates in the cracks of the sidewalk.[3] However, it is with the invention of his idiot characters and the creation of an aesthetics of idiocy that Faulkner achieves the most radical novelty, implicitly denounces the vanity of Western literature's old proper manners, and completes the disfigurement of the individual. All conventions are abolished with Faulknerian idiots, while all of the expectations of the readership, heretofore educated in classical forms, are frustrated: characters and narrators become unrecognizable. In creating his idiocy, Faulkner in turn usurped the right to start a revolution, in the sense intended by Maurice Blanchot in his 1949 essay "Literature and the Right to Death":

> Revolutionary action is in every respect analogous to action as embodied in literature: the passage from nothing to everything, the affirmation of the absolute as event and of every event as absolute. Revolutionary action explodes with the same force and the same facility as the writer who has only to set down a few words side by side in order to change the world. Revolutionary action also has the same demand for purity, and the certainty that everything it does has absolute value, that it is not just any action performed to bring about some desirable and respectable goal, but that it is itself the ultimate goal, the Last Act. This last act is freedom, and the only choice left is between freedom and nothing. (Blanchot, 1995: 319)

With *The Sound and the Fury*, Faulkner assumed the radical liberty of making sound but signifying nothing, with the multiple contradictions of his novel being neither transcended nor resolved in a final unifying movement. Section 4, which closes the novel by attempting to sublimate the confusion of particular consciences and to restore the principle of identity by dint of an omniscient point of view, ultimately does no more than repeat the theme of a "magnificent failure."[4] In writing the monologue of an idiot, Faulkner broke in the reinforced doors guarding stable and faithful forms, behind which unfolds an unbridled—and free—syntax. To paraphrase the words of Virginia Woolf quoted above, *The Sound and the Fury* is built like a succession of "fragments" on the compounded theme of "failure" (failure to live, to say, to make sense), in forms that are as yellowish, unstable, and evanescent as the unhealthy appearance, shambling gait, and limited understanding of idiots. Faulknerian colors are all in half-tones, as if beset by slow dissolution. They are the colors of a world in decline for which these idiot figures serve as an emblem, the antithesis of former heroes, bringing an abrupt and decisive end to the prestigious Southern generations. While Faulknerian idiots embody the end of a time period, they also enable their author—and through him the writing—to explore new, virgin, and fanciful terrain. It is in disintegration itself that new forms and sublime figures emerge. The collapse of a world carries within its chaos fragments that will make up the basis of the world to come. Faulkner's favorite words, of which I have begun to draw up a list here and there, are joined by other forms, whose inevitable disappearance is signaled by the becoming of the gerund but that also provide access, through the combinations in which they are found, to a dizzying beyond. They include "fading," "dissolving," and other related forms that signify all the states of a world in disintegration. Faulkner's world sometimes evokes the pictorial world of Henri Michaux: at times it resembles certain watercolors with yellow, brown, and pallid colors, at other times certain drawings in india ink collected under the label of "drawings of disintegration," which when produced under the effect of mescal are also referred to by the term mescalines, in the same manner as *marines* (seascapes). In one it is color that is in the grip of decomposition and fragmentation, and in the other it is form.[5]

The failure of the synthetic aim of the final section of *The Sound and the Fury* is announced from the very first lines, like a scheduled error: "The day dawned bleak and chill, a moving wall of gray light out of the northeast which, instead of dissolving into moisture, seemed to disintegrate into minute and venomous particles, like dust" (*SF*: 265). The atmosphere of this Sunday dawn announces less a resurrection than the inevitable shakiness of forms ("moving," "dissolving," "gray"), which culminates in their disintegration ("disintegrate") into minute particles, whose disarticulation and scattering bring to mind the distended figures of the bodies and temporality of idiots. Similarly, the death of Addie Bundren coincides with the dissolution of her surroundings: as she is in her death throes, the precariousness of her life—"her failing life" (*AILD*: 47)—endangers the intensity of the light ("the failing light," 48), such that her youngest son, Vardaman, the powerless witness of the disaster looming in the death of his mother, also begins to slowly disappear: "his eyes round, his pale face fading into the dusk like a piece of paper pasted on a failing wall" (49). By way of contamination, amid a landscape whose yellowing imitates how death inevitably degrades bodies, all of the elements of nature descend into chaos:

> In the rain the mules smoke a little, splashed yellow with mud, the off one clinging in sliding lunges to the side of the road above the ditch. The

tilted lumber gleams dull yellow, *water-soaked and heavy as lead, tilted at a steep angle into the ditch above the broken wheel; about the shattered spokes and about Jewel's ankles a runnel of* yellow *neither water nor earth swirls, curving with the* yellow *road neither of earth nor water, down the hill* dissolving *into a streaming mass of dark green neither of earth nor sky.* (*AILD*: 49; emphasis mine)

The outlines of beings and things are threatened by the death of the mother, who is the source of an actual deluge. Distinction is wiped out in favor of that which is blurry and shapeless; the order of things totters in a syntax that increasingly uses grammatical forms that emphasize becoming and change ("clinging," "sliding," "curving," "streaming"), and disappear into the dissolution ("dissolving") of everything (mother "earth") into nothing ("neither [. . .] nor"). And this nothing becomes the subject of a novel of extraordinary virtuosity. Death also unfolds as part of the same movement that gives rise to a vision and birth to a writing, for Darl is as impossible a narrator as Benjy was at the beginning of *The Sound and the Fury* (though for different reasons). He is not present when his mother dies, stuck with Jewel far away in a storm, but he sees this death and describes it with visionary intensity and poetry. Degeneration and disintegration constitute the paradoxical origins of an art.

Part II

To the Roots of the World: Idiocy and Its Objects

> That child, like the other two, never smiled, never stretched his hands to her, never spoke; never had a glance of recognition for her in its big black eyes, which could only stare fixedly at any glitter, but failed hopelessly to follow the brilliance of a sun-ray slipping slowly along the floor.
> —JOSEPH CONRAD, "THE IDIOTS," *TALES OF UNREST*

Chapter 6

IDIOTS HAVE BLUE EYES

> I had forgotten about his eyes. They were as blue as the sides of a certain type of box of matches. When you looked at them carefully you saw that they were perfectly honest, perfectly straightforward, perfectly, perfectly stupid. But the brick pink of his complexion, running perfectly level to the brick pink of his inner eyelids, gave them a curious, sinister expression—like a mosaic of blue porcelain set in pink china.
> —FORD MADOX FORD, *THE GOOD SOLDIER*

In Joseph Conrad's short story "The Idiots," the first appearance of the idiot twins is described in great detail: "The glance was unseeing and staring, a fascinated glance; but he did not turn to look after us. Probably the image passed before the eyes without leaving any trace on the misshapen brain of the creature" (Conrad, 1974 [1898]: 58). The first-person narrator presents multiple paradoxes: the idiot gaze is described as a stare, yet it sees nothing; it is a glance fixed on the world, but over which reality passes "without leaving any trace"; it is a gaze both fascinated and apathetic in which fixedness and impassiveness seemingly go hand in hand. It is also remarkable that the eyes of idiots are almost invariably blue. A comparison of Benjy's physical description from section 4 of *The Sound and the Fury* and that of the idiot from "The Kingdom of God" is once again highly instructive. The eyes of the two idiots reflect the same light, the same transparent clarity, and the same bucolic image of cornflowers:[1] "his eyes were clear and blue as cornflowers, and utterly vacant of thought" ("Kingdom": 55); "His eyes were clear, of the pale sweet blue of cornflowers" (*SF*: 274). They also have the same innocence and serenity: "His eyes were like two scraps of April sky after a rain" ("Kingdom": 60); "his eyes were empty and blue and serene again" (*SF*: 321). The blue eyes of idiots glide along the surface of reality, looking without seeing, seeing without understanding. Ike Snopes's eyes are characterized by their singular emptiness: "the pale eyes which seemed to have no vision in them at all" (*H*: 90); "the eyes above the round mouth fixed and sightless" (95); "his blasted eyes staring aghast and incredulous at nothing" (188). Privatives abound in depictions of these eyes, which seem dispossessed of their elementary faculty, even though nothing hinders their visual acuity. This vast emptiness coincides with the imperturbable tranquility of those who are immune to doubt and anxiety: "when he raised his face it was not even empty, it was unfathomable and profoundly quiet" (*H*: 197). The blue eyes of idiots are the mark of a gaze that—to paraphrase Flaubert insisting on Charles Bovary's bovine stupidity—seems condemned to never encounter thought.[2]

As suggested by the example of Conrad's idiots, Faulkner's idiots are not the only ones who have "cornflower blue" eyes, a color that is as indescribable as it is inexpressive, one that Alfred de Musset would have called "la couleur bête" (the dumb color) (Bachelard, 1998 [1943]: 210). In Steinbeck's *Of Mice and Men*, Lennie also has light eyes, as opposed to George, whose gaze is dark and agitated: "Behind him walked his opposite, a huge man, shapeless of face, with large, pale eyes, with wide, sloping shoulders" (Steinbeck, 1940 [1937]: 9). The indeterminacy of Lennie's silhouette accompanies the limpid and indefinable clarity of his eyes. Similarly, Dostoevsky's idiot is characterized from the beginning by his problematic and disturbing blue gaze, in which a naïve gentleness is combined with curious stasis: "His eyes were big, blue, and intent; their gaze had something quiet but heavy about it and was filled with that strange expression by which some are able to guess at first sight that the subject has the falling sickness" (Dostoevsky, 2003: 6). *The Idiot* suggests that the blue eyes of idiots reflect a reality that is more complex than appears at first sight. By the same token, the idiot that Thoreau depicts in *Walden*, a primal man who is unquestioningly idealized because he is congenitally impervious to the corrupting influence of civilization, evokes a curious collage of opposing forces:

> A more simple and natural man it would be hard to find. Vice and disease, which cast such a somber moral hue over the world, seemed to have hardly any existence for him. [. . .] He was cast in the coarsest mould; a stout but sluggish boy, yet gracefully carried, with a thick sunburned neck, dark bushy hair, and dull sleepy blue eyes, which were occasionally lit up with expression. (Thoreau, 1982 [1854]: 395)

Strength and flabbiness, heaviness and grace are combined with dull, lifeless blue eyes that occasionally light up with expression.

In the symbolism of colors, blue has a duality that confirms the paradoxical impressions sparked by the blue eyes of idiots. Blue, which Antoine Furetière pointed out "is azure in color" (Furetière, 1997: 17), only appears to us as such because of its great distance, "which prompts us to believe that the skies are *blue*, a very distant sea [that] appears to us as *blue*." In this case, the perception of blue is the result of an optical illusion. For classical painters, blue was the fleeting color of the sky and the distance. Due to its likeness to the sky, blue is often associated with the spiritual realm; it is a cold color that supposedly prompts reflection. The *fleur bleue* (literally, blue flower; sentimentality) of Romanticism, which served as the title for Penelope Fitzgerald's novel about the early years of the German poet Friedrich Novalis,[3] evokes the notion of thought taking flight. Most importantly, in Christian iconography, Jesus is represented in blue clothes when preaching the good news of the kingdom of God, for he is announcing the truth and embodying transcendence. However, "we cannot explain why blue is associated with drunkenness (in German *blau sein*, 'to be blue,' means 'to be drunk')" (Cazenave, 1996: 84), although the alcoholism of Malcolm Lowry's consul gives him the "blue expression" specific to certain drunkards.[4] Furetière also observes that "we figuratively say that a man turns totally *blue* when experiencing terrible emotional pain, receiving unfortunate news, or being criticized for something he feels guilty about, because he turns pale and wan" (Furetière, 1997: 18). As a result, from a symbolic point of view blue is at the intersection of two entirely contrary dynamics: thought taking flight on the one hand, idiot and guilty stupor on the other; the transcendence of reality on the one hand, the individual's immanence in the world on the other.

"The blue of noon"[5] is captured in the brightness and pallor reminiscent of a newborn's eyes; the gentleness of an undeniable and vaguely defined innocence; a serenity that converges with dizzying emptiness; and a detachment that restricts one to sluggishness. Did not Christ, dressed in blue, recognize idiots as belonging to the "kingdom of God"? It was most likely Faulkner's reading of the gospel that inspired the title for his first short story about an idiot character: "Blessed are the poor in spirit: for theirs is the kingdom of heaven" (Matthew 5:3). By virtue of their innocence, idiots are promised paradise, the "kingdom of heaven." Yet like the sky, whose temperament changes incessantly, the idiot's gaze is paradoxical, with their "empty" eyes being described in a multitude of ways. While "serene,"[6] their blue is nevertheless lunatic; it is an ineffable gaze showing "solemn detachment,"[7] with blue marking the idiot's strange isolation. François Pitavy has suggested that this transparent gaze draws its vacuity and depth from this blue.[8] Are idiots' blue eyes, and the contradictory qualities emanating from them, the image of a blue-tinged gaze and relation to the world and others? What things are grasped by the idiot's gaze? How is their essence modified by the specter of this gaze? If it is true that "in order for me to be what I am, it suffices merely that the Other look at me" (Sartre, 1992 [1956]: 351),[9] then what am I in the eyes of the idiot? As smooth, flat, and uniform as a spring sky, the idiot's gaze is the filter for a perspectiveless vision, one in which reality is aligned, compressed, and flattened into a singular tableau.

Chapter 7

THE IDIOT GAZE AND ITS REPRESENTATIONS

> The road went on under the moon, vaguely dissolving without perspective.
> —WILLIAM FAULKNER, *SOLDIERS' PAY*

Perspective, which derives etymologically from the Latin *perspicere*, meaning to "see distinctly," is first related to a science closely connected to the field of vision; its purpose is to represent bodies and objects by accounting for the differences that distance and position create in the perception of a figure or color. Perspective is thus at the intersection of geometry, optics, architecture, and the pictorial arts and can be defined as a way of reconstructing visual space and projecting bodies, in which all lines converge on a single point, known as the vanishing point. In its extension to the field of semantics, the word "perspective" refers, in everyday language, to the appearance of objects seen from afar, and more abstractly to the view from which we contemplate certain objects. It is from this latter definition that the more figurative and distant meaning of the geometry of lines comes: finally, the word "perspective" designates an event or a series of events that are presented—amid waiting, fear, and hope—as being probable or possible in a distant future. If we focus on this final meaning, the Faulknerian idiot has no perspective, for his future is saturated by the ratiocinating and atemporal return of the same images and events, and his future is eternally obstructed by an inability to project himself forward. Here I am referring to the notion of perspective chiefly as it relates to the representation of visual space. I will begin by describing the distortions that are characteristic of the gazes of Faulknerian idiots, and test how these gazes break the rules of classical perspective, instead adhering to other ways of perceiving reality characterized by their phenomenological dimension. I will then explore the effects of these idiot gazes as filters for representing a world tinged in blue.

THE PERSPECTIVES OF FAULKNERIAN IDIOCY

For Faulknerian idiots, reality is necessarily univocal, which is to say devoid of equivocation; the word exists only insofar as it is rooted in the thing it designates. The idiot's rootedness in the world and language, in which the fantasy of multiple meanings is sacrificed to the tottering edifice of a single and singular meaning, corresponds to a gaze that looks only in a single direction. The distortions of the idiot's gaze, which are characterized by a frontal, one-dimensional, and fixed relation to the world, can be seen as the initial symptoms of idiocy, those from which all others will flow. The phenomena and signs of idiocy indeed reveal themselves via the idiot's gaze. It is in the singularity of their being-in-the-world—as it is expressed in their gaze—that the vision of idiots is born, at the point where the eye, the spirit, and the world converge. In his 1964 essay "Eye and Mind," Maurice Merleau-Ponty shows how reality and vision resemble one another in a relation of absolute reciprocity: "[T]he same thing is both out there in the world and here in the heart of vision—the same or, if you will, a *similar* thing, but according to an efficient similarity which is the parent, the genesis, the metamorphosis of being into its vision" (Merleau-Ponty, 1993: 128). The qualities refracted by the world's objects have their seat in the body of the beholder and emanate from the vision that defines itself through this body.[1] In the interplay of reciprocal influences, both the vision and the world of idiots[2] assume the same qualities. Embraced by an idiot gaze, the world is condemned to manifest the same signs as the idiot's idiocy—it unfolds as an idiot world.

In *The Sound and the Fury*, Benjy Compson's gaze is first characterized by its fixedness; section 1 actually presents itself as the raw product of this singular gaze. The world that unfurls through the repetitive hiccups of a radically strange syntax is both limited and filtered through this gaze, which is stubbornly fixed on the things that are directly before it. The motif of vision takes shape from the very first words of the novel; the verb *to see* is actually the first active verb that surfaces in Benjy's discourse: "Through the fence, between the curling flower spaces, I could see them hitting" (*SF*: 3). Vision is the initial act from which a world and a work simultaneously proceed. However, we quickly note that this vision is literally hindered: Benjy sees what he sees through a hole in a fence, which is covered by vegetation greatly limiting his field of vision, like a porthole at sea.[3] When his discourse begins, Benjy only sees what appears directly in front of him within the vegetal framework formed by this hole. This first sentence thus appears retrospectively as an emblem of Benjy's abnormal and incomplete vision, as well as an immediate warning that the vision governing the discourse is restricted and problematic. Following on the first paragraph, the verb *to see* shifts into the verb *to watch*: "They went away across the pasture. I held to the fence and watched them going away" (*SF*: 3). In this movement, accidental vision becomes intentional gaze. The appearance of these two verbs on the novel's first page is noteworthy, for they define, precisely albeit elliptically, the nature of the focal point that is the seat for the unfolding perception of reality. The verbs *to see*, which designates both a state of reception and the neutrality of a highly primitive perception, and *to watch*, which is a manner of seeing based on repetition, establish the rules, as it were, for the unfolding story: the objects of Benjy's discourse reside in and are reduced to the things he sees and occasionally looks at. These are entirely concrete objects firmly anchored in the world, for even images of the past are triggered by tangible objects or sensations whose perception is governed by the sense of sight, and that nothing distinguishes from present images, as discussed above. It is remarkable that in spite of their extreme simplicity, the verbs referring to vision occur only rarely in Benjy's discourse beyond this first page. Their first occurrence can therefore be seen as establishing a paradigm, for it presents the modes of a vision that will henceforth be manifested directly, with no reminders for the reader that the strange world from section 1 of *The Sound and the Fury* comes from the vision of the singular *I* presiding over the story.

The "see" sedimented by time and repetition becomes a gaze. However, in spite of the multiple time periods from which it borrows its objects, the idiot's gaze is defined by its stasis: the appearance of the verb *to watch* in the quotation above reiterates the motif of vision's immobility. Benjy has not yet left his observatory, so to speak. What's more, his attachment to the fence reflects his fixed point of view: the gaze incessantly watching for Caddy's arrival is the only control, however precarious and random, he has over a world that presents itself as a series of fortuitous appearances. When they are not directly solicited by surrounding objects or persons, the idiot's eyes remain imperturbably fixed on the objects that directly appear in his field of vision, directly in front of him. The things that trigger the succession of different temporal strata in Benjy's perception reflect this fixedness, for it is through the repetition of the same situation, or the appearance of the same object, that different points in time merge and combine, in which one temporal stratum gives way to another. While the years move on, the objects that transport Benjy from one recollection to another invariably remain the same. Similarly, while the decades alter Benjy's objects of predilection and threaten to make them unrecognizable, their function remains constant and unchanged. This is true of Caddy's cushion, mirror, and slipper, as well as the fire and the rain; the idiot's precarious calm and serenity are based on the permanence of these elements, as is the legibility of the story, for the smallest change in the semblance of order governing Benjy's life sends it teetering into unintelligible chaos and sound. From one point in time to another, and from one image to another, it is as though Benjy's gaze has not moved, as though his eyes are tied to the act of contemplation. The gaze remains imperturbably the same in its posture and orientation: reality is what changes, moves, and transforms, as though objects are the ones that enter and exit, appear and disappear, in the idiot's field of vision. For example, calmed by the spectacle of the fire burning in the hearth, Benjy does not understand why it suddenly disappears when Luster mischievously and deliberately attracts his attention, in order to mock Benjy's subsequent reaction:

> "Here. Look at the fire whiles I cuts this cake." [. . .]
> I ate some cake. Luster's hand came and took another piece. I could hear him eating. I looked at the fire.
> A long piece of wire came across my shoulder. It went to the door, and then the fire went away. I began to cry.
> "What are you howling for now." Luster said. "Look there." The fire was there. I hushed. "Cant you set and look at the fire and be quiet like mammy told you." (SF: 57)

The idiot does not understand that when he turns his head, reality does not make a simultaneous rotation to coincide exactly with his gaze; as a result, he does not understand that some things vanish from his field of vision while others appear within it. Since the idiot's world is attached to his gaze, when reality slips away it sends his entire being reeling. An object's disappearance is experienced as a threat and even a tragedy, one that only the reappearance of the same object—the return of the fire in his gaze—can calm. The idiot does not suspect the power of decision and action that humans can exert over a number of their own visual perceptions: he is unaware that he could see what he wants to see, or that a gaze can be directed toward everything that can be seen; that a *see* can always be transformed into a *watch*, that the world generally remains in its place, and that the center of visual perception is infinitely mobile and free to choose its objects. It is in this respect that Benjy's posture can be qualified as phenomenological: it stands opposite to an objectifying conception of the gaze that places the subject in a position of domination, at the center of vision. Benjy dominates nothing: he is entirely and passively subject to the spectacle of the world surrounding him. From his point of view, objects are the ones equipped with the power to act: his idiocy is manifested here by a kind of animism, in which the things that continually appear and disappear from his field of vision seem to be fully endowed with the terrifying power to move themselves. The idiot is, in a way, the man of magical thinking.[4] Benjy's static gaze makes him a favorite butt for the most elementary jokes. In the passages corresponding to the narrative present, Luster subjects Benjy to the full variety of Tantalus's torments, depriving him of the pleasure of the object he is contemplating. Benjy's absolute naïveté is a source of constant jubilation, for all Luster has to do to drive Benjy up the wall is to remove an object from his sight (the hearth, flowers) simply by making him turn.[5]

These alternating disappearances and appearances can be seen as the continuing symbolic manifestations and repetitions of the one disappearance that matters for Benjy. With this in mind, André Bleikasten established a parallel between these disappearances-appearances of objects and the game of *fort/da*, described by Freud in "Beyond the Pleasure Principle." In the succession of their infantile "gone" and "here," Benjy's visual perceptions resemble the little boy's game observed by Freud, except that for Faulkner's idiot, the absence that is indirectly staged through this dance of objects is, of course, that of his sister. Freud evokes this singular game as follows:

> The child had a wooden reel with some string tied around it. It never crossed his mind to drag it along the floor behind him, for instance, in other words to play toy cars with it; instead, keeping hold of the string, he very skilfully threw the string over the edge of his curtained cot so that it disappeared inside, all the while making his expressive "o-o-o-o" sound [which means "gone" in German, *fort*], then using the string to pull the reel out of the cot again, but this time greeting its reappearance with a joyful "*Da!*" ("Here!"). That, then, was the entire game—disappearing and coming back—only the first act of which one normally got to see; and this first act was tirelessly repeated on its own, even though the greater pleasure undoubtedly attached to the second. (Freud, 2006: 140–41)

Freud observed that the game gives the child a power that he precisely did not have when his mother left: "The experience affected him, but his own role in it was passive, and he therefore gave himself an active one by repeating it as a game, even though it had been unpleasurable." The game thus has a compensatory quality for the child, since through it the boy takes revenge for the affront suffered: "The act of flinging away the object to make it 'gone' may be the gratification of an impulse on the child's part—which in the ordinary way of things remains suppressed—to take revenge on his mother for having gone away from him; and it may thus be a defiant statement meaning 'Alright, go away! I don't need you! I'm sending you away myself!'" (Freud, 2006: 142). While Freud's little boy and Faulkner's idiot both play with reels, and their gestures resemble one another,[6] there is nevertheless a major difference between them: while the child becomes active and plays by transforming what he endured into a controlled gesture, the idiot endures things in an absolute and unsurpassable manner. An eternal child, the idiot is the eternally passive plaything of others' actions, the acutely vulnerable victim of Caddy's departures.

In one of the novel's first temporal changes, the stasis of Benjy's vision and his extreme passiveness appear in a short, iconic scene during a winter day from childhood. Caddy is coming home from school in the afternoon: "Caddy was walking. Then she was running, her book satchel swinging and bouncing behind her" (*SF*: 6). The reader witnesses Caddy advancing through Benjy's gaze, which is firmly snagged on his fence, just as his eyes are fixed on the little dot in the road that gradually becomes his sister. Caddy's appearance in Benjy's field of vision is as sudden as that of her name on the page. This episode coincides with Caddy's first active intervention in the novel, from which she had hitherto been present solely as a phantasmatic presence, but this time Caddy indeed appears to be present.[7] She walks and then runs to meet Benjy, and without ever leaving the trajectory of his gaze comes close enough to talk to him: " 'Hello, Benjy.' Caddy said. She opened the gate and came in and stooped down. Caddy smelled like leaves" (*SF*: 6). Caddy stoops down over her little brother, the smell of trees spreading in the proximity of their bodies; she has regained her real dimensions and is fully identifiable for Benjy. The identification of Caddy on the verge of her gradual transformation from a small distant thing into a small, human-sized girl occurs inside the immutable frame defined by Benjy's gaze: the idiot has still not moved and endures Caddy's progression in an absolutely contingent manner.

The image that best materializes Benjy's fixed gaze is the nail discussed earlier, which on its tiny scale recalls the fence's symbolic function, of which it is an integral part. At times an immobile sentinel posted at the edge of the estate awaiting Caddy's return, at others the victim of his girth, which prevents him from crawling through obstacles,[8] Benjy is nailed to the fence in both a figurative and literal sense. The nail, a phallic symbol representing the obstinacy of his fascination, also signals Benjy's rigid and one-directional visual perception, forever riven on an exclusively frontal world. Before seeing this nail as an evocation of the Arma Christi and a reminder of Benjy's canonical age (which is also that of Christ when he died on the cross on the original Easter Day), the nail should first be considered literally. Just as Benjy cannot pass through the fence without getting snagged, and is irremediably hindered in his freedom of movement by this nail that keeps him prisoner, he can perceive only that small part of the world whose contours are limited by this constraint. The nail thus represents the dual immobility of the idiot's body and gaze.[9]

The limits of the idiot's vision are inscribed within the very limited number of his possibilities. When Benjy sees girls returning from school and hopes to see his long-awaited Caddy among them, the interdependence of bodily movement and the field of vision is explicitly represented:

> I went down to the gate, where the girls passed with their booksatchels. They looked at me, walking fast, with their heads turned. I tried to say, but they went on, and I went along the fence, trying to say, and they went faster. Then they were running and I came to the corner of the fence and I couldn't go any further, and I held to the fence, looking after them and trying to say. (*SF*: 52)

Vision is interrupted when the body's movement is obstructed by the fence, which forms a corner and prevents Benjy from following the schoolgirls, who continue to walk straight and are frightened by the big idiot desperately trying to tell them something. However, just as the gaze's direction and range generally depend on the body and its movement, the cohesion of the idiot's body and the coherence of his movements flow from the sense of sight. This is especially true for Ike Snopes, who needs the world to be visible in order to feel whole within it: "already *cohered* and *fixed* in *visibility*" (*H*: 188), "he backed out of darkness and into *visibility*, turning, *visibility* roaring soundless down about him, establishing him *intact* and *cohered* in it" (189; emphasis mine). Conversely, invisibility compromises his integrity, as the idiot must see in order to deploy the tiny bit of being that he is capable of being: that is why life stops when he is sleeping or enveloped in darkness, for when he disappears he is no longer anything.

While Joseph Conrad's idiots never turn their heads,[10] Faulkner's idiots are frozen stiff in a single direction in a different albeit similar manner. When he appears for the first time, Ike Snopes is walking while looking backward at the toy he is pulling on a string: "the figure of a grown man [. . .] dragging behind him on a string a wooden block with two snuff tins attached to its upper side, *watching over his shoulders* with complete absorption the dust it raised" (90); "Snopes led him toward the door, pushing him on ahead, the other moving obediently, *looking backward* over his shoulder at the block with its two raked snuff tins dragging at the end of the filthy string" (95); "the *backlooking* face" (95; emphasis mine). In this scene, for Ike the world is reduced to the miserable spectacle of this act of looking backward, of this backward gaze: in a single movement, the dual meaning of the adjective and adverb *backward(s)* indicates the direction of the gaze, which looks exclusively "backward" while implicitly denouncing the "backlooking" gesture and the one who performs it.[11]

As a result of their immobile gaze, idiots perceive reality in an essentially interrupted and discontinuous manner. Their singular form of vision prevents them from grasping reality in a global or panoramic way via the inclusion of broad perspectives: their listless reflexes, apparently paralyzed cervical vertebra, and congenital disharmony of various sensory organs prevent idiots from rotating on the axis of their bodies to apprehend the world in its entirety and continuity. This is where the idiot's gaze becomes an idiot gaze, in which the world is divided into successive and distinct slides: the world transforms into an archipelago of distinct worlds, islets adrift. Benjy has to move along the length of the fence to follow the golfers through the course bordering the house: "The man played and went on, Ben keeping pace with him until the fence turned at right angles, and he clung to the fence, watching the people move on and away" (*SF*: 315). The continuity of reality is replaced by a series of distinct vignettes. The final disappearance of the golfers corresponds to the farthest dot, as they gradually distance themselves within Benjy's field of vision. The idiot thus grasps things only partially, interrupted by the absence of transitional links between the different zones of reality. His static gaze is sometimes full, sometimes empty, and potentially full of things that quickly risk disappearing. It is in this manner that the idiot's gaze can be likened to a window:[12] fitted within a solid structure, the window is the impassive contemplator of the exterior spectacle, which momentarily occupies its small unsurpassable frame. The image of the window also emphasizes the unfailing link that suspends the gaze to the body, vision to movement.

The image of Benjy early in the novel as he contemplates golfers through the little window of leafage cut into the fence brings to mind the opening of another remarkable text that preceded it by a few decades, Henry James's evocatively titled 1898 novella (or long short story) *In the Cage*. In the first part of the text, which is subdivided into twenty-seven sections of a few pages each, the third-person narrator provides an initial sketch of the main character and her relation to the space she (an unnamed young woman) occupies, as well as the tasks she performs there. The title quickly takes on its full meaning, as the elements that make up this space are all related to the lexical field of confinement, helping to evoke a cage. The profusion of confinement devices is combined with the lexical field of isolation to describe the extremely enclosed environment (including a grocery store and its smell of cheese) in which the young woman works as a telegraphist and postal worker. Spending her days transcribing messages and distributing stamps, she seems to be imprisoned in a box offering only a tiny opening onto the world: "the gap left in the high lattice." Its tiny microcosm stands in opposition to the great world outside—"outside, as she called it"—that she perceives only through this tiny frame, which reduces it to a few fleeting and fragmented encounters (clients for her are never more than the parts of individuals), and through sensations that are both ephemeral and sterile. On the other side of her little window proceeds the multitude—"the practically featureless, appearances in the great procession" (H. James, 2001:

314). The frame defined in this way illustrates the sordid and alienating working conditions of the emerging modern world;[13] however, this text's extreme originality is that the confined space, which opens only onto a tiny window, restricts the character's vision: the character's point of view coincides with that of the narrative, as the story strictly adheres to what the young woman, who is the focal character, *can* perceive of the world through her little window, "as seen from within the cage" (H. James, 2001: 320).[14] James's text provides no perspective other than the one marked out by the window. The adherence of the narrative point of view to the center of focalization is such that there is no longer any true distinction between the external gaze ("look-out," that of the character onto the world) and an internal gaze ("look-in," that of the world and the readers on the character),[15] with the two converging. The isolation and restricted point of view manipulate the reader's vision, which is captive to the filter of a hindered gaze and forced to sacrifice a panoramic gaze[16] for an extremely fragmented one.

The visual range of Benjy, who similarly serves as a focal character of section 1 of *The Sound and the Fury*, is limited to the two-dimensional plane of verticality and horizontality: the idiot's horizons are restricted by the rigid frame of a window that is sometimes real and sometimes virtual, one that permanently encircles the little patch of world that he can see. A chaotic and fragmented space unfolds through the window of his idiot's gaze, felt by a body that moves heavily, reluctantly, and with difficulty. Yet space is not a flat surface and is defined as being three-dimensional. In the representation of visual space, depth is added to horizontal and vertical planes, and distance is added to width and height. The idiot's singular gaze is therefore not limited to its relative immobility, or to its fragmentary and discontinuous aspect. Its apprehension of this third dimension of depth is subject to restrictions and deformations. The idiot seemingly perceives reality on a single plane: distant objects do not converge on a final vanishing point but are juxtaposed within a relatively flat assembly that evokes, albeit with important differences, what art historian Erwin Panofsky called "aggregate space" (2020 [1991]), which is characteristic of typically medieval pictorial works. In such works, objects are juxtaposed with no consideration for their spatial relations, and without the artist seeking to methodically create the illusion of depth or to place the apparent sizes in relation to one another. Confounding any realistic effect, the sizes of characters are determined subjectively based on social status (the "greats" of this world, aristocrats and those of power, are represented as being large, while the "small folk," the poor, workers, and peasants, always appear small). During the early decades of the fifteenth century in Florence, where the techniques for representing space went through an unprecedented transformation, this vision of space as an aggregate of juxtaposed objects gave way to what Panofsky called the "system space" (2020 [1991]).[17] The representation of this new way of apprehending space was based on geometry, the study of proportions, and the calculation of apparent dimensions; it also included aspects from the field of optics, for "it is based on a strictly defined 'point of view' that the illusion of the third dimension can be constructed geometrically" (Thuillier, November 1984: 1386). The new space conceived in this manner is limitless, with a unity that precedes the objects appearing there. In opposition to this conceptual and abstract conception of space, Merleau-Ponty instead adopts a fundamentally anti-Cartesian perspective, especially in "Eye and Mind." Cartesianism can be seen as the symbol of geometric perspective, in the sense that Descartes believed that art must adopt, under the tutelage of science, a mathematical dimension, therefore making it a scientific project. In a Cartesian perspective, the space perceived corresponds to the space observed and analyzed. Running counter to Cartesianism, phenomenology endeavors to reintegrate life into art: the phenomenology of perception asserts a proximity with the roots of the world. It involves speaking about the visible prior to any scientific objectification, namely by returning to the antepredicative stage of discourse. In *The Visible and the Invisible*, Merleau-Ponty strives to show how the seen object engages the individual's gaze, memory, and flesh.[18] As a result, phenomenology calls for a radical reexamination of the categories of subject and object. The Faulknerian idiot's proximity to the phenomenology of perception resides in his absolute immersion in "the 'there is' of the world" (Merleau-Ponty, 2004: 73).

Space as it is visualized by the Faulknerian idiot clearly adheres to a logic that is deeply disruptive to the meticulous calculations of classical perspective, for it is diametrically opposed to the quattrocento space system. However, (the) idiot('s) space is not similar to medieval aggregate space, either.[19] While at first glance juxtaposed forms appear within it and are "aggregated" on a single plane, the notion of depth is not entirely absent, even though perspective is singularly flattened. This impression of flattening that characterizes the idiot's perception of visual space is evident from the first page of Benjy's monologue as he contemplates the golfers: "They took the flag out, and they were hitting. Then they put the flag back and they went to the table, and he hit and the other hit. Then they went on and I went along the fence. [. . .] They were hitting little, across the pasture" (*SF*: 3). This short passage contains, in a few words, all of the dynamics at work in the idiot's vision: perception of reality in terms of emptiness and fullness, presence and absence (in the alternation between "the flag out" and "the flag back"); and the apprehension of gestures and actions in a fragmentary and accretional manner, coordinated but with no causal connection ("he hit and the other hit"). The restricted and one-directional nature of vision is compensated for by movement of the entire body in order to extend Benjy's vision of the game, which is subsequently divided into a series of vignettes. However, the flattening of reality resides in a few words that can go unnoticed, as demonstrated by their translation, which has proven controversial: "They were hitting little." Faulkner did not write "*a little*," which invalidates the translation proposed by Maurice-Edgar Coindreau: "Ils frappaient un peu, là-bas, dans la prairie" ("They were hitting a little, over there, in the pasture") (*ŒI*: 351). Benjy does not consider how many times the golfers swing their clubs: he may be an idiot, but the translator's interpretation is rather absurd, following no apparent logic. While it may be infinitely opaque and difficult, the discourse Faulkner lends to Benjy is almost infallibly logical.[20] What Benjy experiences after the golfers move to the other end of the pasture is more likely a shrinking of their size within his field of vision; "little" can therefore be more readily interpreted as an adjective than as part of an adverbial phrase truncated for no apparent reason (if we assumed that the article "a" was forgotten due to the narrator's idiocy, this would unusually be the only example of such an omission). What Benjy sees is the golfers hitting, "little," across the pasture. In the thirtieth monologue of *As I Lay Dying*, narrated by Dewey Dell, there is a similar example when the Bundrens' wagon passes before Tull's barn and then drives away. The space that is crossed is measured based on Vernon's size, who has become small behind his plow: "We turn into Tull's lane. We pass the barn and go on, the wheels whispering in the mud, passing the green rows of cotton in the wild earth, and Vernon *little* across the field behind the plow" (*AILD*: 122; emphasis mine). Even though the growing distance is explicitly rendered by repetition of the verb *to pass*, along with other evocations of movement, the change of scale experienced by Dewey Dell is fundamentally similar to the one that opens Benjy's monologue: the primary difference is that in the young girl's vision, the phenomenon is part of an explanatory context, whereas with the idiot it is described in raw form.[21] However, in both cases it is the phenomenon of vision altered by distance that is described literally. One could say that the event unfolding before Benjy's gaze as he contemplates the golfers is the exact opposite of what happens when Caddy returns from school in the scene mentioned above. Benjy perceives proximity in terms of size, with drawing near being synonymous with growing large. Conversely, distance amounts to smallness, and distancing amounts to shrinking. Benjy's vision implements the principle that Ptolemy developed in the second century in his *Optics*, in which he establishes—while taking into consideration the angle of vision and lengths—that the object's apparent size is inversely proportional to its distance from the eye. As a result, even if the idiot's gaze compromises the continuity of visual space marked out by a juxtaposition of infrangible and distinct frames—between which space is replaced by nothing, by blackness, just as the apprehension of space is interrupted by the wall separating two neighboring windows—it does not perceive reality in completely primitive fashion. The spatial representations perceived by idiots are therefore not primitive in the pictorial sense of the word.[22] Even though the idiot's gaze is not aware of the distance separating the object from the eye, it nevertheless phenomenologically presents a perspective that—beyond "the series of speculations and techniques involving the reasoned representation of space" (Thuillier, November 1984: 1386)[23]—indirectly invokes early reflections on the representation of visual space, and serves as a reminder that perspective is a reconstruction built on a certain number of presuppositions, and in no way coincides with real space. The notion of distance is consequently not absent from Benjy's visual perceptions, as demonstrated by the fluctuating size of objects depending on where they are located in relation to the eye within the field of vision. While the size of objects informs the reader regarding their location, the idiot does not associate these variations with the increased or decreased distance separating the object from the eye. Moreover, in Benjy's eyes Caddy and the golfers are apparently endowed with the ability to grow and shrink at will, like Alice under the influence of the magical foods she eats in Wonderland. From his point of view, it is indeed with "magical suddenness" (Bleikasten, 1982: 72) that the size of objects and people varies in space. The impression that space is flattening comes from the fact that distance ultimately appears only insofar as it is deduced and reestablished by the reader's normative perception, which was formed according to the laws of classical perspective, based on decreasing and increasing proportions. Benjy inherently sees space as a two-dimensional plane in which the same thing sometimes assumes the size of a dwarf, and sometimes that of a giant. If we linger a moment longer in the pictorial world, we could say that the way in which space takes form in the idiot's gaze is similar to the structure of Francis Bacon's works. Gilles Deleuze interpreted Bacon's notion of composition in the following manner:

> In fact, the rest of the painting is systematically occupied by large fields [*aplats*] of bright, uniform, and motionless color. Thin and hard, these fields have a structuring and spacializing function. They are not beneath, behind, or beyond the Figure, but are strictly to the side of it, or rather, all around it, and are thus grasped in a close view, a tactile or "haptic" view, just as the Figure itself is. At this stage, when one moves from the Figure to the fields of color, there is no relation of depth or distance, no incertitude of light and shadow. (Deleuze, 2003: 4)

Similarly, the distinction between the ground and the shape—between a foreground and a background, in which all of the strata of reality unfold—blurs in the gaze of idiots. There is no breakthrough toward transcendence, no opening toward the beyond in those ineffable blue eyes deprived of design or project,[24] and hence incapable of projecting anything whatsoever onto the map of reality. Everything is there in an absolutely contingent manner, prehensible in the instant of observation; everything appears and disappears on the same level. In the idiot's gaze, reality unfolds in its raw state without being subject to any arrangement, within a singular contiguity and absolute proximity that restricts and closes the idiot's space.

The impression of flattening that characterizes the idiot gaze momentarily contaminates the entire space of the novel. The perception of the omniscient narrator from section 4 of *The Sound and the Fury* occasionally presents the same visual deformations as the idiot in section 1:[25]

> The road rose again, to a scene like a painted backdrop. Notched into a cut of red clay crowned with oaks the road appeared to stop short off, like a cut ribbon. Beside it a weathered church lifted its crazy steeple like a painted church, and the whole scene was as flat and without perspective as a painted cardboard set upon the ultimate edge of the flat earth, against the windy sunlight of space and April and a midmorning filled with bells. (*SF*: 292)

What is described here is the space that Dilsey and Benjy cross through as they go to Reverend Shegog's service on Easter Sunday, April 8, 1928. Unlike what is happening in section 1, where seeing and saying coincide and fuse in the singular language given to the idiot, here it is a distant narrator who is in charge of narration, evoking, in a language more obviously resembling that of Faulkner, what the characters see but could not express in such an elaborate manner. Yet the differences end there, for the space described strangely resembles the one represented in Benjy's section. In section 4, Faulkner no longer lends a character-narrator words imitating a particular and restricted vision; he lends his own words to this highly singular vision, which he assumes as his own.[26] What occurs in these lines is fairly troubling, as Faulkner discretely comments, from the threshold of his novel, on the subtleties of his approach. Section 1's flat space reappears in the scope of his sentence, which juxtaposes the elements of a set by depriving them of relief: the "scene" and the "earth" are also "flat"; two-dimensional props abound; space is reduced to a backdrop "against" which the world stands out. Moreover, the characteristics of the idiot representation of visual space, which were heretofore only implicitly deduced by the reader, are explicitly announced: "the whole scene was as flat and without perspective as a painted cardboard." Finally, emphasis is placed on the artificiality of this representation and, by extension, the artificiality (*perspectiva artificialis*) of any visual representation of space in the arts. Everything is artificial in this flattened world: repetition of the word *scene* distances any effect of reality by denouncing the theatricality of the *scene[ry]*; the adjective *painted*, which is repeated three times, insists on the painted colors; the materials that make up this space are not those of nature; the profusion of comparative structures replaces the world with images of *a* world. The writing relates what it is doing by pointing at the radical artificiality of the world it is giving shape to: a world as false as a theater set and as flat as a page in a book, whose depth is entirely uncertain (it is never simply a question of point of view), while its perspectives are abandoned to the reader's discretion. This excerpt, which imitates Benjy's vision while illustrating the radical artifice presiding over it, can also potentially be seen as a highly literal manifestation of the failure of this fourth attempt at rewriting, whose clarifying purpose suffers from this final narrator's inability to put the little world of the Compsons into relief.

This opposition between what is flat and what has relief is present at various moments in Faulkner's work. As with Benjy's monologue, the writer replaces the representation of a realist and recognizable space (in which objects are organized to create the illusion of depth) with the representation of a space felt and experienced in a completely subjective way. In *Perspective as Symbolic Form*, Panofsky underscores how the artistic construction of a space that is entirely rational, which is to say infinite, continuous, and homogeneous, is based on two essential presuppositions that disregard reality in the sense of visual subjective impressions (the notion that our vision is the work of a unique and immobile eye, and acceptance that the visual pyramid's intersecting planes can pass for an adequate reproduction of the visual image). The structure of an infinite, continuous, and homogeneous—in a word mathematical—space is opposed to psychophysiological space. Faulkner returns to this space through his idiot's singular vision, one that he occasionally assumes as his own or lends to other narrators. For instance, in *As I Lay Dying*, the fire that engulfs the barn containing the mother's coffin is choreographed against a flat canvas that threatens to disintegrate before the reader's eyes amid the lapping flames. Jewel gesticulates in two dimensions until an object suddenly bursts forth, reestablishing a semblance of depth:

> For an instant longer he runs silver in the moonlight, then he springs out like *a flat figure* cut leanly from tin against an abrupt and soundless explosion as the whole loft of the barn takes fire at once, as though it had been stuffed with powder. The front, the conical façade with the square orifice of doorway broken only by the square squat shape of the coffin on the sawhorses like a cubistic bug, *comes into relief*. (*AILD*: 218–19; emphasis mine)

Darl can be seen as the choreographer for the opening scene of the fiftieth monologue for a number of reasons: he is its narrator-poet and focal point, as well as the cause of the conflagration, which he hopes will end the absurd odyssey of his mother's corpse. Through this act, for which he will be accused of arson, Darl reveals his haste to pay the sordidly postponed homage she is due by incinerating her against everyone's wishes. The moment is important, because it would also mark a resounding victory against Jewel, the younger brother who never ceases to haunt his vision.[27] Jewel appears in the scene as a lunar, impalpable creature ("flat" is repeated in "leanly," which abolishes the dimension of flesh) seemingly cut from tin, bringing to mind the silvery light of the moon. The explosion (which makes no noise: it is a silent ballet; sounds are quieted to better allow forms to occupy the limelight) momentarily threatens his bodily integrity, as he "springs out" and then disappears amid the flames obstructing the view. It is only gradually, through the circumlocution of the sentence that delays its revelation until the final moment, that the setting slowly gains volume: the backdrop of flames reveals forms in which relief suddenly materializes as in a cubist painting, with the features of a large, angular insect. Conical and rectangular forms prefigure the appearance of the only form that matters: "the square squat shape of the coffin." Space regains relief as the mother's coffin suddenly emerges from the flames, saved from the fire (as it was from the waters) by Jewel, who regains his thickness and power of action by transforming Darl's initiative into a stinging defeat that will bring his downfall.[28]

AN IMMUTABLE WORLD, A BLUE WORLD?

The idiot's vision, which is frozen in the instant of contemplation, fragmented by a process of discontinuous accretion, and deprived of perspective in the classical sense of the term, is in keeping with a succession of instantaneous vignettes, snapshots of life. Like Henry James's story narrated from within a cage, his perception of the surrounding world never leaves its frame, which is determined by his immobile eyes, hindered movements, and the rare elements that he can identify and that allow him to remedy the fundamental instability of reality to the extent that is possible. To prevent impressions, by definition fleeting and transitory, from vanishing, they must be framed and preserved within limits that are fantasized as being impassable: they must have cages, they must have books. The few markers that offer a semblance of stability for Benjy, and represent the unsurpassable confines of his tiny world, are the poles of his primary geography: on the one hand are the pasture, the fence, the hill, the barn, the stream, the yard, and the kitchen; on the other are his preferred objects, which invariably have the same soothing effect, namely flowers, Caddy's slippers and cushion, the mirror, and the fire. Benjy's field of reality is entirely framed by these elements, in which everything exists or happens in an entirely uncertain and random influx. This notion of a frame has numerous avatars in Benjy's monologue: the fence, the hearth, the window, the mirror, and the door in particular structure the idiot's vision through the materiality of their edges. In the same movement, these objects fragment reality into a succession of small paintings that create a *mise en abyme* within the larger frames of recollections, successive monologues, and the novel. There are numerous appearances, which, framed by a door, resemble icons: "We went around the barn. The big cow and the little one were standing in the door" (*SF*: 12). The dramatic intensity of a depiction of everyday life in the country is caught and immortalized within a narrow frame. Caddy clearly does not have the constancy of Benjy's preferred objects, although when surrounded by a door, she, too, is fixed in a timeless image: "Caddy came to the door and stood there" (68); "she stood against the door, looking at me" (69). Framed by the door, Caddy becomes the unalterable Épinal image of herself. Her identity is seemingly being stalked by the door (closed in this instance), as though the hour of her deflowering (for such is the context of the cited passages) were forever archived in a snapshot of life, an instant photo that becomes a substitute for itself. The obsessive return of this same image also forms a haunting refrain in Quentin's monologue;[29] it underscores and dramatizes the gravity of this episode in the lives of the two brothers, as well as within the economy of the novel. The mirror plays a similar role to that of the door, framing reality while transforming it and multiplying it in a series of reverberations that have the intangibility of memory:

> Caddy and Jason were fighting in the mirror. [. . .] Jason was crying. He wasn't fighting anymore, but we could see Caddy fighting in the mirror and Father put me down and went into the mirror and fought too. [. . .] Father held her. She kicked at Jason. He rolled into the corner, out of the mirror. Father brought Caddy to the fire. They were all out of the mirror. (*SF*: 64–65)

Here, the mirror is the preferred receptacle for images of childhood and innocence forever lost, reflecting an impalpable dream of reconciliation. Benjy has already showed us what Quentin later reveals about the mirror's calming effect on his younger idiot brother, and the pain he experiences when it is empty: "How he used to sit before that mirror. Refuge unfailing in which conflict tempered silenced reconciled" (*SF*: 170). Benjy vainly seeks the comfort of the mirror's images even after it is moved: "Ben went to the dark place on the wall where the mirror used to be, rubbing his hands on it and slobbering and moaning" (255–56). The black frame on the wall where the mirror of his childhood once hung becomes a symbol for Benjy's dispossession: where there was life and movement there is now only the grime of bygone years.

Benjy has no markers of any kind aside from these few familiar objects that lend his world a precarious stability, and perpetuate it within a succession of icons. His space and time end with them. Beyond the few frames that offer a modicum of structure to his unstable world, Benjy's idiocy turns into a blind terror. Dilsey, who has always taken care of the last-born idiot, is connected to Benjy by a protective instinct and intuitive understanding of his terrors. Despite Dilsey's harshness and momentary irritation, the two of them have a special relationship that the Black servant willingly admits. For Dilsey, Benjy is a child of God, an avatar of sorts of the Christ figure: "You's de Lawd's chile, anyway. En I be His'n too, fo long, praise Jesus" (317). As T. P. prepares to drive Benjy and Mrs. Compson to the cemetery, which they visit regularly to pay homage to their dead, Dilsey warns her son, whom she knows can be mischievous: "And dont start no projecking with Queenie, you hear me. T. P." (10). She forbids him from changing the itinerary, as she is aware that there is only one possible order and direction for Benjy: any change to the one tried and tested by habit and repetition plunges the idiot into chaos. Dilsey's recommendation also prefigures the novel's ending. Over a decade later, as Luster (Dilsey's grandson) is driving the same horse and carriage, he crosses the main square on a whim, skirting the statue on the left. This change of direction, this disturbance in the usual framework, causes Benjy to yell, frightened as he is by the disappearance of his familiar world: "Ben's hoarse agony roared about them" (320). Alarmed by the idiot's cries, and careful not to provoke his grandmother's ire, Luster finally takes the route on the right: panic immediately gives way to calm in the wake of order restored. The idiot's blue eyes regain their limpid serenity: "his eyes were empty and blue and serene again" (321). The illusion of an immutable world is consequently restored.

In the idiot's world, the people and things that magically appear in his field of vision are paradoxically condemned to absolute fixity; the idiot's static and one-directional gaze fixes humans and things, negating their ability to evolve over time. While humans and things appear and disappear without restraint, it is almost invariably in the same form. From the idiot's perspective, humans and things are endlessly forced to repeat the entirety of what they are. If they are transformed by the contingences and necessities of life, for the idiot they quite simply become things other than themselves. This is why Caddy wearing perfume, or Caddy who has become a lover, is no longer Caddy; she is someone else.[30] Caddy has smelled like trees for all eternity and is defined by the permanence of this smell: "I couldn't smell trees anymore and I began to cry" (40). Caddy is recognizable only as this impetuous and dewy figure to her brothers. While Benjy associates Caddy with the smell of trees, she appears in Quentin's monologue imbued with the penetrating fragrance of honeysuckle. The corollary to Benjy's alarm when he no longer recognizes Caddy amid the wafting artificial fragrance is Quentin's pain as Caddy slips from his grasp beneath the veils of her wedding dress: "she ran out of the mirror like a cloud, her veil swirling in long glints her heels brittle and fast clutching her dress onto her shoulder with the other hand, running out of the mirror" (81). His entire monologue is haunted by the altered image of Caddy as a stained virgin. What Caddy did—at "fault" for becoming a woman and leaving behind the little girl she was—she did to her brothers, as suggested by Mrs. Compson: "'You must have done something to him.' Mother said" (41). Her brothers will never get over the loss of her leaving her chrysalis, where they hoped to keep her prisoner.

A raft of portraits and paintings emerge—from the web of words and images of an eternally relived childhood—through the fixed and fragmentary gazes and flattened perspectives of Benjy's idiocy. These portraits and paintings are not strictly speaking figurative, as the idiot is incapable of describing, exhibiting, and arranging reality; they are sensitive rather than descriptive and result from the reader's assembly of elements and details scattered throughout the pages, via words and situations that are not enveloped by any organizing gesture. However, despite their minimalist appearance and elliptical nature, scenes and characters take shape amid the meshwork of repetition and the hollowness of silence. Contrary to the much less innocent narrators who succeed him, and seeking out this particular turn of events in order to justify their actions, the images that emerge from Benjy's monologue radiate a naïve authenticity whose source is the impossibility of lying. In Benjy's discourse, the depiction of certain characters (which, as we have seen, resembles more a fortuitous listing of impressions charged with a certain number of psychological traits) can be simplified to the extreme, with two of them present in the receptacle that is their preferred object. While Uncle Maury is characterized exclusively through his bottle (or its effects)—"Uncle Maury was putting the bottle away in the sideboard in the diningroom" (5); "Uncle Maury was putting the bottle back in the sideboard" (7); "Uncle Maury was sick. His eye was sick, and his mouth" (43)—Mrs. Compson's identity is reduced to the cloth dipped in camphor that constantly covers her head: "We went to Mother's room, where she was lying with the sickness on a cloth on her head" (41); "I could smell the sickness. It was on a cloth folded on Mother's head" (61). Benjy is content with identifying the person with an object, but the association suggested in this way effectively materializes drunkenness and hypochondria, even though these words do not appear in his vocabulary. Other characters seem to emerge from their own absence and subsequently appear in a limited number of situations. For Benjy evokes only what he sees, what is (or was) directly sensible to his perception. The two Quentins, the brother and the niece who are the perfect antithesis of one another, are both characterized by emptiness. The first is the distant and tormented spectator of a childhood to which he no longer fully belongs, already obsessed with a highly developed sense of the forbidden:

> "It's not wet." Caddy said. She stood up in the water and looked at her dress. "I'll take it off." she said. "Then it'll dry."
> "I bet you wont." Quentin said.
> *"I bet I will." Caddy said.*
> "I bet you better not." Quentin said. (*SF*: 18)

This short scene from childhood, which announces future undressings, reveals the full tension that little Caddy's boldness causes for Quentin, who is already assuming an authoritative role toward her. Similarly, his homonym appears exclusively in a highly impressionistic manner through the constant presence of her lipstick: "The fire was in her eyes and on her mouth. Her mouth was red" (*SF*: 67); "Her mouth was red" (71). Quentin is never there, too busy running after men. For Benjy, her presence boils down to lipstick, which stigmatizes the artifice and vulgarity that also characterize the few feminine accessories found in her room in section 4.[31] The two most developed portraits are undoubtedly those of Jason and Caddy, opposed and almost Manichean, a figure of evil and another of good. Jason is constantly depicted with his hands in his pockets; the scenes he appears in are extremely repetitive, signaling both the coherence and limitations of what he is: "'What do you want.' Jason said. He had his hands in his pockets and a pencil behind his ear" (11); "Jason came behind us, with his hands in his pockets" (20, 23). Jason is the one who sneaks up from behind, his hands in his pockets, never responsible for anything.[32] Always innocent, he relentlessly denounces what he considers to be his brothers' and his sister's mistakes, with Caddy clearly being his preferred target: "'Caddy and Quentin threw water on each other.' Jason said" (23); "'I'm going to tell on you.' Jason said" (27); "'I told her not to climb up that tree.' Jason said. 'I'm going to tell on her'" (45).[33] A betrayer, informer, and compulsive liar, Jason is already someone who can be bought: "'Jason wont tell.' Quentin said. 'You remember that bow and arrow I made you, Jason'" (20). Jason is as hard as he is corruptible, as malicious as he is incapable of sympathy. Unlike Caddy, he is furiously ashamed of his idiot brother and does not hide his desire to intern Benjy with his fellows: "I reckon you'll send him to Jackson, now" (52). The Compson "Appendix" reveals that Jason will ultimately achieve his ends.[34]

Caddy, the luminous little girl radiating at the core of the novel—of which she is simultaneously the original impetus,[35] essential "emotion," and major absentee—is characterized by effrontery and indocility: she tirelessly retorts "I don't care" (19, 20, 23) to anyone who will listen, the watchword of her determination to do exactly as she pleases. Fundamentally disobedient, she nevertheless seeks to impose the rules of her own game on her brothers and is very unhappy when they resist her orders: "Besides, he said to mind me tonight. Didn't he didn't he say to mind me tonight" (39). However, the other side of her boldness stems from a deep sense of disgust, which awakens a desire to run far away from a world that her astonishing lucidity deems oppressive:[36] " 'I'll run away and never come back.' Caddy said" (19). For Caddy may be lively, ebullient, and joyous, but she also feels melancholy: "It's still raining, Caddy said. I hate rain. I hate everything. And then her head came into my lap and she was crying, holding me, and I began to cry" (57). For Benjy, Caddy is a bulwark against the constant jokes and bullying to which he is subject. Caddy is the only one who can comfort Benjy and is always attentive to his moaning: " 'Hush now.' she said. 'I'm not going to run away.' So I hushed" (19); " 'You dont need to bother with him.' Caddy said. 'I like to take care of him. Dont I. Benjy' " (63). Her tenderness, which never fails to calm Benjy, is present throughout the initial monologue via the repeated contact of her hands. Caddy rubs Benjy's hands for fear he will catch cold: "rubbing my hand" (6), "Keep your hands in your pockets" (12, 13); she guides him during their escapades, "She took my hand" (7, 22, 48); and simply assures him through her presence, "She put her hand on my hand" (25, 75). Unlike Jason, who hides his hands, Caddy always extends hers toward Benjy. Her great concern can also be seen in her eagerness to carry him: " 'He's not too heavy.' Caddy said. 'I can carry him' " (63). She is the only one for whom Benjy's idiocy is not a burden too heavy to bear. As Caddy is the only one who can quiet him, it is hardly surprising that the idiot's yelling intensifies after her departure. The idiot's cries echo in the narrative present more than anywhere else, whose sound and fury we imagine have occupied the thirteen years of silence between this present and the most recent recollection. A fixed image that is always alike, with no distinction as to the year, for Benjy Caddy invariably has the same gestures and words, which combine, as it were, in the same odor. Beyond this immutable icon there is emptiness, an empty frame on the reverse side of a painting. Since Benjy cannot conceive that people change, any difference signals a departure, and any departure a disappearance. Yet if he does not understand Caddy's departure, Benjy nevertheless feels its reality with intensity. He first senses its imminence, as Caddy's image actually begins to falter with the rocking swing where she meets her lovers, and where her daughter Quentin will one day meet her own; it is a forbidden area, an intolerable spectacle for Benjy: "*Wait, he said. Here. Dont go over there. Miss Quentin and her beau in the swing yonder. You come on this way. Come back here, Benjy*" (46). The back-and-forth of the swing foreshadows Caddy's gradual separation and marks the end of the time of innocence.[37] For Benjy, everything ultimately comes down to a few canonical scenes, where everything has its place and everyone plays their role—an exclusive role that endlessly repeats. This entails being oneself always and forever, and carrying one's moral worth like a birthmark, in an uninterrupted flow of similar and refrangible images unto infinity: "Caddy and Father and Jason were in Mother's chair. Jason's eyes were puffed shut and his mouth moved, like tasting. Caddy's head was on Father's shoulder. [. . .] I went and Father lifted me into the chair too, and Caddy held me" (72). Benjy's monologue more or less ends with this icon: the invalid mother's place is empty, while the father gathers his children and tries to smooth over their disagreements. Jason's eyes are red because he was scolded for his most recent shameful deed, but it makes no difference for Caddy, who quickly hugs Benjy when he joins the three of them on the armchair.

Whether it is entering Benjy's field of vision for the first time or the fiftieth time, a scene is always the original scene, always and ever a unique moment. The notion of narration is distorted by these continual returns. The power of *The Sound and the Fury* resides in the fact that it is an essentially static novel in which nothing happens or moves forward; every image is none other than the repetition of a past image, in which every event has already ceased to exist, in which even time comes to a standstill. The origin of this stasis is Caddy, who embodies the principle of order, all while acting as a catalyst for disorder. Caddy is that from which order is made and unmade, as though her presence canceled itself out between these two contradictory movements, as though between doing and undoing she never absolutely existed. It is hence no coincidence that Benjy's monologue is teeming with images that evoke duality or their opposite, where what is "buttoned" is quickly "unbuttoned," where dressing is always the prelude to a future undressing.[38] Like the game *fort/da*, they can all be interpreted as metaphors and repetitions of the essential event, in other words as Caddy's disappearance, through which time appears to have stopped forever and vision is fixed on the obsessive return of the same. The flood of images borrowed from the time immemorial of an eternal childhood entails a stoppage in the circulation of days, an idiot immobility. Caddy left, Caddy no longer exists, and ultimately there is nothing more to say. If we are to believe Faulkner, the notion of stasis was already inscribed in the genesis of Benjy's character: "That Benjy must never grow beyond this moment; that for him all knowing must begin and end with that fierce, panting, paused and stooping wet figure which smelled like trees" ("Intro *SF*, II": 230). Benjy's idiocy can be defined by his inability to "grow" beyond the loss of Caddy, a loss that is filled by the mechanical reproduction of vignettes preceding her departure, which are relived each time with the intensity of the present. The striking proximity that connects Benjy and Quentin also reveals itself in the repetition and stasis that characterize their perception and discourse. This is emphasized by André Bleikasten:

> All these echoes and cross-references induce a disturbing sense of *déjà-vu*: we are caught with Quentin in a spell-binding set of specular images in which things and events are perpetually duplicated through the giddy interplay of reflections. For Quentin the present is but a mirror held up to the shadows of the past, a theater of ghosts where nothing is ever first, where nothing ever begins. [. . .] In much the same way as Benjy, he seems to hover "between" the present and the past, that is, in the similarity between the two. (Bleikasten, 2016 [1990]: 96)

By virtue of his affinities toward some of Benjy's idiosyncrasies, Quentin can also be seen as a kind of idiot: but like Georges Bataille's depressive hero in *Blue of Noon*, his subtle idiocy is that of suffering.[39] The story of *The Sound and the Fury*, which has one in spite of everything, can be summed up in a few words: Caddy, dishonored, leaves; the lives of her brothers stagnate, standing still at the very moment she loses her virginity. The four successive stories that make up the novel are secretions of this decisive moment, eternal rewritings of the original sin. This is why the same scenes and images continually repeat, until they have infiltrated every page of the novel. It is once again the swing that becomes the emblem for this inaugural moment, for the obsessive return of Caddy's sin. It makes Benjy cry: "Then I could see the swing and I began to cry" (*SF*: 46); it haunts Quentin: "trying not to think of the swing until all cedars came to have that vivid dead smell of perfume that Benjy hated so" (176); and it simply annoys Jason. It is where Caddy loses her honor, and where her daughter forgets her contraceptives.[40] This eternal swinging forever reflects the same images. Pain, dread, resentment, and guilt may be written everywhere in vain, and untiringly repeat their fantasy images, as nothing moves and nobody changes. The stasis that characterizes Benjy's gaze and discourse contaminates every page of the novel, as this unique incident marks the abolition of all possibles.

The representations deriving from Benjy's idiot gaze, to whom we have granted great space simply because he is the only Faulknerian idiot in whom vision and voice agree, define a world of appearances and disappearances marked by its paradoxical immutability. The flat tints that it consists of, in which varied objects aggregate, and its porousness (indiscriminately bringing together heterogeneous temporal images) bring to mind the blue eyes of idiots, and the serenity of a spring sky.⁴¹ What is at play in the singular perspectives of the idiot gaze—a little window onto the world, in which fragmented representations unfold, fleeting and static, flattened and nevertheless profound—is a representation of vision's infancy, the reproduction of a space whose perception is strictly attached to the limited possibilities of the body and feeling. What is depicted through Benjy's idiot eyes is a primitive stage of the world's birth for the gaze. It is the "naive frequenting of the world" (Merleau-Ponty, 1968: 51) advocated by the phenomenological approach.

Chapter 8

IDIOCY'S FETISH OBJECTS

Substitutive Fixations and Logic

> "Here." Dilsey said. "Stop crying, now."
> She gave me the slipper, and I hushed.
> —WILLIAM FAULKNER, *THE SOUND AND THE FURY*

The objects that Faulknerian idiots surround themselves with are endowed with magical powers that are in keeping with the logic of primitive animism. Influenced by his ethnographic reading (notably Sir James George Frazer's *The Golden Bough*, published in 1922), Freud believed that this psychological theory represented the first intellectual system that defined humanity, the first of "three great pictures of the universe" (Freud, 2001: 90) that unfolded over time: an animist vision was replaced by a religious vision, which was in turn supplanted by the scientific vision of modern times. Idiots can be seen as being prisoner to primitive forms specific to an archaic stage of humanity.[1] Our earlier analysis of the perspectives of idiot gazes stressed how Benjy confused the order of his perceptions with the order of nature. Since he does not know that an individual can exert control over his perceptions—and consequently proves incapable of doing so—the inanimate objects of the sensible world seem to possess a free and independent life, and come in contact with his senses only in a purely random and accidental manner. Faulkner's idiots make no clear distinction between humans, animals, and inanimate objects: they consider themselves to ultimately be one object among others. Similarly, their family members seem to be no more than somewhat more sophisticated objects, to which they are connected by a relation of greater proximity. This perception of a world consisting exclusively of independent and animate objects (which is to say objects endowed with a soul)[2]—existing alongside one another on the same level—explains why idiots have the same forms of attachment or aversion toward objects and even animals as they do toward human beings. Things can replace humans due to the extremely precarious border between humans and things in the consciousness of idiots.

Through the unusual use they make of certain objects, invariably reproducing the same patterns of satisfaction, idiots are fixed in childhood experiences and archaic patterns. For idiots, all of the conditions for fixation are met by the intersection of what Jean Laplanche and Jean-Bertrand Pontalis defined thusly in their *The Language of Psycho-Analysis*: "[I]n the first place, it is brought about by historical factors (influence of the family configuration, trauma, etc.). Secondly, it is facilitated by constitutional factors: one partial instinctual component may be more powerful than another one" (Laplanche and Pontalis, 2018 [1973]: 163). The idiot's fixation is therefore located at the point of convergence between exterior traumas, which originate in the family history as well as idiocy's characteristic constitutional limitations. The idiot's "object-relationship" will be at the heart of my reflection, with the notion of object designating the thing, whatever its nature, that is targeted by impulses. This object-relationship unfolds as "an *inter*relationship, in fact, involving not only the way the subject constitutes his objects, but also the way these objects shape his actions" (Laplanche and Pontalis, 2018 [1973]: 278).[3] While the fetish objects of Benjy Compson and Ike Snopes do not exactly grow out of the same needs, in both instances the substitutive logic that governs them similarly responds to the order of desire, and replaces the language of desire.

CADDY AND HER SUBSTITUTES

With his primitive resources, Benjy makes multiple attempts to remedy the disappearance of his chosen object, to remedy Caddy's absence and fill the dreadful emptiness at any cost.[4] The fetish objects he accumulates and fervently worships can all be interpreted as extensions of Caddy: the blue bottle and flowers, the cushion and slipper emerge as the cardinal points of Benjy's world, tangible and paltry substitutions for an intolerable loss. Most of his gestures involve arranging these objects—both connected to Caddy and detached from her—which are ultimately damaged through their repeated handling and use in rituals, as if worn down by the steadiness of the gaze he directs at them. For instance, the slipper that Benjy clutches against himself and venerates like a holy relic is described,[5] in the flow of words related by Benjy and the ensuing monologues, as a dirty and disgusting object: "Has he got to keep that old dirty slipper on the table, Quentin said" (*SF*: 70); "Luster returned, carrying a white satin slipper. It was yellow now, and cracked, and soiled, and when they gave it into Ben's hand he hushed for a while" (316). It matters little that the slipper is in a state of deterioration, like the cushion's round and soft forms, for it invokes the comfort and reassurance of a maternal tenderness that only Caddy could dispense better than these objects. While it echoes the paradigm of Cinderella (who vanishes in the night and is found by the Prince thanks to a slipper lost on the steps of the palace), the slipper can be seen as a metonymic substitute for Caddy, a remainder of what she was, a part evoking the whole. Caddy herself encourages Benjy to use the cushion as a metaphoric substitution for what she represents for him. It is thanks to Caddy that the cushion and its calming effect simultaneously appear: "'Hush.' She said. 'You can go right back. Here. Here's your cushion. See'" (63); "Caddy gave me the cushion, and I could look at the cushion and the mirror and the fire" (71). It is as though Caddy is unconsciously preparing her departure by choosing the emissaries that will replace her kindness, and by designating the objects that will stand in for her absence as fetish objects.[6]

Fetish, which derives from the Latin *facere* and the Portuguese *feitiço* and means both "lining" and "magic spell," is in keeping with a logic of replacement. Freud stated that a fetish is a "substitute for the woman's (mother's) phallus, which the little boy once believed in and which—for reasons well-known to us—he does not want to give up" (Freud, 2006: 91). The fetish thus emerges as "a compromise [...] in the conflict between the force of the unwelcome perception and the intensity of his aversion to it" (91); it is "a very energetic action" through which the revelation that women lack a phallus is denied. Freud also observes that the establishment of the fetish often coincides with "the last impression prior to the uncanny, traumatic one" (92). This explains why shoes are often kept as a fetish. Caddy's slipper can therefore be interpreted as both a phallic symbol and the emblematic object of her departure, in that Caddy's foot is what she uses to disappear: the slipper represents her final visible trace. The fetish takes the place of the phallus and immunizes the fetishist against the fear of castration, which he believes in because of the mother's lack of a phallus. Fetishism is thus a way to deny the alterity of the sexes. For the idiot, fetishism converts the illusion into an ordeal of reality,[7] as the fear of castration vanishes before the horror of emasculation.

By replacing the original thing with fake avatars, the idiot's fetish objects have the same function and soothing qualities as the transitional object does for infants. The child that Donald Woods Winnicott describes in *Playing and Reality* uses a transitional object to re-create the lost proximity to the mother's body. It is this object that enables children to gain their independence and engage with objects. Their first possession—teddy bear, doll, baby blanket, hard or soft object—to which they grow very attached, gives small children (aged between four and twelve months) access to the "intermediate area between the subjective and that which is objectively perceived" (Winnicott, 1971: 3). This transitional object acquires great importance for the child, who sees it as absolutely indispensable when falling asleep, or when threatened by solitude and abandonment (*Hilflosigkeit*). This explains why it is ideal that

> [t]he parents get to know its value and carry it round when travelling. The mother lets it get dirty and even smelly, knowing that by washing it she introduces a break in continuity in the infant's experience, a break that may destroy the meaning and value of the object to the infant. (Winnicott, 1971: 4)

In his monologue, Jason mentions an episode in which Mrs. Compson, helpless in the face of Benjy's yelling, as she is in all of her maternal prerogatives, orders that the slipper be brought to quiet him: "that day when I came home and found Ben bellowing. Raising hell and nobody could quiet him. Mother said, Well, get him the slipper then. Dilsey made out she didn't hear" (*SF*: 207). Through her request, Mrs. Compson recognizes, in spite of her reluctance, the magic power possessed by this object, the only one that can calm Benjy's fear.[8] Dilsey's attitude speaks volumes, for while she implicitly refuses to look for the slipper, it is out of fear of aggravating the idiot's distress, especially under the particular circumstances, which Dilsey is well positioned to know: after a long absence, Benjy has secretly seen Caddy again, who sometimes haunts the vicinity of the family estate in an attempt to have Jason, who reigns like a despot, allow a visit with her daughter Quentin. This is why the slipper, which Jason brought not out of kindness but to test his reaction, has become an instrument of torture when it finally appears in Benjy's field of vision: "I went and got the slipper and brought it back, and just like I thought, when he saw it you'd thought we were killing him" (207). The appearance of Caddy, who has changed and grown older, "never quite the same/never wholly changed," is like an uncanny dream for Benjy.[9] One can readily imagine that this brief interview (which is not described) is the cause of great confusion for the thirty-three-year-old Benjy. In Benjy's little world, the objects that evoke Caddy have taken all of the available space, such that Caddy has ultimately been reduced to the evanescent image that characterizes her through most of the novel; she exists only through the fleeting images and objects that represent her. In the world that Benjy has created for himself, using the paltry means available to him after his sister's departure, he fills the space occupied by Caddy with objects that bring her to mind and thereby replace her, so that there is no more room for Caddy, and even less for a Caddy that does not look like Caddy. Like the sudden appearance of a ghost, Caddy's unexpected return causes fear, for which the slipper's appearance can be seen as the unbearable repetition. In this specific case, the fetish object's ability to soothe is impaired by the appearance of the symbolized (Caddy) behind the symbol (slipper).

For Benjy, Caddy probably disappeared to meet his brother and father at the cemetery he visits regularly with his mother; if she is no longer present, then that is because she is there, like the others whose death he intuitively senses. However, for want of finding Caddy at the cemetery,[10] Benjy makes his own cemetery for her: he symbolically lays Caddy to rest in a blue bottle, which serves as a vase for poisonous flowers, a trifling imitation of the luxurious bouquets that adorn the tombs of Mr. Compson and Quentin. Benjy's immoderate taste for flowers can be interpreted in light of the cemetery he built. Like the idiot from "The Kingdom of God," "he's got to have a flower."[11] Yet unlike the idiot from the short story, who swears solely by narcissuses—the emblematic flower of his idiot solipsism—until the novel's final scene (when he is also decked out with a narcissus, in homage to his predecessor), Benjy has his heart set on flowers that are much less noble, but no less metaphoric: a foul-smelling chamomile,[12] and jimson weed,[13] also known as thorn apple. Benjy squeezes these two flowers, which are characterized by their rank smell and even toxicity, to the point of damaging them. In the above quotation, Luster uses the verb "to wear out," while the narcissus belonging to the idiot from the short story "breaks" and is then "fixed":

> The man looked at his brother for the first time. "His flower is broken, see?" he explained, "that's what he's crying about." [. . .] "I just want to fix his flower for him." [. . .] String was volunteered by a spectator, who fetched it from a nearby shop; and under the interested eyes of the two policemen and the gathering crowd, the flower stalk was splinted. Again the poor damaged thing held its head erect, and the loud sorrow went at once from the idiot's soul. ("Kingdom": 85–86)

This passage can be seen as a preparatory sketch for the final scene of *The Sound and the Fury*, in which Luster "fixes" Benjy's broken narcissus in a very similar manner:

> He came back with a single narcissus. "Dat un broke," Dilsey said. "Whyn't you git him a good un?" "Hit de onliest one I could find," Luster said. "Y'all took all of um Friday to dec'rate de church. Wait, I'll fix hit." So while Dilsey held the horse Luster put a splint on the flower stalk with a twig and two bits of string and gave it to Ben. (*SF*: 318)

While the narcissus he brandishes like a scepter is in keeping with the logic of nature (he's a natural) and the order of God (the church, the kingdom of God, is decorated with narcissuses for Easter), the broken narcissus that Faulkner returns to at the end of *The Sound and the Fury* instills an element of fragility, and can be seen as an image of the idiot's dispossession and total dependence on others (he needs to be fixed). In reference to the mythological hero, the broken narcissus can also be seen as a metaphor for the broken reflection—the cracked ego—of the idiot's threatened integrity. The image of Narcissus is also suggested, in a different form alluding directly to the myth, in the two scenes in which Ike Snopes drinks springwater: "they lean and interrupt the green reflections and with their own drinking faces *break* each's mirroring, each face to its own shattered image wedded and annealed" (*H*: 202); "Again his head interrupts, then replaces as once more he *breaks* with drinking the reversed drinking of his own of his drowned and fading image" (205; emphasis mine). Whether they take the form of his emblematic flowers or are repeated in the initial scene of the reflection in the spring, the allusions to the Narcissus myth depict idiots as individuals who have something "broken," for whom the self-image is a broken and unrecognizable image.

Benjy's cemetery is literally adorned with weeds, continuing the botanical metaphors associated with Caddy: "There was a flower in the bottle. I put the other flower in it" (*SF*: 54). The stink ("rank-smelling") of these poisonous flowers is in keeping with the smell of trees and wet leaves that characterizes Caddy as a child, serving as a parodic version of Caddy's pleasant smell by metaphorically designating her as having become harmful and undesirable. The ambivalence of Benjy's feelings toward his sister, whom he loved (whose smell he loved), but who abandoned him by perverting the pleasure connected to her smell, is implicitly suggested by the interlacing odors.[14] In the continuity of the scene mentioned earlier, Luster's rage—who is frustrated about losing his quarter, thereby compromising his night at the show—is once again directed at Benjy by targeting his flowers and bottle: "Luster knocked the flowers over with his hand" (54). In the ensuing altercation, Luster and Dilsey, the keeper of the cemetery, both use the word "graveyard":[15] "'Is you been projecking with his graveyard.' Dilsey said. 'I aint touched his graveyard.' Luster said" (55). This means that they both see Benjy's little ceremony as the manifestation of a mortuary cult, a miniature replica of the town cemetery. Luster's gesture has all the more impact, for it can be seen as the desecration of a tomb, the voluntary transgression of a taboo: it bears witness to his desire to hurt Benjy with what is most dear to him. The cemetery and its flowers can therefore be included among Benjy's fetish objects and are the most obvious representation of his ambiguous feelings toward Caddy.[16] The creation and maintenance of the cemetery can be interpreted as both the funereal homage that Benjy pays to his missing sister as well as his unconscious desire to be done with her, to punish her by burying her (alive) for what she did.

Contact with the idiot's fetish objects and the child's transitional object similarly creates a sense of security by indirectly invoking the object they represent and replace. However, while the choice of a transitional object and contact with it represent a transition between the child's intense bond to the mother and independence—a necessary stage in "the infant's journey from the purely subjective to objectivity" (Winnicott, 1971: 6)—the idiot is condemned to never move beyond the symbolism of his fetish objects. He does not transition toward anything, for he is haunted by the memory of his intense relation with his sister, and he will never be free of it or gain his independence. While in a case of normal development, the object's "fate is to be gradually allowed to be decathected, so that in the course of years it becomes not so much forgotten as relegated to limbo" (Winnicott, 1971: 5), Benjy's fetish objects are not decathected in any manner; they bear an immutable value that corresponds to the two syllables of Caddy's first name.[17] The idiot Benjy is forever destined to remain in the realm of illusion, as the reality principle enters his sphere of primitive pleasures only accidentally and ephemerally: contact with the slipper, cushion, or flowers always ends up reestablishing the pleasure principle's preeminence over the reality principle.

The vital proximity of the idiot's fetishes—the objects of his pain's primitive worship—is accompanied by quasi-religious rituals that he would renounce for nothing. The primitive cult of the dead, both real and imagined, is one of these rituals. Waiting is another one, contradictory to but nevertheless contiguous with the former: impervious to the years, and in spite of renouncing her long ago and unbeknown to himself, Benjy still stubbornly waits for Caddy to come back from school. However, this act of waiting no longer seems to be entirely sure of its object: the little girl who doesn't come is easily replaced by another, as demonstrated by the scene in which Benjy pursues the Burgess girl. In the end, it is the golfers who draw his full attention behind the fence. In short, waiting is literally emptied of its primary motivation: it is no more than a static pattern for welcoming a multiform reality, a pure act of waiting stripped of an object. Because it is rigid and immutable, the ritual's form ultimately becomes much more important than its content. As suggested by Olga Vickery, all things considered, Benjy does not really know what he is waiting for, what he is missing: "As with the blue bottle which Luster snatches from its place so with Caddy, he is reminded by the small depression in the earth or by the sound of her name that something is missing, but what it is he misses, he scarcely knows himself" (Vickery, 1964: 36). The idiot's stasis also consists of the mechanical repetition of rigid forms vainly applied to emptiness, with uselessness giving shape to what is vain with an almost sacred meticulousness.[18]

CHAPTER 8

THE COW AND THE IDIOT

Chapter 1 of book 3 from *The Hamlet* focuses on the idiot Ike Snopes and his improbable love for a cow belonging to Houston.[19] This chapter consists of three parts: the first focuses on Ratliff, who upon returning to Frenchman's Bend observes, with his quick wit, the changes that have taken place in the hamlet during his absence. A witness to the inexorable rise of the Snopeses to the detriment of Will Varner, the former patriarch who had previously dominated the community, he meditates on the two families that henceforth shape the daily lives of the inhabitants of Frenchman's Bend. Ratliff regularly mentions the ambition of the Snopeses, which has almost become a commonplace, and already senses that the community's future depends on it: "Snopes can come and Snopes can go, but Will Varner looks like he is fixing to snopes forever. Or Varner will Snopes forever—take your pick" (*H*: 179). Adding a new verb to the local vocabulary (to snopes), Ratliff invents snopesism, a concept based on an unprecedented and unavoidable economic logic, namely the decline of great families with genteel practices in favor of mediocre individuals who ferociously and obstinately apply the new laws of the market to the letter, in turn becoming the new lords. While as a talkative philosopher he shares his views with the men who customarily gather on the porch of the grocery store, he also understands that the inhabitants of Frenchman's Bend have found a new source of daily distraction during his absence: "'All right, boys,' the clerk said rapidly, tensely. 'He's started. You better hurry. I cant go this time. I got to stay here. Kind of make a swing around from the back so old Littlejohn cant see you. She's done already begun to look cross-eyed'" (180). With all due respect to Miss Littlejohn, the innkeeper and protector of the idiot Ike, the men rush to see the spectacle on view, whose nature they stubbornly refuse to reveal to the newcomer: "'What's *this*?,' Ratliff said. 'Come on, if you aint seen *it* yet,' one of the departing men said" (*H*: 180; emphasis mine). Hidden behind pronouns with no clear referents, the object of the mysterious spectacle attracting this small rural crowd is literally unspeakable: you have to see it to believe it. Aroused by his pathological curiosity, Ratliff follows the crowd as it moves discreetly toward the scene where the perverted and voyeuristic instincts of the tribe's males burst forth each day, with the exception of a few surprisingly sensible souls, especially the gruff Bookwright, who seemingly has good reason not to follow his peers: "'Go on and see it,' Bookwright said again, harshly and violently. 'It looks like I'll have to, since aint nobody going to tell me,' Ratliff said" (181). The function of this first section, which abruptly ends without identifying the community's new source of jubilation, is to introduce the story of the most pathetic and implausible of romances in an apparently disjointed and discontinuous manner (such that during the first reading of the novel, no clear logical connection appears between the first two sections of chapter 1 from "The Long Summer"). The pastoral for which Ike Snopes is the miserable hero in the second part of the chapter takes place in a reconstructed Eden that stands in sharp contrast to the arid world of economic and financial exchange that the other Snopeses, Flem chief among them, relentlessly pursue.

The beginning of section 2 extends the sense of waiting, and even of suspense, prompted by the preceding scene. The logic governing the first three pages is that of a slow unveiling, delayed by the use of pronouns that replace no noun but stage, by way of successive touches, a strange tête-à-tête between a male "entity"[20] and a female "entity": a "he" that leaves his hearth at dawn to stretch out in the dewy grass near a brook, awaiting a sign or a noise announcing the approach of a "she" that is initially deprived of identity. The pastoral setting of the meeting, which takes place during two simultaneous dawns—of spring and of the day—brings to mind the first daybreak when the first "he" and the first "she," the first man and his first partner, were welcomed after it was peopled by "birds and animals" (*H*: 182).[21] She, the coveted one, the reason for the wait, the fetish object of a fascination that fully assumes its phallic etymology, gradually takes shape in the tenuous sensations that become clearer as she approaches the one who is waiting, awakening his senses from their nocturnal numbness one by one. First, he hears the sound of her footstep on the dewy grass: "Then he would hear her" (182). Then her smell reaches his nostrils: "He would smell her" (183). Finally, she enters his field of vision: "Then he would see her" (183). The use of the frequentative modal auxiliary *would*, combined with repetition of the word *then*, an adverb of time indicating succession, suggests that this is not the first time they have met: it is a ritual whose successive phases repeat each day, as will soon be revealed, in the same order.

In the detailed sensations through which the object of the lover's desire, beaded with humidity, reveals herself to him (and the reader)—readily and traditionally considering that hearing and sight are the senses appealed to by the language of desire—the powerful smell when "she" is still far away strikes a first dissonant note. This olfactory disturbance is quickly confirmed by the appearance of a verb that is totally unexpected in the context of a romantic encounter: "the whole mist *reeked* with her" (183). The desired object smells, reeking of the stable and milk—"the rich, slow, warm barn-*reek* milk-*reek*" (183; emphasis mine). This smell is in no way unpleasant to the lover's nostrils, who takes it in, "smelling and even tasting" (183), with delectation. At the end of the paragraph preceding the beloved's appearance to the lover (but not yet to the reader, who partly resists seeing what is there to be seen), the strangeness of the female entity becomes clear; just as what was heretofore a simple sound now becomes a plop, the sucking sound of a cloven hoof in mud: "hearing the slow planting and the plopping suck of each deliberate cloven mud-spreading hoof" (183). Not only does the beloved stink, but she also has cloven feet. The mystery fades in the limbo of the morning mist,[22] four pages into the section, when the creature is finally named for the one and only time in the entire story: "Probably he did not even know it, was paying no attention at all to where he was going, seeing nothing but the cow" (184). The trembling emblem of *fémellité* that sparks such desire is actually an animal—a cow. Her lover remains to be identified. We know that he lives in the inn run by Miss Littlejohn, who employs him to make the beds. It turns out that the bashful lover is a Snopes who literally cannot say his name: " 'Ike H-mope,' he said. 'Ike H-mope' " (185). It is the village idiot.

The cow is clearly of great importance in the Faulknerian bestiary. In *The Hamlet*, the romance between Ike Snopes and the cow stands as a counterpoint to the mercantile marriage (or more precisely bargain[23]) contracted between Flem Snopes and Eula Varner. The economic arrangement that makes Eula a Snopes stands in sharp contrast to a pure and disinterested love that few—very few—Faulknerian heroes experience. As emphasized by Linda Prior in her article "Theme, Imagery, and Structure in *The Hamlet*," despite its singular object, the purity and intensity of Ike's love prompts admiration and envy, all while representing one of the rare manifestations of hope in a world that is ordinarily marked by harshness and barrenness:

> The second ray of hope which appears in the novel is the love affair between Ike Snopes and the cow. Faulkner here is not satirizing the courtly love tradition—although it is true that Ike's actions conform in many ways to those of the typical thirteenth century courtly lover. And he is not joking about Ike's idiocy or animal passion. The love affair is rather used as a contrast to Eula and her plight. The tragedy is that the cow has a more compassionate lover than Eula will ever have. And again we have the waste: the greatest and purest love in the hamlet is wasted on an unfeeling animal. (Prior, Summer 1969: 239–40)

Eula, who is one of the rare great lovers in Faulkner's novels,[24] will never have the same luck in her romantic encounters as Houston's cow. In *The Hamlet*, she arouses the morbid passion of a schoolmaster named Labove, whose name, formed by crasis, can be seen as the parody of *love* and *bov*ine, a parody that is absent from the romantic idyll of the cow and the idiot. She finally inherits from a decrepit and impotent husband, Flem Snopes, who only has regard for her bargaining value. In *The Town*, her lover, Major de Spain, and her frustrated suitor are not characterized by their courage, or the heroism of their feelings. This absolute love, which Prior considers to be "wasted" on its singular object, makes the cow the most fulfilled of the "*femelles*" in the Faulknerian corpus.

It is not easy to determine what degree of irony and even misogyny is present in this choice. It is unlikely that Faulkner wanted to suggest that no woman deserves to be loved as much as Ike Snopes's cow, or any cow for that matter. He placed too much range and lyricism in his prose—including the cycle of moons and suns, and the fauns and nymphs from his youthful poetry—for us to see (only) irony. The idiot Ike's love is accompanied by aquatic images—dew, a brook, waves, and showers—which suggest the notion of regeneration, of nature's rebirth far from the corrupt world of people. His faith in nature's supremacy and ability to regenerate, personified here by the most natural of lovers (and constituting the framework of *Go Down, Moses*, published in 1942), is too dear to Faulkner for him to mock it entirely. One could instead argue that the section of *The Hamlet* devoted to Ike and his love discreetly pays dual homage to Faulkner's literary past (and what it owes to idiocy) and his most intimate convictions. Taking a step back and pivoting toward the text that probably inspired the portrait of Ike Snopes's cow can help elucidate its symbolism in *The Hamlet*.

In 1937, Faulkner wrote a short story when, of his own admission, he was struggling to get past a hangover: "one afternoon when I felt rotten with a terrible hangover, with no thought of publication" (Blotner, 1977: 245).[25] In the story, Faulkner stages himself as a character who explicitly bears the name "William Faulkner," who is given a secretary who turns out to be his *nègre* (in the figurative sense) (the French word *nègre* means both negro and ghost-writer), and who takes charge of the narration. The story is "Afternoon of a Cow," whose title echoes one of Faulkner's poems, as well as Stéphane Mallarmé's famous poem, both of which are entitled "Après-midi d'un faune."[26] It is not the plot, which involves an act of arson against a stable, that is of interest for us in this short story, but rather the remarkable epiphany (or Joycean parody of epiphany) that it depicts: William Faulkner experiences a crisis (a crisis of the author) in a context marked by its suggestive and scatological intensity. After the cow is saved from the fire, and through an unfortunate chain of circumstances, "Mr Faulkner and the cow were hurled violently to the foot of the precipice with Mr Faulkner underneath" ("Afternoon": 430). The cow, which spent the afternoon in great terror, chooses this precise moment to empty its bowels: "In a word, Mr Faulkner underneath received the full discharge of the poor creature's afternoon of anguish and despair" ("Afternoon": 430). This dung bath will be the source, for William Faulkner, of a singular revelation whose content is not quite revealed[27] but whose effects prompt an endless string of comments in the narrator's ridiculously refined and pompous style:

> As I have indicated, there was a quality almost violent about Mr Faulkner's sedentation; it would be immobile without at all being lethargic,

if I may put it so. He now sat in the attitude of M. Rodin's *Penseur* increased to his tenth geometric power say, since le penseur's principal bewilderment appears to be at what has bemused him, while Mr Faulkner can have had no doubt. ("Afternoon": 431)

This sordidly privileged contact with the intimacy of a cow apparently gave him food for "thought." It is tempting to see the dramatization of this revelation as the unspeakable source for the singular love story that Faulkner the author published three years later: by choosing a cow instead of a woman as the heroine of his most remarkable romantic depiction, Faulkner could say what he was otherwise unable to say about a woman without breaching the rules of propriety. He apparently breached them nevertheless, as the discourse of numerous critics regarding Ike and his cow reveals an ethical resistance that has seen this solely as a zoophilic anecdote or, in the words of Lothar Hönnighausen, as "an unpleasant and uninteresting case of a feebleminded sodomite in Northern Mississippi" (Hönnighausen, 1997: 182). The iconoclastic objective of Faulkner the writer had to use the subterfuge of a strange fable in order to deliver its truth, thereby prompting at least a smile among his most generous readers. Similarly, the story of Ike's love consists of barely tolerable hard facts, mythical finery, as well as raw and prosaic truths, all accompanied by superb lyrical flights; the woman, who may be a muse and a lover, never escapes her absolute ambivalence. Despite the angelic blindness of poets, and their propensity to idealize the object of their fascination, beauty and desire do not exclude—and never erase—the undeniable reality of the woman's bodily functions. This is what is signified by selecting the cow rather than the woman for the leading role as the eternal beloved: it would appear that Faulkner chose to substitute the cow for the woman in order to reveal the truth about the body, which is an integral part of love, regardless of what people want to believe. And to say these things, it was necessary to proceed through the blind and total adoration of an idiot.

This is why Faulknerian cows are often described in an extremely complex manner, one that encourages readers to see them as emblems of femininity;[28] the description of the main cow from *The Hamlet* continues to confuse the reader well after the mystery of its identity has been revealed. Its character contains both the most brutal animality and a highly feminine delicacy. The cow Ike is enamored with is not content with having a cow's body replete with horns, hooves, and teats, a victim of base and irrepressible bodily functions.[29] It is also a woman's and mother's body described in its intimacy, especially through the weight of her teats laden with milk: "the discomfort of her bag" (*H*: 198). In a curious mix of anthropomorphism and animality, it remains a timid and blushing personality that is prey to hesitation, embarrassment, and shame:

When he moved toward her, she whirled and ran at the crumbling sheer of the slope, scrambling furiously at the vain and shifting sand as though in a blind paroxysm of shame to escape not him alone but the very scene of the outragement of privacy where she had been sprung suddenly upon and without warning from the dark and betrayed and outraged by her own treacherous biological inheritance. (*H*: 192)[30]

Trying to escape its seducer, Faulkner's cow is an avatar of the mythological Io, daughter of Inachos and ravishing heifer, who was transformed and condemned to wander by Hera, whose anger she aroused by setting Zeus's heart aflame. In both Faulkner and the Ancients, the cow hides the object of a burning desire. The image of Ike pursuing his cow also evokes that of the lover pursuing his beloved, a motif that is engraved on the Grecian urn celebrated in the ode by John Keats, who was particularly dear to Faulkner.[31] The mad pursuit of Faulkner's idiot leads to a joy that will never be felt by the lover in Keats, whose urn fixes and immortalizes the tension of desire, condemning it to never attain its object. In Faulkner's novel the two distinct entities, the "he" and the "she," are ultimately absorbed into a single pronoun ("they"), bearing witness to the consummated union: "They walk in splendor" (205); "They lie down together" (206). The section actually ends with these final words.[32] The tension fixed by the urn is transcended here in a climactic moment.

Section 3 of chapter 1 from "The Long Summer," the third book in *The Hamlet*, makes an abrupt return to the men's everyday life and the questions that haunt them, beginning with propriety and possession. The first half of the section focuses on Houston, the official owner of she whom we have abusively referred to as "Ike's cow" on account of their affinity. That night, Houston goes back home and notices that his only cow is missing, the only female company he can enjoy: "Since the death of his wife three or four years ago, the cow was the only female creature on the place, obviously" (*H*: 206). The peculiar relation, to say the least, between Houston and his cow confirms our intuitions: while in horror he accuses Ike of the worst perversions, his own attachment to the cow is not without ambiguity. The cow crystallizes what is presented as his obsessive "fixation" with the female sex: "the savage fixation about females which the tragic circumstances of his bereavement had created in him" (207).[33] Houston rushes out not only after his property but also in search of his substitute partner. He knows right away where to look for her, as this is not the first time his cow has disappeared:[34] he sets out in search of the idiot with full knowledge of the facts. His exasperation reaches its limit through the act's repetition, and he decides to give the idiot a lesson. Houston is behind the first (and most charitable) of solutions that are successively proposed by the community to cure Ike of his amoral passion: "He would cure the idiot forever more of coveting cows by the immemorial and unfailing method: he would make him feed and milk her" (209). When he finds the idiot and his cow, Houston proposes transforming the idiot into a *garçon-vacher*, a cowboy of sorts with no mount, responsible for the beast's comfort through the performance of the most thankless tasks. Houston's project is never realized and proves futile for a number of reasons. How could Houston help the idiot be aware of his beloved's brute animality when he himself is far from being convinced? How could "professional" proximity to the cow's bodily functions kill the idiot's desire, given that he already devotes his time to her most intimate needs and finds no task distasteful? The idiot's feelings toward the cow are based on total abnegation, as pointed out by Lyall Powers in *Faulkner's Yoknapatawpha Comedy*:

> Ike Snopes is an idiot, yet his devotion to his beloved is as selfish as true love always is: he *wants* the object of his love, and, at the same time, he is as ready for selfless sacrifice, for gallant protection, for unstinting care for the wants and needs of the beloved as a true lover always is. Ike goes through the fire to save his beloved from the burning barn; he gets food for her, graces her brow with a garland of posies, gives her the relief from a heavy udder that milking affords. (Powers, 1980: 147)

When a neighboring farmer finally returns his cow after the idiot flees, Houston chooses to renounce his mission of moral improvement.[35] His admission of failure, which comes before any response on his part, reflects his acceptance of the cow's preference for another, as he renounces his vain struggle against the forces of attraction, against which he is powerless. Acknowledging his impotence, he decides to give the cow to the idiot, to abandon her to him. Torn between the notion that one should not sell one's partner, even if she is a *whore*, he even hesitates to accept the idiot's money that Mrs. Littlejohn hands him, to unambiguously conclude their bargain and formalize the change of owner. Houston gets rid of his cow like an unfaithful woman: "She drew the clean, knotted rag from her pocket. 'I dont want money,' he said roughly. 'I just dont want to see her again'" (*H*: 216). In this way, the lover defeated by an idiot can obtain a meager sense of satisfaction, for at least he is the one initiating the separation.

This is the moment the narrator returns to at the end of section 1—where the thread of this more or less linear story had been left—in order to recount the idyll of the idiot and the cow. When Ike and the cow are reunited, the story reconnects with the narrative present. What the reader is momentarily tempted to interpret as a happy ending, with Houston's words reflecting the fact that the cow and the idiot now form a single entity, or couple, in the eyes of the community—"Goddamn it, keep *them both* away from my place. Do you hear?" (216; emphasis mine)—soon turns into a nightmare. While the idiot and the cow are united, it is behind a wall of planks forming a small pen abutting Mrs. Littlejohn's house. Lump Snopes designed this cage, whose solid walls are as tall as a man, with a movable plank allowing the voyeur's gaze to enter:

> He pulled that plank off! At just exactly the right height! Not child-height and not woman-height: man-height! He just keeps that little boy there to watch and run to the store and give the word when *it*'s about to start. Oh, he aint charging them to watch *it* yet, and that's what's wrong. That's what I don't understand. What I am afraid of. (*H*: 218; emphasis mine)

Ratliff's indignation reconnects with the succession of referentless pronouns that had already helped to withhold information at the end of section 1: however, the reasons for choosing these voluntarily opaque pronouns have changed. Now that he has "seen," now that he has given in to his curiosity and "knows," the horrified Ratliff still cannot verbalize this new object of fascination for the male community of Frenchman's Bend. His intuitions are confirmed, for he saw something he never wanted to see.[36] The pen where Ike now lives in the company of his cow has been transformed into a "peep-show." The story remains silent about what is visible by using ellipsis, which protects readers from their own voyeuristic instincts; the sordid spectacle only occurs implicitly. The attention of the narrator, whose compassion and anger coincide with Ratliff's outbursts, briefly lingers on the rows of faces craving these dramatic images, but this is not described either, for the focus is on their rush and hunger. The creation and success of the peep show can be explained by the irresistible attraction of what is taboo, which Freud defines in the following manner in *Totem and Taboo*: "Anyone who has violated a taboo becomes taboo himself because he possesses the dangerous quality of tempting others to follow his example: why should he be allowed to do what is forbidden to others?" (Freud, 2001: 38). Through their voyeurism, behind the facade of healthy and moral propriety, normal men reveal not only their deviant lust but also and especially their desire and regret at not being idiot (enough) to satisfy their forbidden desires. The use of ellipsis helps denounce the true horror of this chapter. Where the idiot has replaced the lover with a cow, the crowd of males replace the pleasure they probably do not experience with their wives with their voyeuristic impulses, pornography by proxy. In denouncing vice, they give free rein to their own perversions. In short, where there was love, there is now only depravity. They are therefore the true zoophiles, who displace their paranomic dreams onto an innocent person, whose love is thereby transformed into a cathartic outlet for their secret debasement. Ratliff is consequently revolting against not only

Lump Snopes, the instigator of this peep show, but also against the weakness and herd instinct of the hamlet's men. Faulkner does not commit the error of making him a white knight of propriety, for while Ratliff decides to end the snubs suffered by the idiot, it is not to do good or right wrongs, but simply because he is "stronger":

> I aint never disputed I'm a pharisee. [. . .] Or that besides, it aint any of my business. I know that too, just as I know that the reason I aint going to leave him have what he does have is simply because I am strong enough to keep him from it. I am stronger than him. Not righter. Not any better, maybe. But just stronger. (*H*: 219)

In doing so, he holds the community's men to their own rules, especially Lump, who uses their vices for even more vicious ends. It is this notion of might makes right that, driven by collective appetites, perverts an individual's love; the same notion will also bring an end to this "scandal."[37] It is once again Ratliff who proves to be the cleverest, for in this story so deeply marked by shame and dishonor, he bases his strategy on the respect and dignity of the family name. Since Ike is a Snopes, his degradation could tarnish the honor of an entire clan that already possesses little and is desperately seeking more.[38] It is by arousing their dubious sense of honor, in the disguised form of blackmail, that Ratliff is able to convince the Snopeses to hold a family conference—"We'll have a conference. Family conference" (*H*: 223)—to simultaneously rehabilitate the idiot and the name, in an effort to exorcise the wrong:[39]

> That ere wont do. That's it. Flesh is weak, and it wants but little here below. Because sin's in the eye of the beholder; cast the beam outen your neighbor's eyes and out of sight is out of mind. A man cant have his good name drug in the alleys. The Snopes name has done held its head up too long in this country to have no such reproaches against it like stock-diddling. (*H*: 222)

Despite being convinced of the absolute contingency of morality, reeling off his individualistic philosophy in a constant flow of commonplaces, Snopes is flattered by the interest prompted by his name, and takes the bait. The family conference takes place that same afternoon in the presence of Ratliff and Reverend Whitfield,[40] who is familiar from *As I Lay Dying*. In a speech marked by his morbid pragmatism, the latter soon recommends his superstitious remedy:

> You take and beef the critter the fellow has done formed the habit with, and cook a piece of it and let him eat it. It's got to be a authentic piece of

the same cow or sheep or whatever it is, and the fellow has got to know that's what he is eating; he cant be tricked nor forced to eating it, and a substitute wont work. Then he'll be all right again and wont want to chase nothing but human women. (*H*: 223)

According to Whitfield, in order for the idiot to be purified of his abnormal desires—in order for him to be "right again" and chase after only "human women"[41]—he must undergo an ordeal that is a pagan Eucharist of sorts, intolerably cruel. Even though Ike's cow cannot truly be considered a totem,[42] the ingestion of her flesh by he who loves her can nevertheless be interpreted as a taboo due to cannibalism. With this in mind, Whitfield's recommended cure consists of forcing the idiot, who violated a first taboo by mating with an animal, to commit a second one that will eliminate the first: the fault of the monstrous act of mating will be washed away by performing another monstrous gesture—having the idiot eat the "cooked" flesh of his beloved, so that he feels, in both mind and body, that the object he "formed the habit with" no longer exists.[43] The horror of this scene, with Ratliff actively contributing to its conclusion—somewhat tarnishing his status as a champion despite his initial good intentions—concludes with an absurd bargain whose aim is to determine who will buy Ike's cow from Mrs. Littlejohn. She once again backs away and refuses, through her passive resistance, to allow the community to do as it pleases with the idiot: "—only Mrs Littlejohn wont let us have the cow" (*H*: 223). Chapter 1 of "The Long Summer," as well as the idyll of the idiot and the cow, end with this technical obstacle and its financial consequences. The Snopeses, brothers and cousins, fear that saving the family's honor will cost them too much. Everything comes down to a matter of small change—"'Sixteen dollars and eighty cents?' I. O. said. 'Hell fire'" (*H*: 224)—but the nature of the punishment itself fails to raise any eyebrows.

This is where the narrator abandons the idiot Ike and his sorry fate; while Ratliff sets out on the road again in search of clients who will go into debt to buy his sewing machines, he continues the story of this long summer by evoking two other stories of love and death, which soon prove to be darker and more inglorious than that of Ike Snopes. By way of a long analepsis, the narrative first focuses (in the first part of the second chapter from "The Long Summer") on Houston and the circumstances in which he met, married (after vainly trying to avoid her), and lost his wife Lucy Pate—circumstances that make him regret the cow's presence. The second part of the story focuses on another unusual Snopes, who, following only his own rules, frees himself—like Ike, but for different reasons—from the clan's imperatives: it is the somber idealist Mink, who decides that summer to kill Houston. These two stories replace the horror of the sacrifice of Ike's cow, which, like the peep show, is not described. In section 3, when he returns to Frenchman's Bend at the beginning of fall—marking, as it should, the end of "The Long Summer"[44]—Ratliff finds a small community that, after the sound and the fury of extraordinary events, has recovered the order and calm of "these blue and drowsy and empty days filled with silence" (*H*: 287). Mink is in prison awaiting his trial, and the idiot has paid for his unusual love. His punishment is not just the expiation of a personal sin but also the ritualized repression of the entire community's paranomic desires, as they are unleashed for a moment through the voyeuristic spectacle of the tiny peephole. Such is the ironic destiny of the idiot Ike, whose love for the cow makes him the scapegoat of the community. Neither Ratliff (who ultimately emerges with his hands clean) nor the reader is present at this ceremony, although neither can escape a vision that provides the full measure of Ike Snopes's tragedy. It is, incidentally, with this vision that book 3 of *The Hamlet* ends:

> Then Bookwright went on, and he untied the team and drove the buckboard on into Mrs Littlejohn's lot and unharnessed and carried the harness into the barn. He had not seen it since that afternoon in September either, and something, he did not know what, impelled and moved him; he hung the gear up and went on through the dim high ammoniac tunnel, between the empty stalls, to the last one and looked into it and saw the thick, female, sitting buttocks, the shapeless figure quiet in the gloom, the blasted face turning and looking up at him, and for a fading instant there was something almost like recognition even if there could have been no remembering, in the devastated eyes, and the drooling mouth slacking and emitting a sound, hoarse, abject, not loud. Upon the overalled knees Ratliff saw the battered wooden effigy of a cow such as children receive on Christmas. (*H*: 294–95)

Through increased use of coordinating conjunctions, prepositions, and postpositions indicating advancing movement, the syntax of the paragraph, which is cited here in its entirety, imitates Ratliff's slow progression as he approaches the barn, enters, and advances toward the last stall. The tension hovering over his approach, in the darkness and amid the powerful odor of ammonia, dramatizes the discovery that awaits him at the end of the aisle, of which he has a vague intuition ("something, he did not know what"). What appears in the last stall is the vision of a desperately idiotic idiot: after this long summer, in which love transfigured him by sublimating his congenital disabilities,[45] Ike has actually fallen into the most irreversible and abject idiocy. He presents all of the idiosyncrasies of idiocy, as his body, which braved enemies and obstacles for love—rain, cold, and dark—has lost its composure, reduced to a heap of sagging flesh. His slack, drooling lips emit an inarticulate sound, muted and plaintive. The purification ritual he was subjected to simply purified his idiocy, making it more whole and absolute. His face reveals terrifying pain, one that makes him regress into gloomy inertia. His beloved, with whom he desperately seeks contact and struggles to grieve over, is now present in the form of a diaphanous metonymy: the smell of ammonia, the barn, and her fellows, who resemble she who was once his. She is also present in the miserable effigy of a little wooden cow, the paltry substitute for the idiot's great love that Eck Snopes gave him in a bout of compassion, and that is already worn out by Ike's tender affections: "Yes. I felt sorry for him. I thought maybe anytime he would happen to start thinking, that ere toy one would give him something to think about" (*H*: 296).

Chapter 9

THE EXACERBATION OF SENSATION

> She would be still invisible, but he could hear her; it is as though he can see her—the warm breath visible among the tearing roots of grass, the warm reek of the urgent milk a cohered shape amid the fluid and abstract earth.
> —WILLIAM FAULKNER, *THE HAMLET*

Above, I discussed the logic of the idiot's gaze, and how this singular gaze carves up reality and petrifies it in a succession of immutable little scenes. The Faulknerian idiot's gaze is marked by its immobility, which generates an immobilism that can be seen as an unconscious disposition to refuse change, a blindness to the mutability of the world. However, analysis of the sources of the idiot's perception cannot be limited to the study of vision and the visual field, despite the close relationship the eye and the gaze have with issues relating to narration (the terminology for many tools in narrative art borrows from the field of vision), and with writing in general. If sight has often been considered the noblest sense, it is nevertheless closely linked to other senses in forming impressions and knowledge.[1] The writing of Faulknerian idiocy emanates from a gaze that is both the metaphor and the crucible for singular narrative choices; it is a writing of feeling, which decomposes how the idiot's external and internal stimulations cause specific modifying effects on his perception and its affects. The Faulknerian aesthetics of idiocy is rooted in a singular esthesia, in which all of the senses are summoned and heightened such that their distinctions tend to disappear in the blurred forms of *syn*esthesia. The writing of idiocy therefore marks a decisive stage in Faulkner's writing: it is striking that the development of an aesthetics of idiot sensation should involve one of the most striking characteristics of Faulkner's style, namely the systematic primacy of sensations over sentiments.

Sensation is distinguished from sentiment through its more marked physiological basis (its seat is the body rather than the soul) and its immediate nature (it is not entangled with any meditative or reflexive discourse, and immediately concerns tangible elements). Perception opens onto exteriority, onto the world's objects, rather than being reduced to an experience of its own state, which does not rule out the fact that, as something that can be sensed, perception includes a dimension in which the perceiver experiences or affects him or herself. What radically distinguishes the perception of sensations from sentiment, imagination, and memory is that the perceived is present in person, in flesh and blood, and not simply as something else, such as an image or intangible memory. Benjy's "memories" are really perceptions. Abstraction of the past does not exist for idiot characters, as the past suddenly appears in their consciousness in the fragmented form of present perceptions triggered by tangible and actual objects. Beyond Benjy, a number of Faulkner's protagonists reveal a tendency to sense rather than feel: the sentiments that readers attribute to them often derive from the intermingling of sensations. Faulkner generally has little to say about sentiments: the ethereal and reflexive discourse of sentiment is remarkably absent in his work, which is more interested in how bodies react to the inducements and stimulations of the sensible world, and how free will and his characters' actions are altered by it. For Faulkner, sentiment is always rooted in sensing, in the profusion of concrete impressions and sensations. Faulkner is in no way a sentimental writer, but one for whom everything is literally related to sensation.

Even though the immobilism of the idiot's vision gives rise to a perception of the world that is essentially static, as though entangled in the stagnation of time, it nevertheless reveals a surprising vivacity when it occurs. Such is the paradox of idiot perception, as the instant of a petrifying vision (one that makes the organic structure of life mineral) welcomes the teeming sensations of life. The idiot's relation to the world is based on a constant engagement of all the senses, as minimal and practically nonexistent intellectual capacities are compensated, as it were, by an exacerbation of sensation. For the idiot, the places abandoned by reason are consequently flooded by the senses. "Benjy's pasture" (*SF*: 94) becomes the preferred field for all that is sensible.

The word "sensation" derives from the Late Latin *sensatio*, which means "comprehension." For Faulkner's idiots, sensation is the preferred mode for comprehending the world, although the term must shed the connotation with cold intelligibility it has in everyday language and return instead to its more elementary aspects. The word "*comprendre*" (to understand, to comprehend) includes "*prendre*" (to take); idiots "take" the world, they grasp it "with" what their bodies sense, "with" what their bodies become under the effect of sensation. This is the only thing they are equipped with. The development of the idiot's logic of sensation renews the close relation that Faulknerian idiocy has with certain words of a phenomenological order. With regard to sensation, Faulknerian idiocy is once again in an awkward position with respect to objective thought, in that idiots, who are here the subjects of the perception, have a leading role as sensing beings. Their perceptions are not handled by Faulkner's writing as exterior objects, with idiot characters fortuitously serving as the site for their realization. What truly happens in the idiot's sensation, to use Maurice Merleau-Ponty's formulation, is "a re-creation or re-constitution of the world at every moment." It is an endless return to how the world offers itself as a subject (and vice versa)[2] within a relation of immediacy that precedes the objectifying discourse, and hence radically frees itself of its requirements.

As a consequence of his extremely limited capacity of intellection, Benjy has an immediate relation to the world. For him, the world can be reduced to its sensible dimension, and his entire knowledge of the world proceeds from sensation, and results from his senses. The cave in which Benjy finds himself does not open onto a beyond consisting of the conceptual world of ideas. It is fundamentally foreign to the world of representations—it contains only pure presences. The few words of his little language all resemble sensations and are characterized by their unfailing rootedness in the sensible world. A word has meaning for Benjy only insofar as it is connected to a concrete sensation, which contains its unequivocal and invariable reference. The idiot's limited understanding does not conceptualize sensation: he apprehends the world in terms of raw sensations, in the sense that their grain is not refined by the filter of thought. The world thus unfolds as an incessant buzzing of diffuse sensations, whose very confusion underpins a singular poetry, let alone a poetics. While sensation is the idiot's central relation to reality, it also necessarily restricts its scope: the world of ideas is wiped out by the world of things, which is the exclusive and solipsistic world of idiocy. The idea of things never transcends sensible things themselves. For the idiot, the world's objects can be reduced to those that are perceptible through the senses, in other words material, concrete, tangible, visible, and sensible to the senses of hearing and smell. In Clément Rosset's terminology, the idiot adds "value" to things in order to integrate them within an "intellectual circulation of sense" (Rosset, 1986: 35). The Faulknerian idiot's perception of reality is an exclusively sensible circulation of sense. The idiot's world is ultimately no more than an amalgamation of sensed things, but just as nothing is thought within it, nothing is literally felt, as demonstrated by the radical absence of terms referring to sentiments and emotions in his discourse. The very forms of thought and sentiment are sacrificed for those of sensation, which is heightened by the exclusive hegemony of the senses and the sensible world. That is why, in *The Hamlet*, the appearance of the verb *to know* in the omniscient narration of the central event from Ike Snopes's little life is so suspect: "he *probably knew* generally where she would come from each morning, since he *knew* most of the adjacent countryside and was never disoriented" (*H*: 185; emphasis mine); "But his bare feet would *know* the dust of the road" (186). These examples show how much Ike's "knowing" is rooted in the contiguity of sensations, in this instance spatial and tactile. This verb *to know* is imposed on the narrator for lack of a more appropriate solution for referring to the idiot's singular knowledge, while his hesitation (as demonstrated by the many adverbs), and its resulting nuances with regard to his first choice, reveal his discomfort: "his feet *knew* the dust of the road again though *perhaps* he himself was unaware of it, *possibly* it was *pure instinct functioning* in the desolation of bereavement" (196). *To know*, a verb usually reserved for rational knowledge and understanding, gives way to the term *instinct*, taken from the vocabulary used for animal behavior.[3] The narrator reconsiders: as Ike nears the coveted cow, his idiot's humanity is described in an increasingly animal manner. This strategy seeks to reassure common people regarding human nature (Ike should be excused for the errors of his ways, for deep down he is no more than a strange animal).[4] What is at stake in the changing vocabulary referring to the idiot's (com)prehensions is the transition from a human to an animal, from conscious life to twilight.[5] However, the narrator, struck by remorse or simply fascinated by the tenacity of Ike's human, all too human, desire for his cow, is not content with his discourse on the instincts. He ultimately rehabilitates the humanity of Ike Snopes by granting him the grace of a certain knowledge, however curious it may be: "his sightless hand which knows and remembers" (*H*: 199). Here, synesthesia refers to the actual knowledge of sensing.

Benjy Compson's discourse is not encumbered with such lexical hesitation: to use a commonplace of narratology, his monologue shows more than it tells. No word is needed to designate his paradoxical sensible knowledge, because the objects of this knowledge precisely appear in his discourse through the singular confusion of their sensible emergence. The other side of this poetic immediacy, as well as its primary paradox, resides in the reader's difficulty—mired in the requirements of comprehension and unsatisfied with simple prehension—in untangling the sense of what is shown amid the confusion of the senses.[6] Despite the remarkable vivacity of his senses, the idiot is entirely incapable of forming the least conscious judgment. If all the objects of his perception are mixed up in the continuity of the same prehension of the senses, it is because the idiot does not distinguish between what he is and what is other: the world, and the beings and things that inhabit it, are mere extensions of his own body. The idiot's singular perception is similar to the mechanisms of an infant consciousness. We can also trust the narrator's dithering in Ike Snopes's idyll and interpret the absolute proximity between the idiot and the world as a kind of instinct that brings idiocy and animality closer together. This is notably the reading of Erwin Straus, who advises us to think along these lines:

> What the animal understands does not become an independent object, as it is for the knowing subject. The animal merges with the object in an immediate communication, forming a community of direction and pathway with it. This subjugates it and disposes of it, whereas the knowing subject has knowledge at its disposal, and through it the known object. (Straus, 1989: 328)

Like the animal, the idiot "merges with" the world: the world has no autonomy except for the "direction" and "pathway" he imprints on it. However, this independence is intolerable for the idiot, who does everything to abolish it. Still, and this is where an idiot is different from an animal, when the world accidentally escapes the order of the idiot's needs and desires, it is inevitably the source of tremendous dread. In general, it is the idiot's fundamental imperfectability that prompts us to compare him to an animal rather than a child: "Animals [. . .] create no new worlds; they invariably remain the prisoner of their adaptation to their own world" (Straus, 1989: 316). While Benjy certainly shows an absolute inability to evolve, in the sense that his adaptation to the world around him—determined once and for all of eternity—is impermeable to any change, he is nevertheless "creative." From the strictly literary point of view that concerns us, the idiot's unfailing rootedness in the world of things and his immersion in the sensible are central to the creation of a radically new literary world. For where a normative perception summons concepts and ideas, in the idiot's conscience and the writing that underpins it, only sensible things and events are described, minutely and in their most intimate mechanisms.

Benjy's animality is reinforced by the animal references that abound in his discourse and fix its borders, as if marking out his territory, and that can be defined as an encroachment of the animal on the human, or vice versa. Some pages from his monologue are particularly representative of this: within the spatial subordinates that do not identify the object of the main clause to which they are connected, Benjy's impressions are regularly rooted in the evocation of places occupied by animals: "where the cow was lowing" (SF: 19), "where we could smell the pigs" (20), "where the pigs ate" (20), "where the cows ate" (21). The animal world offers Benjy a range of preferred markers that afford him an identification of sorts, as cows and pigs feed, low, and grunt just like he does.[7] Hearing, smell, and sight contribute to the topographical tracing of the narrow field of his familiar perceptions, within the spatial markers defined by the sensible presence of farm animals. Nothing in his discourse suggests that Benjy perceives a difference between the animals and human beings that surround him, for he mentions both within the same continuum, with no distinction of species.[8] Prince, Queenie, and Fancy (12), and Dan (29), appear in the novel's first section in the same way as humans, for their names are stripped of any antecedent identifying what they are; they are presented only through these names, which reveal nothing about their identity. It is only by slowly gathering disparate elements that the reader finally learns that the first three are horses and the last one a dog, and that Benjy seems entirely unaware of this fact.[9] To Benjy's ears, even language is deprived of any distinctive value: the words of men are like noises, just like the yells of animals. In *The Five Senses*, Michel Serres observes that "voices make noise, so do things. [. . .] Before making sense, language makes noise: you can have the latter without the former, but not the other way around" (Serres, 2016 [2008]: 120). In the idiot's consciousness, language returns to its primordial relation to the other sounds that arise in the world, in which humans are reminded of their essential animality.

The world appears much closer to the Faulknerian idiot than to us readers, who are weighed down by the accouterment of objectifying thought, which makes this remarkable world—extraordinarily dense and opaque (because alien to the concept's transparency)—so stubbornly unintelligible. In the final analysis, the reader has no choice but to reestablish the categories and causal links in order to generate sense from the confusion of the senses.

However, the one-dimensionally sensible world inhabited by the idiot is also the primary world in which sensible forms welcome and give rise to the second—and secondary from the perspective of Faulkner and phenomenologists—discourse of thought.[10] Through the idiot, Faulkner placed himself counter to the metaphysical tradition, which, since the Platonic injunction to grasp only the essence of things as true, has always designated phenomenality as being harmful to truth. From the metaphysical perspective, there is no being in appearing. Yet, if the Faulknerian idiot is, unbeknown to himself, aligned with a phenomenological perspective, it is because the truth is precisely rooted in appearing, which contains all of the being to which he has access. A thing exists for him only insofar as it is part of the spatiotemporal fabric of the here and now. Just as phenomenologists conceive of consciousness not as a substance independent of the world but as one that even makes it exist (in other words, in and for the world), the idiot's consciousness indisputably has no other mode of being than rootedness in a sensed world. For Merleau-Ponty, the painter's approach best illustrates this privileged relation that the senses have with the prescientific life of consciousness. Through their opposition to the partiality of a scientific form of thinking, which treats all beings as an object and manipulates things without inhabiting them, painters have an unmediated relation with reality: "Only the painter is entitled to look at everything without being obliged to appraise what he sees. For the painter, we might say, the watchwords of knowledge and action lose their meaning and force" (Merleau-Ponty, 1993: 123). The Faulknerian idiot is also freed of "being obliged to appraise," although what is part of a voluntary artistic approach for the painter is experienced and endured by the idiot because of the psychic dysfunctions characteristic of idiocy. While painters immerse themselves in the sensible world by choice, idiots are forced to do so by their nature. Perhaps the relation idiots have with reality is even more complete because of this, even more ideally naïve than that of painters. The idiot is an emblem of this relation to raw being, the innate relation beyond all knowledge that Clément Rosset has described as a "rough contact that bumps into things and draws nothing from them but the sentiment of their silent presence" (Rosset, 1986: 43).

As an eminently sensitive being, the idiot reacts to sensory arousal. The sensation that triggers the most violent reactions in Benjy of course bears the name Caddy, whichever of her numerous metamorphoses is involved: her smell, her slipper, or the common phrase heard on golf courses. All of Benjy's instincts are determined by Caddy's traces, by her absence, by the traces of her absence. Benjy's sharp senses return everything to Caddy, that initial loss of an indefinable something that signifies a certain freshness and well-being for him, and that is entangled with the roots of being, to the impalpable source of sensation. Even when present, Caddy only reveals herself to Benjy through the intermingling of gentle and pleasant sensations associated with the brisk cold, the warm hearth, or the green scent of trees. Faulkner defines Caddy as she emerges from the confluence of the idiot's senses: "that fierce, courageous being who was to him but a touch and a sound that may be heard on any golf links and a smell like trees, into the slow bright shapes of sleep" ("Intro SF, II": 231). But one sense is predominant: Caddy, whose physical appearance is never really described, is essentially present through her smell. It is in this respect that Paul Carmignani observes, in his article "Olfaction in Faulkner's Fiction," that "Benjy, the idiot, is the archetype of the character dwelling in the fragrant aura emanating from feminine presence. [...] Though unable to reason, Benjy is nonetheless perfectly able to find out things by the sense of smell. The world around him is one big nosegay" (Carmignani, Summer 1990: 308). Yet the sense of smell, the sense of animality, is generally relegated to a subordinate role when compared to the nobility of the other senses, as its close proximity to a shameful body discredits it in relation to the other senses. It is with this in mind that Michel Serres opposes the singularity of the sense of smell with the abstract universality of sight and sound, and the rootedness of taste within the network of cultural habits:

> Smell seems to be the sense of singularity. Forms reappear, invariant or recurrent, harmonies are transformed, stable across variations,

specificity is countersigned by aroma. With our eyes closed, our ears stopped, feet and hands bound, lips sealed, we can still identify, years later and from a thousand other smells, the undergrowth of such and such a place in a particular season at sunset, just before a rainstorm, or the room where feed corn was kept, or cooked prunes in September, or a woman. (Serres, 2016 [2008]: 169–70)

Smell is the sense of *idiôtès*; it is also the idiot's keenest sense. Benjy's perception of the world is an uninterrupted chain of smells, scents, and stinks, even though he has none of these words available to describe the odors that reach his nostrils. As previously mentioned, his neurasthenic brother Quentin is also particularly sensitive to smells: they both associate Caddy with the scents of the "Immemorial Earth."[11] If for both of them smell is the most prominent sense, with their respective monologues actually unfolding like "bouquets" of smells, it is because the sense of smell, like Proust's madeleine dipped in verbena tea, is the preferred sense of recollection. Therein lies Caddy's disappearance: the inexorable vanishing of sensations that once came in an uninterrupted flow, epitomized by Benjy's smell of trees and Quentin's scent of honeysuckle. In the emptiness of her physical absence, the obsessive permanence of Caddy's memory merges with the present like a smell that can appear at any moment and repeat, in its airy wake, the precious configurations of childhood:

Improbable, blended, specific, singular odours, their time and place uncertain. Now suppose that a rare blend should appear a second time in the random turbulence of the air, that this unique confusion should recur, improbably: the knot gathers in its threads, the apex pulls up its base, the tributary subsets burst forth as they intersect, a whole world rushes in: bodily position, enchantment, colour, circumstances crowd around, rarity reappears, richly ornamented and decorated; here, for want of frequency, memory is not transformed into knowledge, but we are dazzled, ecstatically, by our proximity to this overabundant memory.

The sense, therefore, of the confusion of encounters; the rare sense of singularities: our sense of smell slides from knowledge to memory and from space to time—no doubt from things to beings. (Serres, 2016 [2008]: 170)

Volatile and unforeseeable, the odor of trees and the scent of honeysuckle appear in the discourses of Benjy and Quentin Compson—lovesick heroes of their now intangible sister—with the tenacity and insistence of an obsessive memory. Each time these odors randomly repeat in the daily life she long ago deserted, Caddy's image bursts forth with all of the sadness and frustration that have been grafted onto her departure. As opposed to the virginal and immaculate smell of trees, honeysuckle reflects the sophisticated associations that haunt Quentin: the fragrance of honeysuckle, "getting the honeysuckle all mixed" (*SF*: 129), carries with it the ideal images of the antebellum South, of innocent young girls in flower in crinoline dresses on the porches of large plantations. For Quentin, the scent of honeysuckle is distorted into a suffocating smell that calls to mind, amid the confused images emanating from it, the twin falls of the South and of his sister. However, for Benjy the smell of trees that he loves more than anything is a literal smell: it is not coupled with any symbolic value. In a perfect equivalency, the smell of trees *is* Caddy's smell: "Caddy smelled like trees and like when she says we were asleep" (6); "Caddy smelled like trees in the rain" (19). It is a smell associated with the gentleness of sleep, with rain, a smell that haunts section 1 like a throbbing refrain: "Caddy smelled like trees" (42, 43, 44, 48); "She smelled like trees" (43, 72). In his *Baudelaire*, Sartre defined smell as "[a] body with the flesh removed, a vaporized body which has remained completely itself but which has become a volatile spirit" (Sartre, 1950: 174). Caddy has indeed become a "volatile spirit" for her brothers, vanishing amid the wrenching sensations she consisted of, appearing only in the unforeseeable, ephemeral, and fragmentary quality of a smell.

Paradoxically, the heightening of these senses is what brings the idiot closer to animals but also gives him a superior and almost superhuman intuition. If, as Rosset has said, for idiots "the thing is forever as it is itself, without any sign or signification" (Rosset, 1986: 44), this entails that his relation to reality is the closest that can be imagined. Entirely impervious to the principles of reason, idiots take the path of immediacy: they choose the shortest path in order to gain access to things. Upon the death of Mr. Compson, Roskus observes that Benjy may not be as much of an idiot as he appears: " 'He know lot more than folks thinks.' Roskus said. 'He knowed they time was coming, like that pointer done. He could tell you when hisn coming, if he could talk. Or yours. Or mine' " (*SF*: 31–32).[12] Here, Roskus uses a popular commonplace regarding idiots, one that is most often associated with madness, as demonstrated by the fear sparked by Darl Bundren's visionary gaze in *As I Lay Dying*: those abandoned by reason have access to a kind of higher understanding akin to divination. Just as Darl "knows" that his mother is terminally ill and guesses his sister's pregnancy through the fabric of her dress,[13] according to Roskus, Benjy "knows" when death takes one of the house's occupants. The preferred objects of this wordless divination, which draws its power from the silence in which language is annihilated ("if he could talk," "without the words"), are death and sex, *grande mort* (big death) and *petite mort* (little death), the exhalation of the final breath, the pleasure that engenders life.[14] Like Benjy, the idiot Lonnie from "Hand upon the Waters" does not understand what death is, which for all that does not prevent him from "knowing": "where the deaf-and-dumb youth probably still waited for him to come home, knowing that something had happened, but not how, not why" ("Hand": 73). Death is a sensation for Faulkner's idiots. Recurrent use of the verb *to know* in order to designate the clairvoyant truths accessible to idiots and madmen does not truly betoken knowledge but instead a sensible experience: "Sensing is an emphatic experience. In sensing, we feel ourselves in the world and with the world. [...] The ego's relation to its world is, in connection with sensation, a kind of être-relié [connected being] that must be entirely separated from how knowledge is situated before the world" (Straus, 1989: 333). In addition to knowledge, we willingly attribute to the idiot direct and total access to a reality that is reluctant to reveal itself to those who are overly fond of generalizations, a kind of prescience of what cannot be the object of rational knowledge. To develop this topic, the transcendentalist poets of the nineteenth century lent great importance to the child. For instance, in the first chapter of "Nature" (1836), Ralph Waldo Emerson establishes that one must be a child in order to be fully receptive to nature's truths: "The sun illuminates only the eye of the man, but shines onto the eye and the heart of the child. The lover of nature is he whose inward and outward senses are still truly adjusted to each other; who has retained the spirit of infancy even into the era of manhood" (Emerson, 2000: 6). One must be nothing in order to see and sense everything;[15] one must be devoid of prejudice and preconceived notions, entirely fresh and virgin—ideally idiot—to accede to the most intractable secrets. This is the predominant image of Benjy in Quentin's stream of ideas, a combination of personal impressions and related words: "Benjy knew it when Damuddy died. He cried. *He smell hit. He smell hit*" (*SF*: 90). Without understanding it, Benjy smells death just as he smells Caddy and her proximity, her misguided ways, and her absence. Sadness and joy, an increasingly rare feeling in the degenerating world of the Compsons, are concentrated in the smells that momentarily waft upon the air before vanishing. Like the smell of trees, the smell of death is cyclical, repeating, ever the same. It is also a strong smell that invades the entire space of the novel. The passages evoking Damuddy's death, Quentin's suicide, and the deaths of Mr. Compson and Roskus have the same elliptical, suggestive, and impressionistic character as the scenes set against the backdrop of Caddy's marriage, which like her sexual initiation is also sensed by Benjy—but not exclusively by him—as a kind of death.[16] In the tangle of temporal strata that underpins Benjy's monologue, these occasions are presented in a relation of proximity, such that the sensations relating to death ultimately converge with those stemming from the sister's marriage, bearing in their wake the initial and initiatory memory of the grandmother's death. These deaths and Caddy's marriage are linked through the similar impressions they elicit: in both cases there is a rupture, a threshold that is irreversibly crossed;

both cases accentuate the increasing distance from the innocent games of childhood along the riverbank. This is why Benjy associates them with the "memory" of the first disappearance, that of Damuddy, by evoking a scene in which the Compson children believe that the adults have gathered around the grandmother for a "party" from which they have been excluded: "'They aint moaning.' Caddy said. 'I tell you it's a party'" (37). In *Reading Faulkner: "The Sound and the Fury,"* Stephen Ross and Noel Polk note that on similar occasions, Faulkner does not use italics where we would normally expect them: "perhaps to indicate how completely and inextricably Caddy's wedding and Damuddy's funeral are related in Benjy's mind" (Ross and Polk, 1996: 26). This increases the lack of distinction between events, which are reduced to similar sensations. Benjy is removed from the home on both occasions; it is hardly coincidental that the shameful symbol of the lineage's bastardization is cast out—"Can you take him out of the house" (*SF*: 34)[17]—during rituals striving to bolster a tottering family institution (here it is the son's death by suicide that is being commemorated) with normative models, which leave no room for error. Doubly absent through his physical distance and stupefied contemplation of other realms, Benjy nevertheless "smells" death,[18] that unnamable thing—"I could smell it" (34)—while simultaneously showing heightened attention to his darkened surroundings.

The adjective "dark" is repeated constantly: "The bones rounded out of the ditch, where the dark vines were in the dark ditch, into the moonlight, like some of the shapes had stopped. Then they all stopped and it was dark, and when I stopped to start again I could hear Mother, and feet walking fast away, and I could smell it" (34). The darkness coincides with a succession of somber images: "The ditch came up out of the buzzing grass. The bones rounded out of the black vines" (35). The ditch appears in Benjy's field of vision and reveals the mare's bones, just as death engages his senses, giving rise to a world haunted by shadows. The news of the eldest son's suicide is not clearly stated: Benjy has all the fewer words to express it, given that the family hid it from him and excluded him from the ceremony. In Benjy's discourse, Quentin's death disappears as much as it appears, giving rise to one of the great strategies of Faulkner's writing, one that is echoed in numerous narratives to come, namely the almost systematic retention of crucial information in favor of the impressions and sensations—described in the confusion of their sudden occurrence—that gravitate around this central moment and appear severed from both their origin and cause.[19] In order to give an account of this intimate confusion of the senses, and the apparent disorder that nevertheless reflects a singular order, the idiot's discourse sacrifices the preestablished rules of causality, replacing them with a combination of effects, or what Édouard Glissant has called the "inextricable."[20] While it can be readily interpreted as the opposite of logic, the manner of apprehending the world that characterizes idiocy in Faulkner, a complex union of animality and infantilism, nevertheless consists of regular and repetitive motifs that respond to logic, namely the logic of idiot sensation.

In addition to being eminently olfactory, Benjy's sensations also give a prominent role to the effects of light and darkness, which serve almost systematically as a backdrop for his inner scenery. Benjy's highly visual monologue includes the play of light and dark in which the mysterious given of light—whose constancy the idiot grasps without understanding its origin—weakens or grows, appears or disappears. For him, light is the condition sine qua non of all possibilities: the world vanishes with it at sundown, when all the lamps are extinguished. Section 1 of *The Sound and the Fury* finishes with the complete darkness that comes with sleep. This sleep is free of the fear present in similar moments in the future, for Caddy is there holding Benjy, who is lulled by the illusion that things will always be this way: "Caddy held me and I could hear us all, and the darkness, and something I could smell. And then I could see the windows, where the trees were buzzing. Then the dark began to go in smooth, bright shapes, like it always does, even when Caddy says that I have been asleep" (*SF*: 75). Instead of signifying the end of day, gradual darkness represents the slow disintegration of the world. Benjy's senses are dulled and softened, and seem to lose the vividness that characterizes them when he is awake, yielding languidly to the formless forms of dreams, in which sensation continues more loosely and vaguely. However, all of his senses are confusedly aroused during the ceremony of sundown: touch through contact with Caddy's arms; hearing ("*hear*") through his concentration on his breathing; smell ("*smell*"), which is stimulated by the intimacy of the bed he is sharing with his sister; and finally sight ("*see*"), which declines with the darkness.[21] Benjy's monologue closes with a vast synesthesia in which darkness can be heard and smelled: intertwining sensations from different sources give rise to the idiot's ephemeral comfort, with which the world can once and for all be extinguished. In Benjy's vision, the world always appears against a luminous substrate, as his gaze fills with the sudden appearance of a light source and empties with darkness.[22] In the immediacy of a comma or a period, Benjy's unusual syntax reproduces both the gradual flood of light and its abrupt withdrawal. For Benjy, the world unfurls against the wide and nuanced range of light, with all shades of daylight and twilight[23]—from lunar pallor to total darkness—succeeding one another in an uninterrupted flow of extremely varied sensations that, despite their apparent simplicity, become more complex through the interplay of striking combinations:

> I went around the kitchen, where the moon was. Dan came scuffling into the moon. [. . .] The grass was buzzing in the moonlight where

my shadow walked on the grass. [. . .] It was dark under the trees. Dan wouldn't come. He stayed in the moonlight. Then I could see the swing and I began to cry. (*SF*: 46)

Caddy and I were running. "Caddy." Charlie said. We ran out into the moonlight, toward the kitchen. (*SF*: 48)

In this passage consisting of fragments intertwined across several pages, like a pattern weaving threads of darkness and light, bright moonlight pervades two distinct memories, two scenes on the swing: in one, Caddy meets Charlie, and in the other Quentin meets the man with the red tie. The moon's diaphanous light accentuates the resemblance of the two strangely similar scenes by favoring the substitution of the mother's and daughter's faces, fifteen years apart. Benjy identifies the moon as the only reassuring element in the darkness sought out by the lovers, in this night that forever steals Caddy and her avatars from him. Like the dog Dan, he has an instinctive fear of the night and what can occur during it. This is why he pulls Caddy toward the light, "in the moonlight," the protected area where he senses that Charlie will not follow. "His song," his lament, "melts in the calm light of the moon."[24] Whatever its source, for Benjy light is an invariably familiar element, thanks to which he can situate himself, or evoke that which he does not understand: "When we looked around the corner we could see the lights coming up the drive" (37), which are those of Caddy's wedding procession. Benjy, who has been kept away for the occasion, nevertheless reveals his pathetic desire to see: "I clawed my hands against the wall" (38, 35). Yet since he has been secluded, the various evocations of Caddy's wedding are strictly limited to the space of the little window where he is standing, through which the waves of intertwining sounds and lights end their journey in his frustrated senses. This image of Benjy sequestered in the cellar—standing atop a box before a little window, and falling off the box while desperately trying to understand a situation he senses is crucial—becomes an obsessive icon in Quentin's imagination. It is continually repeated throughout the second monologue of *The Sound and the Fury*: "He lay on the ground under the window, bellowing" (94). It is as though Quentin, who attended the ceremony and its preparations, found his pain echoed in the seclusion of his idiot younger brother. It is odd that Quentin's discourse does not expand upon the evocation of Caddy's wedding with any additional visual images: through Benjy, it trusts in the perception of the hazy lights that gradually lead Caddy away from the world of their childhood; it adheres closely to the expression of a nameless pain, for this may also be all that it can say.

In general, Benjy and Quentin share the same fascination for the shadows cast by an understated sun that is almost entirely absent in section 1 of the novel. In Quentin's stream of consciousness, there is no doubt that shadows have a symbolic value that goes hand in hand with his obsession with time and the prospect of his imminent end, with his shadow forever awaiting him at the bottom of the river.[25] For Benjy, they possess a much more literal signification. Benjy does not at all understand why this unfailing double—"We went along the brick wall, with our shadows" (35)—always follows him and sometimes precedes him: "We went along the fence and came to the garden fence, where our shadows were. My shadow was higher than Luster's on the fence" (4). He is missing the causal link explaining that shadows—their size and direction—are cast by the position of the sun or the moon. However, for both Benjy and Quentin, shadows are similarly the intangible imprint of an inconsolable absence, the unceasing albeit elusive memory of she who haunts both of them, and who, having become immaterial, will never return. The ubiquity of shadows in Benjy's monologue is part of a broad network of synesthesia.

Because it awakens all of the senses, synesthesia is the preferred form of Benjy's sensible perception. Deriving from the Greek *sunaisthêsis*, which means "perceive together" or "simultaneous perception," synesthesia can be defined as the combination of sensations, the simultaneous engagement of multiple senses, or the response of multiple senses to the stimulation of one of them. In Benjy's discourse, synesthesia is a figure of combination and confusion. It originally denoted a sensorial condition, or according to the definition in *Le Robert*, a "sensorial perception disorder characterized by the perception of an additional sensation to the one normally perceived, in another part of the body or involving another sensorial domain." Considering the differences in the natures and effects that distinguish one sense from another, Erwin Straus pointed out the improbability of such intersensory effects (*Mitempfindungen* in German): "The eye and the ear have as little inherent interconnection as do sound and light when considered as physical agents, or color and sound considered as distinct modalities; hence the amazement when faced with synesthesia" (Straus, 1963: 204). Benjy's inability to make distinctions between the different fields of experience gives rise to sensorial and syntactical juxtapositions and combinations that freely associate heterogeneous elements: the absolute primacy of sensation is attested to by the many instances of synesthesia, in which a process's cause is sacrificed for its effect ("*We could hear the roof*," *SF*: 66), as well as phrases that coordinate various objects as though they had shared characteristics ("We could hear the fire and the roof and Versh," 70). The synesthesia that characterizes the idiot's perception is an intensified version of the mechanisms of accumulation and agglomeration that generally underpin

Faulkner's writing. Glissant described this writing of raw things, which scorns abstraction and the fantasy of transcendence, in the following terms:

> For any storyteller, the most familiar way to describe something is through *accumulation*, by piling up the component parts of this so-called reality, or at least the elements whose presence he can detect. To describe or present what exists by multiplying details of its constituent parts means challenging the pretension of penetrating the sense of things in a single shot. The list is one of the vectors of baroque thought, in opposition to the "search" for depth. (Glissant, 2000: 198)

In its least developed form, synesthesia is in keeping with the "something I could smell" (*SF*: 75) that ends Benjy's monologue and that is grafted onto his customary visual sensations: "There was a fire. It was rising and falling on the walls. There was another fire in the mirror. I could smell the sickness. It was on a cloth folded on Mother's head. Her hair was on the pillow. The fire didn't reach it, but it shone on her hand, where her rings were jumping" (61). Sickness is revealed here through the conjunction of two sensations: a cloth placed on his mother's head, and an unusual smell that the idiot cannot name (camphor). In similar fashion, fire, the sparkling concentration of light, spreads its flames through a combination of sensations made all the more complex by the mirror's doubling. The fire is perpetual movement: its elusive character is featured in this movement's reflection as it flickers on the walls of the room. Simultaneously in the hearth, in the mirror, and on the walls, the contagious fire has seemingly set the entire space ablaze and threatens to reach the pillow where his mother is resting; but it stops at her hands, sweeping the rings on her fingers along in a jumping dance. The object of unparalleled fascination, fire is also the element that allows Benjy to characterize, by association, Caddy and her daughter Quentin, with their resemblance being suggested by the similar images to which they are connected: "Caddy's head was on Father's shoulder. Her hair was like fire, and little points of fire were in her eyes" (72); "Quentin looked at the fire. The fire was in her eyes and on her mouth. Her mouth was red" (67). Through its improbable degree of sophistication, Benjy's comparison ("like fire") is an exception in his discourse: it is inspired by a literal understanding of the fire's reflection, which it sees as the fire's extension into Caddy's hair and Quentin's eyes and mouth. But Benjy does not say that the mother and daughter are on fire, consuming their desires just as flames consume themselves (it is up to the critic to ascribe ethereal symbols to his literal sensations). What Benjy perceives is simpler, more original, and ultimately prettier.

In Benjy's discourse, synesthesia is actually the source of constant poetic improvisations: the idiot's poetry dismisses causal explanations. The idiot neither asks nor answers any questions: his discourse unwinds like a rosary of affirmations that dismantle the law of causality.[26] In the examples cited above—"the trees were buzzing" (75); "the grass was buzzing" (46)—to which we can add other, similar ones—"the rattling leaves" (6); "the bright rustling leaves" (7)—the natural elements that make up Benjy's landscape are endowed with an autonomous language (here a buzzing, there a rustling) consisting of pure effects that contain and simultaneously eliminate the causes that produce them. Is it the wind or an insect that is making the trees and grass buzz? (We can assume that footsteps are what crush and rustle the dead leaves.) Benjy's discourse is one that shows, with a wholly disconcerting simplicity, how the most common and obvious phenomena first reveal themselves through sensation and the senses. The fascinating dance of light materializes in the fire: "Jason threw into the fire. It hissed, uncurled, turning black. Then it was grey. Then it was gone" (72). Attentive to his brother's only movement, Benjy notes his gesture without considering his motivation: a pure gesture, "throwing" has no object. All that matters is the fire's effect on the unspecified object, which is described step by step in its continuity: hissing, uncurling, blackening, graying, disappearing. The process unfolding before the idiot's and the reader's eyes is ordinarily referred to by the noun "combustion." However, this generic scientific term is completely silent regarding the fire's materiality, which Benjy's elementary poetry renders so precisely that readers experience a revelation, as though they were (re)discovering fire through the idiot's senses, with the idiot. Unable to decipher the relation of cause and effect producing it, the idiot "knows" only the phenomena and the proliferation of sensations through which they unfold. On a number of occasions in Benjy's discourse, there is (con)fusion between an act's agent and object: given that he only perceives the changes that result from an act, he attributes both the act and the power to act to the object. There are innumerable examples of this. During the dinner scenes, the ingestion of food is indicated by the rising steam—"It steamed up on my face" (24)—and the back-and-forth of the spoon, which seems to move on its own up to Benjy's mouth: "The spoon came up to my mouth" (25). Rain is represented through the music of the roof, "We could hear the roof" (66), while the reader infers the existence of the jewelry box thanks to its sparkle: "It was full of stars" (41). These few examples are only some of the many instances in Faulkner that illustrate the dismantling of causality that is characteristic of idiot perception. The scene in which Benjy burns himself is a summary of the full logic of the idiot's sensation:

> *I put my hand out to where the fire had been.*
> "Catch him." Dilsey said. "Catch him back."
> My hand jerked back and I put it in my mouth and Dilsey caught me. [. . .] My voice was going louder every time.

> "Get the soda." Dilsey said. She took my hand out of my mouth. My voice went louder then and my hand tried to go back to my mouth, but Dilsey held it. My voice went loud. She sprinkled soda on my hand. (SF: 59)

Captivated by the fire, whose flames have momentarily decreased in intensity, Benjy reaches his hand into the hearth. Dilsey rushes to stop his dangerous gesture. As though animated by an autonomous force, his hand is abruptly pulled away from the fire and raised to his mouth, while under the shock and pain of the burn, his voice rises into what we assume is a moan. Benjy establishes no relation between the experience of the burn and the experience of pain. Pain is a pure event: it boils down to the hand's compulsive movement to the mouth and a raising of the voice. Interpreted by the reader as a clue, Dilsey's attention makes no sense to Benjy. All of the sensations that beset him are exacerbated by the fact that nothing prepares him for them or helps him anticipate them—they occur, suddenly and independently, an incessant flow of surprises. They have the freshness of the first time a phenomenon is experienced (rain, fire, a burn, or water turning into ice), one that nevertheless becomes timeworn through its familiarity.

The very mechanisms of sensation place the sensing subject and the sensed object in a symbiotic relation in which any notion of hierarchy is abolished. To repeat an analogy mentioned earlier, in his book chapter "Painting and Sensation," Gilles Deleuze provides the following definition of sensation as it relates to painting:

> Sensation has one face turned toward the subject (the nervous system, vital movement, "instinct," "temperament"—a whole vocabulary common to both Naturalism and Cézanne) and one face turned toward the object (the "fact," the place, the event). Or rather, it has no faces at all, it is both things indissolubly, it is Being-in-the-World, as the phenomenologists say: at one and the same time I *become* in the sensation and *something* happens through the sensation, one through the other, one in the other. (Deleuze, 2003: 24)

Deleuze's reference to phenomenology is not haphazard, as his definition of sensation repeats the motif of the necessary and unavoidable ambivalence of all sensing, as theorized by Merleau-Ponty.[27] Just as when the *I* senses via the intermediary of touch—"touch it touching" (the touched object being, in the same movement, the object that touches)—the body can, in its total openness to the world, be defined as "the sensible sentient" (Merleau-Ponty, 2004: 254). The logic of idiot sensation is in keeping with this twin movement, which invalidates the categories of object and subject, because the fluid and permeable expressions of the sensing subject and the sensed object become interchangeable. Sensation refers not only to the idiot's singular and exclusive being-in-the-world but also to the world's singular and exclusive being-in-the-idiot. The idiot becomes only in relation to what happens through and within sensation: his becoming is inextricably rooted in the becoming of the world he inhabits. By correlation, the idiot's world is perceptible only through the net of his sensations. Sensation thus contaminates all of Benjy's perceptions and shapes the world that emerges from his discourse. Causality is dismantled and replaced by a mode of fluid association, one that follows the traces but does not grasp the continuity of this twin movement: the occurrence of the sensed thing, and the becoming of the sensing subject. This minute attention to the detail of sensibility, including its most subtle nuances, imbues Benjy's discourse with a poetry that is firmly committed to things, and describes them in their initial phenomenality. Benjy's idiocy is in keeping with a world full of the singular music of rustling leaves and buzzing trees, in which sensation pursues its incessant murmur.

Chapter 10

IDIOCY, ALCOHOL, AND OTHER ILLICIT SUBSTANCES

"A Derangement of All the Senses"

> —He dreamed of an amorous pasture, where shining
> Swells, natural perfumes, golden puberties
> Move calmly and take flight!
> —ARTHUR RIMBAUD, "SEVEN-YEAR-OLD POETS"

The idiocy filtering the gaze and voice of the first monologue from *The Sound and the Fury* is akin to an extreme experience that redefines the novel as a genre and deeply challenges the reader's traditional prerogatives and expectations. Caught in the net of an idiot consciousness, readers are engaged, with all due respect, in seeing and perceiving like an idiot. They are prompted to awaken the idiocy lying dormant within them. If they refuse to play the game, the novel will remain an implacably opaque and unreadable object; but if they accept, they submit themselves to a gaze and voice that, as unconventional as they may be, enjoy a sovereign hegemony. No intrusion by the author or intervention by an external narrator will frame the story or transcend its confusion by ultimately reestablishing elements of sense. What the novel's first section proposes to the reader is the unprecedented experience of an unequivocal and total immersion in idiot being and sensing. Even though it is temporary and takes place by proxy, this reading experience, which radically alters the gaze and perception of those who engage in it, has irreversible effects. The radical singularity of reading *The Sound and the Fury*, and the shock of many of Faulkner's texts written in its wake, make it impossible to relegate them to the drawer of once-read and familiar books. They will forever be the extraordinary objects of an experience that requires readers to participate as human beings, to compromise their certainties, convictions, and very rootedness in the world. They are fabulous objects approached only with a certain feverishness.

In a very famous letter addressed to Georges Izambard in 1871,[1] Arthur Rimbaud wrote that being a poet means being a seer. Seeing entails dismissing the *I* that makes the individual a subject; it entails accepting the other in oneself, abandoning the known world, abandoning oneself to the "unknown" through the "derangement of *all the senses*":

> Right now, I'm encrapulating myself as much as possible. Why? I want to be a poet, and I'm working to turn myself into a *seer*: you won't understand at all, and it's unlikely that I'll be able to explain it to you. It has to do with making your way toward the unknown through the derangement of *all the senses*. The suffering is tremendous, but one must bear up against it, to be born a poet, and know that's what I am. It's not at all my fault. It's wrong to say *I think*: one should say *I am thought*. Forgive the pun.
>
> I is someone else. (Rimbaud, 1993: 28)

Despite the attraction of such a hypothesis,[2] my purpose is not to suggest that the reader immersed in Benjy Compson's idiocy become a poet and seer in the manner of Rimbaud. Yet there is no doubt that the reader's immersion in idiocy, following in the author's footsteps, disrupts the "laziness" and "customs" of readers as well as their conception of self: their intimacy with the idiot telling this tale brings forth the other in them, exposing them, like the poet on a quest, to a singular alterity that threatens the primacy of their status as a subject over the world of objects, and disrupts the logic governing their perception by fundamentally challenging its reliability. Like the poet, the reader is submitted to the "offensive of things."[3] It is also true that the pleasure and even jubilation of such an experience come from effort, and something akin to suffering. Numerous analogies can be made between Faulknerian idiocy as the experience of writing and reading, and what Henri Michaux called "the great ordeals of the mind." This expression (and the essay that defines it) brings together Michaux's experimental alienations through the consumption of drugs and other neuroleptics, in an effort to discover and ultimately describe what happens to subjectivity after reasoning has disappeared under the effect of these substances:

> Since the body (its organs and functions) became known and revealed not through the prowess of the strong, but through the disorders of the weak, ill, infirm, and wounded (for health is silent, and is the source of that incredibly mistaken impression that everything goes without saying), the disturbances of the mind and its dysfunctions will be my teachings. More than the overly excellent "savoir-penser" [knowing how

to think] of the metaphysicists, it is the madness, ecstasy, agony, and "ne plus savoir-penser" [no longer knowing how to think] that are truly destined to "discover us." (Michaux, 1966: 14)

As for the poet (and like Rimbaud, Michaux was a poet), abandoning "savoir-penser" is a quest, the search for an idiot sensing and thinking. Drugs are hence just a pretext and means in the service of "disruptions of the mind":

> In other ways, a great many other ways, drugs betray, discover, and unmask mental processes, bringing consciousness where we had none, and similarly removing it where it was always present, a strange game of drawers in which some close in order for others to open. Hence delectable the many functions hidden during a natural state, I set out to find them—calmly. (Michaux, 1966: 12)

Faulkner was no stranger to these states: he was an inveterate drinker, chronically seeking a similar numbing of his *savoir-écrire* (knowing how to write) and *savoir-être* (knowing how to be).[4] According to Joseph Blotner, Faulkner once commented, addressing a young actress, on alcohol's effect on his self-perception: "When I have one martini, I feel bigger, wiser, taller. When I have a second, I feel superlative. When I have more, there's no holding me" (Blotner, 1974: 227). Far from us to interpret Faulkner's chronic inebriation, and even less to imagine how his senses were altered by it. It is, however, nice to think that he found pleasure in it, and that while drunk he resembled less the consul from Malcolm Lowry's *Under the Volcano* than Guy Debord's self-portrait in *Panegyric*:

> Among the small number of things that I have liked and known how to do well, what I have assuredly known how to do best is drink. Although I have read a lot, I have drunk even more. I have written much less than most people who write, but I have drunk much more than people who drink. I can count myself among those of whom Baltasar Gracián [. . .] could say: "There are those who got drunk only once, but that once lasted them a lifetime." (Debord, 2004: 29–30)

What interests us in Faulkner's chronic alcoholism is that he was familiar with these extreme states in which "there's no holding me," and that this faltering state was a compulsive need for the creator. It is especially remarkable that the hyperesthesia of his idiots is not very different from certain manifestations of drunkenness. In fact, whether it results from consuming alcohol or other forbidden substances, drunkenness presents itself as a way of circumventing the tyrannical primacy of clear and rational thought, whose tools exert control over a world in order to better conceal another. This is what Michaux also suggested:

> The danger of an excessive preference given to communicable, demonstrable, detachable, and useful thought, an exchange value to the detriment of deep thought that continually grows deeper. The danger of its all-too-constant socialization.
>
> The particular danger of excessive control, of the heavy use of the directive power of thought that constitutes the particular stupidity of "great studious minds," who now only know directed thought (voluntary, objective, calculating) and knowledge, neglecting to allow intelligence to roam free, to remain in contact with the unconscious, the unknown, with mystery. (Michaux, 1966: 30)

People drink a lot in Faulkner's novels; they sometimes drink until they fall into an ethylic coma, as demonstrated by this brief sketch of Thomas Sutpen's father in *Absalom, Absalom!*: "his father began the practice of accomplishing that part of the translation devoted to motion flat on his back in the cart, oblivious among the quilts and lanterns and well buckets and bundles of clothing and children, snoring with alcohol" (*AA*: 181). For Faulkner, alcoholism is one of the essential prerogatives of masculinity.[5] However, if one were to select a central scene involving drunkenness in the work of Faulkner, it would once again be from the first monologue of *The Sound and the Fury*, with Benjy being the one who experiences it. This scene emerges from a number of fragments from the past: it is Caddy's wedding day, and Benjy has been excluded from the festivities, but he and T. P., who are still children, have drunk something that reminds them of sarsaparilla[6] but produces the effects of champagne (bought for the occasion by Mr. Compson). Drunkenness increases the idiosyncrasies of the idiot's perception, as though his idiot's idiocy is amplified by the idiocy of drunkenness. In this scene, the evocation of Benjy's own gestures is replaced by how the world proceeds under the influence of his drunken movements: T. P. laughs and can't stand, while Benjy whirls. What emerges is a chaotic and burlesque world altered by the frenzy of his sensations: "The ground kept sloping up and the cows ran up the hill. T. P. tried to get up. He fell down again and the cows ran down the hill. [...] He was still laughing, and I couldn't stop, and I tried to get up and I fell down, and I couldn't stop" (*SF*: 21). The precarious balance of the body, which keeps falling, is presented via the trajectory of the cows, who sometimes appear to be climbing the hill and sometimes to be hurtling down it, according to the perspectives that change each time Benjy falls. Building on this scene, when Benjy is made to swallow more champagne, the changes the body undergoes under the influence of alcohol are described in detail as they appear:

> They held me. It was hot on my chin and on my shirt. "Drink." Quentin said. They held my head. It was hot inside me, and I began again. I was crying now, and something was happening inside me and I cried more, and they held me until it stopped happening. Then I hushed. It was still going around, and then the shapes began. Open the crib, Versh. They were going slow. Spread those empty sacks on the floor. They were going faster, almost fast enough. Now. Pick up his feet. They went on, smooth and bright. I could hear T. P. laughing. I went on with them, up the bright hill. (*SF*: 22)

Imbibing alcohol is likened to a burning, which begins in the throat and travels down the chest. Benjy is probably about to be sick, which would explain why everyone is busy trying to protect the floor. The world continues to slowly spin around him, then come the smooth and bright shapes that ordinarily accompany sleep, replacing the sharp outlines of diurnal objects with the vague and hazy forms of a vision yielding to sleep. The words related here are entirely free of punctuation: all of the impressions—gustatory and tactile, visual and sonorous—are uniformly caught in the same continuum. Benjy is too drunk to recognize the familiar voices surrounding him. At this point, his monologue includes another scene that greatly resembles the evocation of drunkenness, namely the implicit description of the anesthesia preceding his castration: "I tried to get it off of my face, but the bright shapes were going again. [. . .] But when I breathed in, I couldn't breathe out again to cry, and I tried to keep from falling off the hill and I fell off the hill into the bright, whirling shapes" (53). The whirling and vague shapes are once again present, anesthetizing the habits and customs of propriety. They give free rein to the writer's alcohol-fueled dreams, give body to the disconnected images of the idiot consciousness, and bring forth the vision of the poet-seer. It is no coincidence that Georges Bataille compares the birth of art to drunkenness:

> Upon various occasions, when hitherto listless, passive and as though asleep, man touched by that electrifying, seemingly heaven-sent passion, has stood suddenly up, clear-eyed and renewed, and has set forth to conquer; then, the gates of the possible swung wide, as though suddenly waked, he sees within reach what hitherto appeared in dream, only furtively to his eye. This passing from winter's torrid standstill

to the springtime's rapid efflorescence seems always to have been like a transition from pale sobriety to drunkenness: as if, the life in him quickened, man were seized by a dizzying exhilaration which like some strong drink gives a feeling of power. A new life begins: it has lost none of the material harshness which is life's constant thorny essence, it is no less a perilous struggle, but the fresh possibilities it brings with it have the winy taste of delight. (Bataille, 1955: 22).

Part III

"Trying to Say"

Every day I set less store on intellect. Every day I see more clearly that if the writer is to repossess himself of some part of his impressions, reach something personal, that is, and the only material of art, he must put it aside.
—MARCEL PROUST, *BY WAY OF SAINTE-BEUVE*

Chapter 11

THE FURY OF ORIGINS, THE RINGING OF SOUND

> In its beginnings, art had unavoidably to summon forth that leap of free spontaneity which we usually call genius. At Lascaux it is this free movement we sense most deeply, and that is why, writing about cave-art, I have spoken of art's beginnings. We can do no better than roughly date these paintings. But whatever their real date, they were something new: out of nothing, they created the world they figure.
> —GEORGES BATAILLE, *LASCAUX; OR, THE BIRTH OF ART*

When questioned by critics or students seeking advice about being a writer, or when called upon by his editors for new editions of his works, Faulkner constantly returned to his fetish novel, the only one that mattered and that he kept faith in, the one he proudly said would be his best: "This one's the greatest I'll ever write" (Wasson, 1983: 84).[1] At the same time, gripped by an unhabitual optimism, Faulkner wrote to his dear aunt Bama that it was "the damnest book I ever read" (Blotner, 1977). This book, which he never recovered from and never stopped mentioning—whose origin myth he embellished with variations over time (the apple tree that Caddy climbs sometimes becomes a pear tree)—was also the occasion for multiple rewritings that sought to rekindle the singular emotion he experienced while composing it. The four sections of the novel, the four voices that successively "try to say" Caddy's story and the destiny of the Compson family, were followed nearly twenty years later by the Compson "Appendix," which presents the oldest roots of the Compson genealogy. In the meantime, there had been two introductions to *The Sound and the Fury*, which in all likelihood were written in 1933 and were forgotten until James Meriwether drew attention to them in 1972. I will look closely at these two texts, which are fairly similar but have notable variations, for they are among the rare occasions when Faulkner used his incomparable eloquence to make reflective comments about his art.

The introductions present *The Sound and the Fury* as a space marked by two related acts of learning: learning how to read, namely the indirect implementation of decades of reading, and learning how to write. The novel was both the crucible for all his learning as well as the milestone marking the end of his training as a writer. While Faulkner's sententious phrase should be approached with caution—"With *The Sound and the Fury* I learned to read and quit reading, since I have read nothing since. Nor do I seem to have learned anything since" ("Intro *SF*, I": 226)—its solemnity, as well as its mythical and even eschatological overtones (Faulkner interprets the ultimate end of his experience as a reader), are important. In 1933, when he had already published three of the masterpieces from the years of miraculous productivity following *The Sound and the Fury*—namely *Sanctuary*, *As I Lay Dying*, and *Light in August*—and was working on the short stories that would develop into *Absalom, Absalom!*,[2] Faulkner felt he had never experienced the same emotion while composing these works as he did when writing *The Sound and the Fury*, when he was bursting with joy and a sense of absolute liberty. Nor had he learned anything since, surely because he had nothing left to learn. Everything was there in the pages of this best-loved novel, like a mother who shows special love for the most unruly and undisciplined of her children: "that one which caused me the most grief and anguish, as the mother loves the child who became the thief or murderer more than the one who became the priest" (Stein, Spring 1956: 73). In 1933, when the rest of his progeny inspired only "cold satisfaction," the beloved child remained a source of "ecstasy": "So when I finished it [*As I Lay Dying*] the cold satisfaction was there, as I had expected, but as I had also expected the other quality which *The Sound and the Fury* had given me was absent: that emotion definite and physical and yet nebulous to describe: that ecstasy, that eager and joyous faith" ("Intro *SF*, I": 226). In these introductions, Faulkner paradoxically evokes the supreme inspiration he felt while writing *The Sound and the Fury* through two highly contrasting images; his dramatization of this singular state evolved from one introduction to the next, with its fury intensifying. The first introduction describes *The Sound and the Fury* as Faulkner's genius child, conceived without premeditation, effort, or pain, as though by the grace of divine intervention. Inspiration is symbolized through the gentle and holy images of the immaculate conception: "This is the only one of the seven novels which I wrote without any accompanying feeling of drive or effort, or any following feeling of exhaustion or relief or distaste" ("Intro *SF*, I": 227). This long, negative description, whose syntax features the privative preposition *without*, describes a painless delivery. The second introduction depicts its brilliant genius through the violent and devastating image of exploding dynamite: "[T]he entire story [...] seemed to explode on the paper before me" ("Intro *SF*, II": 230). It is as though the dynamite that Faulkner had carefully approached in *Soldiers' Pay* suddenly exploded in his hands,³ shattering the constraints and awkwardness that still held his writing back. This is when the vision of the first images of *The Sound and the Fury*, expressed through the anaphoric repetition of "I saw,"⁴ emerged from the cataclysm; the revelation came with the suddenness and roar of an apocalypse. Faulkner's writing burst forth through the fragments of a world seen through an idiot's perception.

Yet the rewriting of *The Sound and the Fury* was not limited to these self-reflexive texts that tirelessly rehashed the novel's unique and exemplary nature. In a much more discreet and dispersed manner, Faulkner's tribute to his dearest novel extended throughout his oeuvre in the form of traces. With the publication of *Absalom, Absalom!*, Faulkner became the cartographer for Yoknapatawpha County, returning to the central locations evoked in his novels and adding information about two sites where the Compson family's destiny is linked to the history of the idiot Benjy. The family home is evoked through the pasture of which Benjy was deprived: "Compson's. Where they sold the pasture to the golf club so Quentin could go to Harvard";⁵ and the statue of the Confederate soldier prominently featured in the center of town is described through the filter of Benjy's idiocy: "Confederate monument which Benjy had to pass on his *left* side" (*AA*: 314–15). Such were the images that came to the author over seven years after writing *The Sound and the Fury*. The theme of the idiot's dispossession and the disturbing dynamics of his perception endure as the novel's most lasting features. Through the legend for the map, which encompasses the entire existing work, passing the Confederate soldier "on his left side" is implicitly recommended for the county's other characters, as well as the reader. It is a signage system internal to the work. The permanence and consequences of idiot sensation are symbolized by driving instructions that are imposed on the writing, which continues to proceed on the left, as required by Benjy. The origin for the distortions of Faulkner's writing—its deformations, alterations, and deviations from normative syntax—is subsequently marked in the very cartography of Yoknapatawpha.

The fury of genius also impacted the emergence of sounds in the novels to come, ranging from rustling to growling. The following novels' allegiance to *The Sound and the Fury* is likely to recur in sentences where the initial fury continues to resound, as a distant echo.⁶ *Absalom, Absalom!* pays direct homage to the quotation from Shakespeare that gave *The Sound and the Fury* its title: "all the voices, the murmuring of tomorrow and tomorrow and tomorrow beyond the immediate fury" (*AA*: 232). Faulkner's phrase is built on the triple repetition of the adverb *tomorrow*, which reflects Macbeth's rhythmic speech,⁷ and offers a kind of synthesis for it via the association of sound ("voices," "murmuring") and "fury." *Absalom, Absalom!* also signals its connection to *The Sound and the Fury* through the theme of memory, which underpins the structure of both novels: "the hate and the fury and the unsleeping and the unforgetting" (*AA*: 238). The fury and the permanence of memory are revealed in the same breath. Finally, in the last pages of the novel, it is the idiot Jim Bond who imperceptibly invokes his predecessor by intertwining the words *sound* and *fury* (the latter appearing in the form of the adjective *furious*): "Quentin could see it: the light thin furious creature making no sound at all now, struggling with silent and bitter fury . . ." (300),[8] ". . . and there was only the sound of the idiot negro left" (301). The only sound that endures in these tales of collapsing worlds is that of idiots; the only lasting fury is that of the writing ensuring their survival. Faulkner's other texts including idiot characters extend the memory of Benjy and perpetuate the memory of a writing that originated from the chaos of his consciousness. In the section of *The Hamlet* about Ike Snopes, the rain that falls on him and his cow is first described in terms of "noise and fury"; the narrator returns to the phrase a few lines later, as if concerned about authenticating the source of inspiration. In the wake of the shower, the echoes of the earlier novel's title have multiple effects:

> Although the rain had not seemed to last long, yet now it is as if there had been something in that illogical and harmless sound and fury which abrogated even the iron schedule of grooved and immutable day as the abrupt unplumbable tantrum of a child, the very violence of which is its own invincible argument against protraction, can somehow seem to set the clock up. (*H*: 204)

The rain shower, which interrupts an otherwise mild day, is a metaphor for the impact of *The Sound and the Fury* on the rest of Faulkner's work. The summer shower provides an opportunity to return to the place where Faulkner's writing found its source, where it chose to ignore preestablished rules (whose rigidness is featured here through the semantics of fixedness) and to instead follow only those of its own making (the clock, like the one Dilsey hears, is set to a singular time beyond time). The effects of the rain shower echo how Faulkner's writing abandoned widely accepted constraints to give free rein to the "illogical" and "unplumbable." Comparing this effect of rupture with the anarchical violence of an angry child also conjures the memory of Benjy's unfathomable yelling. The burdensome thought patterns that hinder the flow of time are opposed by the abrupt and unpredictable nature of a cool rain shower, of a fresh new writing; the novelty and rupture respond to the suffocation of experienced things. As suggested by André Bleikasten, "*The Sound and the Fury* marks Faulkner's decisive encounter with Literature, his final entry into its infinite text, a space in which novels are endlessly born out of novels. With *Flags in the Dust* he had discovered that his experience as a southerner could be used for literary purposes; with *The Sound and The Fury* he came to realize that, far from being the mere expression or reflection of prior experience, writing could be in itself an experience in the fullest sense" (Bleikasten, 2016 [1990]: 42). This constant temptation to return to his fetish novel reflects Faulkner's recognition that occupying the consciousness of an idiot was a stroke of genius; it also expresses his desire to summon the fury of the very beginning and extend it indefinitely, be it to evoke a summer rain.

Chapter 12

THE AESTHETICS OF IDIOCY

Writing and Aphasia

> The language of the novel can perform its function only through lies, and paradoxically that is the only function it can accomplish in truth.
> —LOUIS-RENÉ DES FORÊTS, *VOIES ET DÉTOURS DE LA FICTION*

TO SAY OR NOT TO SAY: FIGURES OF FAILURE

Benjy Compson's discourse presents multiple paradoxes. It is first a discourse narrated by a narrator deprived of speech. An aphasic tale springing from the destitution of an idiot mind, it nevertheless dramatizes numerous discourses. The narration in the past tense of the day of April 7, 1928, whose anchoring in the novel's present is revealed through multiple allusions to the events that will serve as a framework for Jason's monologue,[1] are quite often replaced by words related in direct speech, which reflect fragments of conversations perceived and recorded by the idiot in a more or less distant past. The importance of the speech of others in Benjy's monologue is present in the typography of his tale via the extremely frequent presence of new lines (followed by indentations), which usually signal changes in speaker. Visually, the tale is spaced out, in contrast to the density of Quentin's monologue, a harbinger of the disconcerting compactness of *Absalom, Absalom!* The many blank spaces in the text materialize the inevitable gaps of an idiot tale and symbolize the chaotic jolts and starts of the idiot's perception, which does not proceed from any temporal distinction and freely assembles the most disparate objects and events. The omnipresence of direct speech—in which Benjy, who does not speak, never directly participates—makes way on a few rare occasions for more elaborate discursive forms, which can only surprise the reader, who has grown accustomed to the regular rhythm of his discourse and to the alternation of his singular language of the senses with the speech of others. Indirect speech makes a brief appearance in the jumbled evocation of Damuddy's wake and Caddy's wedding. These two episodes from the Compson family history are without a doubt the two central events in Benjy's monologue: "'They haven't started yet.' Caddy said. *They getting ready to start, T. P. said*" (SF: 38). Here it is a word, or more precisely the phonetic realization of a word, which initiates the shift between two different temporal strata. Perched in the tree, Caddy comments on what she sees inside the house: the "party" from which the children think they have been excluded has not started. The acoustic form *started* triggers the memory of another occurrence of the verb *to start*, namely T. P. commenting on the start of the wedding ceremony. The two scenes present other similarities in addition to the repetition of the same verb,[2] which explains the parallel between them: Caddy and T. P. are both peeping in on an event from which they have been excluded. Moreover, the two scenes are built on a logic of inversion that reveals the proximity of a feeling of loss: if death is evoked as a party awaiting an orchestra, the wedding celebration is implicitly evoked as a bereavement. The use of free indirect speech is even more surprising:

> Versh closed the door black. I could smell Versh and feel him. You all be quiet, now. We're not going up stairs yet. Mr Jason said for you to come right up stairs. He said to mind me. I'm not going to mind you. But he said for all of us to. Didn't he, Quentin. I could feel Versh's head. I could hear us. Didn't he, Versh. Yes, that right. Then I say for us to go out doors a while. Come on. Versh opened the door and we went out. (SF: 27)

The source of the utterance, the voices that are in dialogue, seem familiar to Benjy, but their identification is made difficult by the darkness and its corollary, the joint disappearance of vision and the visible world. This is why, contrary to what ordinarily occurs when words are reported, the snatches from the little conference in the dark are transcribed in a continuous flow without being attributed to their speaker.[3] Tactile and olfactory impressions are heightened to compensate for the disappearance of visual perceptions. Finally, Benjy's discourse resumes its usual mode of operation when Versh opens the door, revealing the light of the evening and the world. The idiot's desire to "say" and its repeated failures thus appear in contradictory fashion, in the coexistence of different types of more or less complex discourses. Benjy's aphasia is revealed through multiple syntactical forms and is characterized by a singular use of the verb "to say."

In Benjy's discourse, the verb "to say" is used in an intransitive and absolute manner: it remains without an object.[4] The desire to say as a theme is initiated by Caddy in her first appearance in the novel, in the first scene where Benjy clings to the fence waiting for her to come home from school: "What is it.

What are you trying to tell Caddy" (6); "'What is it.' Caddy said. 'What are you trying to tell Caddy'" (7). Moved by the generosity of her feelings, Caddy is the only one who considers Benjy dignified enough to utter speech. While everyone sees him as either an indefinable thing—as something hopeless and shameful, "Your mamma too proud for you" (70)—or as an animal that must be isolated and even confined—"'You, Benjamin.' Mother said. 'If you don't be good you'll have to go to the kitchen'" (5)—Caddy is the only one who asserts that Benjy belongs to the human race. Because speech represents the dividing line between animals and humans, Caddy patiently and vainly tries to act the midwife in giving the idiot access to the act of saying. Tirelessly trotting out the same injunctions (the verbs *to try* and *to tell* are inseparably linked), she tries to understand Benjy, to explain his reactions and (re)establish their meaning: "'What is it, Benjy.' Caddy said. 'Tell Caddy. She'll do it. Try'" (41). Yet faced with Benjy's inability to formulate the least utterance, she often responds hypothetically to her own questions: "I couldn't smell trees anymore. [. . .] 'What is it, Benjy.' Caddy said. 'Is it this hat'" (40). By dint of sheer effort (she is indeed the one "trying to say"), she succeeds in explaining Benjy's confusion: "'Oh.' she said. She put the bottle down and came and put her arms around me. 'So that was it. And you were trying to tell Caddy and you couldn't tell her. You wanted to, but you couldn't, could you. Of course Caddy wont. Of course Caddy wont'" (42). Everything is explained by "the bottle" of perfume that dramatizes her increasing eroticization, and the disappearance of her innocent smell of trees. Benjy is, so to speak, the guarantor of Caddy's purity.

Despite appearances, their relation is not unambiguous; Caddy is not entirely selfless, as she has as much to gain from Benjy's presence as he does from hers. In moving too far away from him, she will lose almost everything she had—brothers, parents, a home, and later a husband and a child. Few critics have noted that Benjy is a mirror of sorts constantly directed at Caddy, and how Caddy is sensitive to this reflection that shows her most imperceptible changes, and sees him as the person in charge of her morality. When, after erring, she swears, promises, and makes resolutions ("Tell Caddy. She'll do it"; "Of course Caddy wont"), she speaks more to herself and her own bad conscience than to Benjy, who after all has not asked her for anything. Her sacrifices—she offers her bottle of perfume to Dilsey and asks Charlie to go away to please Benjy[5]—can be read as aborted attempts to correct her own image, to rediscover her original purity and thereby regain her brother's trust. But this does not account for her strong desire, which will never stop corrupting her promises. The complexity of Caddy's attitude toward Benjy can also be seen in how she infantilizes him, how she idiot*izes* him under cover of a discourse pretending to see his worth: "You're not a poor baby. Are you. Are you. You've got your

Caddy. Haven't you got your Caddy" (9). When she addresses Benjy, Caddy is speaking of herself in the third person and reduces her own person to the status of an object (*your Caddy*), foreshadowing the replacements Benjy comes up with to remedy her absence. Her reassuring little chant is the reverse side of a threat: Caddy simultaneously makes herself indispensable and condemns her brothers' world to reel, as they no longer have "their Caddy" to comfort them or crystallize their desires and frustrations. However attentive and protective she may be, Caddy is the source of deceptive illusions[6]—she generates mirages. It is no coincidence that she should be the source of fiction: "[I]n *The Sound and the Fury* I had already put perhaps the only thing in literature which would ever move me very much: Caddy climbing the pear tree to look in the window at her grandmother's funeral" ("Intro *SF*, I": 227). Weighed down by the conflicts driving her, Caddy can be seen as Faulkner's fictional double, as she imitates within the novel—albeit with less success—the author's intention when he chose to attribute a discourse to the idiot. Caddy and Faulkner are the only ones who believe that Benjy has something to say that is worthy of being heard. Benjy's wanting to say is inseparably associated with Caddy, with the source of emotion and the deceptive powers of the imagination.

After Caddy's departure, Benjy's intention to say remains hanging, as it were, on the fence, which has not moved. By staying posted at the place and time when Caddy usually appeared in his field of vision, Benjy assumes that he will eventually see her again. In a certain way, and regardless of what T. P. may believe,[7] this imitative magic trick works:

> I went down to the gate, where the girls passed with their booksatchels. They looked at me, walking fast, with their heads turned. I tried to say, but they went on, and I went along the fence, trying to say, and they went faster. Then they were running and I came to the corner of the fence and I couldn't go any further, and I held to the fence, looking after them and trying to say. (*SF*: 52)

When the little girls coming home from school appear, taking the same route as his sister a few years earlier, his desire to say resurfaces. This scene is a repetition with variation of the initial scene of Caddy's return from school. The number of girls has increased, as the single Caddy has been replaced by the plural "the girls," and Caddy's joy in the earlier episode makes way for the malicious and suspicious curiosity of the schoolgirls. Benjy, who is impervious to these changes and sees the little girls as avatars of his lost sister, persists in "trying to say" (the expression is repeated three times); the more he tries, the more frightful he seems. This scene is repeated a third time during the assault of the little Burgess girl when the fence is inadvertently left open one day: "I was trying to say, and I caught her, trying to say, and she screamed and I was trying to say" (53). However, this supposed aggression is only suggested by the proximity of the syntagms "I caught her" and "she screamed"; nothing indicates that Benjy hurt or sought to hurt the little girl. Seeing him as a lecher because he came a little too close to her is tantamount to approving the public's condemnation, and justifies the legitimacy of the mutilation he suffers as punishment for his supposedly doubtful intentions. Why not imagine that the idiot was not once again simply trying to say the thing that is condemned to remain unsaid? In the narrative present, it is the golfers who ultimately complete the dynamic of waiting: "How can I make them come over here, if they aint coming. Wait. They'll be some in a minute. Look yonder. Here they come" (51); "*Here some come*" (53). Thus Benjy, who is castrated for accosting a little girl reminding him of his sister and engaging in an unusual conversation with her, finds himself reduced to contemplating the golfers who spend a good deal of their time looking for balls on the other side of the fence.[8]

The twin themes of trying to say and the failure to say are rooted in idiocy as well as in the dynamic that undergirds any intention to write. It is repeated on numerous occasions and in various forms in "Monk," for instance in the characterization of the eponymous idiot: "he tried to make his speech, trying to tell them something of which they could make neither head nor tail and to which they refused to listen" ("Monk": 40). Like Benjy, Monk is severely aphasic, and at first glance his discourse seems as senseless as Benjy's monologue; because it is disturbing and does not develop in the right way, some "refused to listen," and therefore to understand. Yet unlike Benjy, while he does not fulfill his desire to say, Monk nevertheless succeeds in releasing it in a flow of words, however unintelligible they may be: "He just kept on trying to say whatever it was that had been inside him for twenty-five years and that he had only now found the chance (or perhaps the words) to free himself of" (44). However, what is striking in these two quotations is that the object of his desire to say and the object of Monk's discourse are just as vague as they are in Benjy's case: the intransitive use of the verb *to tell* has simply given way to radically indeterminate objects ("something," "whatever"). But the question of the idiot's intentions is not at all elucidated. On the other hand, a desire for discourse—one that fears remaining unfulfilled—determines the narrator's reflexive comments at the opening of the short story. "Monk" is a story in the first person, narrated by Charles Mallison; it is based on an investigation led by his uncle, Gavin Stevens: "He told my uncle" (45); "nobody except my Uncle Gavin seemed to be concerned about Monk" (46). The community's indifference toward Monk is counterbalanced by the interest shown by Chick, who wants to establish the only written account of the idiot's life by correcting the inaccurate gossip and accounts from his trials:

> I will have to try to tell about Monk. I mean, actually try—a deliberate attempt to bridge the inconsistencies in his brief and sordid and unoriginal history, to make something out of it, not only with the nebulous tools of supposition and inference and invention, but to employ these nebulous tools upon the nebulous and inexplicable material which he left behind him. Because it is only in literature that the paradoxical and even mutually negativing anecdotes in the history of a human heart can be juxtaposed and annealed by art into verisimilitude and credibility. ("Monk": 39)

For Chick, the expression of a duty to remember is combined with a moral duty to alleviate the community's failures toward its feebleminded members. However, upon closer inspection, this opening to the story, which from the outset advances the formula that characterizes Benjy's idiocy and resonates in Monk's idiocy ("I will have to try to tell," "I mean, actually try," etc.), proves highly unusual. Its great solemnity, which does not reflect the best of Faulkner's writing, strangely brings to mind the emphasis of some of Faulkner's speeches on his art,[9] especially the one he delivered in Stockholm on December 10, 1950, when he was awarded the Nobel Prize in Literature. Speaking on this occasion to the writer who will one day take his place, Faulkner offers some advice:

> He must teach himself that the basest of all things is to be afraid; and, teaching himself that, forget it forever, leaving no room in his workshop, for anything but the old verities and truths of the heart, the old universal truths lacking which any story is ephemeral and doomed—love and honor and pity and pride and compassion and sacrifice. (*PF*: 723–24)

These two speeches, by Chick the Faulknerian narrator and by Faulkner the writer at the peak of his glory, reveal the central issues and intentions of narration (the first focuses on the notion of "history," the second speaks of "literature" in general). The desire to say thus gains access to the object that idiocy stubbornly keeps for itself. For Faulkner, a story is an account of hidden truths, and both of these speeches recognize that they are truths "of the heart." In other words, stories assert the great values (and Faulkner did not tire of repeating the list) stifled by "fear." Chick's preliminary remarks are less abstract about how to detect and "try to say [them]." His discourse is built on the notion that only literature—with the help of "nebulous tools" ("supposition," "inference," "invention")—can give tangible form and coherence to the fundamentally "ephemeral," "sordid," and "nondescript" nature of life. Only literature can transcend the paradoxes and contradictions "of the heart" and confer upon them the "verisimilitude" and "credibility" that life has denied them. There, it has been said; but fortunately not everything has been said. After these metafictional interludes, the story continues, and gains the upper hand. In doing so, it suggests that things go far beyond this long list of moral prerogatives—that they are opaque, hidden, and sometimes contradictory. Faulkner the writer who "tries to say" is, of course, infinitely more endearing than the one who has found something to say and explains what he is doing. To echo a remark made by Louis-René des Forêts in *Voies et détours de la fiction* (The Paths and Detours of Fiction), the chaotic search of the creative process is incomparably richer than statements of objects found and methods deployed: "Often we do not know what we are looking for, and the purpose of our search we see only vaguely, in the sudden appearance of a sunny spell" (Des Forêts, 1985 [1962]: 16). This fundamental paradox of writers—who are perhaps the most poorly placed individuals to speak about their own language—was identified by Virginia Woolf in "An Introduction to *Mrs Dalloway*" (1928): "It is difficult—perhaps impossible—for a writer to say anything about his own work. All he has to say has been said as fully and as well as he can in the body of the book itself. If he has failed to make his meaning clear there it is scarcely likely that he will succeed in some pages of preface or postscript" (Woolf, 1994: 548). Why try to transcribe into the language of the world what is said in the unique language of the work?

The difficulty and even impossibility of a self-critical discourse is especially pronounced with Faulkner, whose reflexive remarks are often contaminated by the theme of trying, of attempting, and whose semantics contain the specter of failure. Trying entails the risk of not succeeding, of not achieving one's ends; it reveals one's desire by acknowledging the risk that it may not be fulfilled. In rereading the interviews and addresses collected in *Faulkner in the University*, I identified over fifty pages that contain the expression *try[ing] to* (with sometimes up to five occurrences on a single page). The verbs that are most often associated with it are essentially variants of *to tell*, and refer to the quest of the creative process: *to say, to write, to paint, to describe, to find, to get*—in a word, *to do*. More rarely, the expression "try to" is combined with verbs that betray an intention of edification and refer to the finality of the work rather than its means: *to teach, to explain, to change,* and finally *to cope*. With Faulkner, the expression *try[ing] to* can therefore be considered a verbal tic. Rooted in the aphasia of idiots, it ultimately contaminates the novelist's discourse: its repetition sends his efforts to explain his project juddering to a halt. The notion of an aborted attempt recurs each time Faulkner commented on the conditions in which he wrote *The Sound and the Fury*, and the impact of these conditions on the novel's structure:

> I wrote the Benjy part first. That wasn't good enough so I wrote the Quentin part. That still wasn't good enough. I let Jason try it. That still wasn't enough. I let Faulkner try it and that still wasn't enough, and so about twenty years afterward I wrote an appendix still trying to make that book what—match the dream. [...] You try and you try and you try to do the best you can to make something which to you was passionate and moving, so passionate and moving that it wouldn't let you alone you had to write it. (*FU*: 84–85)

If we omit the abstraction of certain nouns, one could say that through the extreme paucity of their syntactical structures, continual repetition, and chaotic movement, these lines bring to mind Benjy's discourse. The verb *to try* assumes a status that is as absolute as the verb *to tell* is for Benjy. It nevertheless helps define the creative process in a much more illuminating way than the pompous dramatizations of the act of writing mentioned above. Writing involves trying and persevering in one's dogged attempt to conjure the "dream[ed]" and "passionate" forms that ceaselessly haunt the writer. The genius of *The Sound and the Fury* resides in the permanence of this doggedness—its success is the result of its own failures. Through the multifaceted, contradictory, and fleeting figure of Caddy; through its structure in four parts, each of which successively tries to remedy the preceding one's failure; and through the ubiquity of this fragment of a motto ("trying to"), which signals the desire to say and transforms into an incantatory formula for the desire to write, *The Sound and the Fury* metaphorically embodies the "elusive object"[10] obsessing the writer, as suggested by des Forêts:

> Threatened by both his success and his failure, every writer is in a permanent state of insecurity. As we have seen, one must seemingly say only one thing and nothing else, but are we ever assured of being able to say it? What's more, it may also seem to us that what we are saying is not what is most necessary to say, or that it could be said with fewer words. (Des Forêts, 1985 [1962]: 16)

THE IDIOT'S INTERIOR MONOLOGUE

The idiocy of Benjy Compson emerged at the same time as it engendered a highly original discursive mode in the body of American literature, the interior monologue. This mode allowed Faulkner to stage the idiot's aphasia and to simultaneously surpass it. His use of the interior monologue was of course in keeping with canonical texts, but he also blazed extreme paths that sketched out a definition for the genre.

As opposed to the monologue in traditional theater, which involves a scene in which characters speak to themselves or think out loud, the interior monologue unfolds in the silence of the character's psychological processes. The silent voice of the character-narrator, which is generally conveyed in the first person, represents the voice of the character's "interiority" and can therefore only be heard when sought out by the act of reading. In *Ulysses* (1922), James Joyce explores and exploits the initial potential of this discursive mode, which tries to retrace the flow of thought as it takes shape, both consciously and unconsciously;[11] through erratic and disorganized forms that transcribe the chaotic succession of permanently evolving psychological states, it creates the illusion of an internal verbal outpouring. It was also Joyce who ensured the belated posterity of Édouard Dujardin's 1887 novel *Les Lauriers sont coupés* (*We'll to the Woods No More*),[12] which first used the interior monologue as an exclusive and coherent narrative strategy, one that radically broke with the traditional requirements of fiction. As the story's only center of perception, Daniel Prince is an absolutely subjective character-narrator: the world exists only when he perceives it. The interior monologue presents itself as a raw text that accumulates various objects by retracing the heterogeneous perceptions through which they are grasped. Here is the opening to chapter 2 of Dujardin's novel: "Red and gold, a glare of light, the café; a white-aproned waiter; pillars hung with hats and overcoats. Anyone here I know? Those people are watching me come in" (Dujardin, 1990 [1938]: 20). In its fragmentary style and nominal syntax, the text continually adds various observations. The location (the Café Oriental) is identified through sensations of color and light; then, once the observer is in the crowd, there comes a brief reflection on the gaze of others and one's self image. A text in the making, the interior monologue relies on the illusion of its incompletion. The method it is based on seems paradoxical at first sight: rupture, disorder, and confusion (fleeting visual impressions are combined with class consciousness) go hand in hand with the continual ebb and flow of sensations through juxtaposed fragments. In the primary texts that feature the interior monologue as the framework of the story—whether it is divided among multiple character-narrators or not—the continuity of the stream of consciousness (and unconsciousness) is reinforced by the story's duration, which often spans a very short period of time. *Les Lauriers sont coupés*, *Ulysses*, Virginia Woolf's *Mrs Dalloway* (1925),[13] and each of the monologues in *The Sound and the Fury* are, strictly speaking, the accounts of a single day.[14] Focusing on "interior" life, the interior monologue gives little importance to action and plot: it is driven by details, the little nothings of life, which are paradoxically presented with meticulous care. In any event, the story is engendered by the context of utterance, which, as Coralie Vauchelles has observed with regard to Dostoevsky's "A Gentle Creature," "never leaves the field of the text, even when it is in the past. The speech act unfolds without narrative mediation, within the here and now summoned by the beginning of the short story, and in the only appropriate form for an opening in an interior monologue, which is to say *in medias res*" (Vauchelles, 2004: 31). Despite the back-and-forth between times, during which it mentions the first letters exchanged and the first disappointments with Leah (a minor actress at the Théâtre des Nouveautés), Daniel Prince's monologue remains focused on his rendezvous. His impatience and difficulty to anticipate how it will unfold are the story's only central themes. The first perplexing sentiment that accompanies the reader's entry within the here and now of an interior monologue comes from the absence of reference points shedding light on the mode of utterance or on the nature of the situation in which the focal narrator-character appears rooted for eternity. It is up to readers to free themselves from the demands and expectations of a distantiated and panoramic story; to renounce their familiar world in order to slip into the interiority of a character, and accept seeing and perceiving only what the latter sees and perceives. It is up to readers to move beyond the text's apparent opacity and the disbelief of their first impressions, in order for this internal voice to find an audience within them. Dujardin remarked that his novel should "be acted, which is to say MENTALLY acted by the reader" (Dujardin, 2001 [1887]: 132). The discomfort prompted by the interior monologue stems not only from the fact that it is an intrusion upon an intimacy, but that it also engages the reader's person by disrupting the way in which they see for them to become the actors of an interiority alien to their own. In *Les Lauriers sont coupés*, the narrator is pleased that his love for Leah is platonic, just as his desire emerges for the evening to take on an advantageous turn: "Must dress now; but what's the use of changing? I shan't be able to stay on at Leah's; I shall have to come back here. Still, after all, one never knows the turn things will take; anything might happen, some lucky coincidence" (Dujardin, 2001 [1887]: 52). In fragmentary syntax, the duty dictated by the rules of decorum is confronted with the contingent power of instincts. By placing the focal character's passing impressions on the same level as the values dictated to him by his sense of morality, as well as his most ferociously suppressed desires, and by allowing them to pour forth in the same flood of language, the interior monologue sheds light on the conflicts and contradictions induced by the mechanisms of thought. This is noted by Joseph Danan in his *Le Théâtre de la pensée* (The Theater of Thought), who ventures to define the "truth" of the interior monologue while mentioning Dujardin:

> It belonged [...] to Dujardin to invent this elliptical writing that decomposes reality according to the order of perceptions: the text's discontinuity and division into "shots," which lead the reader along with their fluidity in an uninterrupted movement forward, help make *Les Lauriers sont coupés* the longest tracking shot in the history of literature. Moreover, there are no stops in the novel's unfolding. [...] What is important is first the "truth" of this perception of the external world, offered when it is *à peine* [barely] formulated in words—and everything resides in this à peine, which is rendered by brief notations, the rhythm, and noun clauses, as though halfway between the image and sensations on the one hand, and the words in which consciousness readies to translate them on the other. (Danan, 1995: 47–48)

The information that flows in the interior monologue is not organized in any kind of hierarchy. In its imitation of psychological mechanisms, interior monologue claims to abolish the principles of sorting and selection; it establishes the supremacy of the trivial alongside the noblest of thoughts. For example, Daniel Prince's great love sits side by side with his inspection of the cleanliness of his shirt collars: "[T]he novel that wants to express the life of the soul will incessantly sway between poetic exaltation and plain, vulgar everyday life" (Dujardin, 2001 [1887]: 126). We see the emergence of a literature consisting of apparently insignificant individuals (idiots or housewives are given the rank of perceptive and narrative centers) and previously neglected trivialities (the combustion of a piece of paper in a chimney, or the death of a moth against a windowpane, become literary objects in their own right). In "Modern Novels" (1919), Virginia Woolf defines the prerogatives of the modern novelist in terms that, without mentioning them directly, bring to mind the methods of the interior monologue:

> The mind, exposed to the ordinary course of life, receives upon its surface a myriad impressions—trivial, fantastic, evanescent, or engraved with the sharpness of steel. From all sides they come, an incessant shower of innumerable atoms, composing in their sum what we might venture to call life itself; and to figure further as the semi-transparent envelope, or luminous halo, surrounding us from the beginning of consciousness to the end. Is it not perhaps the chief task of the novelist to convey this incessantly varying spirit with whatever stress or sudden

deviation it may display, and as little admixture of the alien and external as possible? (Woolf, 1988: 33)

According to Woolf, the modern novelist's "chief task" is to grasp the atomic nature of life, which consists, at its most everyday and banal, of a profusion of infinitesimal objects. It sets out to present the continuity and permanence of impressions that appear chaotically and suddenly in its perceptual field, without distinguishing between fleeting and lasting impressions, and by blocking out any external interference. The modern novel's primary object is therefore present in the incessant swarm of ever-changing impressions that form around the novelist's "mind" like a "luminous halo." It is in this hazy area that impressions generate life, and it is this life that makes up the novel's material.

The "truth" of the interior monologue subsequently resides in its indiscriminate acceptance of all forms of perception, regardless of their nature, intensity, or importance. However, the interior monologue's naïve sincerity, running counter to the hypocrisy of social relations, is paradoxically a wholly artificial construct. The central artifice of the interior monologue involves the approximation (Danan's *à peine*) of a language that chaotically emerges as the psyche is engaged by the world's external objects. It uses trial and error and a voluntarily rickety syntax to sketch out a process that is being completed. It entails fixing, within the permanence of a text (however dismantled and disfigured it may be), the perpetual, conflictual, and even cyclothymic appearance of perception on "the mind's surface." The interior monologue seeks to represent how states of perception reveal themselves before they are put in words and organized within a reasoned discourse. However, as these forms necessarily consist of words, the authors who use the interior monologue are aware of this paradox and therefore generally choose to use language chaotically. In their attempt to imitate the inner perceptual flow—verbalizing the nonverbal and putting the jumble of perceptions into words—they often choose to warp language in order to create the illusion of a preverbal discourse that escapes the organization of the senses via reason. They shred usual syntax, sometimes reducing it to fragmented segments (Benjy Compson's monologue) and sometimes dissolving it into interminable blocks of words (Molly Bloom's monologue at the end of *Ulysses*), in which ordinary sensations and unwelcome impressions are intertwined and are in no way controlled by an overarching plan or curbed by any form of censorship.

By using the interior monologue, Faulkner placed himself within the tradition of the major modernist novels published on the other side of the Atlantic. The composition of *The Sound and the Fury* marked his beginning in this regard.[15] However, Faulkner's perspective when he set out to write his first interior monologue was markedly different from the Joycean project. The primary distinction lies in the referential system in which the monologues in question are situated. Unlike Joyce, who for the monolith of *Ulysses* assembled a multitude of "protean" cultural references both popular and erudite,[16] Faulkner opens *The Sound and the Fury* with the firm stance of a total lack of culture. Where Joyce combines all aspects of his erudition, Faulkner renounces the wide reading that put him on the path of literature; of course, he returns to it in Quentin Compson's internal monologue, but for a time, for the time it took him to begin his novel, he chose to be an idiot. By inhabiting the most unsophisticated psyche possible, he pushes the limits of the interior monologue even further than his predecessors. The exemplary nature of Benjy's Compson monologue has prompted many critics to see Faulkner's text as an extension of those by Joyce and Woolf. However, Benjy Compson's monologue calls for a more precise reflection. It is not simply a masterpiece of the genre; it is a singular internal monologue whose uniqueness brings to mind another experimental text, Natsume Sōseki's *I Am a Cat* (1905). The novel is a first-person narrative whose exclusive narrator is, as the title suggests, a cat who observes, recounts, and comments on the acts and gestures of his owner (a teacher), and the students and colleagues who visit him daily. Throughout the story, the cat never gets over his initial surprise upon discovering humans: "[T]his must have been the very first time that ever I set eyes on a human being. The impression of oddity, which I then received, still remains today" (Sōseki, 2002: 3). Over the course of the seasons, this cat, who can express himself in perfectly clear language (notably combining academic jargon and slang from the suburbs of Edo), presents what he feels, hears, and sees without ever leaving the tiny area marked out by his owner's house and its immediate surroundings, where he attends to his occupations as a cat. His narrative point of view includes a complex combination of both naïve objectiveness (not belonging to the world of humans, the cat describes their behavior with distance, without ever passing judgment) and conjectures about communication between animals (the cat has very pragmatic conversations with Kuro, a neighborhood cat given to boasting about the number of mice he catches). A quirky vision of Meiji-era Japan emerges from the discrepancy between the animal nature (and its requisite ignorance) of the center of perception and the knowledge of certain dialogues confronting the teacher and his students. *I Am a Cat* nevertheless remains very traditional despite its highly original point of view and cannot strictly speaking be considered an interior monologue. Still, it is similar to the monologue of Faulkner's idiot in the sense that both narratives are built on an impossible discourse articulating sensible perceptions and mental images that are all the less verbal for being in the head of a cat and the consciousness of a mute idiot. In both cases, the first-person narrator is a being deprived of speech. For all that, Sōseki does not meet the challenge of inventing a feline language. He has his cat arbitrarily speak like a human, although like Benjy the cat does not speak in the proper sense of the word (except to other individuals of his kind); he simply recounts the tribulations of his owner without understanding them, taking full advantage of the naïve surprise and astonishment of his unprecedented point of view.[17] Faulkner, however, does not simply attribute language to the idiot—he invents an idiot language. In doing so, he places himself at the intersection of two structural impossibilities. On the one hand, in keeping with Dujardin and later Joyce, he gives words and voice to a silent process, creating a discourse from a multitude of sensible elements that precisely escape discourse. On the other, in keeping with Sōseki, he produces an impossible discourse whose function is not simply to compensate for the idiot's mutism and congenital inability to pronounce intelligible speech, but also—and this is where he differs from his predecessor—to provide an account of the highly particular perception that is (or could be) that of an idiot. As such, the idiot's internal monologue is a dual aberration, for it embodies an unparalleled singularity and solitude.

Most interior monologues seem to pursue a kind of silent dialogue with the world despite their monological structure and anchoring in an individual's interiority. In his analysis of two narratives by Arthur Schnitzler, Philippe Chardin points out the incongruity of the notion of an inner self:

> What therefore triumphs, in what is supposed to be the fortress of *pensée propre* [particular thought], are the *common*places of an inculcated code; interior monologues of this type [*Lieutenant Gustel* and *Fräulein Else*] clearly reveal that the supposed inner self can paradoxically harbor, in many cases, the most naively and tragically socialized thought possible. (Chardin, 2004: 12)

As demonstrated by the excerpt from *Les Lauriers sont coupés* cited above in which the narrator corrects himself in order to avoid breaking the rules of propriety, the speech does not escape its social dimension; or, to echo Mikhail Bakhtin's terminology, the monologue is paradoxically dialogic:

> Every conversation is full of transmissions and interpretations of other people's words. At every step one meets a "quotation" or a "reference" to something that a particular person said, a reference to "people say" or "everyone says," to the words of the person one is talking with, or to one's own previous words, to a newspaper, an official decree, a document, a book and so forth. [. . .] [I]n the everyday speech of any person living in society, no less than half (on the average) of all the words

uttered by him will be someone else's words (consciously someone else's), transmitted with varying degrees of precision and impartiality (or more precisely, partiality). (Bakhtin, 1981: 338)

The two sections of *The Sound and the Fury* that directly follow Benjy's interior monologue are no exception to the law of dialogism, which simultaneously determines both "practical language"[18] and the language of fictional characters in a novel. Similarly, the successive monologues in *Absalom, Absalom!* can be seen as long, interrupted dialogues in which the character-narrator finds a privileged albeit imaginary interlocutor in another character (Miss Rosa Coldfield addresses Quentin, Quentin addresses Shreve, etc.). In their respective monologues, Quentin and Jason Compson continue to discourse with the world and observe its laws and principles, if only to be more indignant about them. They both have a preferred interlocutor, the father for Quentin and the mother for Jason. The father and mother are the respective and fantasized recipients of monologues built around their obsessive presence. Quentin meticulously prepares his suicide while being haunted by his father's maxims.[19] Jason justifies diverting the money Caddy sends to her daughter by evoking Mrs. Compson's failures as a mother, pretending to protect her all the better to abuse her. As contradictory as it may seem at first glance, most major monological texts include dialogical elements, if only due to the frequency of the words related, both directly and indirectly. This is also true of Benjy Compson's interior monologue, which continually and automatically repeats snatches of conversations caught in the continuum of heterogeneous perceptions:

> The bowl steamed up to my face, and Versh's hand dipped the spoon in it and the steam tickled into my mouth.
> "I dont want any more." Quentin said. "How can they have a party when Damuddy's sick."
> "They'll have it down stairs." Caddy said. "She can come to the landing and see it. That's what I'm going to do when I get my nightie on." (*SF*: 26)

Quite unlike his brothers, Daniel Prince, or Stephen Dedalus, when Benjy relates the speech of others, he does not know what he is saying or what it means. For him, other people's speech is just one sensory element among others: it is sound, a noise stripped of signification, emerging from the steam that rises from his dinner plate and "tickles" his senses. The absence of discrimination between the perception of speech and the solicitation of other senses is marked by the neutral syntax of Benjy's monologue, which provides no information regarding voice inflections; the emotions conveyed by questions and exclamations are expurgated from the text. Nothing is accentuated in Benjy's discourse: all of the information is strung out on the same plane and is of the same importance. The idiot is incapable of orchestrating the speech of others within the flow of his own perceptions; he can only note the alternation of sound and silence. It is impossible for him to inhabit the speech of others, to use and interpret it.[20] As a result, in Benjy's interior monologue, speech is deprived of a social dimension. Reduced to a succession of sound elements, it is flattened and neutralized, and thereby stripped of its pathetic dimension. In the idiot's interior monologue, speech is no more than one of the world's objects, with fury taking atonal form amid the confusion of sound. In reference to Bakhtin, whose typology of literary genres distinguishes the novel from poetry based on the constitutive dialogization of the language, the idiot's alienation from the world and its dialogues lends his internal monologue a uniquely "poetic" dimension:

> In genres that are poetic in the narrow sense, the natural dialogization of the word is not put to artistic use, the word is sufficient unto itself and does not presume alien utterances beyond its boundaries. Poetic style is by convention suspended from any mutual interaction with alien discourse, and allusion to alien discourse. (Bakhtin, 1981: 279)

In Benjy's interior monologue, the "discourse's natural dialogization" makes way for a singular language that diverts the speech of others from its chiefly communicative function. It is a monologue in the strictest sense of the term, for no considerations external to the continual perceptions assailing the idiot's psyche are taken into account. The idiot's interior monologue, its specific and unique poetry, derives from disappearance of the referential system shared by all speaking humans. For Benjy, the abstract systems that form the political, social, and cultural worlds—as well as the world of exchanges—simply do not exist. His idiot world is exclusively anchored in the density of things, in which language is reduced to its status as a thing; it takes on a dense materiality that is reminiscent of its use in poetry, which carves language up into little nuggets of words and bursts of sound. Like poetry, Benjy's interior monologue frees itself from the central requirement of meaning. Signifieds decamp amid the melody of signifiers; they can be recaptured only after a laborious hermeneutic quest, whose outcome is, from the very outset, condemned to approximation and incompleteness. Like a poem, Benjy's monologue is stripped of direct and communicable information, but if we play its game, its opacity opens onto a multitude of meanings.[21] It is an "abolished bauble, sonorous inanity" (Mallarmé, 2006: 69); it melts into a language of small objects, which abolishes the common meaning but gives rise to an interior music that cannot be forced into signification. Here we are once again approaching the monologue in *Macbeth* that gave *The Sound and the Fury* its title, and bears repeating here:

> Life's but a walking shadow, a poor player
> That struts and frets his hour upon the stage,
> And then is heard no more: it is a tale
> Told by an idiot, full of sound and fury,
> Signifying nothing. (*Macbeth* 5.5.24–28)

The interior monologue sets out to provide an account of the trivial, ephemeral, and incoherent nature of the perceptions that precariously anchor humans within a world where they are simply temporary travelers. It tries to show that the transcendence of meaning is just an illusion, for life, which unfolds in the confusion of instantaneous perceptions, signifies nothing; it is a mirage to believe otherwise. The interior monologue therefore has an awkward relation to a novelistic art that orchestrates reality and places it within a hierarchical structural framework: it opposes the order of a traditional story with the disorder of real life, whose essentially senseless and unmotivated nature is exacerbated by the idiocy of Faulkner's narrator. Still, in denouncing one trick, the interior monologue sets up yet another. This is demonstrated by Benjy's interior monologue, which bears the paradoxical stamp of an organized disorganization, a talkative mutism, a silent fury. The artifice of creating a "psychological voice" is implicitly denounced by Benjy's mutism and imperviousness to language. His unfathomable silence is therefore a symbol for the silence of the consciousness.[22] The silence of idiocy and the silence of consciousness can be broken only artificially, through the production of a singular language that is not echoed by practical language. What Faulkner depicts through the composition of this first interior monologue is precisely the artificiality of the process, and more generally the artificiality that defines literature. Claude Simon asserts this artificiality in his 1986 *Discours de Stockholm*, in response to his detractors who "denounce in [his] works the product of a 'laborious' and therefore 'artificial' effort." He goes on to say that "the dictionary gives the following definition for this word: 'To do artfully,' and 'That which is the product of human activity and not that of nature'" (Simon, 1986: 12). Benjy's interior monologue is exemplary because it implicitly contains a reflection on the dual artifice of language and literature. As paradoxical as its title may seem, *The Sound and the Fury* reflects on the silence that underpins any work of art, on the emptiness that follows reading (and the contemplation of any art object) and the curiosity of the very act of reading, which involves conjuring an intangible world from the silence, and doing so silently. This world does not have its double in the mirror and vanishes as soon as the book object is closed.[23]

This reflection is pursued in the two other parts of the Faulknerian monological triptych, namely *As I Lay Dying*, where no sounds are audible and nothing happens outside of the psyche of the character-narrators, and *Absalom, Absalom!*, the magisterial novel that dramatizes the essential artificiality of all stories, and in which a series of silent voices rise and then stop—"the long silence of notpeople in notlanguage" (*AA*: 5)—constructing a world and a story that are as dark as they are doubtful. Through their "neverending rehashing of words" without words, their solipsistic "mutism" that destroys the possibility of a shared world, and their singular language that simultaneously emerges and threatens to vanish, these three novels—each of which in its own way is perhaps Faulkner's best—can be seen as extensions of the idiot('s) interior monologue, which retrospectively assumes an initiatory dimension. They are located at the point of convergence between silence and literature, which Maurice Blanchot defines in the following manner:

> One can, then, accuse language of having become an interminable resifting of words instead of the silence it wanted to achieve. Or one can complain it has immersed itself in the conventions of literature when what it wanted was to be absorbed into existence. That is true. But this endless resifting of words without content, this continuousness of speech through an immense pillage of words, is precisely the profound nature of a silence that talks even in its dumbness, a silence that is speech empty of words, an echo speaking on and on in the midst of silence. And in the same way literature, a blind vigilance which in its attempt to escape from itself plunges deeper and deeper into its own obsession, is the only rendering of the obsession of existence, if this itself is the very impossibility of emerging from existence, if it is being which is always flung back into being, that which in the bottomless depth is already at the bottom of the abyss, a recourse against which there is no recourse. (Blanchot, 1995: 332)

Seen through the filter of Blanchot, all three of *The Sound and the Fury*, *As I Lay Dying*, and *Absalom, Absalom!* apparently belong to the novelistic genre identified by Louis-René des Forêts (whom Blanchot read avidly), namely ontological novels.[24] Benjy Compson's idiocy constitutes both the prelude and the touchstone for an uninterrupted exploration of being and the conditions for its existence. The idiot's existential silence is succeeded by the madman's obsession for the constitutional void of his being; then there are the insane who exist only in a past that is not theirs.²⁵ In *As I Lay Dying*, silence and emptiness, existential reflection and literature converge in the theme of falling asleep (a recurring topic in major monological texts).²⁶ In the novel's seventeenth monologue, a few pages from Addie's death, Darl sketches out a little theory of the loss experienced by the subject when it falls asleep: "In a strange room you must empty yourself for sleep. And before you are emptied for sleep, what are you. And when you are emptied for sleep, you are not. And when you are filled with sleep, you never were. [. . .] And since sleep is is-not and rain and wind are *was*, it is not" (*AILD*: 80). Lying in a strange bed far from his family home, while his mother lies dying, Darl follows the twists and turns of his thoughts and sensations, which are all the more insistent and insidious since the appeal of the external world has momentarily ceased. Yet in these specific cases, the theme of sleep, which is associated with the need to "empty yourself," takes the unexpected form of a struggle against sleep. The soft, fluid, and incoherent forms in Darl's discourse are replaced by a rigorously logical syntax in which all of the sentences are built on the same model. Anaphoric repetition of the coordinating conjunction *and* is featured in the continual process of accretion characteristic of the interior monologue, and simultaneously introduces a succession of circumstantial complements that help define different states of being. When considered the other way round, Darl's demonstration reflects on the impossible definition of his individual identity. Being is definitively annulled during sleep: this state of nonbeing is expressed through a superlative adverb and a past tense signaling a bygone past ("you never were"), both of which evoke death. In the transitory state between sleeping and waking, when the emptying of the day's being occurs, the invalidity of the subject that—dispossessed of its power to act and react—has ceased to be, is marked by the latency of the present ("you are not"). During the waking state, the affirmation of a state of being makes way for an interrogation ("what are you") that, albeit not accentuated (it is indistinctly grasped in the flow of ratiocination), shows how troubled Darl is through the objectifying interrogative pronoun *what*, which reveals that he does not consider himself to be a subject. The waking state is thus implicitly evoked as the most anxiety-inducing state of being. The "is-not" of past rain or of his mother, whose death he senses, is opposed with the nonbeing of Darl, who is awake but unable to grasp *what* he is. He understands that his only possibility of being is grammatical, hence linguistic: "And so if I am not emptied yet, I am *is*" (81); it notably occurs through the transformation of the verbal copulas *is* and *was* into qualifying adjectives that feature existence or death. For Darl, the only way to complete the proposition "I am" is to affirm his awakened existence: "I am *is*"—I am a thing that is. To make up for his inability to define what he is, and to remedy an uprooting that is all the more disturbing given that the maternal figure is falling into eternal sleep,

Darl's monologues are fraught with objects and with words. It is as though Darl were seeking, at all costs, to fill his essential void through the uninterrupted evocation of perceptions and intuitions, whose emergence is the only proof of his existence. All things considered, Darl indirectly offers reminders that his is a literary and fictional character; he is made up strictly of words, and exists only if these words are extracted (by the writer, and later by the reader) from the inexorable sleep in which they sink.

Through the idiot's interior monologue, Faulkner aligned himself with the rupture and questioning that defined literary modernity. He used the filter of Benjy's psyche to develop an intimate understanding of the central issues and paradoxes of literature—its artificial authenticity (its authentic artificiality), as well as the irreversible silence that precedes, accompanies, and succeeds it. It was also thanks to his idiot narrator that Faulkner mastered his art and defined its idiosyncrasies: the writer's profession of faith took form behind the idiot's monologue. Finally and especially, at a great distance from the precious and stuffy accents of his youthful poetry, Faulkner became, via the intermediary of Benjy's voice—that "voice from elsewhere"[27]—the poet he had given up on being: "I've often thought that I wrote the novels because I found I couldn't write the poetry, that maybe I wanted to be a poet, maybe I think of myself as a poet, and I failed at that, I couldn't write poetry, so I did the next best thing" (*FU*: 4). Benjy's monologue is probably the most poetic text in the Faulknerian corpus.

FAULKNERIAN CIRCUMLOCUTIONS

In Benjy's interior monologue, the failures of practical language, along with the processes of selection and combination on which it is based, are replaced by strategies of circumvention and avoidance that engender a language in which words do not symbolically designate things but describe and evoke how their physical, material, and sensible characteristics affect the subjectivity that perceives them. In the idiot's language, the constitutive match of the linguistic sign between a concept and its acoustic image is often challenged. Benjy nevertheless possesses a certain number of words that appear to function conventionally. He can indeed refer to a certain number of objects directly by associating a signified with the signifier required by usage,[28] for instance *fence*, *flag*, and *balls*, or *cows*, *pigs*, and the *barn*, with these two subgroups demarcating the familiar landscapes inhabited by Benjy. With these signs, the abstract and symbolic function of the signifier is abolished by the almost systematic use of the definite article *the*, or possessive and demonstrative adjectives. Indeterminacy is rare in Benjy's discourse, where most of the objects are already familiar. Here are two examples: "T. P. had lightning bugs in *a* bottle" (*SF*: 32);

"she was lying with the sickness on *a* cloth on her head" (41; emphasis mine). In the first instance, Benjy distinguishes *a* bottle from his bottle (the one he erected as a cemetery); in the second, the indeterminacy of the cloth placed on his mother's forehead (perhaps it is not the same one each time, or having been changed it has perhaps changed color) is cancelled out by the overdeterminacy and repetition of the context ("*the* sickness"). Indefinite articles therefore play a contrasting role in Benjy's discourse, occasionally helping to identify strange elements that have been grafted onto familiar objects. However, the objects designated in this way are always familiar; the first occurrence of a word is always accompanied by a definite adjective. One can therefore say that Benjy's use of articles inverses the rules of common usage.

Yet given his limited lexicon, Benjy is often confronted with situations for which he does not possess the appropriate sign to refer to the thing. On such occasions, the concrete reality of the object or sensation calls on other signs that are similar. It is the proximity or similarity between a signified deprived of a signifier and another signified equipped with a familiar signifier that lead to certain singular expressions. These give rise to coinages, the lexical creations and syntactical inventions that give the idiot's monologue its poetic dimension. For instance, the terms "the flower tree" (*SF*: 3) and "the firedoor" (56) are built on the associations of impressions that grasp the object through its external qualities, but do so without explicitly naming it. The juxtaposition of known signifiers can fill in the gaps of the unknown. In the first example, two general names ("flower" and "tree") refer to a specific object, a particular tree in flower that the reader cannot identify. This tendency, which can be seen as a kind of spontaneous synecdoche, is symptomatic of the phenomenon that Freud called "paraphasia":

> The appropriate word is replaced by another less appropriate but has a certain relation to the right word. [. . .] One also speaks of paraphasia when two intended words are fused into one malformation, such as "*Vutter*" [Fother] for "*Mutter*" [Mother] or "*Vater*" [Father]; by common consent circumlocutions by which a specific noun is replaced by a very general one ("dings," "machine," "chose") or by a verb, have also been regarded as paraphasia. (Freud, 1953: 21–22)

In the end it matters little if the tree is a magnolia or a laurel; what is important is that it is a tree in bloom. The extreme simplicity of the association between tree and flower gives rise to the fresh and vernal odor from which Caddy emerges. In the second example, the door's materiality and function of separation are associated with the immateriality of the fire and Benjy's fascination with it: "the firedoor" metonymically refers to the wood-burning stove that has pride of place in Dilsey's kitchen—it is literally the object that preserves the fire.

In his book chapter "Two Aspects of Language and Two Types of Aphasic Disturbances," Roman Jakobson distinguishes between aphasics who show a deficiency in selection and those who manifest contiguity disorder. Benjy Compson seems to belong to the first category: "The more his utterances are dependent on the context, the better he copes with his verbal task. He feels unable to utter a sentence which responds neither to the cue of his interlocutor nor to the actual situation. The sentence 'it rains' cannot be produced unless the utterer sees that it is raining" (Jakobson, 1971: 56).[29] Benjy will make an utterance only in response to a sensation of innervation rooted in the immediate context. What is not directly accessible via the senses does not exist for him: "We could hear the fire and the roof. *Dilsey said, All right. You can come on to supper. Versh smelled like rain. He smelled like a dog, too. We would hear the fire and the roof*" (SF: 68). With its impersonal structure and subject that designates nothing and nobody, "it rains" is too abstract an utterance for Benjy to declare, although he repeats it in a version made more complex by the idiomatic grammar of Quentin as a child, who already feels regret: "*I wish it wouldn't rain, he said*" (66). The rain is directly evoked by the combination of auditory and olfactory sensations: the crackling of the fire and the sound of the roof (with raindrops falling) bring to mind the memory of a dinner scene when Versh comes back wet, smelling like a wet dog. This short excerpt exemplifies how Benjy's discourse deconstructs the orders of perception and language all in the same movement: the word "rain" has no reason to be included, except by virtue of the immediately perceptible effects of rain. The comparison suggested by the association of rain with the smell of dog should also be understood literally, as a juxtaposition of impressions that appear in the syntax through differentiated propositions, repetition of the comparative preposition *like*, and the appearance of the adverb *too*. Benjy therefore sees no causal link in the conjunction of these two odors. Strictly speaking, this should not be seen as an image but as a real impression (wet clothes that smell like dog) that practical language converts into a cliché. While it may be tempting to liken Benjy's aphasia to one of the types highlighted by Jakobson, and consequently identify it more precisely with one aspect of language, Benjy's case resists such definite categorization. While his disorder essentially reveals itself in word choice, and he is incapable of substituting one word for another or performing the exercise of "equational predication" (Jakobson, 1971: 58),[30] his discourse cannot be reduced to the metonymic pole that Jakobson associates with selection disorder. Even though metonymy actively compensates for the gaps in Benjy's language, his discourse is not exempt from metaphors, or at least from "quasi-metaphoric expressions [. . .] since, in contradistinction to rhetoric or poetic metaphors, they present no deliberate transfer of meaning" (Jakobson, 1971: 64). In Benjy's discourse, metonymy and metaphor are diverted from their status as tropes and obviously do not spring from rhetorical intentions. Still, poetry blooms there involuntarily, as if by default. Metonymy slips into the idiot's syntax to alleviate his lexical shortcomings by referring to a particular concept via the evocation of a related concept combined with it out of necessity (cause for effect, container for contents, etc.): for instance, the roof stands in for rain, the flower for the flowering of a tree, the "firedoor" for the stove. Similarly, the almost systematic use of definite articles is based on a metonymic reflex, revealing that the idiot considers a particular object to be the only representative of its kind, as though the inventory of the world stopped with the limited repertory of these single objects. With regard to metaphor, it is not so much featured in the idiot's discourse as it represents one of its structural principles. By using the effect of resemblance, it serves to transpose, transport, and arrange Benjy's interior monologue. It is through similarity that one topic leads to another, and one temporal layer leads to another. In the example cited above, rain is the element that brings about the analogical substitution of one scene for another, in permeable fashion and without the intermediary of a formal element to introduce comparison.

Faulkner deliberately submitted himself to the trial of Benjy's aphasia in his effort to twist and distort everyday language, to compress it and extract the essence of his style. Through the aphasia of his idiot, Faulkner denounces and surpasses the arbitrariness of the sign, thereby freeing himself from the principle defined by Ferdinand de Saussure: "[T]he individual does not have the power to change a sign in any way once it has become established in the linguistic community" (Saussure, 2011: 69). The idiot or the poet, on the other hand, has this power. The decision to ascribe a discourse to the idiot coincides with the emergence of forms that push language in its retrenchment and divert its referential methods and symbolic function to reconnect with the "voice of things."[31] Through the filter of Benjy's idiocy, Faulkner meets the challenge of dismissing the word in order to grasp the thing itself hidden and vanishing within it. In "Literature and the Right of Death," Maurice Blanchot shows how any literary production necessarily involves destruction:

> A word may give me its meaning, but first it suppresses it. For me to be able to say "This woman," I must somehow take her flesh-and-blood reality away from her, cause her to be absent, annihilate her. The word gives me the meaning, but it gives it to me deprived of being. The word is the absence of that being, its nothingness, what is left of it when it has lost being—the very fact that it does not exist. [. . .] The meaning of

speech, then, requires that before any word is spoken, there must be a sort of immense hecatomb, a preliminary flood plunging all of creation into a total sea. (Blanchot, 1995: 322–23)

Benjy's language restores the presence of the thing, threatened by the emergence of the word. For Faulkner, idiocy was a way of forgetting that there is a word to say a thing, thereby freeing himself of the word so as to better attain the thing. Idiocy consequently serves as an escape from the naming of things: by reducing the number of words, it paradoxically increases the number of things to be perceived. The idiot's discourse provides a short poetic-physical lesson on the process of combustion and orchestrates the (re)discovery of the different states of water: "She broke the top of the water and held a piece of it against my face" (*SF*: 13). Here Benjy describes in a factual, elementary, and rigorously exact manner the fact that in certain circumstances,[32] water can literally "break" into little solid fragments. The invention of an idiot language prompts Faulkner to reconnect with the elementary particles that make up the world's objects, to disarticulate phenomena whose complexity is flattened and even denied by being designated (combustion, freezing). Naming involves a synthesis that is detrimental to the essence of things and erases the contingency of their being in the world. Faulkner takes the opposite path. To recapture the objects driven away by language, he chooses dissociation, dissolution, and convolution. He chooses to circumvent the word in order to deprive it of its power to destroy the thing. In order to do so, he chooses other words that draw concentric circles around the thing, and summon it by analogical substitution without naming it. Blanchot describes the essential contradiction of language in the following manner:

> My hope lies in the materiality of language, in the fact that words are things, too, are a kind of nature—this is given to me and gives me more than I can understand. Just now the reality of words was an obstacle. Now, it is my only chance. A name ceases to be the ephemeral passing of non-existence and becomes a concrete ball, a solid mass of existence; language, abandoning the sense, the meaning which was all it wanted to be, tries to become senseless. (Blanchot, 1995: 327)

It is as though the paradoxes that underpin literature wash up in the figures of idiocy: as silent words, as a teeming empty life, literature threatens the world's objects, all while serving as the sole protector of their permanence. Idiocy establishes its supremacy over reason in the first lines of *The Sound and the Fury*, with insignificance taking the place of the sign and senselessness that of sense. Through the language that invents itself within it, idiocy offers a second life to the insignificant and senseless trivialities that practical language obscures behind the omnipotence of the sign. Faulkner's work thus found both its form and object.

The circumlocutions that define Benjy's monologue influenced the novels to come. They essentially reveal themselves through the theme of withheld information, with respect to both the writing and the novels' structure. Critics have referred to this method as a strategy of the empty center, or as the erasure of the central event. André Bleikasten has described it as "an 'economy' of the narrative that systematically skirts around the event" (Bleikasten and Moulinoux, 1995: 10). Édouard Glissant has shown how the causes and effects of an event always appear separated from the event itself: "[T]he relationship of the text to the subject generally stops the moment the act begins, leaving open gaps at these sites of exasperation, suggested more by their locale than through clinical description" (Glissant, 2000: 169). The two examples that are most often given are Temple Drake's rape in *Sanctuary* and Addie Bundren's burial in *As I Lay Dying*. In both cases, the suspense and expectation created by the context are frustrated. The event is replaced by an ellipsis, a blank, a textual void that remains silent regarding the most spectacular or intense dramatic element. *Sanctuary* is built around the absent center that the novel's first thirteen chapters lead up to, with the ensuing seventeen chapters exploring its many repercussions and consequences. This strategy, which defines the structure of these novels on a macroscopic scale, also operates in a minor mode, crafted by the narration of secondary anecdotes.[33] The ellipsis of Temple Drake's rape is foreshadowed in a burlesque mode at the end of *As I Lay Dying*, in the scene opposing Dewey Dell and MacGowan, the Jefferson pharmacist who has promised to administer an abortion remedy. It is clear that MacGowan, who happens to be the narrator of one of the novel's final monologues, is not impervious to the young girl's rustic charms—"She looks pretty good for a country girl" (*AILD*: 242)—and intends to take advantage of the situation and her naïveté. After seeing Dewey Dell's determination to rid herself of her burden, MacGowan informs her about the risks he is taking by helping her[34] and then engages in thinly veiled blackmail: "You come back at ten o'clock tonight and I'll give you the rest of it and perform the operation" (247). The nature of the "operation" in question is not directly revealed, but the phrases "the rest of it" and "perform" support conjectures of all kinds. However, rather than follow Dewey Dell and MacGowan into the cellar, the story takes the point of view of Vardaman. He accompanies his sister to the pharmacy that night and waits for her on the sidewalk—"She has been in there a long time" (251)—and then objectively recounts, without understanding, her annoyance when she comes out and is forced to admit that she has been manipulated: "She looks at me. 'It aint going to work,' she says. 'That son of a bitch' " (251). As demonstrated by this avoided scene—which takes place in the blank typographical space separating two monologues and the textual spaces that interrupt Vardaman's perceptions[35]—the abortion Dewey Dell wants will not take place. The novel's future will have to contend with a soon-to-be-born child. The theme of abortion shifts, in very unusual fashion, from the girl bearing life to the dead mother, for it is Addie who undergoes an abortion of sorts, with her burial serving as the aborted conclusion of *As I Lay Dying*. The mother's funeral is reduced from its status as the major event behind the novel, one that justifies its dynamic, to an ancillary event that is not entirely worth our time. In this case, the omission of the central event does not function as a litotes; it does not diminish the event's importance in order to further emphasize its pathetic dimension. Its erasure should be understood literally, for in view of everything that has preceded it, this scene no longer is important. What is important for the novelist took place in the fifty-eight monologues preceding the mother's burial, whose telling boils down to the paltry detail of the shovels borrowed from citizens of Jefferson: "we stopped there to borrow the shovels" (*AILD*: 258). What's more, this omission reveals the artificiality of the pretext (literally, what precedes the text) on which the entire novel is built, in addition to the naïve credulity of readers, who conscientiously wait for their questions to be answered and expectations to be satisfied. Yet with Faulkner, the climax that the story appears to be building toward only appears between the lines, like a palimpsest; the peak of the dramatic tension is resolved in the silence of what is left unsaid. In book 2 of the Snopes trilogy, the most emotionally charged event is most certainly the suicide of Eula Varner Snopes, an ordeal and shock that the reader shares with the characters who are affected. Eula seems to take her decision in good conscience; before taking her life, she visits a beauty parlor for the first time in her life, and pays a visit to Gavin Stevens, who clearly is not aware of her intentions. Stevens describes how their last meeting ended—Eula's final appearance in the Faulknerian corpus—in the following terms:

> "Thank you," she said. "Good night," and turned and I watched her, through the gate and up the walk, losing dimension now, onto or rather into the shadow of the little gallery and losing even substance now. And then I heard the door and it was as if she had not been. No, not that; not *not been*, but rather no more *is*, since *was* remains always and forever, inexplicable and immune, which is its grief. That's what I mean: a dimension less, then a substance less, then the sound of a door and then, not *never been* but simply *no more is* since always and forever that *was* remains, as if what is going to happen to one tomorrow already gleams faintly visible now if the watcher were only wise enough to discern it or maybe just brave enough. (*T*: 293)

This fleeting portrait of Eula at the threshold, the liminal space that foreshadows her permanent disappearance, takes the place of the description of her suicide (which occurs in the ellipsis separating two chapters), whose circumstances will be clarified only in the final volume of the trilogy,[36] and whose intimate motivations will remain resolutely opaque. As she walks away from Gavin Stevens, who watches her (with the reader) from the sidewalk, Eula seems to lose (the verb *to lose* is repeated) one by one the qualities that kept her rooted in the world: her "dimension" and "substance" are threatened by the shadows of the porch. An intangible figure, already her own ghost, she disappears with the slam of a door—a sound that can, in retrospect, be interpreted as the sound of a detonating revolver. It is hardly coincidental that the syntax of this excerpt, where life meets death, borrows from Darl's existential grammar. Like Darl, Gavin corrects himself: "No, not that; not *not been*, but rather no more *is*, since *was* remains always and forever, inexplicable and immune, which is its grief." He rejects the bygone and definitive character of the past perfect and past simple tenses, whose use grammatically kills the subject, preferring an unusual phrase instead ("no more *is*"), which snatches Eula back from her own disappearance by opening the possibility of a reappearance. However, this *was*, which like an ill omen conveys the obviousness of finitude, persists (the expression "*was* remains" is repeated twice). Through her sober and irrevocable final words, Eula says thank you and goodbye to her audience: "'Thank you,' she said. 'Good night.'" Then, dignified and elegant, she disappears into *was*.

While many critics have noted the recurrence of the phenomenon, few of them have asked why Faulkner chose to so systematically remain on the margins of the event instead of broaching it directly. The argument that he is following the implicit rules of propriety is not plausible. The opening to chapter 28 of *Sanctuary* invalidates this claim. Confronted by the jury empaneled for the trial of Lee Goodwin, who has been falsely accused of murdering Tommy and raping Temple, the prosecutor brandishes the corncob that was used to rape the young girl: "The district attorney faced the jury. 'I offer as evidence this object which was found at the scene of the crime.' He held in his hand a corn-cob. It appeared to have been dipped in dark brownish paint" (S: 283). The phallic substitute is presented abruptly and brutally; the reader is spared no detail (including the gynecologist's report). Faulkner therefore did not spare the reader from anything—his intention resides elsewhere.[37] Perhaps it should be sought in the gaze and voice of the idiot, which do not understand the world and its objects—or language in general—and are hostile to established and proven facts. For the idiot, things are condemned to flux, variation, and change, and Faulkner the writer shows a similar defiance to supposedly conclusive events. He is not so much interested in the nature of an event—which, because it cannot escape the subjectivity of those involved, is subject to caution and cannot be evoked in its entirety—than that which announces and results from it, the multiplication of its sensible effects on a limited number of individuals (the most radical restriction being accomplished by the interior monologue). This is how, in Faulkner's work, the impossible objectivity of the action is sacrificed for the radical subjectivity of the reaction. If the event is abandoned, so to speak, to the hollowness of the text, that is because it signifies nothing as such; it is also because words fail to grasp some of its aspects and hence fail to say. Faulknerian circumlocutions are so many echoes of this singular desire to say, whose central concern is the dogged attempt rather than its success. It is less a matter of reaching a goal than drawing near it.

Chapter 13

THE DISORDERS OF PREDICATION AND THE ORDER OF A WORLD

The Idiot Idiom

> The book, the written thing, enters the world and carries out its work of transformation and negation. It, too, is the future of many other things, and not only books: by the projects which it can give rise to, by the undertakings it encourages, by the totality of the world of which it is a modified reflection, it is an infinite source of new realities, and because of these new realities existence will be something it was not before.
> —MAURICE BLANCHOT, "LITERATURE AND THE RIGHT TO DEATH"

In late winter 1928, Faulkner began writing a short story entitled "Twilight," which he thought would take up around a dozen pages. The story came to him first in the form of a "story without plot" (*LIG*: 146), built around the central figure of the young girl Caddy, who has three brothers. The story's seminal image is crafted around two situations that dramatize the four children. There is a death that has not be revealed to them (the death of Damuddy), and a brook where they play and splash, left to their own devices:

> I just began to write about a brother and a sister splashing one another in the brook and the sister fell and wet her clothing and the smallest brother cried, thinking that the sister was conquered or perhaps hurt. Or perhaps he knew that he was the baby and that she would quit whatever battles to comfort him. When she did so, when she quit the water fight and stooped in her wet garments above him, the entire story, which is told by that same little brother in the first section, seemed to explode on the paper before me. ("Intro *SF*, II": 230)

From the outset, the narrative perspective is rooted in the naïveté of childhood games and the blind confidence that a young boy—the benjamin—has for his older sister. She is the preferred object of his attention; he worries for her but is also convinced that she belongs to him. It is through his novice eyes that the story begins to take shape, distorted by the filter of childhood. Like Caddy, who has to "stoop" to comfort him, by choosing this little boy as the narrator Faulkner put himself at the boy's level, seeing things exclusively through his eyes. Faulkner was then "struck" by a stroke of genius: "[T]he idea struck me to see how much more I could have got out of the idea of the blind, self-centeredness of innocence, typified by children, if one of those children had been truly innocent, that is, an idiot" (*LIG*: 146). Faulkner intuited that his choice of narrator stood much to gain if it crystallized the qualities of childhood and heightened them further. The perspective of idiocy then replaced the approach of childhood: the idiot Benjy was born. Not simply content with climactically featuring the "self-centeredness" and "innocence" of childhood, Faulkner cast the idiot to literally be the center of a singular world. The present task was to have him speak. For Faulkner, the creation of an idiot idiom was not solely the next stage of his project; it was the decisive leap that marked his entry into literature. Perhaps he had already understood this, for one day in 1956, looking back at his body of work from a distance, he described Benjy in the following terms: "He was a prologue, like the grave-digger in the Elizabethan dramas" (Stein, Spring 1956: 74). If Benjy can be seen as the prologue for a novel, he is also the prologue for Faulkner's writing and work, the singular space in which they took form.

Faulkner never pretended he was creating a realistic and plausible portrait of an idiot. If this had been his intention, he would not have chosen the narrative strategy of the interior monologue. He was aware that his choice was based on an aberration and represented a risk, but it was one he took deliberately. He based his idiocy neither on an investigation nor on improbable accounts of it (until evidence to the contrary, a deaf-and-dumb idiot has never provided an account of their lot); it reflects no preexisting reality or tangible foundation. It is a pure literary object whose creation was based on an experimental gesture and a high-wire act of imagination, which entailed inventing what an idiot sees, smells, and feels—how he perceives the world. Faulkner ultimately gave free rein to idiocy so that it could express itself in the first person. The groundwork for such a discourse was as considerable as it was problematic. It involved abandoning, in the same destructive gesture, the perceptual logic and linguistic structures governing the world of ordinary humans, for whom the idiot is often an affront, one that shocks, disturbs, and displeases. Instances of Benjy Compson's idiocy indisposing those around him are mentioned on numerous occasions in *The Sound and the Fury*: "How come you cant behave yourself like folks" (*SF*: 14); "*Cant you get done with that moaning and play in the branch like folks*" (19). As demonstrated by repetition of the phrase "like folks," in light of which the idiot is defined by default, he is characterized by his outrageous difference and fundamental inability to behave "like folks." He is a disturbing element because he does not do anything "like folks," which is also why he proves to be such an unusual narrator. It is by focusing on his conduct, which seems to defy common sense, that Faulkner imposed this direction on his writing in the first monologue of *The Sound and the Fury*. The subterfuge that underpins his project led him, in paradoxical fashion, to use his full reasoning abilities in order to deprive reason of its supremacy. In other words, Faulkner used all of his talent and inventiveness for innocence and ignorance to take charge of his discourse. Incomprehension thus became an ordering principle for his writing.[1] Rooted in an iconoclastic and revolutionary stance, the writing of Faulknerian idiocy is based on an essential presupposition: contrary to his creator, the idiot narrator is deprived of initiative and intention. "He dont know what he want to do" (14): he goes nowhere and wants nothing. His being-in-the-world is marked by an extreme passiveness; he suffers the assault of the world. The corollary of his great impotence resides in his virgin expectations. He is innocent because he is incapable of anticipating or explaining what happens—"in all innocence, unsuspecting, unforewarned" (*T*: 248). The world happens to him in one long movement of perpetual astonishment. His perception of the world is, consequently and necessarily, both disorganized and chaotic. It is this astonishment and disorganization, this chaos, that Faulkner strived to establish as a system.

To provide an account of the singular perception of his idiot, Faulkner deliberately distorted his vision and language. He invented a different and singular language built on deviations, flaws, and gaps—one capable of intimating the distortions of an idiot's perception. The idiot's categorical disorders affect the order of his perceptions and generate syntactical disorders. It is precisely these disorders of idiot predication that engender a remarkable writing, one that defines its issues through idiocy and later exports them to future works.[2] Behind the appearance of chaos, the idiot's language follows a strict and precise logic corresponding to a primary determinant, the exclusive primacy of sensation. Benjy's discourse compensates for the failures of his intelligence with respect to the most basic physical phenomena, as well as his partial understanding of key events in his family history due to an overinvestment of sensation. The idiot's senses mark out the field of his experience. The silence of sensation—the substrate of sound—is replaced by a language of sensation, which performs the miracle of putting the preverbal confusion of the senses into words. In creating his idiot narrator and the idiot idiom that reveals the world he perceives, Faulkner initiated a philosophical reflection on the nature of perception, whose principles are dismantled by Benjy's monologue. By virtue of his idiocy, the perceiving subject from the first monologue of *The Sound and the Fury* reveals the twin movements that determine all perception (simultaneously giving access to reality and the subject's experience thereof),[3] and deepens the gap separating perception from knowledge. The following example highlights how the perceived object is dependent on the subjectivity of the perceiver, and reciprocally how the perceiving subject is affected by the perceived object. Mrs. Compson and Benjy are preparing to go to the cemetery in the carriage. Benjy evokes their departure in the following manner: "The carriage jolted and crunched on the drive. [. . .] We went through the gate, where it didn't jolt anymore" (*SF*: 10). The carriage is clearly evoked as an extension of its occupants: the subjects "the carriage" and "we" are indistinctly subjected to the same effects. The verbs "jolt" and "crunch" can be interpreted as metonymies: they designate the complex sensation arising from the carriage's movement as it is affected by the ground's surface (probably gravel). However, the causal relation between what Benjy perceives (the jolts, starting, and crunching) and the source of his perceptions (the unevenness of the ground) is erased by the extreme simplicity of the syntax, which puts the word "carriage" in the position of an active and responsible grammatical subject. In the same movement, Benjy is implicitly reduced to the status of an object that is literally jolted by the versatility of sensations. After passing through the gate, he regains his tranquility when the carriage drives over less uneven terrain, with the change of surface being suggested by a negation of the state evoked just before ("where it didn't jolt anymore"). The primacy given to sensation clearly shows that the Faulknerian idiot possesses no knowledge; he cannot strictly speaking be considered a subject, being irremediably deprived of the ability to apprehend the world's object via both senses and ideas.

On a fundamental level, the idiot does not have the slightest idea about things: he simply has no ideas. He perceives the world solely through the intermediary of his sense organs: he only has sensations. With each one constituting a collection of sensations, the objects of his world are perceived in their radical singularity as particular and unique objects: in that respect, they can be considered idiot objects, deprived of doubles. The repetition of their appearance in no way changes their absolutely exceptional character. For the idiot, these objects never acquire the character of sameness. The sensible object is never transcended by the categorization and generalization of concepts.

In his treatise *On the Soul*, Aristotle defines sensation as the first moment in the soul's perception of a thing; the soul is open to things, and sensations represent the imprint of things on the soul. Aristotle distinguishes between the "proper" perceptible object (a color is perceived by sight, a sound by hearing, etc.), the "common" perceptible object[4] (movement is specific to touch and sight), and the "co-incidental perceptible object": "A perceptible object is also called 'co-incidental,' for instance, if the white object might be the son of Diares; for one perceives this co-incidentally, because this object which one perceives co-incides with the white" (Aristotle, 2018: 33). In "apophantic" language,[5] the language of signification, a substance, which is to say a thing that shows itself through its presence, is ascribed a kind of being through the intermediary of predicates that correspond to categories (location, quality, quantity, etc.) in the Aristotelian vocabulary. Apophantic language therefore involves giving an essence to substances based on categories. Yet in Benjy's language, there is often a reversal that paves the way for what can be called an aesthetic language in that it is the sensation (the "white" in the quotation above) that finds itself in the position of subject or substance: "The roof was falling. The slanting holes were full of spinning yellow" (*SF*: 12). In this example, sensation, which associates the color yellow with a spinning movement, takes the place of the thing it refers to. The identification of this thing (it is in fact sunlight passing through cracks in the barn roof) disappears behind the listing of its sensible qualities. The description of Quentin moving through the dark is presented in similar fashion; it is noteworthy that the excerpt in question brings to mind the white of Diares's toga: "His shirt was a white blur" (23). The context of the words that come before this quotation inform the idiot (and the reader) regarding the character's identification and spatial position, who is clearly identified by Mr. Compson and located by Versh: "'Where's Quentin.' He said. 'He coming up the walk.' Versh said. Quentin was coming slow" (23). However, where his father and keeper see the substance (Quentin drawing near), the idiot Benjy emphasizes the scene's common sensible characteristics. Quentin's slow advance is combined with a nighttime sensation of distancing, thereby reducing him to the appearance of a shirt—"a white blur," a vague white form that stands out against a dark background—which appears to be moving on its own. Its sensible qualities metonymically stand in for the naming of the object. In the process, Quentin disappears behind a synecdoche, a part of himself (his shirt), whose substance appears compromised by the predominance of the sensations that simultaneously evoke and revoke it. Apophantic and aesthetic language are based on a similar structure (in which A is B). But their essential difference is that aesthetic language makes the coincidental ("spinning yellow," "white blur") a subject or a substance. This characteristic is behind the recurrence of hypallages in Benjy's discourse.

Hypallage (which etymologically means "exchange" or "inversion") characterizes objects obliquely and mixes up habitual perceptions. As suggested by Catherine Fromilhague in *Les Figures de style*, it proceeds with a "more or less complex transfer of characterizing elements" (Fromilhague, 1995: 43) by using syntactical displacement or transformation of the adjective into a noun. Benjy's description of the cold is particularly revealing in this regard: "I could smell the bright cold" (*SF*: 6). The complexity of the idiot's sensation of cold is revealed in the simultaneous perception of an odor; or, more precisely, by how smell is affected both by an anesthetizing cold (the odor described by Benjy can also be interpreted as an odor by default) and by light (daylight, as the impression of cold coincides with the moment Benjy goes outside). Synesthesia is doubled by a hypallage attributing a tint ("bright") to an intangible element. This logic is confirmed and reversed when Benjy and Caddy go back into the house: "We ran up the steps and out of the bright cold, into the dark cold" (7). As the succession of prepositions shows, objects—whether they are hard like steps or immaterial like the cold, air, or light—are all perceived on a single plane, as a succession of sensations evoking a succession of states. The "bright cold" transforms into the "dark cold," which in a second hypallage materializes the hostility of the atmosphere in the Compson home: the cold endures and is joined by darkness. These two examples illustrate the specific process and effect of hypallage, which is based on "restructuring the perception or impression that is emphasized: the object that is the medium of the perception becomes secondary" (Fromilhague, 1995: 44). The recurrence of certain stylistic features in Faulkner's writing is hardly accidental, as they form the framework of the aesthetic language he developed to dramatize his idiot's categorical disorders. They feature the deformation of language as well as the diversion of its apophantic methods. In *Metaphysics*, Aristotle shows that mental activity occurs in the transition from sensation to a synthesis wrought by the intelligence. In the example from the treatise *On the Soul* cited above, once the sensation of white has been associated with the substance of Diares, the final conclusion is that Diares is (in) white. Apophantic language is consequently built only afterward, as aesthetic language comes first. However, this synthesis does not occur normally in the case of Benjy, whose discourse is rooted in aesthetic language that remains a simple utterance indicating a presence, contrary to apophantic language, which signifies how a thing is, based on the categories of time, place, quality, and so on. Aesthetic language is therefore not a language of signification. It places in the position of subject that which is ordinarily just a predicate or an attribute, thereby making the sensation perceived the subject of the sentence.[6] In Faulkner's writing, this primary language, the language of the senses and presence, is built around the predominance of comparison and metonymy.[7]

Analysis of one of the prominent phrases from Benjy's monologue, "Caddy smelled like trees," clearly reveals that the comparison is built on a three-part structure involving a *comparé* (the compared term, *Caddy*), a *comparant* (the comparing term, *trees*), and a theme (*smelled*), whose signified is a property shared by the *comparé* and the *comparant*; in this case it is an odor. Despite appearances, the comparison is a highly complex figure from Benjy's point of view. As opposed to the hypallages that naturally reveal the uninterrupted continuum of intertwining sensations, comparison involves a deliberate association. It characterizes the objects in light of other known objects. Fromilhague has observed that in the act of comparison, "the *comparant* keeps its literal sense and designates an autonomous albeit virtual referent; it has the most prominent figurative power of all micro-structural figures" (Fromilhague, 1995: 75). In the way it summons and brings together heterogeneous objects, comparison generates lasting images. Because they represent exceptional occasions in which the idiot moves a little closer to his desire to say, these images ensure the permanence of his discourse. If stunned readers retain anything after their first reading of Benjy's monologue, it is surely "Caddy smelled like trees." Most of these images stand out by virtue of their highly concrete nature. The same trees that appear when Caddy is compared to them disappear, along with the comparison, under the artifice of perfume and behind the bridal veil: "I couldn't smell trees anymore" (*SF*: 40). Comparison thus establishes a relation of either resemblance or difference.[8] Its recurrence in Benjy's language stems from the keenness of his senses, as the perception of an object very often prompts another perception through synesthetic comparison. Most of the comparisons scattered throughout the idiot's discourse are thus built around a perceptual theme; their detailed analysis highlights two senses—smell and sight—as well as a few objects precisely characterized by their propensity to prompt analogies. The common feature of these objects, however heterogeneous they may be, resides in the fact that when they engender a comparison, they are a source of pleasure for Benjy. The list of such objects is very short: Caddy obviously occupies a central role,[9] but there are also the "bright shapes," T. P. (who of all his keepers Benjy shows the greatest attachment toward), rain (variously associated with Mr. Compson, Quentin, and Versh),[10] and the mirror. By associating these few favorite objects in various combinations, comparison generates a small anthology of idiot images. Some of them are marked by their repetitive and even tautological dimension: "The pig pen smelled like pigs" (35). In this example, surprise paradoxically comes from an obvious sentiment. If similar comparisons are generally left unsaid, that is because they do not compare anything, the *comparant* and *comparé* being (almost) identical. Their truth is nevertheless undeniable—that is the definition of a truism—and the description of the odor of the "pig pen" (Benjy apparently doesn't know the word *pigsty*) could not be more scrupulously exact. Most of the comparisons in the idiot's discourse show an inventiveness that is poetic. Rather than provide an exhaustive list,[11] here are two particularly illuminating examples in their context. They are visual comparisons whose operating method appears somewhat more complex than olfactory comparisons. Both involve the mirror:

> The windows went black, and the dark tall place on the wall came and I went and touched it. It was like a door, only it wasn't a door. (*SF*: 61)

> He rolled into the corner, out of the mirror. Father brought Caddy to the fire. They were all out of the mirror. Only the fire was in it. Like the fire was in a door. (*SF*: 65)

In the first case, the comparison tries to identify an unknown object; the theme comes down to the auxiliary verb *to be*. This object is first mentioned paraphastically around a very general noun ("place"), whose particularity language tries to grasp through the addition of simple attributive adjectives ("dark," "tall"). The comparison itself comes in the wake of a tactile impression ("touched"): the unknown *comparé* ("it") is assimilated with a familiar object ("a door"). This example shows how Benjy summons the few words he knows to refer to the objects in his world. But the ensuing concession is a rarity in his discourse. The expression "only it wasn't a door" can be read on two levels. It can be interpreted as a commentary on the artificiality of methods of comparison, which arbitrarily associate dissimilar objects. But it also shows how Benjy conceives of the comparison as a relation of strict equivalence. If, in this specific case, he deems his comparison invalid, it is because in all of the other cases, comparison expresses the similarity of his sensations as satisfactorily as in the undeniable "The pig pen smelled like pigs." The second example is particularly striking in terms of syntax. Unlike the preceding example, the "mirror" object is clearly identified. The mirror represents the infrangible frame that I previously suggested (de)limits Benjy's rigid and univocal visual field: characters appear and disappear within it based on their movements. What is remarkable is that the word "mirror" no longer interests Benjy, who is more focused on his memory of the comparison that previously enabled him to get around the absence of the word mirror: "Only the fire was in it. Like the fire was in a door." It is as though, giving it second thought, the word "door"—another frame in which objects appear—appeared more apt to define his sensation. This is to say that in the fire's reflection in the mirror, the idiot does not see a reflection but rather the object itself. For him, the objects of the world cannot be doubled in virtual images. He grasps them literally and unilaterally. That is why the mirror object inspires vague discomfort in the idiot, which he remedies by referencing the door's materiality, as the tangibility of the objects appearing within it is undeniable.

Comparison and metaphor function similarly but are different on a number of levels: while the *comparé* and the *comparant* are necessarily expressed in comparison, that is not the case with metaphor. While comparison establishes a verifiable resemblance between the *comparé* and the *comparant*, metaphor is based on a symbolic analogy. It is this latter aspect that explains why metaphors (in the narrow sense of the term) are so rare in Benjy's monologue. However, the very structure of his discourse can be considered metaphorical, as it associates a *comparé* and a *comparant* via a shared sensible theme, but without the intermediary of tools that signal comparison, thereby transitioning indistinctly from one temporal stratum to another. Metaphor plays a negligible role in the idiot's language, for it is based on forms that are too abstract for an idiot and is therefore always coincidental. In comparison, the referents of the *comparé* and the *comparant* remain formally distinct, whereas in a metaphor they fuse together, hence the potential appearance of confusion. The child narrator Vardaman shows a resistance to understanding metaphorical expressions that is comparable to that of Benjy. Vardaman understands metaphor literally, as when he involuntarily produces one:

"When will we get to Mottson, Darl?" I say.
"Tomorrow," Darl says. "If this team dont rack to pieces. Snopes must have fed them on sawdust."
"Why did he feed them on sawdust, Darl?" I say. (*AILD*: 196)

Here, Darl metaphorically suggests that if their present team may "rack to pieces," it is because Snopes, who sold them the mules, fed them on sawdust. Vardaman's question reveals that he has understood the poor treatment inflicted on the mules[12] literally: he is genuinely taken aback that one could subject animals to such a diet, and asks for an explanation.

One of the most decisive features of the idiot idiom in Faulkner's writing is metonymy, which I discussed above in its relation to aphasia. Among the different forms of metonymy that can be distinguished, the one that is the most represented in Benjy's monologue involves giving the effect for the cause, or evoking an abstract principle through its concrete manifestations. Catherine Fromilhague has shown that in circumventing the requirement of discursive development, metonymy responds to a principle of economy—"[T]he power of metonymy comes from its power of condensation" (Fromilhague, 1995: 68)—as well as a principle of impropriety: "[I]n its literal sense, the term violates the rules of distribution. [. . .] Attributive adjectives are often the object of semantic distortion" (69). Metonymy is one of the preferred figures in the idiot's discourse because its use satisfies both the search for density and the desire to give an impression of incongruousness. In naming a phenomenon by describing its effects, metonymy entirely dispels the discourse's pathetic aspect. Its use instinctively resembles that of litotes, for instance in the following scene in which Caddy resists Charlie's advances in order to comfort Benjy:

> "Go away, Charlie." Caddy said. Charlie came and put his hands on Caddy and I cried more. I cried loud.
> "No, no." Caddy said. "No. No."
> "He cant talk." Charlie said. "Caddy."
> "Are you crazy." Caddy said. She began to breathe fast. "He can see. Dont. Dont." Caddy fought. They both breathed fast. "Please. Please." Caddy whispered.
> "Send him away." Charlie said.
> "I will." Caddy said. "Let me go."
> "Will you send him away?" Charlie said.
> "Yes." Caddy said. "Let me go." Charlie went away. "Hush." Caddy said. "He's gone." I hushed. I could hear her and feel her chest going. (*SF*: 47)

Caddy's desire is not explicitly indicated, but Benjy precisely shows its consequences on his sister's words, gestures, and body. Yet this scene that Benjy interprets in his favor (he temporarily snatches Caddy away from Charlie's embrace) ironically denounces how Caddy is split in two, and the duplicity that results. Through Benjy's naïve eyes, Caddy is torn between her allegiance as an older sister and her desire as a woman. It is truly a struggle ("Caddy fought"), although Benjy is mistaken regarding the reason: Caddy is not fighting against Charlie but rather against her own impulses. Temptation manifests itself in what Benjy interprets as her resistance: "no" is a hidden "yes," "please" is both a supplication and an invitation, with quickening breath attesting to growing desire. While Benjy finally calms down, believing that he has regained his monopoly over his sister's attention, the scene ends on an irresolute note suggesting that Caddy has gone to the other side of the mirror, and that she insincerely takes advantage of her brother's credulity to satisfy her desire.

The deaths of Mr. Compson and Roskus are revealed in the same movement, in an even more suggestive manner and with very few words. The two events are associated through the presence of "moaning" (*SF*: 32–33), which is prompted by the memory of Damuddy's death. The death of the father is inscribed in the shift from "It wasn't Father" (repeated twice[13]) to the odd noise made by Mrs. Compson: "we could hear Mother" (34). Death and crying are suggested by syntactical structures and words that are elementary and general—a simple negation of the father's presence and the verb to "hear"—that underdescribe the event and, from a formal point of view, dispel its pathetic dimension. As a result, the discourses of desire and death are left indeterminate, replaced by factual descriptions of their immediate manifestations (we see how in any other discourse "breathing" and "moaning" could be considered metaphorical expressions of desire and death, whereas with Benjy they are metonyms). Still, the effect produced on the reader is no less striking. The factual nature and juxtaposition of such scenes indirectly prompt the emotion that Benjy, who does not understand what is happening, does not feel. From the reader's point of view, this emotion proves all the more intense, as it flows from channels where tears give way to extreme sobriety.

By avoiding naming the thing clearly, the idiot's language paradoxically situates itself at the heart of things. The strategy of predicative avoidance coincides with grasping the thing itself, even as it is deprived of a name. Gaps, extreme concision, and things left unsaid are sometimes more eloquent than the proliferation of words.[14] This is further confirmed by the reflections of Rosa Coldfield, who in the fifth chapter of *Absalom, Absalom!* begins to reveal to Quentin the nature of the humiliation that Thomas Sutpen inflicted on her the day he proposed his sordid transaction:

> *I will tell you what he did and let you be the judge. (Or try to tell you, because there are some things for which three words are three too many, and three thousand words that many words too less, and this is one of them. It can be told; I could take that many sentences, repeat the bold blank naked and outrageous words just as he spoke them, and bequeath you only that same aghast and outraged unbelief I knew when I comprehended what he meant; or take three thousand sentences and leave you only that Why? Why? and Why? that I have asked and listened to for almost fifty years.) But I will let you be the judge and let you tell me if I was not right.* (AA: 134–35)

Like the idiot Benjy but for different reasons, Rosa Coldfield is unable to say what she is "trying to say." She emphasizes the effects of her announcement, even though what "can be told" will not be revealed but rather drowned in an emphatic and overcharged syntax that kills emotion by dint of exacerbating it. Perhaps this is precisely her goal: deadening the horror behind an uninterrupted flow of words. The mortifying revelation that refuses to leave her lips is replaced by a metalinguistic discourse on how to reveal, the tone to adopt, and the number of words needed to say ("*three words* [. . .] *three thousand words*"). This "digression" (I am referring to the excerpt's punctuation) ultimately takes over the entire discourse. The revelation as such is deferred to the next chapter (where the point of view is that of Shreve, who reformulates the story that Quentin told him as he heard it from Rosa Coldfield). Yet when it occurs, drowned in uncertainty due to the numerous intermediaries needed to access it, this revelation—"that they breed together for test and sample and if it was a boy they would marry" (*AA*: 144)—is no longer truly important. The only true and reliable information is found in reticence.[15]

The function and effects of metonymy in the first monologue of *The Sound and the Fury* are diametrically opposed to how it is used in *Absalom, Absalom!* In both cases, metonymy helps circumvent information. While in the case of Benjy it compensates for his lexical shortcomings by featuring things in a paradoxically direct, tangible, and effective way, in *Absalom, Absalom!* it wraps itself in a reflexive and abstract discourse, distancing things. In the first case the thing is grasped in a relation of absolute proximity, while in the second it is set aside by a flood of words that irremediably separate the intention to say and the act of saying. Benjy Compson's monologue in *The Sound and the Fury* and *Absalom, Absalom!* can be considered as the two ends of the spectrum of Faulkner's writing. The extreme starkness of one stands in contrast to the overabundance of the other; the first is a minimalist poem, the second a dense and incessant flowering; one is a lesson in things, the other a lesson in words. While *Absalom, Absalom!* distinguishes itself through its hyperbolic prose that incites things to withdraw, there is an obvious proximity between Benjy's metonymic discourse and certain monologues in *As I Lay Dying*. In the latter work, metaphors are predisposed to transform into metonymy, and the expression of pain alternates between the two singular registers of euphemism and dark humor, which may seem antithetical at first glance, but actually and strangely converge. Narrated by Darl, despite the fact that he does not witness the scene, the twelfth monologue of *As I Lay Dying* literally relates Addie's death. The scene depicts Dewey Dell, Vardaman, Cash, and Anse around Addie's deathbed, and describes how each of them reacts to the imminence of death. This death is announced in the monologue's last lines: "*Jewel, I say, she is dead, Jewel. Addie Bundren is dead*" (*AILD*: 52).[16] However, the slow extinction that precedes it is suggested by the repetitive evocation of a single object, the fan. The fan's movements[17] stand in for the explicit figuration of Addie's death throes, indirectly informing us regarding their duration—"the fan still moving like it has for ten days" (48)—as well the powerlessness of those who can do nothing except witness the inexorable outcome: "the fan still moving steadily up and down, whispering the useless air" (48–49). The vainness of Dewey Dell's efforts is thus emphasized, for she is simply moving "useless air." The fan symbolizes both the moment of death—"the fan in one hand still beating with expiring breath into the quilt" (49)—as well as death itself: "the clutched fan now motionless on the fading quilt" (50). The choice of this object in such a dramatization was not made by chance: in the shift from persistent movement ("still moving," "still beating") to immobility ("now motionless"), the fan serves as a metaphor for Addie's death throes and their result, with which it is implicitly compared through its movement and cessation. The circulating air (personified as "whispering") evokes her failing breath, while the fan functions as a metonym for the dying person, who is no more than a held breath that it vainly tries to prolong through the air it generates. The pathetic dimension of Addie's death is therefore contained between the thin ribs of the fan. During the funeral escort for Addie's coffin to the Jefferson cemetery, the buzzards that Darl and Vardaman spot in the sky are given similar treatment: "'See them?' I say. High above the house, against the quick thick sky, they hang in narrowing circles" (94). Their first appearance is dramatized by the fact that pronouns without referents replace their clear designation, which is delayed until the following page: "Motionless, the tall buzzards hang in soaring circles" (95). At first the buzzards are characterized by their paradoxical immobility, sometimes suggested by repetition of the word *hang*, and sometimes by the image of the nail: "He is looking at the sky. The buzzard is as still as if he were nailed to it" (122). Similarly, the inexorable approach of buzzards seems to be refuted by insistent references to their distance: the adjective *tall* is almost systematically used to describe them—"motionless in tall and soaring circles" (104). Yet just as it designates the elevation of the buzzards in the sky, the attributive adjective *tall* materializes the scope of the threat they represent, which grows with their number. The increasing number of buzzards fascinates and obsesses Vardaman, who keeps track of the grim figure: "Now there are seven of them, in little tall black circles. [. . .] 'Yesterday there were just four,' I say. [. . .] Now there are nine of them, tall in little tall black circles. [. . .] Now there are ten of them, tall in little tall black circles on the sky" (194–97). In this final example, repetition of the adjective *little* clearly plays a reassuring role,[18] minimizing the threat hanging over the corpse, whose carrion smell is suggested implicitly. The slow circling of buzzards around the coffin stands in for the direct evocation of what happens to the corpse. The growing number of concentric circles expresses their great hunger and imitates the convolutions of language, which chooses to designate the unnamable thing and process[19] by mentioning their effects. The buzzards, whose proximity signals the putrefaction of the mother's body, also threaten to become its metonymic vessel by cutting it to pieces and ingesting it.

The metonymic functioning specific to Benjy, along with the largely metonymic language that emerges in his monologue, had a decisive influence on Faulkner's writing, in which objects often signify tragedies and sensations replace the language of sentiments. Faulkner's writing found its preferred forms and figures in idiocy, with Benjy's idiot idiom defining its logic. In Faulkner, catastrophe—in its dual sense as an upheaval and the apex of a story—is only evoked through its premises and consequences. The latter are less the subject of a coherent discourse than they are determined by a language in which concepts are invalidated by the ubiquity of things. Put another way, the elevation of ideas is compromised by the tangibility and weight of the sensible world. When the abstraction of concepts and ideas takes center stage, it is always to point out that which it precisely is unable to say. The excess of words is generally the symptom of an inability to grasp an object. It is often an avowal of failure, the sign of a loss. It can sometimes also reveal the breakdowns in an individual's rootedness in the world they inhabit. Benjy's discourse of idiocy is radically different from a singularly talkative madness, as demonstrated in varying degrees by the monologues of Quentin Compson, Darl Bundren, and Rosa Coldfield. For the latter, language conceals the collapse of things but also denounces their irreversible distancing. The madman's language is a language of transcendence; one of its primary characteristics denies the sensibility of experiences that it does not enjoy. That is why Caddy's sensuality is unbearable for Quentin, who, for lack of personal experiences, increasingly uses bookish quotations and ruminations on the past, forced to borrow from the experiences of others. This pathology of language is also present with Darl, who is the narrator with the most monologues in *As I Lay Dying*. Darl sees and describes things transparently, without lingering over their specific qualities. He sees what he is not there to see: "Darl [. . .] that sits at the supper table with his eyes gone further than the food and the lamp, full of the land dug out of his skull and the holes filled with distance beyond the land" (*AILD*: 27). Darl is elsewhere; the objects he is contemplating are "further" than the ordinary and tangible objects (the table, the meal, the lamp) of everyday life, the very ones that exclusively occupy the idiot's field of perception. The world in which Darl lives is not the world of shared experience; it is a world "dug out of his skull"—a world whose holes are precariously filled with tools as impalpable as the emblematic "distance" separating things in themselves from the words referring to them. What fills his vision ("full," "filled") is also pierced with "holes," which shows the discontinuity of his being-in-the-world. The distance separating *full* and *filled* can be seen as the failure of being *fulfilled*, as the possibility of its realization fizzles into nothing. In similar fashion, Rosa masks the absence of life that is characteristic of her life, which is entirely lived by proxy,[20] through the proliferation of stories and poems devoted to the Confederate armies that her father precisely tried to escape,[21] and through her tormented confessions that incessantly turn around an object that resists speech. For the Faulknerian madman, language is the final barrier before the void; for the idiot, it immanently manifests the plenitude of things. The beauty of Faulkner's writing fluctuates between these two poles, but it is in idiocy that it "digs" the idiosyncrasies that will, by way of contrast, enable it to develop those of madness. Idiocy is the first gesture, and Quentin's monologue is the second; it follows that of the idiot and is defined in relation to it.

The second monologue of *The Sound and the Fury* extends the reflection on the modes of experience and the possibility of a language rooted in things. Yet it also shows its reverse side, which is to say the opposing temptation of language to rise above things. In doing so, it also exhibits its own reverse side, namely how its elevation condemns language to miss out on things. Earlier I discussed how Addie Bundren's only monologue theorizes language's failure to coincide with its objects. But in retrospect, it should perhaps also be seen as one of the most explicit formulations of the Faulknerian project as undertaken through idiocy: "I would think how words go straight up in a thin line, quick and harmless, and how terribly doing goes along the earth, clinging to it" (*AILD*: 173). The idiot idiom actually aims to trace, on the sensible surface of the earth, the crawling movements of "doing," which in the same movement encompasses the subject, perception, and objects. It is this original intimacy with the earth, with the ground and its roots—"The ground was hard, churned and knotted" (*SF*: 4)—that gives most of Faulkner's stories set in Yoknapatawpha County their earthy flavor. The opening of *Light in August*, enveloped in "its slow palpable aura of somnolence and red dust" (*LA*: 11), is one of the most memorable scenes in this regard. What takes shape in Quentin's monologue is the twin strategy of borrowing and differentiation that defines Faulkner's writing with regard to its original idiom, which is to say the idiot idiom. To conclude this chapter, instead of expanding the list of their visible differences, I will try to show the similarities between the idiot's monologue and that of his neurasthenic and suicidal brother, and to reveal how Quentin—even as he distinguishes himself from it—is the first to extend the decisive legacy of the idiot idiom. This proximity is particularly evident in the long scene fluctuating between fantasy and memory that unfolds like a double in the mirror—a reflection in the water—of the initial and initiatory scene of the children's games in the river. Quentin and Caddy, now young adults, have returned to their childhood river, whose unruly flow imitates the form of this little story within the story. Assorted images and impressions are indiscriminately associated with one another, and the absence of punctuation eliminates the distinctions between the voices and their inflections. Questions and exclamations are reduced, as in Benjy's monologue, to blank affirmations that betray no emotion. Repressed in this way, the emotion of this scene is nevertheless all the more striking for it:

> the air seemed to drizzle with honeysuckle and with the rasping of crickets a substance you could feel on the flesh
> [. . .]
> get out of that water are you crazy

but she didn't move her face was a white blur framed out of the blur of the sand by her hair
[...]
the water sucked and gurgled across the sand spit and on in the dark among the willows across the shallow the water rippled like a piece of cloth holding still a little light as water does
hes crossed all the oceans all around the world
then she talked about him clasping her wet knees her face tilted back in the gray light the smell of honeysuckle (SF: 150)

The discourse of pain is replaced by a procession of synesthetic sensations. The simultaneous perception of an odor ("honeysuckle") and a sound ("the rasping of crickets") is expressed as a tactile sensation ("drizzle"), whose sensuality is heightened by the alliteration associating *feel* and *flesh*. Sensation, which by definition is elusive and fleeting, assumes an unusually solid form. In the waning light of dusk, Caddy is a hazy shape, almost without a face ("her face was a white blur").[22] Her hair can still be distinguished, but her face is a cloud, a vague shape that stands out against an equally hazy background. The object that Quentin's vision is trying to "frame" slips away. This moving and fleeting portrait that fails to discern its object reflects how Caddy resists her brother's grasp—how Caddy is already no longer Caddy. Like when she was a child, Caddy jumps in the water, and Quentin tries to pull her out. Throughout the scene, from which I have reproduced only an excerpt, Caddy is constantly described as being "wet" and "humid." In her case, water does not have the quality of a purifying ritual but is instead the physical manifestations of her eroticism and symbol of her sexual experience. It is the river that Quentin does not want her to dive into, the river in which he refuses to become wet himself. Quentin will enter the water, Caddy's element, only to drown there. Throughout the text, Caddy's lover and the gestures of love are referred to using pronouns without referents—*he, him, it*. For Quentin, the man that took Caddy from him and from the childhood in which he remains (in the company of Benjy, who like him will stay stuck there his whole life), is impersonal and interchangeable, while sexuality remains unspeakable. These lines clearly show that Quentin's tragedy resides not only in the fact that Caddy lost her virginity, but that he is not "him" (for her or anyone else), and has never done "it." This scene is unusually similar to Benjy's monologue by virtue of its great simplicity, and the paradoxical confusion and heightening of sensations that reveal it. What distinguish it are the references and allusions to canonical texts that abound in Quentin's monologue. In its idiot austerity, this scene implicitly weaves two major Shakespearean themes via the discreet evocation of two couples of star-crossed lovers: Othello and Desdemona, and Romeo and Juliet. The excerpt cited earlier is a rewriting of sorts of "The Willow Song," Desdemona's song of betrayed love in *Othello* (4.3), from which I will cite an excerpt:

> The poor soul sat sighing by a sycamore tree
> Sing all a green willow;
> Her hand on her bosom, her head on her knee,
> Sing willow, willow, willow:
> The fresh streams ran by her, and murmur'd her moans;
> Sing willow, willow, willow;
> Her salt tears fell from her, and soften'd the stones; —
> (*Othello* 4.3.41–47)

Numerous elements from Shakespeare's text are echoed in the scene described by Quentin, beginning with "the willows." There are also "streams," "tears," and even Caddy's position ("clasping her wet knees"), which is like that of the woman from the song ("her head on her knee"). In the extension of the text, a tearful Quentin attempts a final heroic gesture by replaying the death scene of the banished lovers that closes *Romeo and Juliet* (5.3), replacing the poison of Shakespeare's lovers with a knife. Repeating "yes" like an erratic refrain, Caddy appears resigned to the ceremony orchestrated by Quentin and the values he sanctions. The repetitive evocation of Caddy's throat culminates with the expression "I held the point of the knife at her throat" (*SF*: 152). But despite Caddy's encouragement, Quentin does not have the courage to thrust the blade in: "no like this youll have to push it harder" (152). The failure of death with his sister prefigures his solitary death for—or at least because of—his sister. This remarkable scene contrasts with the obvious pedantry in other parts of Quentin's monologue, in which the excessive flow of words poorly masks the great precariousness of things. Dream or memory, it represents a rare moment where, despite his tears, Quentin seems to accept the sensible order of the world. Benjy is not far, and it is no coincidence that he is evoked in the first enjambments of this fifteen-page prose poem: "is Benjy still crying / I dont know yes I dont know / poor Benjy" (150). With a language where small sensations play a big role, in which solemn words are used only with irony or circumspection (if not quite simply sacrificed)—a language whose austerity and sobriety bring to mind the extreme reticence of the idiot idiom—Quentin's monologue finds its bearings in Benjy's monologue and then distinguishes itself by exploring the themes specific to his character. Faulkner's writing has found both its touchstone and its cadence.

Chapter 14

TRYING TO READ FAULKNER

> A big demand *has* been made, the biggest of all. Your work by simply existing is a claim without a stop, made on our understanding.
> —EUDORA WELTY, *ON WILLIAM FAULKNER*

Dewey Dell's first interior monologue in *As I Lay Dying* highlights the decisive influence exerted on it by the idiot idiom: couched in highly spare syntax, it is steeped in repetitions and does not go to the trouble of clarifying its subjects. It includes clues that readers must associate and compare if they want to extract plausible avenues of interpretation. The abundance of details has a singular corollary in missing information. The effect of saturation in the discourse through repetition of the same motifs, structures, and words is counterbalanced by the retention of the meaning. The event in question is clarified only after multiple readings, which sometimes must take the form of painstaking analyses. At first glance, this text, which is emblematic of the reserved circumlocutions of Faulkner's writing, remains as opaque and mysterious as the "the secret shade" (*AILD*: 27) it mentions on multiple occasions. In Faulkner's writing, things are done and undone by way of suggestion,[1] whose necessarily variable effects are based on the reader's subjectivity. The truth that is revealed at "the end of the row" in which Dewey Dell and Lafe are filling their sacks with cotton cannot help but be precarious and doubtful. After the expectation sparked by the text's opacity, the story does not end conventionally with the meaning's emergence. Faulkner's writing presupposes that the reader will agree with a disorder that is not transcended by a final ordering of the story. The hypotheses advanced by Faulkner's readers are, for the most part, unverifiable; reading his work is therefore often condemned to irresolution. For all that, what can be read in Dewey Dell's first monologue? What are its explicit and implicit contents? What shapes does the perpetual evasion of meaning take?

The first part of the text includes minimalist but significant sketches of Dewey Dell's father and three older brothers.[2] Anse is stigmatized by his inertia:

"Pa dassent sweat because he will catch his death from the sickness so everybody that comes to help us" (*AILD*: 26). Convinced that he will die if he breaks out in a sweat, Anse takes his favorite posture, exploiting his world. Jewel is marked by his nonchalance: "And Jewel dont care about anything he is not kin to us in caring, not care-kin" (26). His indifference is suggested by the triple repetition of the word *care*, which is twice combined with the adjective *kin*, and signals his strangeness by showing how different he is from the rest of his siblings. The coinage "not care-kin" reveals Dewey Dell's intuition of what no one dares yet reveal—that Jewel is actually not part of the Bundren family. As is often the case in the monologues that precede the departure to Jefferson, Cash is reduced to the movements of his saw as he produces the planks for the unnamable object: "nailing them to something" (26). The imminence of Addie's death, which is discretely mentioned through a pronoun referring to an object that is so obvious its referent need not be identified—"She is going to die" (28)—along with the need for a coffin, are simultaneously suggested and relegated to the margins of the unspeakable. Darl is the brother who captures Dewey Dell's attention the most, a configuration that prefigures his preeminence over the entire novel. His gaze, and the insistent repetition of the phrase "without the words" (27) in connection with the verb *to know*, make him seem like both a threat and an object of loathing: "And that's why I can talk to him with knowing with hating because he knows" (27). Not only is the visionary Darl he who "knows" beyond words, he also "knows" something that could compromise Dewey Dell. This impression is confirmed by changing tenses: Dewey Dell's discourse imperceptibly shifts from "he knew" to the emphatic phrase "he did know," and culminates in the present with the absolute "he knows," which definitively marks Darl's ascendancy over his sister. But what does Darl "know" that Dewey Dell prefers he didn't? This question takes the reader back to the beginning of the monologue, which opens with the evocation of a certain Lafe, heretofore unknown: "The first time me and Lafe picked on down the row" (26). His importance for Dewey Dell, who includes his name at the beginning of her narrative, is confirmed by the transformation of the initial "me and Lafe" into a *we*, which is to say an entity that apparently goes beyond the grammatical level. The two appear to have made an agreement that, while not being clearly formulated, involves a *sack* (the word is repeated multiple times). This object metonymically refers to the activity carried out by the characters (who are filling sacks with cotton), but will soon be doubled by erotic allusions. I will cite the central paragraph of this monologue in its entirety:

> We picked on down the row, the woods getting closer and closer and the secret shade, picking in into the secret shade with my sack and Lafe's sack. Because I said will I or wont I when the sack was half full because

> I said if the sack is full when we get to the woods it wont be me. I said if it dont mean for me to do it the sack will not be full and I will turn up the next row but if the sack is full, I cannot help it. It will be that I had to do it all the time and I cannot help it. And we picked on toward the secret shade and our eyes would drown together touching on his hands and my hands and I didn't say anything. I said "What are you doing?" and he said "I am picking into your sack." And so it was full when we came to the end of the row and I could not help it. (*AILD*: 27)

Filling Dewey Dell's sack by the end of the row of cotton is the central issue, as demonstrated by Lafe eagerly filling the young girl's bag instead of his. The sack is the symbolic container of a promise—evoked by the constant repetition of the indefinite pronoun *it* deprived of an antecedent—that Dewey Dell wants to be fulfilled, just as she fears the consequences ("I said will I or wont I"). The proximity of the woods plays a crucial role in their affair: their approach brings to mind the final scenes of *Macbeth*, in which despite the threat of the armies assembled to dethrone him, the eponymous character feels protected by the impossible fulfillment of the witches' prediction:[3] "Till Birnan Wood remove to Dunsinane / I cannot taint with fear" (*Macbeth* 5.3.2–3). Unlike Macbeth, Dewey Dell willingly attributes the ability to move to the woods. In seeing the woods approach, she refuses to admit that she is the one drawing near; aware of the imminence of her destiny, she can offer no resistance other than procrastination and ratiocination. Her syntax reflects her efforts to clear herself of any responsibility for what is waiting in the wood's "secret shade," a twin symbol for dissimulation and the unknown. Her discourse shifts from hesitation—"it dont mean for me to do it"—to the evocation of a duty—"I had to do"—whose execution is independent of her will, as she continually repeats. The transition from the present ("I cannot help it") to the past tense ("I could not help it") affirms her belief that circumstances alone decided her fate, and that regardless of how she resists, "it" will happen. This formula signals the finality of her fate and also reveals the scope of her desire. Moreover, the retrospective aspect of the story suggests that it is too late to turn back: "it" is now part of her history and herself. One could indeed consider that the pronoun *it* refers to the promise of love, as well as Lafe and Dewey Dell's lovemaking in the shaded woods, just as it foreshadows the embryo she carries within her. Similarly, in retrospect the word *sack* assumes sexual connotations: this sack, whose volume increases as it is filled with cotton, serves as a triple metaphor for intensifying desire, for the subsequent transformation of Lafe's genital organs, and for Dewey Dell's pregnancy. "It" finally occurs in the typographical blank separating the paragraph cited above from the paragraph that follows, which begins: "And so it was because I could not help it. It was then" (*AILD*: 27). Here, the pronoun *it* assumes the status of a grammatical subject: in the continuity of the paragraph, it ultimately dissimulates Dewey Dell's guilt as projected by Darl's gaze, who she is convinced "knows," and will give her no respite.[4] The difficulty of reading this text, which is also a challenge for the translator, is that its structure, syntax, and words implement the elliptical strategy characteristic of Faulkner's writing: everything paradoxically happens when the language distinguishes itself through its understatements.

When Jean Stein asked Faulkner, in their famous interview, about the problems caused by the reception of his work—"Some people say they can't understand your writing, even after they read it two or three times. What approach would you suggest for them?"—he answered without batting an eye: "Read it four times" (Stein, Spring 1956: 76). This pragmatic adage concisely sums up the difficulty of reading Faulkner. Whether we admit it or not, Faulkner is best appreciated through trial, effort, and repetition. Whether we like it or not, the pleasure created by his writing is accompanied by a perversion that one could call masochistic.[5] Many readers resist it, seeing it as a topic of irritability or even worse as a source of boredom, and ultimately conclude that Faulkner is the hobbyhorse of obsessed academics. This impression is supported by the fact that Faulkner's work verifies the observation made by Roland Barthes in *The Pleasure of the Text:* "The text of pleasure is not necessarily the text that recounts pleasures" (Barthes, 1998 [1975]: 55). The little world of Yoknapatawpha County is predominantly marked by confrontation, rupture, chaos, and negative passions: it is a heavy and trying world in which characters seldom experience states of grace. As shown by the truncated story of Dewey Dell's love (who will spend the rest of the novel literally carrying the weight of her guilt), common and shared experience only occurs on the margins of the county, and in the silent margins of the story. Idylls are rare in Faulkner and hew very closely to their etymological definition: short lyric poems (like the episode of Ike's love for his cow) that are fragmentary (as with the relation between Eula Varner Snopes and Manfred de Spain) or relegated to what is left unsaid (the tenuous happiness of Mink Snopes and his wife is related in few words). Most often, they end badly. This heaving and painful world contributes to the difficulty of reading his work, and also makes a theme out of its difficulty. Yet with Faulkner, the pleasure of the text is neither "precarious" nor "precocious":

> The bliss of the text is not precarious, it is worse: *precocious*; it does not come in its own good time, it does not depend on any ripening. Everything is wrought to a transport at one and the same moment. This transport is evident in painting, today's painting: as soon as it is understood, the principle of loss becomes ineffective, one must go on to something

else. Everything comes about; indeed in every sense everything *comes—at first glance*. (Barthes, 1998 [1975]: 52–53)

Unlike the process described by Barthes, the pleasure of the Faulknerian text "come[s] in its own good time" and depends on a long and slow "ripening." It does not transport in one single moment but requires two, three, or four readings, after which, far from being exhausted, its bliss increases so much that it is sometimes difficult to "go on to something else." As difficult as it was for writers who were contemporaries of Faulkner to write during his lifetime or in his wake, from the reader's point of view Faulkner continues to make the work of many writers pale in comparison, regardless of place or time.[6] During a conference in Macon, Georgia, in 1960, Flannery O'Connor evoked the specter of Faulkner in the following way, with the caustic tone that is her own: "The presence alone of Faulkner in our midst makes a great difference in what the writer can and cannot permit himself to do. Nobody wants his mule and wagon stalled on the same track the Dixie Limited is roaring down" (O'Connor, 1999: 45). In retrospect, these words have broadly surpassed the microcosm of Southern writers and have taken on a universal and timeless dimension. Among the endless answers to the question of how this is so—how *The Sound and the Fury* is a "text that obsesses [. . .] more than a memory" (Pétillon, 2003 [1992]: 53)—there are two that strike me as being particularly convincing. These two answers are disconcertingly simple. The permanence and durability of the pleasure provided by Faulkner's writing reside first in an inexhaustible "sentiment of presence," like the one felt by Georges Bataille when, gazing upon the frescoes in Lascaux, he witnessed the miracle of "the birth of art":

> Directly we enter the Lascaux cave, we are gripped by a strong feeling we never have when standing in a museum, before the glassed cases displaying the oldest permanent remains of men or neat rows of their stone instruments. In underground Lascaux we are assailed by the same feeling of presence—of clear and burning presence—which works of art from no matter what period have always excited in us. (Bataille, 1955: 12)

Throughout Benjy's monologue in *The Sound and the Fury*, we have the striking sense of witnessing a beginning. "A new life begins: it has lost none of the material harshness which is life's constant thorny essence, it is no less a perilous struggle, but the fresh possibilities it brings with it have the winy taste of delight" (Bataille, 1955: 22). The singular emotion that comes with reading Faulkner is akin to the one felt during the experience of a birth: the birth of a writing; of an art stripped of doubles and peers within the "horizon of expectations of its first public" (Jauss, 1982: 54), one that continues to be talked about despite the many labels that have endeavored, for decades now, to grasp and "display" its essence; and finally, the birth of an art of reading. Faulkner's writing creates its own reader and the specific demands for its reading. It is actually in these very demands that I see the second explanation for the singular pleasure sparked by the Faulknerian text. Through its novelty and strangeness, it is an inexhaustible resurgence of "discoveries," the principle that Wolfgang Iser argues, in *The Implied Reader*, is one of the fundamental origins of aesthetic pleasure: "[D]iscovery is one form of aesthetic pleasure, for it offers the reader two distinct possibilities: first, to free himself—even if only temporarily—from what he is and to escape from the restrictions of his own social life; second, actively to exercise his faculties—generally the emotional and the cognitive" (Iser, 1974: xiii). Faulkner's writing is both an escape and a teaching,[7] both freedom and its exercise, one that is all the more arduous given that the gap "between poetic language and practical language, imaginary world and everyday reality" (Jauss, 1982: 54) is deep. Reading Faulkner is rarely pleasant, but it is always stimulating; it is not an ornament for the senses, but a challenge for the mind; it is no entertainment, but requires continued investment on the part of the reader. It does not divert readers from the activity of their consciousness, but engages them all the more fully within it, in its slow convolutions and endless circumlocutions, giving pride of place to what is "hidden."[8] The sacrifices made in reading Faulkner, and even more so in critiquing Faulkner, are considerable: it takes patience and hence time—a time that increases given that one's entry into the text is littered with obstacles. Great persistence is sometimes needed, and it requires even greater renunciation: by "stripping" readers of their ordinary expectations and traditional markers, it exposes their vision to bareness and their world to nudity, both of which spark fear. As suggested by Virginia Woolf in her 1926 essay "How Should One Read a Book?," the writing of "great writers" "bend" and "break" the reader.[9] Some readings are undeniably a threat to the reader's integrity. The vista that opens with the first sentence of a Faulkner text is a thousand miles from the facile distractions of "culinary" novels:[10] its exoticism is a kind of giddiness.

The first reading of Benjy's monologue, the one whose remarkable memory we strive to preserve, prompts a sense of profound strangeness. The readers who enter Benjy Compson's consciousness have no bearings; their powerlessness before the text unfolding before their eyes reflects Benjy's position toward the world. They are idiots, suddenly struck with idiocy through an opaque language that resists making sense. The initial monologue of *The Sound and the Fury* uses various images to transform one's difficulty reading it into an implicit theme. The scene in the narrative present that opens the novel is a little parable on the process of reading: "'Wait a minute.' Luster said. 'You snagged on that nail again. Cant you never crawl through here without snagging on that nail'" (*SF*: 4). Benjy tries to pass through the "broken place" in the fence, but he gets stuck, his passage hindered. Similarly, while the verb *to snag* refers to the state of being caught, the noun *snag* signals the hitches and pitfalls hidden in the text. The verb *to crawl* reflects both Benjy's position as he crawls and the position of readers, who must slip, to the best of their ability, into an awkward syntax. It also refers to the pace of reading, which is slowed by obstacles, for the reader is often forced "*to go at a crawl.*" The obstacles are materialized through the repeated theme of thwarted action: "Mrs Patterson's dress was caught on the fence" (14). Like Mrs. Patterson, the reader is often stuck, stagnating and going nowhere in the act of reading. Preventing a smooth advance are the causal flaws and missing information interspersed throughout Benjy's monologue, which incidentally makes multiple references to objects with holes in them, beginning with the previously mentioned fence—"the broken place" (4)—or the pocket—"this here hole in my pocket" (14)—that Luster's quarter fell through. In Faulkner, the reader's expectations are partially satisfied (and will remain shot through with holes) only through perseverance, and on the condition of accepting the *différance* of meaning.[11] The wise words that Dilsey shares with the children, instead of informing them of their grandmother's death, are also intended for the reader: "You'll know in the Lawd's own time" (25, 26). If there is "knowledge" in Faulkner, it is always connected to the future. With all due respect to Dilsey, its deferred revelation is more the result of the reader's effort than divine revelation. The simultaneous effect of the process of reading and the process of writing—in other words the impression that the idiot's consciousness develops its singular forms simultaneously with the reading of them—is symbolized by how Benjy and Luster base their movement on that of the golfers on the other side of the fence: "they stopped and we stopped" (3); "They went on. We went on along the fence" (54). In these examples built on repetition of the same verb, as well as the substitution of *we* for *they* as the grammatical subject, the idiot is an apish double of the golfers: his fascination with the golfers prompts him to imitate them and follow them closely. Reading the text is a *mise en abyme* of Benjy's gestures, with the reader being similarly condemned to adapt, as best as possible, to the erratic movements of his body and consciousness. "To read a book well, one should read it as if one were writing it," wrote Virginia Woolf (1994: 390). To read Benjy's monologue as it should be read requires reading it the way Faulkner wrote it: by assuming the narrator's idiocy as one's own, and renouncing for a time the implicit criteria of normality. Reading the initial monologue of *The Sound and the Fury* clearly requires new modes of thought and ways of imagining: it asks not so much to be understood as to be experienced in the resistance that characterizes it.

It is easily understandable that Benjy's monologue in particular, and Faulkner's writing in general, create diverse and extreme impressions on readers. Confronted with this monologue, some feel the reverential admiration with which one contemplates a jewel, seeing it as "full of stars": "It was full of stars. When I was still, they were still. When I moved, they glinted and sparkled" (*SF*: 41). The more the reader advances and digs into the text, the more the glint and sparkle of these stars grows. Others—and sometimes they are the same—experience a fatigue and frustration similar to that of Luster, who spends his days watching over an idiot: "Dont you reckon folks get tired of listening to you all the time" (54). Even for those in the first category, it is undeniable that reading Faulkner sometimes causes irritability. Readers sometimes feel they have been ill treated, given no regard. It is true that when he began writing his foundational novel, Faulkner did not care about being understood or appreciated. As pointed out by Noel Polk, his strategy was even directly opposed to such preoccupations: "He chose a deliberate misdirection, a miscommunication, or perhaps *dys*communication with his reader *and* with his narrator" (Polk, 1996: 103). With Benjy's monologue, Faulkner's writing takes off in earnest. It develops its own aesthetics based on the dysfunction of idiocy, and engages with its readers by exposing them to the unpleasantness of total and absolute incomprehension. Faulkner's indifference to conventions and refusal to establish clear and recognizable contact with his readership are sometimes interpreted as a kind of arrogance. The aesthetics of idiocy, along with the reader's transformation into an idiot—despite the fact that immersion in Benjy's idiocy requires readers to make great intellectual efforts—can paradoxically be seen as forms of elitism. Still, Faulkner was aware that there is no work without readers, and that, as demonstrated by Mikhail Bakhtin, reading is a condition for a work to be possible, the gesture that "embraces it, informs it, completes [it]" (Bakhtin, 1978: 71). Contrary to appearances, this logic is heightened in Faulkner, as Benjy's monologue, at the origin of the writer's great oeuvre, shows how reading represents an activity in its own right. This activity is based on an effort of (re)construction, which Stephen Ross has shown resembles an exercise in translation:

> Each utterance [Benjy] makes tends to stand alone, side by side with other statements but not connected to them by the speaker himself—sentences are joined with "and" but never with "because" or "so," forcing the reader to translate the simple sequence of sentences into familiar causal relationships. That readers can accomplish the translation is just the point of Faulkner's method: such images and syntax retain the form of objective description but they arrange phenomena in odd patterns that the reader must "conventionalize." (Ross, 1989: 172)

With this in mind, Benjy's monologue opens with a remarkable dialogue with readers, implicitly requiring them to elicit the meaning of the utterances, simple but opaque because of their radical strangeness, by reestablishing the missing links. It asks readers to fill the void, the literally blank space between two successive utterances by inserting "because," "so," and "for," the unquestionable explanatory tools of a normal discourse. The existence of Benjy's monologue is based on the reader's skill in filling in the gaps and piecing together its scattered and deficient utterances. The uniqueness of reading Faulkner therefore resides in the task imposed on the reader, namely producing a kind of retrospective discourse—most often immaterial and silent—in an effort to gather the text within a final organizing gesture and grasp its hidden intelligibility. Pierre Bergounioux has described this retrospective process as follows:

> This intelligibility—someone is this, some else does that—is not provided for the reader by someone, the author, who tells the story, paying little regard to that which is not as he says—doing so clearly, in this order that comes only from him—that things happened in reality when it was the present, the only real time, for those who took part, but in the obscure, truncated light of minds dominated by anxiety, tormented by migraines, struck with idiocy. [...] We can summarize the story, locate its peripheries over the course of time, list the characters and their relations, construct the structural theme governing the entire story. But the author abandons to the reader the task of drawing, for his own account, the second equivalent, careful of what he said, as those who are within would do if they were not thereby unable to do so. (Bergounioux, 2002: 123–24)

However, it is essential to accept the precariousness of this second discourse: Faulkner's writing is not a scattered puzzle for the benefit of a third party; its beauty resides less in its subsequent recomposition into a picture of "conventional" images than in the dissemination of its pieces.[12] Some critics such as Richard Gray consider the reading of Benjy's monologue as a "game," one with no givens and constant repositioning.[13] Unlike the idiot, whose condition cannot be improved, the reader's situation gradually does get better. It gradually appears that Benjy's chaotic world reveals itself in a syntax adhering to clearly defined patterns. The impression of chaos is not the doing of a chaotic writing but grows out of a perfectly mastered score. If the modes of idiot perception and idiom frighten the reader, it is first because they sacrifice the distance of conceptualization. The reader's skill and pleasure ultimately consist in grasping the sense of the senses by following its digression and evasion, in understanding it and then disentangling oneself from it, in order to keep intact the paradoxical volatility of a writing otherwise rooted in its objects.

The strategy of deferred clarification that characterizes Faulkner's writing is reflected at all levels of the work:[14] it is present in the idiot's syntax but also governs the structure of *The Sound and the Fury*; it is central to the persistent fantasy prompted by the novel; and it determines the evolution of Faulkner's work. On numerous occasions in Benjy's monologue, the reader's confusion regarding factual phenomena that the idiot cannot name ultimately decreases, thanks to the information contained in the speech of others that is reported throughout the monologue, as well as in Benjy's own discourse. Even though the idiot cannot understand their import and meaning, he provides indirect explanations for the reader who is at first perplexed by the strategies of avoidance characterizing the poetry inherent to his idiom. In other words, if readers are unable to grasp the phenomena described by the idiot in the bare words and heightened sensations that define his discourse, assuming they are attentive, there is almost always someone to help them get things straight. For instance, the factual albeit periphrastic description of the water that breaks is followed by the appearance of the word "ice" spoken by Caddy, the appropriate signifier for the signified in question: "Ice. That means how cold it is" (*SF*: 13). This example also confirms that Caddy is the only one who deems Benjy worthy of explaining. Similarly, when they hear the unusual sound made by Mrs. Compson upon Damuddy's death—"then we heard it again"; "then we couldn't hear it" (25)—it is Quentin who points out the source and nature of the sound: "'That was Mother.' Quentin said. [. . .] 'She was crying.'" (25). Consequently, the opacity of Benjy's discourse is less absolute than appears at first sight. After testing his reader's ability to be an idiot and apprehend the world like one, Faulkner sometimes uses, via other characters, the practical language shared with readers, as though he wanted to ensure that his readers understand correctly.[15] That is how certain elements undergo deferred clarification, even when the reader no longer expects it.

The novel's structure also reflects a similar consideration: one section of the novel can "clarify" the language of a preceding one. All of Faulkner's comments on the composition of *The Sound and the Fury* include the semantics of clarity: "I took three more sections, all longer than Benjy's to try to clarify it" ("Intro *SF*, II": 231). Even though, from one section to another, Faulkner had the sense that he was "delaying," things are indeed clarified little by little. For instance, after the confusion and density of Benjy's and Quentin's monologues, the readability of Jason's monologue is all the more disconcerting, given, as Wolfgang Iser has remarked, that the reader has made considerable efforts to *not* see clearly for over half of the novel: "[W]hen total comprehension seems to be out of the question, the Jason monologue provides the reader with the privilege of overall vision that has been withheld from him till now" (Iser, 1974: 148). This logic is expanded in section 4, which symbolically opens at dawn with the all-embracing gaze of a third-person narrator: "The day dawned bleak and chill, a moving wall of gray light out of the northeast" (*SF*: 265). This dawn partially lifts the veil over the opaqueness of the preceding texts: section 4 finally shows, from an external and omniscient point of view, what the three other tales did not. For instance, when the big man-child with the shambling gait truly appears for the first time, the reader has already spent multiple hours in his company, with greater or lesser degrees of proximity. Yet in seeing him, the reader has difficulty recognizing him. There is great surprise in seeing what was heretofore only imagined, especially realizing that one had, as it were, not seen anything. None of the three successive monologues of the Compson brothers contains a full portrait. All things considered, none of the three monologues shows the reader Benjy's pasture, or the sparkling little Caddy or loyal Dilsey. As a result, things and characters take full shape just before the end of the novel. Until now they were only words, immaterial and versatile. It is as though Benjy's portrait had been deferred for so long that the reader ultimately gave up waiting for it and tacitly accepted doing without it. That is why the late descriptions of Benjy (the character, as opposed to the narrator) that are disseminated in the narration closing the book inevitably come as a shock. They come at a late hour and wipe out the mental images that the reader had unconsciously formed, replacing them with other images imposed in authoritarian fashion. Faced with the curious gallery of portraits that begins approximately fifty pages before the novel's end, the reader is beset by a strange feeling of surprise and vague disappointment. Having accepted hesitation, change, and evanescence as the mode of the story, the subsequent precision, detail, and clarity of section 4 seem to be an infringement on the story, and even a personal affront to one's capacities as a reader. Even when deprived of faces, Caddy and her brothers have a certain depth and familiarity—in a word, an existence—that the reader had forgotten are based on radically subjective images. Moreover, as the mist clears during the morning of the final section, the appearance of portraits in the traditional sense of the term come with a disagreeable aftertaste, which stems from the fact that Benjy and his pasture do not resemble—cannot resemble—the images readers created for their own use in the ellipses and silences of the first three monologues. That is why the initiative of the author, who serves as the novel's fourth narrator, in order to remedy the extreme singularity of the three voices preceding his own, is doomed to fail: "[I]t was still not complete" (Stein, Spring 1956: 74). The failure of section 4 of *The Sound and the Fury*, the ineffectiveness of the "final turn of the screw" ("Intro *SF*, II": 232), results, as it were, from too much light, from an excess of clarity that introduces dissonant notes in the story rather than harmonizing and completing the novel. It is interesting that this feeling of failure materializes through the incessant repetition of the verb *to try* and never gives way to the expression of accomplishment or completion (*manage* and *achieve* are rare words in Faulkner's writing) that pursued Faulkner long after the novel's publication.

He returned to it in the form of the "Appendix/Compson, 1699–1945," which is based on the fantasy of a fifth voice. But by providing unwanted answers, this retrospective chronology of the Compson family only heightens the disappointment of section 4 of the novel. The didactic efforts of this hybrid text, which develops as an odd afterthought, add nothing to the novel's quality. On the contrary, reading the "Appendix" generates a sense of frustration in which readers are tempted to "try" to forget the gallery of overly explicit and dated heroes parading before their eyes. The efforts that the author-narrator of the "Appendix" makes to correct the idiocy of the original text seem counterproductive, even damaging. The process of deferred clarification reaches its limits here and somehow creates an effect of saturation. When the "Appendix" revisits the destiny of Caddy—who is deliberately the great absent in *The Sound and the Fury*—the list of her failed loves[16] and the revelation of her promiscuity with a Nazi officer are not only unnecessary but are harmful to her character's characteristic volatility. Published in 1946 in the final section of *The Portable Faulkner*, the anthology edited by Malcolm Cowley, the text appears in a chapter aptly entitled "The Undying Past": for both Faulkner and the reader, the irresolution that dominates the text of *The Sound and the Fury*, despite the accumulation of clarifying voices, effectively inscribes the work in an "undying past" that refuses to be quiet and never fuses with the bygone past. In fact, rather than helping dissipate the work's obscurity, these successive and retrospective attempts to clarify its meaning paradoxically serve only to increase the doubt and uncertainty of the reader, who ultimately ends up in an unusual position of rebellion, albeit a silent one, in relation to the author and the excess of information. After writing the "Appendix," and believing that his fetish novel had finally found its (re)solution, Faulkner wrote to Cowley: "I should have done this when I wrote the book. Then the whole thing would have fallen into pattern like a jigsaw puzzle when the magician's wand touched it." He goes as far as recommending that the "Appendix" be read as a prologue to *The Sound and the Fury*, suggesting to his editors at Random House, who were preparing the novel's publication for the Modern Library imprint, to publish the "Appendix" before Benjy's section. Here I will allow myself to contradict Faulkner and to affirm that it is especially important not to follow his recommendation. I prefer to see the "Appendix" as an independent text, comparable to "That Evening Sun," the short story published in 1931 in which he once again staged characters from the Compson family, or as a test of exegesis that should be handled with precaution and moderation. On a basic level, *The Sound and the Fury* is sufficient unto itself; its beauty largely flows from its stubborn resistance to its many rewritings. It is crucial that reading the text—and ideally reading all of Faulkner—begin with the idiot's monologue. Despite the intense satisfaction that Faulkner felt upon completing the "Appendix," this final attempt at clarification still does not provide a definitive answer. He was still trying ten years later, when he published *The Mansion* in 1959. Faulkner's penultimate novel offers obvious proof of how the idiot Benjy and the idiocy of *The Sound and the Fury*, that failed but favorite novel, had not lost their grip. Chapter 14 of *The Mansion* opens with a digression that, in the space of a few lines, picks up the thread from a thirty-year-old story, which Faulkner finally tries to bring to an end (note the recurrence of the adverb *finally*):

> Jason, the middle one, finally got rid of Benjy too by finally persuading his mother to commit him to the asylum only it didn't stick, Jason's version being that his mother whined and wept until he, Jason, gave up and brought Benjy back home, where sure enough in less than two years Benjy not only burned himself up but completely destroyed the house too. (*M*: 619)

The final solution available for him is to annihilate the Compson estate and its idiot in the same fire: Benjy dies by immolation under circumstances similar to those that Jim Bond survived in the final pages of *Absalom, Absalom!* After producing a final novel, published on June 4, 1962, one that was never taken seriously by critics or by Faulkner himself, a final farce entitled *The Reivers*, Faulkner in turn passed away, in the middle of the night on July 6, 1962.

The unusual accessibility of Faulkner's final novels, in which the monologue disappears before the supremacy of dialogue and solipsism makes way for exchange and sociability, are the culmination of the strategy of *différance* that characterizes most of his work. While it does not dispel Faulkner's obsession for his first novel, by revisiting the questions left unanswered and imposing answers on them, the "Appendix" nevertheless brings an end, however arbitrary it may be, to the waiting. It was normal and necessary for Faulkner to choose that moment in the history of his work to try something else. Given the history of his time (World War II, the social changes that irremediably transformed the South), it was perhaps logical for him to focus on new subjects, to open his work up to the "Americanization of the county," which coincided with the end of the Faulknerian epic, as noted by Édouard Glissant.[17] The tone of the folkloric anecdotes—"that was part of our folklore, or Snopeslore, if you like" (*T*: 129)—scattered throughout the Snopes trilogy offers lighter fare, as do its accounts of social climbing, score settling, and the blandness of daily specials served at roadside diners.[18] Yet it is simplistic to say that the clarity of the late novels is synonymous with failure. While it may apparently be less intricate, "Snopesian writing" is, in its own way, a writing of jubilation:

> I have suggested that the writing in the trilogy is flat. Certainly, relative to what is revealed of the county's lofty damnations, it is. But even if this Snopesian writing does not fall into the abyss, it is composed with a dense complexity in which the real must be disentangled from people's motivations and the minutiae of their actions. (Glissant, 2000: 188)

Unjustly dismissed by critics, Faulkner's final novels are those of an aging writer at peace with the "county's lofty damnations," and with the fears of the past. They are the novels of a writer in his maturity who has nothing left to prove (to himself), who explores the preoccupations and idiosyncrasies of thirty-five years of writing and presents the changes of his time, deliberately choosing to have fun while doing it. The singularity of Faulkner's writing endures and continues, in a conversational mode, his perpetual tribute to his early discoveries; but with time, it grew calmer.

The exemplary nature of Benjy's monologue is confirmed, from the reader's point of view, by the fact that his text serves as a training exercise for reading Faulkner. Like the idiot's monologue, the later novels assume a readability that they would potentially not possess without this earlier test. Just as the first monologue of *The Sound and the Fury* represents the initiatory focal point for Faulkner the writer, for the reader it is like an initiation rite ladened with pitfalls: "But when I wrote Benjy's section, I was not writing it to be printed. If I were to do it over now I would do it differently, because the writing of it as it now stands taught me both how to write and how to read, and even more" ("Intro *SF*, II": 231). Faulkner learned how to write, while the reader learned how to read—"and even more."

Conclusion

FICTION OF ORIGIN AND THE ORIGIN OF FICTION

> I was over thirty. I hadn't written a line. I randomly read *Absalom, Absalom!*, which had just been published in a new pocket edition: from the first pages I found a father, a brother, something akin to *the father of the text*.
> —PIERRE MICHON, *TROIS AUTEURS*

For lack of releasing the language of his idiot characters, Faulkner releases their thoughts through the miracle of narrative strategies, giving them a voice and words, delivering and freeing them from their silent torpor. The singular originality of Faulkner's writing took shape and form from the creation of an idiocy and its shapelessness, eliciting what Georges Bataille has called "marvelous forms,"[1] whose radical novelty Georges Didi-Huberman has commented on thusly:

> Laying claim to shapelessness does not mean laying claim to non-forms, but rather engaging in a *labor of forms* akin to what would be a *labor* of childbirth or death throes: an opening, a ripping, a heartrending process putting something to death and, within this very negativity, inventing something absolutely new, bringing something to light. (Didi-Huberman, 1995: 21)

The birth of new forms results from the death of older forms, forms smooth and worn with time. Novelty proceeds from an act of tearing, from a heartrending, from the sacrifice of long-felt forms and expectations. In Faulkner, the transition from a writing weighed down by heritage and tradition to a radically new and resolutely modern writing takes place via idiocy.[2] Idiocy in Faulkner—the painful birth of unusual forms both difficult and marvelous—is a kind of initiation. In its infancy, it demands the cruel sacrifice of readability.

As a transition, idiocy expresses the progress of writing. This is the crucial detour that Faulkner could not have taken, a detour that transformed the laborious apprentice into an undisputed master.

In Faulkner, idiocy is embodied by characters who frequently appear in his work. The idiots of Yoknapatawpha County contribute to the local color of the South depicted by Faulkner all while expressing, on an individual scale, how the nation tends to perceive the most distinctive of its regions. The presence of idiots in the community initiates a game of opposites in which the other, less singular members are implicitly defined. The innocence of idiots stands in opposition to the machinations of fellow citizens trying to achieve their ends,[3] while the incorruptible infancy of their world view preserves them from the county's damnations. Idiocy also concentrates Faulkner's great obsessions, namely a temporality "decapitated" of its future, in which the past suddenly appears alongside the present; it is built on the insoluble dialectic opposing the unusual individual and his or her community, which experiences difference as an affront. Idiocy is a posture whose uncorrupted freshness is a suitable place for the author to regain, as it were, his lost virginity. The singularity of the idiot's gaze, which is neither predetermined nor perverted by any arbitrary law, resides in the fact that it is perpetually born in the world as the world is reborn, pristine and new, in each of his gazes. Through the fiction of an emerging world, in which things show more than they tell and burst forth forever exceptional in the collection of sensible qualities—necessarily changing and versatile—there comes the birth of an idiom whose characteristics bring to mind those of original languages as defined by Rousseau in his 1781 *Essay on the Origin of Languages*: "What the ancients said most vividly they expressed not by words, but by signs; they did not say it, they showed it." Rousseau evokes a language built on "presenting arguments to the eyes" and points out that "the most energetic language is the one in which the sign has said everything before one speaks" (Rousseau, 1998: 290). It is a similar language, at the source of the sensible, that Faulkner invents through his idiot narrator. It is through the "mute eloquence" (291) of the idiot's idiom that Faulkner's writing finds its remarkable color and assumes its preferred forms.

For all these reasons, the Faulknerian idiot, the incarnation of an extreme alterity, can be considered as the "conceptual persona" of Faulkner's fiction. I have borrowed this concept from Gilles Deleuze and Félix Guattari, who in their *What Is Philosophy?* attribute this singular status, halfway between the discourse of literature and that of philosophy, to what they call the "Idiot" of Descartes's *cogito*,[4] the "Antichrist" and "Dionysus crucified" of Nietzsche, and the Socrates of Plato. Deleuze and Guattari defined this notion of a conceptual character in the following way:

> Conceptual personae carry out the movements that describe the author's plane of immanence, and they play a part in the very creation of the author's concepts. [...] Conceptual persona are the philosopher's "heteronyms," and the philosopher's name is the simple pseudonym of his personae. I am no longer myself but thought's aptitude for finding itself and spreading across a plane that passes through me at several places. [...] But conceptual persona is not an abstract personification, or a symbol or allegory, for it lives, it insists. (Deleuze and Guattari, 1996 [1994]: 63–64)

As the creator of fictional situations and characters, Faulkner is obviously not a philosopher. One could even claim that in the wake of his aesthetics of idiocy, his writing shows symptoms that are allergic to the concept. When the concept blossoms, in his late novels in particular, it is often to denounce the conceitedness of certain characters: for instance, Gavin Stevens, who was educated at Harvard and the University of Heidelberg, shows a propensity to use abstract notions that reveal his superiority over the county's oafs, who, for that matter, are all respectful toward him. But the idiolect particular to Stevens also serves to show how disembodied his relation to the world is. With this in mind, his declaration to Linda Snopes that he loved her platonically—after having a similar adoration for her mother—is especially eloquent: "*I am happy I was given the privilege of meddling with impunity in other peoples affairs without really doing any harm by belonging to that avocation whose acolytes have been absolved in advance for holding justice above truth I have been denied the chance to destroy what I loved by touching it*" (M: 656). Fulfilled by the prudent and distant enjoyment provided by the grandiloquence of words, Stevens takes joy in not having experienced ("*without really doing*") or possessed ("*I have been denied*"). He interprets his privations favorably as so many "chances." There is no doubt Faulkner is having fun with his character. By giving him a stodgy, dry, and obsequious discourse, whose ridiculousness is emphasized through the repetition of pompous words beginning with the letter "a" (and hence borrowed from the first pages of the dictionary: "*absolved*," "*acolytes*," "*advance*," "*avocation*"), he makes the county's intellectual into the idiot's opposite double. For one, the absence of sensible experience is masked by the predominance of conceptual language, while for the other the exclusive preeminence of sensible experience yields to the idiocy of a minimalist idiom.

If the idiot can be seen as Faulkner's conceptual persona, it is because he is present throughout his work and somehow "lays out the plane." For Faulkner, he represents a kind of *in*aptitude of thought, one that shapes the identity of his creator and determines the shape of his entire body of work. In Deleuze's words, it is a character that is not at all abstract because it "lives" and "insists" until the final pages of his work, which echoes until the very end the jolts and starts of the writing of idiocy. The idiot's idiocy marks out a certain number of figures whose recurrence lends Faulkner's style a certain stability. Meanwhile, it leaves the imprint of instability on Faulkner's novelistic world. Determined by this conceptual persona, which emerges at the origin of fiction and embodies the fiction of its origin, Faulkner's writing is built on sudden appearances and reflects the perpetual variations of sensible perception: objects "jump" in its syntax as they "jump" out within the idiot's gaze. Benjy's discourse is peppered with the verb *to jump*, sometimes referring to a sudden appearance—"The cows came jumping out of the barn" (*SF*: 20)—and sometimes evoking a disappearance: "The cellar door and the moonlight jumped away" (40). The same image is repeated to capture the fire's reflection on Mrs. Compson's rings: "Her rings were jumping" (61); "Her rings jumped on Caddy's back" (62). The emotion specific to Faulkner's writing comes from this primitive and jumping dance of sensation, which according to Bataille also characterizes the earliest masterpieces: "At Lascaux, gazing at these pictures, we sense that *something is stirring, something is moving*. That something touches us, we are stirred by it, as though in sympathy with the rhythms of a dance; from this passionate movement emanates the beauty of the paintings" (Bataille, 1955: 130).

NOTES

INTRODUCTION

1. The literary experience of idiocy that Faulkner pursued with his full faculties of reason has many points in common with the singular experience described by Georges Bataille in *Inner Experience*: "Inner experience responds to the necessity in which I exist—and human existence with me—to challenge (question) everything without acceptable rest. [. . .] I wanted experience to lead me where it was leading, not to some end given in advance. And I say at once that it does not lead to a harbor (but to a place of bewilderment, of nonsense)" (Bataille, 2014: 9).

2. The quotation is from the first of two introductions written by Faulkner in 1933 for the new edition of *The Sound and the Fury*. Neither of these two texts, which have many similarities but differ on certain subjects (which I will discuss below), was published during his lifetime. James B. Meriwether tracked them down, and then edited and published them in 1972 and 1973 in the *Southern Review* and the *Mississippi Quarterly*, respectively.

3. Largely truncated and reworked by his publisher, the novel that appeared in one form in 1929 under the title *Sartoris* was unrecognizable to its author.

4. "One day I seemed to shut a door between me and all publishers' addresses and book lists. I said to myself, Now I can write" ("Intro *SF*, I": 227).

5. "A book is the product of a self other than that which we display in our habits, in company, in our vices" (Proust, 1984 [1958]: 12).

6. The actual name of William Faulkner's great-grandfather was Colonel W. C. Falkner.

7. Bud is short for Budweiser, a famous brand of American beer.

8. Joseph Blotner likely drew inspiration from Benjy Compson's obsessive memory in his evocation of the idiot from Oxford, Mississippi, who was permanently pressed up against the fence marking out both his front yard and the extent of his possibilities: "She [Annie Chandler] lived with her family on Pierce Avenue, a few blocks southeast of the Falkners. She and her sisters were charged with the care of their brother, Edwin, who could be seen playing in their front yard behind a high fence. The family had learned early in his childhood that Edwin was retarded. He would never be normal, though he lived past the age of thirty. Annie Chandler gave to her pupils the kind of love that her family gave its own perennial child" (Blotner, 1974: 21). In 1928, when Faulkner was writing *The Sound and the Fury*, Edwin Chandler was still pressed up against the iron fence: "Just a few blocks away

Miss Annie Chandler, his first-grade teacher, still lived, and her brother, Edwin Chandler, who could speak and play simple games but whose mind would never grow to adulthood as his body had done years before. Faulkner had seen him behind his iron fence since childhood" (Blotner, 1974: 210).

9. What especially drew Faulkner's attention in the sixty-three poems of *A Shropshire Lad* was the hero's rootedness in an eminently sensitive and tangible world. This relation to the world prefigures the singular being-in-the-world of Faulknerian idiots to come, a full-throated version of which is announced here: "Here was the reason for being born into a fantastic world: discovering the splendor of fortitude, the beauty of being of the soil like a tree about which fools might howl and which winds of disillusion and death and despair might strip, leaving it bleak, without bitterness, beautiful in sadness." This evocation of Housman's collection is taken from an article Faulkner wrote on poetry and the influence it had on his life (*EPP*: 117). *A Shropshire Lad* had a profound influence on Faulkner throughout his life, who continually paid discrete tribute to this central work in his development as a writer, such as in *Soldiers' Pay*, in which the veteran Donald Mahon, who is a shadow of his former self, carries a copy of the collection.

10. The entry for "idiocy" in the *Dictionnaire des termes techniques de médecine* (Dictionary of Medical Terminology) also points out that "idiocy almost always coincides with arrested development of the encephalon, which can occur either during intrauterine life or after birth, and can be caused by heredity or a particular illness" (Garnier and Delamare, 1972).

11. In the hierarchy established by Voisin, "congenital or acquired imbecility" and "mental debility" were minor forms of idiocy. Imbecility is characterized by "the rudimentary existence of all intellectual faculties, instinctive or moral, by the perversion or instability of these faculties," whereas debility coincides with "the weakness or imbalance of faculties" (Voisin, 1893: 79–80).

12. As a specific form of mental debility, cretinism is connected to a very precise cause (thyroid deficiency) and manifestation (goiters).

13. Séguin's discourse brings to mind the negative theology that defines God in light of what he is not.

14. This is how Sartre describes Flaubert the child in his *The Family Idiot: Gustave Flaubert, 1821 to 1857*: "Gustave was a simple soul, improbably, pathologically credulous; he frequently fell into long stupors—his parents searched his features and feared he was an idiot" (Sartre, 1981: 7). In *Les Mots* (1963), Sartre describes himself as a child idiot and entertains the notion of a lineage connecting him to Flaubert. It is noteworthy that Sartre actively contributed to Faulkner's recognition in France, to the extent that his novels were translated into French. The lineage connecting Sartre and Flaubert also included Faulkner and his idiots.

15. It is significant that the term "madness" is absent from psychoanalytic terminology. If the notion of madness was not included by Jean Laplanche and Jean-Bertrand Pontalis in their *Vocabulaire de la psychanalyse* (1967; *The Language of Psycho-Analysis*), that is because Freud did not consider madness to be a stable state. Freud invented concepts that replaced the notion of madness in an effort to identify the dynamics of unconscious impulses, which can take pathological forms.

16. In the first state of nature identified by Rousseau, humans were "savage" in the sense that they lived outside any kind of society. Deprived of any conscience or moral liberty, they were not civilized: like animals restricted to pure sensations. Rousseau recognized that this state of nature was a theoretical fiction—a myth—whose function was not so much to rehabilitate the savage as to denaturalize the description of social beings.

17. Faulkner made this idea his own, in a somewhat different form, in connection with Benjy Compson's thirty-three years of age: "You mean, he been three years old thirty years" (*SF*: 17).

18. The *Oxford English Dictionary* points out that this is an archaic sense: "One naturally deficient in intellect."

19. Pierre Senges suggests this in his *L'Idiot et les hommes de paroles* (The Idiot and the Men of Words): "All idiots [. . .] are tempted by the mystical (or we are ourselves tempted by a mystical reading of their adventures): this direct relation, from mouth to mouth (gaping mouth to gaping mouth), not just from the idiot to God but also from the idiot to all things, with an immediacy that causes concern or laughter, is what characterizes our idiot" (Senges, 2005: 86).

20. The incorruptibility of the idiot is highlighted by Flannery O'Connor in the character of Bishop from *The Violent Bear It Away*: "'And that one,' the old man would say, beginning to brood on the schoolteacher's child again, 'that one—the Lord gave him one he couldn't corrupt'" (O'Connor, 1955: 77).

21. "And I like this readiness of yours, Prince, you're really very nice" (Dostoevsky, 2003: 29).

CHAPTER 1. IS THE IDIOT A MONSTER?

1. On the contrary, Nietzsche insisted on the virtues and advantages of illness, especially with regard to composition. In *Ecce Homo*, in the chapter entitled "Why I Am So Wise," he evokes the conditions in which he wrote "Daybreak": "In the following winter, the first I spent in Genoa, that sweetening and spiritualization which is virtually inseparable from an extreme poverty of blood and muscle produced 'Daybreak.' The perfect brightness and cheerfulness, even exuberance of spirit reflected in the said work is in my case compatible not only with the profoundest physiological weakness, but even with an extremity of pain" (Nietzsche, 2004 [1986]: 8–9). Similarly, in "Daybreak" he devotes an entire paragraph to the topic of "On the Knowledge Acquired through Suffering": "The condition of sick people who suffer dreadful and protracted torment from their suffering and whose minds nonetheless remain undisturbed is not without value for the acquisition of knowledge—quite apart from the intellectual benefit which accompanies any profound solitude, any unexpected and permitted liberation from duties" (Nietzsche, 1997 [1982]: 69).

2. It is interesting that Verlaine's list of the monster's "dreadful" characteristics includes an explicit reference to the distention of skin, bringing to mind and possibly foreshadowing descriptions of Faulknerian idiot bodies: "The skin, limp, was yellow and dirty . . ." (Verlaine, 1962: 129–30).

3. In her book *Faulkner: Le Roman de la détresse* (Faulkner: The Novel of Distress), Aurélie Guillain's description of Popeye, the main character in *Sanctuary*, indirectly

denounces the monstrousness that presides over its composition: "Popeye seems to consist of a hodgepodge, as though he had summarily been created for an improvised ritual from recovered materials, scraps of tin and bits of black rubber" (Guillain, 2003: 122).

CHAPTER 2. THE FLABBY FLESH AND FLACCID BODIES OF IDIOTS

1. The narrator of "The Kingdom of God" makes multiple references to containers without contents: "a burlap bundle" ("Kingdom": 78), "the sack" (80), "the other sack" (80); the vagueness surrounding the delivery of these bags is described through adverbs such as "briefly" (78) and "swiftly" (80). Fear ("scared," 78) and "sweat" (80) contribute to a state of tension culminating in the fear sparked by the police, with the shift toward increasingly determinate articles making the threat increasingly tangible: "some bull" (80), "a bull" (80), "a policeman" (80).

2. This meaning appears in Plato's *Sophist*, in which the "unskilled" person is opposed to the "sophist" (Plato, 1985: 221c).

3. "Monk" was published in *Scribner's* in May 1937 before being included with five other detective stories in the collection published under the title *Knight's Gambit* in 1949. In publishing *Knight's Gambit*, Faulkner expressed his desire, as he had done earlier with *The Unvanquished* and *Go Down, Moses*, to collect short stories that had previously had an independent existence. All of the short stories in *Knight's Gambit* dramatize the character Gavin Stevens, a lawyer who assumes the role of a detective. In "Monk," Gavin Stevens secures the acquittal of the idiot Monk Odlethrop, who was unjustly imprisoned for a murder he did not commit. Stevens then discovers that Monk was the victim of the machinations of another inmate in prison, who took advantage of his feeblemindedness to incite him to commit another murder, for which he is ultimately hanged.

4. In "Hand upon the Waters," Gavin Stevens investigates the mysterious death of feebleminded Lonnie Grinnup, who is incidentally the last descendant of the founders of Yoknapatawpha County. Lonnie Grinnup, whose real name (which he apparently has never known) is Louis Grenier, was himself the protector of an individual even more idiotic than himself, a deaf-and-dumb orphan named Joe whom he welcomed into his hut in the woods: "the deaf-and-dumb orphan he had taken into his hut ten years ago and clothed and fed and raised, and who had not even grown mentally as far as he himself had" ("Hand": 66).

5. Aurélie Guillain interprets the absence of shape that is characteristic of idiots as a metaphor for their amorality: "Since Benjy is a creature that does not know what is forbidden, and does not act like a selfish and guilty self, he has no *contours*. An amoral being is too scattered, too conflated with the matter of the world for us to identify with him" (Guillain, 2003: 82).

6. In John Steinbeck's 1937 novel *Of Mice and Men*, the characteristics of the idiot Lennie bring to mind those of Faulknerian idiots. A comparison of the descriptions of Lennie and George, in the very first pages of the novel, emphasizes how the idiot is associated with flabbiness and the normal man with what is hard and defined:

The first man was small and quick, dark of face, with restless eyes and sharp, strong features. Every part of him was defined: small, strong hands, slender arms, a thin and bony nose. Behind him walked his opposite, a huge man, shapeless of face, with large, pale eyes, with wide, sloping shoulders; and he walked heavily, dragging his feet a little, the way a bear drags his paws. His arms did not swing at his sides, but hung loosely. (Steinbeck, 1940 [1937]: 9)

This parallel dual portrait underscores the recurring physiological attributes traditionally associated with idiocy: enormously disproportionate corpulence, the absence of shape (we find the adjective "shapeless"), the distended nature of members, and a dragging and clumsy gait reminiscent of a bear. The idiot is thus defined as the opposite of the normal human, who is small and alert with clear and sharp characteristics, and is made up entirely of nerves, muscle, and bones in a structure with clearly defined contours.

7. "He [Jewel] squats there, staring straight ahead, motionless, lean, wooden-backed, *as though carved squatting out of the lean wood*" (*AILD*: 231; emphasis mine).

8. They appear on pages 94, 95, 103, 108, 209, and 231; in a spillover effect, Dewey Dell also perceives her older brother as being made of wood: "Jewel sits on his horse like they were both made out of wood, looking straight ahead" (*AILD*: 122).

9. The adjective "comical" is used rarely enough by Darl to justify its emphasis here: "After that I thought it was right comical" (*AILD*: 131).

10. While the Bundrens are either perched atop or hitched or roped to the wagon carrying their mother's coffin, Jewel is the lone horseman, preceding his kin on his mount.

11. This characteristic is also present in Steinbeck's idiot: "They sat by the fire and filled their mouths with beans and chewed mightily. A few beans slipped out of the side of Lennie's mouth. George gestured with his spoon" (Steinbeck, 1940 [1937]: 31).

12. "You mean, he been three years old thirty years" (*SF*: 17). The idiot is described as having reached full maturity at the age of three, which cannot be surpassed despite the number of years.

13. The idiot from "The Kingdom of God" remains passively seated in the car during the entire story, impervious to the agitation around him.

14. "We go along the fence" (*SF*: 4). In *The Hamlet*, Ike tirelessly follows the cow, with the consistency of his trajectory being marked by the repetition, in various forms, of the verb "follow" (*H*: 184–85).

15. The awkwardness of the idiot's gait is also marked, in both Faulkner and Steinbeck, by the recurrence of the adverb "heavily": "He ran heavily" (*H*: 186). Ike's clumsy running exposes him to a number of falls.

CHAPTER 3. INARTICULATE VOICE AND STORY

1. I have borrowed this neologism from the translators of *Du Sens des sens* (The Sense of the Senses) by Erwin Straus (1989: 322).

2. The quotations are from *AILD*: 172–73.

3. Equating words and deeds necessarily occurs through the absence of language and voice; it is ultimately possible only in silence.

4. On two occasions in the final lines of *The Sound and the Fury*, the text evokes the idiot's extreme pain in terms of "agony," an English word that refers to intense fear and great suffering, to death throes.

5. Here we follow Coindreau's interpretation of the verb "to cry," which he translates as "*crier*" (to yell) rather than "*pleurer*" (to shed tears). This choice is confirmed by numerous citations that signal the absence of tears: "But he bellowed slowly, abjectly, without tears" (*SF*: 316).

6. The successive expressions referring to his cries as those of an animal include: "making an urgent whimpering sound," "that rapid whimpering," and "still whimpering" ("Hand": 64).

7. After a long absence traveling far and wide, Ratliff discovers the existence of the most innocent of the Snopes, whom he is seeing for the first time: "'I dont know as I would believe that, even if I knowed it was true,' Ratliff said. 'You mean he just showed up here one day?'" (*H*: 90).

8. "'I cant take you down home bellering like you is.' T. P. said. 'You was bad enough before you got that bullfrog voice. Come on'" (*SF*: 35).

9. "... with Ben's voice mounting to its unbelievable crescendo" (*SF*: 320).

10. The diversity and indeterminacy of the possible content of the idiot's cry could be stated in the same terms that Faulkner used at the end of his first novel to describe the songs accompanying the Sunday service of Blacks: "It was nothing, it was everything" (*SP*: 315).

11. In his argument that the singular ground of *The Sound and the Fury* was prepared by the texts that preceded its publication, from which the novel makes a series of formal borrowings, Kreiswirth holds that *Soldiers' Pay* and *Flags in the Dust* also begin, albeit to a lesser extent, with no regard for narrative conventions. This takes the form of a short and at the very least disconcerting sketch that catches the reader off guard: the first novel begins with a military farce surrounding the character of Julian Lowe, who is remarkably absent from the rest of the novel; the second begins with a chaotic recitation of the Sartoris family legend by Will Falls, a secondary character. Sacrificing the notion of exposition for that of immediate presentation and immersion without mediation should thus be included among the idiosyncrasies of Faulknerian writing.

12. "At very least an unsettling narrative non sequitur; at most it is a monstrous violation of the fictional tradition that identifies a 'narrator,' especially a first person narrator, with a point of view and demands that narrators be self-conscious enough to describe what is happening to others and themselves" (Polk, 1996: 100).

13. The term "stream of consciousness" was first used by William James, brother of Henry, in *The Principles of Psychology* (1890), to refer to the uninterrupted stream of perceptions, thoughts, and feelings in a waking mind. In literature, modernism appropriated this term to refer to a singular narrative mode that endeavors to reproduce, without the intervention of an organizing narrator, the disorderly and constant flow of heterogeneous elements in a character's psyche: sense perceptions, more or less (un)conscious thoughts, memories, expectations, feelings, random associations, and so on. It is important to note that behind the appearance of anarchy and radical liberty, the stream of consciousness is nevertheless based on a whole series of literary conventions.

14. Genette based his remarks on the words of James Joyce, as related by Valéry Larbaud: "what has been quite unfortunately christened 'interior monologue,' and which it would be better to call *immediate speech*: for the main point, which did not escape Joyce, is not that the speech should be internal, but that it should be emancipated right away ('from the first

lines') from all narrative patronage, that it should from the word go take the front of the 'stage'" (Genette, 1980: 173–74).

15. It is an idiot language in all senses of the term. Let us recall that the Greek adjective *idios*, from which the word "idiot" derives etymologically, means simple, particular, unique, and singular, in the sense of that which has its own character, and by extension that which is not reflected in the double of a model or a mirror (see Rosset, 1986).

16. "By immersing us directly in Benjy's talk, Faulkner establishes the persona of the narrator, allowing us to respond first to a literary convention—that of first-person narration—and only later to the violation of that convention. By the time we fully realize who or what Benjy is, we are already listening to him talk" (Ross, 1989: 171).

17. This expression is borrowed from a rejoinder in Lars von Trier's film *The Idiots* (1998), which was produced in Denmark in compliance with the Dogme 95 Manifesto. Its characters, who are self-proclaimed idiots, are actually normal people seeking their "inner idiot," an expression denoting an idealist return to the fantasy of primal simplicity and authenticity, beyond the normativity of consumer society.

18. The phrase "Benjy's discourse" is not entirely appropriate. It does not truly refer to Benjy's discourse, but rather to discourse given to Benjy. I will nonetheless use this phrase out of convenience, although I will not lose sight of its profoundly paradoxical aspect.

19. "Moreover, reported conversation (by people of normal intelligence) occupies more than half of Benjy's monologue—a monologue which, strictly speaking, is no monologue at all but rather a *polylogue*, a mosaic or patchwork of many voices seemingly recorded at random by an unselective mind. Yet Benjy's own idiolect stands out the more startlingly for being interwoven with the speech of others. Throughout the section it forms a closed system, a strictly private code, designed to suggest the functioning of an abnormally limited consciousness" (Bleikasten, 1976: 68).

20. There are nevertheless a few exceptions to this rule: in certain cases, the use of the pronoun to refer to the source of the speech is justified by the fact that a gesture or physical contact accompanies the words. In such cases, identification is made not only by hearing but also through a number of other senses (sight, touch, and smell in the following example) that make it obvious: "Caddy took me to Mother's chair and Mother took my face in her hands and then she held me against her. 'My poor baby.' she said" (*SF*: 8). Here, the use of a pronoun as the source of the speech reveals something that is obvious for Benjy.

21. An example of Faulkner's indignation regarding his publishers' persistence in correcting his choice of punctuation appears in a letter to Horace Liveright from October 1927: "He's been punctuating my stuff to death; giving me gratis quotation marks and premiums of commas that I dont need" (Blotner, 1977).

22. Clément Rosset would say their idiocy. "The world and all the bodies within it forever lack their complement in the mirror. They are eternal idiots" (Rosset, 1986: 43).

23. Guillemin-Flescher (1996) observes that the adverb *then*, which ordinarily identifies a specific moment in time, is diverted from its primary use. In Benjy's speech, it is either used to link a verb expressing an event or a situation with a verb evoking a state (as in the previous example), or to link two verbs expressing ongoing states or situations, as in the following example, in which the notion of acceleration is not mentioned: "Caddie was walking. Then she was running" (*SF*: 6). "In other words, in Benjy's case *then* simply marks

a break in time between two stages of the same process, or between two distinct situations. It never represents a transition from the initial to the final stage of a process, or a relation between events" (Guillemin-Flescher, 1996: 51).

CHAPTER 4. FAULKNERIAN IDIOTISMS: THE MECHANISMS OF REPETITION

1. Caddy's brief reappearance in Benjy's adult life is the source of a disturbance to which I will return in my analysis of idiocy's fetish objects. It is worth noting that Faulkner, who is speaking about the novel nearly thirty years after it was written, does not seem to remember this episode, which he presents as a hypothetical situation.

2. Jason is depicted in this same vein in the short story "That Evening Sun" (1931), in which he cunningly handles the art of blackmail and the threat of denunciation despite his young age.

3. Faulkner had initially planned to distinguish the different temporal layers by printing Benjy's section in different colors. Indeed, if the reader uses colored pencils to rectify what the publication of the novel did not allow, its reading becomes somewhat clearer: "One time I thought of printing that first section in different colors, but that would have been too expensive. [. . .] But if it could have been printed in different colors so that anyone reading it could keep up with who was talking and who was thinking this and what time, what moment in time, it was . . ." (*LIG*: 147).

4. Faulkner defined his work as being an exercise in repetition: "I am telling the same story over and over, which is myself and the world" (Blotner, 1977: 185). Repetition occurs at all levels of Faulkner's work, from the microscale of coordinating conjunctions to the macrocosm of the county. It is structurally present through the reuse in his novels of texts already published as short stories (this is notably how *The Unvanquished* was written), as well as the continuation of plots (from *Sanctuary* to *Requiem for a Nun*) and the reappearance of the same characters (the idiot Benjy is at the heart of *The Sound and the Fury* but reappears in "Appendix/Compson, 1699–1945" and *The Mansion*). It is the linguistic realization of repetition and its idiotisms that are of particular interest here, as they relate to idiocy.

5. The repetition of the verb "imagine" highlights the fluctuating and random foundations of the story, which is ultimately no more than the uninterrupted addition of imaginations: "I can imagine them as they rode" (*AA*: 85); "And I can imagine how Bon told Henry, broke it to him" (86); "So I can imagine him, the way he did it" (87). Édouard Glissant has noted how repetition is an "elocutionary wandering [that] sends the certainties of the edict into divagation" (Glissant, 2000: 201).

6. The keyword in the destiny of Thomas Sutpen, the term "design," is repeated insistently beginning with the seventh chapter (*AA*: 194ff.); its exact meaning is clarified a few pages later: "The design—Getting richer and richer" (209). It is worth noting that in the second part of this chapter devoted to Sutpen's biography, the boundless ambition of Sutpen's "design" is tempered by his "mistake." Repetition of the word "mistake" combines with that of the word "design" to depict an inexorable sense of failure: "his conviction that it had all come from a mistake and until he discovered what that mistake had been he did not intend to risk making another one" (215).

7. I have borrowed this terminology from Gilles Deleuze and Félix Guattari's *What Is Philosophy?*: "Percepts are no longer perceptions; they are independent of a state of those who experience them. Affects are no longer feelings or affectations; they go beyond the strength of those who undergo them. Sensations, percepts, and affects are *beings* whose validity lies in themselves and exceeds any lived. They could be said to exist in the absence of man because man, as he is caught in stone, on the canvas, or by words, is himself a compound of percepts and affects. The work of art is a being of sensation and nothing else: it exists in itself" (Deleuze and Guattari, 1996 [1994]: 164).

8. This notion of mechanism was precisely inspired by the mechanics of the text, especially in the evocation of pistons, which on a number of occasions describe the determined, uninterrupted, and machine-like gestures of Cash completing his funereal task: "The saw has not faltered, the running gleam of its pistoning edge unbroken" (*AILD*: 77); "Yet the motion of the saw has not faltered" (77); "He takes up the saw again; again it moves up and down, in and out of that unhurried imperviousness as a piston moves in the oil" (77).

9. As stressed by Jurij Lotman, "the repetition of a word in a text, as a rule, does not mean the mechanical repetition of a concept. Most of it points to a more complex, albeit unified, semantic content" (Lotman, 1977: 127).

10. Monk slavishly and without understanding repeats the words that another prisoner teaches him for not entirely commendable purposes: "And now I am going out into the free world, and farm" ("Monk": 49, 52). The idiot's serenity partially derives from his psittacism: "it was just a serene reiteration of the fact" (40). In John Steinbeck's *Of Mice and Men*, Lennie repeats the lessons and wise advice that George dictates to him with all the zeal of which he is capable, doing so to such an extent that the latter ultimately becomes irritated by his friend's devotion: "Jesus Christ, Lennie! You can't remember nothing that happens, but you remember ever' word I say" (Steinbeck, 1940 [1937]: 179).

11. Aurélie Guillain identified psittacism to be a symptom of distress: "Psittacism affects all characters stunned or overcome by pain, grief, or terror. [. . .] Repetition of the message is a symptom of distress" (Guillain, 2003: 24).

12. In the opening to his article "Faulkner's Art of Repetition," which focuses more on the phenomenon of repetition than Faulkner, Donald Kartiganer shows how repetition is central not only to fiction, but also to life:

> What does it mean to repeat something? A great deal, if not the bulk, of modern thought and literature revolves around that question. Within the ranges of repetition we have discovered the way of our knowing as well as the impossibility of knowing; the name of our bondage to what has already been as well as the name of our release—indeed, an invitation, in the face of aimless recurrence, to will the world. Repetition is our disease, our compulsion to reenact endlessly old, forgotten desires, and our cure, compulsion redeemed into dialogue, in which we revise the past, retrieving new possibilities from determinate origins. (Kartiganer, 1989: 21)

13. Benjy has another notable syntactical failure that I mentioned earlier: central to the repetition of the same words is the syntax's continual repetition of the coordinating conjunction "and," which places all elements of reality in a relation of absolute contiguity: "*We went* along *the fence and came to* the garden *fence*. [. . .] *We came to the* broken place *and went* through it" (*SF*: 4; emphasis of repeated words mine). In its connection to repetition,

the persistence of coordination can thus be seen as an additional sign of Benjy's inability to consider reality in the abstract, to perceive it in relations of contrast and hierarchy.

14. Deleuze stresses the apparently contradictory link between repetition and difference: "Does not the paradox of repetition lie in the fact that one can speak of repetition only by virtue of the change or difference that it introduces into the mind which contemplates it? By virtue of a difference that the mind *draws from* repetition?" (Deleuze, 2004 [1994]: 90).

15. The skill with which Sacks hollows out the notion of memory is remarkable.

16. Aki Kaurismäki's film *The Man without a Past* (2002) is built around similar themes. The hero for whom the movie is named is deprived of his past after an accident whose circumstances he does not recall, and is condemned to hebetude; he is a man both new and helpless, seemingly struck with idiocy in a world he fails to understand.

17. The word *hiatus*, which Sacks uses to describe his patient's amnesia, is also one of Faulkner's favorite words. It notably appears on the last page of *The Sound and the Fury*: "For an instant Ben sat in an utter hiatus. Then he bellowed" (*SF*: 320; it is remarkable in this example that the hiatus is precisely materialized by the succession of vocalic sounds). The word also appears in the third monologue of *As I Lay Dying*, in a passage that describes Jewel on his horse: "They stand in rigid terrific hiatus" (*AILD*: 12). In both examples, the notion of hiatus refers, by default, to the blankness lying behind space, to what is terrifying, what is kept quiet: the utter dread of the idiot, the monstrous coupling of the man and his mount.

18. Despite his investigations with those close to the lost mariner (whom the latter did not recognize, with their images being, by force of habit, drastically changed in relation to the memory that he kept of them from thirty years earlier), Sacks was unable to identify the source of his patient's unusual amnesia. He could simply offer a few guesses:

There is a great blank. We do not know what happened then—or subsequently.... We must fill in these "missing" years—from his brother, or the navy, or hospitals he has been to.... Could it be that he sustained some massive trauma at this time, some massive cerebral or emotional trauma in combat, in the war, and that *this* may have affected him ever since?... Was the war his "high point," the last time he was really alive, and existence since one long anti-climax? (Sacks, 1986: 29)

19. The paradox lies in the fact that familial repetition comes to an end in an individual that everything condemns to repetition.

20. In her admitted preference for Jason, Mrs. Compson repeats that she sees him as one of her own: "he is more Bascomb than Compson" (*SF*: 103).

21. The earliest recollections in Benjy's narrative present bear the trace of his birth name: "'Let him tell.' Caddy said. 'I dont give a cuss. Carry Maury up the hill, Versh'" (*SF*: 20). However, upon her youngest son turning five years old (around 1900), Mrs. Compson calls him by his new name: "*He was just looking at the fire, Caddy said. Mother was telling him his new name*" (56).

22. It is interesting that the son of Jacob and Rachel also had his name changed, as his mother, who died shortly after giving birth to him, had named him *Ben-Oni*, which literally means "son of my sorrow." His father changed his name to *Benjamin*, "son of happiness." Benjy Compson is thus the ironic successor of the son of resentment who became the favorite son.

23. "'Candace.' Mother said. 'I told you not to call him that. It was bad enough when your father insisted on calling you by that silly nickname, and I will not have him called by one. Nicknames are vulgar. Only common people use them. Benjamin.' She said" (*SF*: 63–64).

24. This word should of course be understood as a generalization, for what is true for the Snopeses is also true for most modest and common Faulknerian families such as the Bundrens and others.

25. Deaf to the cruel but realistic declarations of Luster, who desperately tries to make him understand that nothing will come along the road—"They aint nothing over yonder but houses" (*SF*: 14)—Benjy's idiocy is perfectly coherent in this regard, for he will wait for Caddy, in spite of good sense, for more than thirty years.

26. *Vertigo*, which was released in 1958, is a film about memory and repetition. Spirals also appear in various forms beyond the film's title sequence and poster: spiral staircases, Madeleine's (Kim Novak's) bun, the concentric circles that appear in tree stumps, and Johnny's (James Stewart's) endless shadowing through the twisting streets of San Francisco all incessantly repeat the same coiling. Hitchcock's camera movements, which combine zooming in with backward tracking shots, add to the feeling of being trapped in the spirals of memory.

27. The reader will soon learn that beneath its glorious appearance, the end of this section, which takes on the appearance of a pastoral myth, with the love between the idiot and the cow seeming to triumph over sterile repetition and a logic hostile to humans, is actually a prelude to a denouement of rare cruelty. The ritual of adoration developed by the idiot will be replaced by the purgatorial and cannibalistic ritual that the men of the community imagine as punishment for his heinous zoophilia.

28. Benjy's monologue is bursting with similar examples, in which his kin appear in a halo of light that brings to mind the iconography of holy images: "'Oh.' Father said. Light fell down the steps, on him" (*SF*: 23); sometimes, under similar circumstances, Benjy appears to himself: "He stooped and took me up, and the light came tumbling down the steps on me too" (24).

CHAPTER 5. STATES OF A WORLD IN DISINTEGRATION

1. Notwithstanding the remarks of Jean-Yves Jouannais, the radical liberation from any sense of being connected or belonging to a movement strikes me as a myth. Faulkner never claimed to belong to the modernist movement (and for good reason, for was it not a label created afterward by critics to gather together disparate works with formal similarities?), but his admiration for the radicalism of his contemporaries was already a form of allegiance (which obviously takes nothing away from the extreme originality of the stances adopted by Faulkner). Faulkner gave James Joyce and Sherwood Anderson a leading role in modern letters and recognized their influence on him: "The father of modern literature, Faulkner thought, is probably James Joyce, but the father of modern American literature is Sherwood Anderson" (Green and Allen, 1999: 79).

2. Jacques Pothier observed: "[O]ne is not born Faulkner, one becomes him. As if to symbolize this distance between the man and the work, the young Faulkner began to add a "u" to his name starting in 1918" (Pothier, 2003: 32).

3. Michel Gresset suggests that the best term for Horace Benbow is "unmanned": "[A]t the end of his journey, we find a character who has suffered a kind of general iconoclasm. Nothing remains of what he lived for and hence *through*; deprived of his panoply of fictions, he ends up being 'without qualities' (which is splendidly expressed in a single English word, unmanned)" (Gresset, 1982: 244).

4. Faulkner repeated, in a number of different ways, that the feeling of failure characteristic of *The Sound and the Fury* was accompanied by a paternal attachment that was as privileged as it was unfailing: "It was the best failure. It was the one that I anguished the most over, that I worked the hardest at, that even when I knew I couldn't bring it off, I still worked at it. It's like the parents feel toward the unfortunate child, maybe. The others that have been easier to write than that, and in ways are better books than that, but I don't have the feeling toward any of them that I do toward that one, because that was the most gallant, the most magnificent failure" (*FU*: 61).

5. Geneviève Bonnefoi discusses Michaux's mescalines in her monograph *Henri Michaux peintre* (Henri Michaux the Painter). One could imagine that she is describing Faulkner's world: "For the first time, these works did not include references to his usual world. An almost entirely abstract universe, in endless transformation, decomposition, and recomposition, a world of undulations, spasms, whirlwinds, and vibrations, a world of collapses and cracks, of terrific geological shaking in which traces of humanity appear only rarely, a kind of debris floating or frozen in a cataclysm, admirably expressed by the vibrant writing of which it is composed" (Baatsch, 1993: 146).

CHAPTER 6. IDIOTS HAVE BLUE EYES

1. In *The Town*, a bouquet of blue flowers is used to describe the eyes of Eula Varner Snopes, the bovine and idiot little girl in *The Hamlet*, who has become a mother, spouse, mistress, and muse to an entire town: "the eyes not the hard and dusty blue of fall but the blue of spring blooms all one inextricable mixture of wistaria cornflowers larkspur bluebells weeds and all, all the lost girls' weather and boys' luck and too late, the grief, too late" (*T*: 292). Eula got this gaze from her father, Will Varner, the "baron" of Frenchman's Bend, whose eyes are described as "little hard bright innocently blue eyes" (*H*: 6). However, in this case the narrator's emphasis on Varner's blue innocent eyes at the beginning of the novel is clearly ironic: the ensuing four hundred–odd pages stand in stark contrast to this initial announcement, for Varner is anything but innocent.

2. The exact quotation is: "if his eyes, just once, had read her thoughts" (Flaubert, 2004: 37).

3. In *The Blue Flower* (1995), the budding poet's blue flower is a child of twelve, simple and even simpleminded and dull, whom he falls in love with to the great bewilderment of his friends and family.

4. "He had assumed the blue expression peculiar to a certain type of drunkard, tepid with two drinks grudgingly on credit, gazing out of an empty saloon, an expression that pretends he hopes help, any kind of help, may be on its way, friends, any kind of friends coming to rescue him. For him life is always just around the corner, in the form of another drink at a new bar. Yet he really wants none of these things. Abandoned by his friends, as

they by him, he knows that nothing but the crushing look of a creditor lives round that corner" (Lowry, 1984 [1947]: 353).

5. We have borrowed this expression from Georges Bataille's 1957 novel *Blue of Noon*. It is striking that this novel, which includes the word "blue" in its title, is a history of idiocy of sorts: "In my idiotic heart, idiocy is singing its head off. I HAVE PREVAILED!" (Bataille, 2002: 16).

6. The permanently serene eyes of the idiot Monk, even when he is on the scaffold, are almost disquieting: "wan and small behind the dingy glass, yet wearing that expression questioning yet unalarmed, eager, serene, and grave" ("Monk": 46); "that expression serene, sympathetic, and almost exalted" (48); "That serenity was still there, but for the moment something groped behind it: not bafflement nor indecision, just seeking, groping" (48). Eula Varner's blue gaze is also described in terms that stress its improbable serenity: "that blue serene terrible envelopment" (*T*: 83); "the unbearable and unfathomable blue, speculative and serene" (83).

7. "But the idiot only stared at him in solemn detachment" ("Kingdom": 57).

8. "A transparent gaze, intensely blue, like cornflowers, or the sky, whence the idiot's eyes derive perhaps their vacuity as well as their ineffable depth" (Pitavy, 1983: 102).

9. In *Being and Nothingness*, Sartre shows that the gaze is present at the point where both eyes converge and should not be confused with the eyes themselves: it is never, strictly speaking, the eyes that look. On the contrary, the eyes are hidden within the gaze: "It is never when eyes are looking at you that you can find them beautiful or ugly, that you can remark on their color. The Other's look hides his eyes, he seems to go *in front of them*" (Sartre, 1992 [1956]: 346–47). What's more, a dual relation to the Other is established in the gaze, which can be defined as a relation of reciprocal objectification: when my gaze makes the Other the object of my vision, I become the object of the Other's gaze. "This is because to perceive is to *look at*, and to apprehend a look is not to apprehend a look-as-object in the world (unless the look is not directed upon us); it is to be conscious of *being looked at*" (347). The gaze's dual status is embodied by Charles Bon in *Absalom, Absalom!*: "the watcher and the watched" (*AA*: 97, 98). As a result, the term *regarder*/to watch is connected to the vocabulary of control and vigilance in both French and English: *garder*/to ward (over). In English, the expression *to watch and ward* refers to the act of watching over, which is notably the duty of a sentry.

CHAPTER 7. THE IDIOT GAZE AND ITS REPRESENTATIONS

1. "Quality, light, color, depth, which are there before us, are there only because they awaken an echo in our body and because the body welcomes them. Things have an internal equivalent in me; they arouse in me a carnal formula of their presence. Why shouldn't these correspondences in their turn give rise to some tracing rendered visible again, in which the eyes of others could find an underlying motif to sustain their inspection of the world?" (Merleau-Ponty, 1993: 125–26).

2. I will consider the implications of the subjective genitive, which highlights the vision and world "specific" to idiots (remembering that this is the first meaning of the adjective

idios), as well as those of the objective genitive, which uses a normative point of view to designate a vision and world in which idiots are the objects.

3. "I could see" (*SF*: 3)—the modal *can* is understood here in both senses, referring to the physiological and psychological capacity of the vision specific to an individual, as well as the possibility of vision, which is limited here by external elements.

4. Ethnology opposes magical and rational thinking: magical thinking admits the existence of supernatural powers inherent to certain objects or individuals (*mana* in archaic societies), and supposes an anthropomorphism in which the world contains wills that act on people; rational thinking tends to reduce this belief to a supernatural and symbolic causality.

5. "I tried to pick up the flowers. Luster picked them up, and they went away. I began to cry. 'Beller.' Luster said. 'Beller'" (*SF*: 55). Unlike Luster, who never tires of taking his frustration for having to take care of him out on Benjy, Caddy and Dilsey ensure, like kindly godmothers, that Benjy is always surrounded by his fetish objects: "*You can look at the fire and the mirror and the cushion too, Caddy said. You wont have to wait until supper to look at the cushion, now*" (66).

6. "Luster cried and Frony came and gave Luster a tin can to play with, and then I had the spools and Quentin fought me and I cried" (*SF*: 30). This game also evokes the image of Ike Snopes and the toy he drags on a string, whose disappearance is a tragedy for him.

7. This feeling of presence is not a simple illusion, as Caddy is the great absence from Benjy's present as well as the years separating this present (dated 1928) from her marriage and permanent departure in the spring of 1910.

8. "'Wait a minute.' Luster said. 'You snagged on that nail again. Cant you never crawl through her without snagging on that nail'" (*SF*: 4).

9. The restricted vision of the idiot encumbered by his bodily movements is a caricatured manifestation of the elementary rule that, according to Maurice Merleau-Ponty, generally presides over all visual perceptions: "Moreover, it is also true that vision is attached to movement. We see only what we look at. [. . .] All my changes of place figure on principle in a corner of my landscape; they are carried over onto the map of the visible. Everything I see is on principle within my reach, at least within reach of my sight, and is marked upon the map of the 'I can.' Each of the two maps is complete. The visible world and the world of my motor projects are both total parts of the same Being" (Merleau-Ponty, 1993: 124). This brings to mind the novel's inaugural "I could see" (*SF*: 3).

10. "The glance was unseeing and staring, a fascinated glance; but he did not turn to look after us" (Conrad, 1974 [1898]: 95).

11. Similarly, it is odd that Jewel Bundren's gaze in *As I Lay Dying*—contrary to that of Ike Snopes in the preceding examples—is invariably described as being directed before him: "Jewel sits the horse, gazing straight ahead" (*AILD*: 121); "Jewel sits on his horse like they were both made out of wood, looking straight ahead" (122); "[He] squats there, staring straight ahead, motionless, lean, wooden-backed, as though carved squatting out of the lean wood" (231). The immobility of Jewel's unshakably frontal gaze is in keeping with the hardness of carved wood; Darl continually repeats that his gaze is "rigid"—"the pale rigidity of his eyes" (128); "*He had that wooden look on his face again; that bold, surly, high-colored rigid look like his face and eyes were two colors of wood*" (181)—meaning by "rigid" implacable and obstinate. Jewel's gaze riveted straight before him reflects his determination

to do things as he sees fit, deaf to the recriminations of his kin and blind to their pain, alone at the front of the procession.

12. It is noteworthy that the window was used to theorize classical perspective and construct a homogeneous space, one that is objective and deprived of qualities, in other words a purely geometric space. With Benjy, the window of course plays a role in marking out his perspective, but it is certainly not an artifice in the service of the geometric construction of his world.

13. In the wake of the American transcendentalists, Herman Melville similarly denounced, in his 1853 story "Bartleby, the Scrivener," industrialization's disastrous consequences for the individual: as in James's story, it is the claustrophobic space in which the extravagant copyist Bartleby works, stuck in a corner between a screen and a window with a view of a wall, that best depicts his alienation (Melville, 1985).

14. This explains why the young woman in question is never named or described: doing so would require an external perspective to describe her physical appearance.

15. I have borrowed these terms from William Gass's essay on Henry James's text in *Fiction and the Figures of Life* (Gass, 2000 [1970]: 168).

16. The panorama originally referred to a large circular painting placed around a rotunda, allowing the viewer to see the represented objects as though he or she were discovering the surrounding horizon from a certain altitude. By analogy, the noun panorama applies to vast stretches of country seen from a height, without the observer's view being hindered in any direction. The gaze's circularity around the body's axis is thus central to the notion of a panorama; however, it is precisely this ability, to embrace the surrounding world by naturally accompanying the gaze with a rotating movement, that Faulkner's idiots lack, and of which James's focal character has been deprived.

17. The first to make conscious and systematic use of linear perspective by rigorously applying the technique of the vanishing point was Tommaso di Giovanni Guidi, known as Masaccio, who painted his *Trinity* on a wall of the Santa Maria Novella Church in Florence in 1425. The first theorist of the fundamental principles of perspective (even though he never used the term itself) was the ecclesiast Leon Battista Alberti, who wrote a didactic treatise in 1435 entitled *On Painting*. In "Espace et perspective au quattrocento" (Space and Perspective during the Quattrocento), Pierre Thuillier defines a "space system" as one in which "objects occupy precise situations in relation to one another and are organized in an orderly and unitary manner" (Thuillier, November 1984: 1384).

18. This is notably what occurs with the hand that both feels and is felt: "And finally a veritable touching of the touch, when my right hand touches my left hand while it is palpating things, where the 'touching subject' passes over to the rank of the touched, descends into the things, such that the touch is formed in the midst of the world and as it were in the things. [. . .] Since the same body sees and touches, visible and tangible belong to the same world. [. . .] [E]very movement of my eyes—even more every displacement of my body—has its place in the same universe that I itemize and explore with them, as, conversely, every vision takes place somewhere in the tactile space" (Merleau-Ponty, 2004: 251–52).

19. This tempting but false argument is advanced by Noel Polk, who establishes an implicit parallel between Benjy's perspective and the aggregate space of primitive painting: "As on a primitive painter's canvas, [scenes] appear in size and proportion as he originally experienced them, neither increased nor diminished nor distorted by perspectives of time

and position" (Polk, 1996: 110). The size of the world's objects in the idiot's perspective is in no way symbolic but is instead the result of sensible perceptions that are perfectly coherent in spite of appearances.

20. This is why the perspectives of Benjy's gaze are not "ridiculous" in the painter William Hogarth's sense of the word, whose 1754 engraving developed a satire on false or "ridiculous perspective," which the painter commented on thusly: "Whoever makes a Design without the knowledge of Perspective will be liable to such Absurdities as are shown in this Frontispiece" (McCarthy, January 6, 2021). This famous caricature is packed with the most ridiculous errors in applying the rules of perspective, and a whole that consists of disparate elements with no unity. To give just a few examples, on a hill in the background an exaggeratedly large traveler lights his pipe on a candle that an old woman holds out to him through the window of a dwelling in the foreground; and a row of sheep, arranged by size, walk along a path turning toward the left, but their representation inverses the laws of perspective, such that the farthest one is the size of an elephant, and the closest that of a mouse. The perspectives present in the Faulknerian idiot's gaze are not absurd like those in Hogarth's work, as they follow an unusual albeit coherent internal order.

21. The clear context in which this change of scale occurs also explains why Coindreau's translation is highly relevant in this case. Coindreau translates Dewey Dell's vision as he should have translated Benjy's: "Nous prenons le sentier de Tull. Nous passons devant la grange et nous continuons; les roues chuintent dans la boue, entre les rangées vertes de coton dans la terre sauvage; et Vernon, *tout petit* dans le champ derrière sa charrue" ("We take Tull's lane. We pass in front of the barn and continue; the wheels whisper in the mud, between the green rows of cotton in the wild earth; and Vernon, *very small* across the field behind his plow") (*ŒI*: 975; emphasis mine). However, I will argue that this translation's punctuation breaks the continuity of Dewey Dell's vision: there is no reason to isolate Vernon within a noun phrase separated from the body of the sentence with a semicolon. Repetition of the verb *to pass* suggests that Dewey Dell lists all of the elements, things, and people, both near and far, that "pass" through her vision as the wagon carrying the Bundrens to Jefferson "passes" before them. Vernon is just one of the elements, along with the barn and the rows of cotton, in relation to which this passage occurs.

22. Which is to say, in western Europe before the Renaissance.

23. This is Pierre Thuillier's definition of *perspectiva artificialis* during the quattrocento, as opposed to the meaning of the word "perspective" in the Middle Ages, which denoted the science of optics (*perspectiva communis*).

24. "The heavenly blue eyes gazed at him without intent" ("Kingdom": 57).

25. This is true of the beginning of the fourth section, in the form of barely perceptible clues and allusions. This is notably how Dilsey appears to Mrs. Compson: "Dilsey said nothing. She made no further move, but though she could not see her save as a blobby shape *without depth*, Mrs Compson knew that she had lowered her face a little . . ." (*SF*: 272; emphasis mine). As in Benjy's monologue, the dimension of depth appears to have been abolished here.

26. One could object that since Benjy is not alone, it is Dilsey who is at the center of the vision (as opposed to the first three monologues, the fourth section of *The Sound and the Fury* has sometimes been called the "Faulkner section" or the "Dilsey section"). However, the way in which Benjy and Dilsey each perceive the space of this scene tends

to converge in the narrator's syntax. Their proximity (Faulkner went so far as to use the same words to describe both of them, with the notable recurrence of the adjective *dropsical* in their respective portraits; *SF*: 265, 274), in addition to the similarities in their vision, are constantly stressed in this last section, in which Dilsey asserts her affinities with the simplicity and innocence of the white idiot, whom she considers worthy—by virtue of what he represents and in spite of the reluctance of her kin—of entering a Black church:

"I wish you wouldn't keep on bringin him to church, mammy," Frony said. "Folks talkin." "Whut folks?" Dilsey said. "I hears em," Frony said. "And I knows whut kind of folks," Dilsey said. "Trash white folks. Dat's who it is. Thinks he aint good enough fer white church, but [n-----] church aint good enough fer him. [. . .] Tell um de good Lawd dont keer whether he bright er not. Dont nobody but white trash keer dat" (*SF*: 290).

In the fourth section of *The Sound and the Fury*, Dilsey and Benjy both resemble the "poor in spirit" whom God welcomes into his kingdom.

27. This flat portrait of Jewel can be seen as the manifestation of Darl's jealous desire to "flatten" his brother.

28. It is of course after the barn fire that everyone declares Darl to be mad, and the decision is made to intern him in order to avoid paying damages. The pragmatic Cash presents the situation in the following manner: "It wasn't nothing else to do. It was either send him to Jackson, or have Gillespie sue us, because he knowed some way that Darl set fire to it. I dont know how he knowed, but he did" (*AILD*: 232).

We will not look more closely at Darl because the logic governing the madman's vision appears, for the most part, to diverge considerably from that of the idiot's vision. While the idiot's gaze is rooted in a relation of immanence toward things, the madman's gaze is visionary: it transcends objects and looks through and beyond their material contours, "with his eyes gone further than the food and the lamp, full of the land dug out of his skull and the holes filled with distance beyond the land" (*AILD*: 27). The solitary and fascinated world that Darl contemplates is located in an inaccessible and frightening beyond. This is why his gaze is disturbing: "them queer eyes of hisn that makes folk talk" (125). This is also why Dewey Dell feels threatened by her brother's gaze, which she is convinced sees through her and undresses her: "The land runs out of Darl's eyes; they swim to pin points. They begin at my feet and rise along my body to my face, and then my dress is gone" (121). Darl understands through his eyes rather than through words: "He knew without the words" (27).

29. "She stood in the door" (*SF*: 92); "the twilit door the twilight-colored smell of honeysuckle" (95); "she was standing in the door" (124); "She stood in the door looking at us her hands on her hips" (136).

30. Olga Vickery has noted this as well: "[A]ny alteration in Caddy makes her not-Caddy" (Vickery, 1964: 35). Caddy, aware of the intimate and irreversible changes she is experiencing, feels shame and distress. Her younger idiot brother's gaze prompts her to feel guilty and makes her feel like a stranger to herself: "Caddy came to the door and stood there, looking at Father and Mother. Her eyes flew at me, and away. I began to cry. It went loud and I got up. Caddy came in and stood with her back to the wall, looking at me. I went toward her, crying, and she shrank against the wall and I saw her eyes and I cried louder and pulled at her dress. She put her hands out but I pulled at her dress. Her eyes ran" (*SF*: 68–69). Caddy cannot bear Benjy's gaze, even though he does not understand anything.

She twice averts her eyes and literally shrinks, cornered by her sense of guilt. The cries of Benjy, who no longer recognizes her smell or her gaze as a deflowered young girl, are accompanied by a repeated gesture that the idiot—without understanding what has happened to his sister—instinctively directs at the issue and cause of Caddy's unbearable metamorphosis: the dress, which he pulls on two occasions, is a metonymic image of her forbidden lovemaking, with Benjy's gesture reversing that of the lover, who lifted it to strip his sister bare. Quentin rewrites this scene in the second monologue, identifying with Benjy: "she touched him then he yelled she stood there her eyes like cornered rats" (149).

31. "On the floor lay a soiled undergarment of cheap silk a little too pink, from a half open bureau drawer dangled a single stocking" (*SF*: 282).

32. Jason washes his hands of everything and never takes part. His hands, which are always in his pockets, also suggest his greed and venality, a theme that is widely developed in the novel's final two sections. His hands signal both a fear of losing and a repulsion to giving.

33. This phrase, "I will tell on you," which is invariably addressed to everyone around him, also defines Jason's uncharitable attitude in "That Evening Sun": " 'If you go, I'll tell,' Jason said" ("Sun": 300); " 'Jason is going to tell,' Caddy said" (301).

34. "Committed to the State Asylum, Jackson 1933" ("Appendix": 213).

35. This is how Faulkner evoked the exceptional character of his dear Caddy (whom he called "my heart's darling"): "[I]n *The Sound and The Fury* I had already put perhaps the only thing in literature which would ever move me very much: Caddy climbing the pear tree to look in the window at her grandmother's funeral while Quentin and Jason and Benjy and the negroes looked up at the muddy seat of her drawers" ("Intro *SF*, I": 227).

36. " 'Hush, Mother.' Caddy said. 'You go up stairs and lay down, so you can be sick' " (*SF*: 64). Caddy's lucidity clearly identifies her mother's hypochondria, aware that she needs a specific context (silence, solitude) so she "can" be sick in peace.

37. The swing's suggestive back-and-forth appears elsewhere in Faulkner's work as a preferred symbol of sexual awakening: numerous young women experience a sensual epiphany or renounce their innocence on swings, including Cecily Saunders in *Soldiers' Pay* and the eponymous heroine from the short story entitled "Elly" (1934) as well as Caddy and her daughter Quentin. This is also true of Jeanne in Émile Zola's novel *Une page d'amour* (1878; *A Love Episode*).

38. The alternations between "button"/"unbutton" (*SF*: 7–8, 18–19) and "dress"/"undress" (31–35, 73), along with their respective opposites, appear just a few pages apart throughout Benjy's monologue.

39. "I no longer even felt any pain, or the least anxiety; inside my head, I was aware of nothing but absolute stupidity, it was like a state of perpetual childishness. I was shocked by the madness enacted by my wild state of mind whenever I had wanted to tempt fate, and I recalled the irony and courage I had shown; and, of all that, the one thing left was the feeling that I was some kind of idiot, extremely touching perhaps, but in any case ludicrous" (Bataille, 2002: 33).

40. " 'Agnes Mabel Becky.' [. . .] 'Damn if one of them didn't leave a track' " (*SF*: 50).

41. I am thinking of the sky-sea of the lagoon where Friday wanders in Michel Tournier's novel *Vendredi ou les limbes du Pacifique* (published in English translation as *Friday*), in a scene where vision, obliterated by so much blue, can no longer discern distance and, even less so, the very scale of the landscape: "On the wet mirror of the lagoon, I see Friday

coming toward me with his calm and steady gait, and the desert of sky and water is so vast around him that nothing can provide scale, such that it is possibly a three-inch Friday placed within my grasp, or on the contrary one that is six measuring rods long and half a mile away" (Tournier, 1972 [1967]: 221).

CHAPTER 8. IDIOCY'S FETISH OBJECTS: SUBSTITUTIVE FIXATIONS AND LOGIC

1. With this in mind, the idiot reveals the link between ontogenetic (genesis of the individual) and phylogenetic (genesis of the line or species) mechanisms, as theorized by Ernst Haeckel. "Haeckel's Law" stipulates that ontogenesis (the history of individual development) recapitulates phylogenesis (the history of evolution).

2. The Latin *animare* first means to be endowed with life, to breathe life into a person or thing. Freud discussed the term "*animatism* [which] has also been used to denote the theory of the living character of what appears to us to be inanimate objects" (Freud, 2001: 88).

3. This interrelationship is highlighted by the preposition *de* (of) (as opposed to *à* in relationship *to* the object), thereby indicating that neither the subject nor the object preexist their relationship.

4. In his analysis of the novel, which revolves entirely around the theme of loss, John Matthews sees loss and dispossession as being fundamental to the idiot's world: "Benjy's world has been punctured by loss. From his section's first scene through its last, Benjy is tormented by the sensation of loss, and struggles to rectify or replace what is missing." He implicitly considers Benjy Compson to be a primitive incarnation of the loss (and defeat) suffered by the South after the Civil War: "Benjy comes into existence in the novel as the embodiment of a primitive response to loss" (Matthews, 1990: 35, 37). This reflection can be extended by emphasizing that a substitutive and compensatory logic also presided over the novel's composition. This, in any event, is what Faulkner suggests in the second introduction to *The Sound and the Fury*: "I did not realise then that I was trying to manufacture the sister which I did not have and the daughter which I was to lose, though the former might have been apparent from the fact that Caddy had three brothers almost before I wrote her name on paper" ("Intro *SF*, II": 230). Faulkner is referring to his first daughter, Alabama, who was born in January 1931 (after the publication of the novel), and died after just nine days. The actual lack of a sister and the death of a daughter are retrospectively associated with the same sentiment of loss felt by the idiot Benjy and embodied by Caddy.

5. "I went to the fire and sat on the floor, holding the slipper" (*SF*: 61); "*I squatted there, holding the slipper*" (72).

6. In *Faulkner, Mississippi*, Édouard Glissant notes that beyond idiocy, fetish objects are recurring figures in Faulknerian stories:

> Miraculous objects, signs of the obscure, things that double the Jeffersonian real. They are ordinary items, diverted from their everyday use or at any rate "loaded" with the supernatural weight of obsession. [. . .] By nature or in the urges they excite, they inhabit this other world where one must go to find answers to "the question." Their effect is like the elusive but reassuring happiness that the fire's warmth and reflections provide for Benjy. (Glissant, 2000: 160–61)

Glissant provides a nonexhaustive list: the lock for the small community of Jefferson (*Requiem for a Nun*), Issetibbeha's red shoes ("Red Leaves"), Gavin Stevens's eccentric red car (*The Town*), and others all have the same crystalline and soothing qualities as the idiot's fetish objects.

7. One can speak of an idiot fetishism in the sense that the illusory dimension characteristic of fetishism, as defined by Freud, is approached literally in Faulkner. Idiocy has its roots in this literality.

8. Mrs. Compson's attitude toward the objects that her son feels affection for, and that have the power to reassure him, is highly disparate; she makes recourse to these objects in absolute emergencies but ordinarily looks unfavorably on them. In the scene cited earlier, in which Caddy provides her cushion to Benjy, Mrs. Compson tries to prevent it: "'Dont, Candace.' Mother said. [. . .] 'You humor him too much.' Mother said" (*SF*: 63). This scene continues (or repeats) on the following page: "'Take that cushion away, like I told you.' Mother said. 'He must learn to mind.' The cushion went away. 'Hush, Benjy.' Caddy said. 'You go over there and sit down.' Mother said. 'Benjamin.' She held my face to hers. 'Stop that.' she said. 'Stop it.' But I didn't stop and Mother caught me in her arms and began to cry, and I cried. Then the cushion came back and Caddy held it above Mother's head" (64). This sketch exposes Mrs. Compson's complete powerlessness and blindness. She desperately tries to play her role as a mother by denying the power of these objects, which mitigate her own deficiencies: her gestures (she breaks down crying), which she knows are useless, only increase the idiot's crying. On the other hand, she refuses to admit that her idiot son is not perfectible ("he must learn"); she vainly struggles against the shame of his idiocy by insisting he be given a "normal" name (Benjamin instead of the diminutive Benjy), and by imposing "normal" behavior (seeking his mother for consolation rather than a cushion). Benjy's fetish objects are unbearable for Mrs. Compson, because they remind her of her own futility. Mrs. Compson's character corresponds to what Winnicott has implicitly described as a bad mother, as opposed to a "good-enough 'mother' [. . .] who makes active adaptation to the infant's needs" (Winnicott, 1971: 10). Mrs. Compson shows no sincere devotion to Benjy or attentiveness to his needs, and is precisely characterized by her refusal to adapt to anything whatsoever. It is thus hardly surprising that Caddy once again has the final word: Caddy defies maternal interdictions and creates a little trick to show Benjy the cushion behind Mrs. Compson's back; it is Caddy who has the actual role of the good mother, offering the child (doubled here by an idiot) the objects she hopes he will grow attached to in order to better detach himself from her.

9. *Heimlich* gives way to *unheimlich*; Paul Verlaine's "familiar dream" transforms into a nightmare (Verlaine, 2019: 12).

10. After her marriage and banishment in 1910, Caddy's rare appearances in the novel occur precisely at the cemetery near her family home—where she is no longer allowed to go—at the tomb belonging to Quentin and Mr. Compson, who died in 1910 and 1912, respectively. The fact that she appears in the cemetery confirms the notion that she now resembles a ghost, and that Jason and her mother consider her to be dead.

11. "Is your brother sick, or dead, that he's got to have a flower?" ("Kingdom": 86); "'Here. You dropped your jimson weed.' He picked it up and gave it back to me. 'You needs a new one. You bout wore that one out'" (*SF*: 54).

12. "He was playing with that bottle full of dogfennel" (*SF*: 56). "Dogfennel" is defined by Calvin Brown in *A Glossary of Faulkner's South* as: "Mayweed, an acrid, rank-smelling

weed (*Anthemis cotula*) bearing a daisylike flower" (C. Brown, 1976: 72). The *Oxford English Dictionary* points out that this flower's name comes from its bad odor and the form of its flowers, which bring to mind those of fennel.

13. "You sit down here and play with your jimson weed" (*SF*: 14). This plant is defined by Brown as: "Jamestown weed, common thorn-apple (*Datura strambonium*), a large, rank-smelling, poisonous weed, common around barns" (C. Brown, 1976: 111). It was used for contraception and abortion.

14. Similarly, the blue bottle that serves as a cemetery once contained poison.

15. While it is repeated automatically, this word is not part of Benjy's vocabulary; he prefers the word *bottle*, literally designating the nature of the thing that is the object of a symbolic ritual. Mrs. Compson uses the word *cemetery*, derived from the ecclesiastical Latin, to refer to the place where the family's dead are buried. It is worth noting that Dilsey makes no distinction between Benjy's cemetery and the family cemetery, which she invariably refers to using the word *graveyard*, ascribing to both the same religious respect: "'You knows de way now?' she said. 'Up de street, round de square, to de graveyard, den straight back home'" (*SF*: 318).

16. In his 1924 essay "Fetishism," Freud notes that "affection and hostility towards the fetish, corresponding to the denial and acknowledgment of castration, combine in unequal proportions in each different case, so that one or the other is more clearly discernible" (Freud, 2006: 94).

17. The fourth principle of the theoretical study of transitional objects and phenomena indicates that "the transitional object may eventually develop into a fetish object and so persist as a characteristic of the adult sexual life" (Winnicott, 1971: 9). The idiot's fetish objects can thus be interpreted as transitional objects whose function is subverted and condemned to endure indefinitely, thereby becoming intransitional objects.

18. One could say that the idiot inhabits what Clément Rosset has called "the site of insignificance":

> *The site of insignificance*, a place where all roads coexist and merge, can apparently not be described as a state, for it is instead the negation of all states, but could just as well be described as the state par excellence: possessing the virtue that lacks the most tenacious of stabilities, the most lasting organizations—that of *not being subject to any change*. There is, at least here, total assurance about the future: nothing will happen that could ever contradict the principle of insignificance (everything that will happen will always be the same thing, simultaneously determined and ordinary). The paths of the future already belong to the present confusion of paths. (Rosset, 1986: 20)

19. There is a similar couple, embodied by Fernandel and a certain Marguerite, in the film *The Cow and I* directed by Henri Verneuil in 1959, and inspired by Jacques Antoine's novel *Une histoire vraie* (A True Story).

20. "It was the actual thin depthless suspension of false dawn, itself, in which he could already see and know himself to be *an entity* solid and cohered in visibility" (*H*: 182; emphasis mine).

21. The English text evokes this mysterious partner through the expression "the flowing immemorial female" (*H*: 183). The English substantive *female* does not clarify the species of the female *entity* that is being depicted, in that it does not have to choose between *femme* (woman) and *femelle* (female animal). René Hilleret's French translation (revised by Didier

Coupaye and Michel Gresset) renders it as: "principe fluide de la féminité immémoriale" ("fluid principle of immemorial femininity") (*ŒIII*: 408). Perhaps the cow's *fémellité* (state of being a *femelle*) is overtranslated.

22. This dramatization brings to mind the opening to section 4 of *The Sound and the Fury*, which begins like an epiphany as it pierces the morning mist.

23. If Flem Snopes accepts to marry the very young Eula Varner, whom everyone knows to be pregnant by a certain Hoake McCarron (who takes flight as soon as he hears the news), it is surely because Will Varner offers him a deal that will speed his upward economic and social mobility: by "selling" his daughter as one would a cow, Varner is trying to save the family's honor. However, this gesture serves especially to establish, definitively and irreversibly, the primacy of Flem Snopes over the hamlet's affairs, and soon over those of the town.

24. Desire is an endlessly regenerating natural force in her: "a simple natural force repeating itself" (*T*: 88).

25. The short story was published in its original version only in 1947, after Maurice-Edgar Coindreau, to whom Faulkner had offered it as a gift, published it in a French translation in the journal *Fontaine* in 1943.

26. Mallarmé's poem dates from 1872, while Faulkner's poem is actually the first text he ever published, appearing in the *New Republic* in August 1919.

27. "His reaction would *reveal* that actual character which for years he may have successfully concealed from the public" ("Afternoon": 431; emphasis mine). Ike Snopes is the victim of the same accident under similar circumstances: "he, lying beneath the struggling and bellowing cow, received the violent relaxing of her fear-constricted bowels" (*H*: 192).

28. When fleeing the home where his mother has just died, little Vardaman seeks comfort in the barn from a cow that seems to feel and share his sorrow: "The cow is standing in the barn, chewing. [. . .] She nudges me, snuffing. She moans deep inside, her mouth closed" (*AILD*: 55). More generally, the cow's symbolic value across various cultures is invariably positive: its simple warmth and patient gestation make it the very symbol of the Earth Mother, the expression of the *maternel végétatif* (vegetal motherliness). The cow personifies the maternal and nourishing power of the earth, while its horns and femininity also make it an attribute of the lunar world.

29. The cow grazes: "once more she stopped to graze" (*H*: 184); chews: "She stands as he left her, tethered, chewing" (201); and ruminates: "fodder and flowers become one inexhaustible rumination" (203). I also noted above that its "bellowing" (190–94, 198) sometimes reveals a voice: "he actually heard the cow's voice" (189); "the intolerable voice" (190).

30. The cow from "Afternoon of a Cow" was already the product of a similar collage, with its bovine corporality coinciding with its supposedly feminine intuitions and heightened sense of decorum: "the poor creature (a female mind; the lone female among three men) [. . .] knew by woman's sacred instinct that the future held for her that which is to a female far worse than any fear of bodily injury or suffering: one of those invasions of female privacy where, helpless victim of her own physical body, she seems to see herself as object of some malignant power for irony and outrage" ("Afternoon": 430).

31. The urn described by John Keats in "Ode on a Grecian Urn" (1819) also depicts the ritual sacrifice of a heifer symbolically adorned in the finest array: "To what green altar, O mysterious priest, / Lead'st thou that heifer lowing at the skies, / And all her silken flanks

with garlands dressed?" (Keats, 1988: 345). In his chapter "Out of the South: The Fiction of William Faulkner," from his retrospective on literature from the American South entitled *Writing the South: Ideas of an American Region*, Richard Gray provides a list of the many references and allusions to Keats's Grecian urn that appear in Faulkner's stories (Gray, 1997: 206–7).

32. The shift from one behind the other (a position representing the quest of desire) to one with the other (*they*) marks the (temporary) end to the idiot's moaning, who now experiences a rare moment of peace and plenitude.

33. This gender confusion is confirmed when Houston first catches her fleeing with her lover and addresses her in the following terms: "Git on home, you damn whore!" (*H*: 194).

34. Houston and his dog had already intercepted the idiot Ike and his cow a few pages earlier: "Houston found them there" (*H*: 193). Taking pity on Ike, Houston paternalistically offers the idiot fifty cents as compensation for his forced separation: " 'There,' he said. 'Now git! Home! Home!' he shouted. 'Stay there! Let her alone!' [. . .] Then Houston took a handful of coins from his pocket and chose a fifty-cent piece and came and put it into his shirt pocket" (195). But the idiot throws the coin into the river (196), symbolically refusing any compromise, for money has no value for him.

35. "Not mere revenge and reprisal, but redress" (*H*: 213).

36. "He knew not only what he was going to see but that, like Bookwright, he did not want to see it, yet, unlike Bookwright, he was going to look" (*H*: 217).

37. Here we find one of Faulkner's fetish words: "He ceased, having talked himself wordless, mute into baffled and aghast *outrage*" (*H*: 219; emphasis mine).

38. In *The Town*, Ratliff pursues his crusade against the Snopeses, who continue to spread like vermin: "But he [Ratliff] had put into my mind too, just like into Gowan's, that idea of Snopeses covering Jefferson like an influx of snakes or varmints from the woods" (*T*: 98). He ultimately grasps that the quest of the patriarch Flem Snopes is not to amass ever more money, but to gain "respectability" in the community: "When it's jest money and power a man wants, there is usually some place where he will stop; there's always one thing at least that ever—every man wont do for jest money. But when it's respectability he finds out he wants and has got to have, there aint nothing he wont do to get it and then keep it" (227–28).

39. Freud notes: "It is no doubt the transmissibility of taboo which accounts for the attempts to throw it off by suitable purificatory ceremonies" (Freud, 2001: 24).

40. We cannot help but interpret the appearance of Reverend Whitfield in the role of the great priest restoring morality as a clearly ironic intertextual nod, for in *As I Lay Dying* the good reverend is Addie Bundren's lover and the progenitor of Jewel, whom he subsequently sees as the incarnation of his sin, "a living lie" (*AILD*: 177). Whitfield and Addie's relationship can be seen as a modern and countryside version of *The Scarlet Letter*, which Nathaniel Hawthorne published in 1850. Yet unlike his predecessor Reverend Dimmesdale, who is struck with remorse, Reverend Whitfield's dubious lifestyle does not end with his frequenting a married woman who already has two sons. In the only monologue that he narrates (immediately after Addie's only monologue and revelations), he goes as far as being implicitly relieved by her death, as she will take their secret to the grave, sparing him the shame her confession would have sparked: "let me not be too late; let not the tale of mine and her transgression come from her lips instead of mine" (178).

41. It is odd to find this implicit distinction between human women and other women, which began with the characterization of Eula and is repeated in various forms throughout *The Hamlet*, here in the mouth of a man of God.

42. Ike's cow hardly falls under Freud's definition of a totem: "What is a totem? It is as a rule an animal (whether edible and harmless or dangerous and feared) and more rarely a plant or a natural phenomenon (such as rain or water), which stands in a peculiar relation to the whole clan. In the first place, the totem is the common ancestor of the clan; at the same time it is their guardian spirit and helper, which sends them oracles and, if dangerous to others, recognizes and spares its own children. Conversely, the clansmen are under a sacred obligation (subject to automatic sanctions) not to kill or destroy their totem and to avoid eating its flesh (or deriving benefit from it in other ways)" (Freud, 2001: 3).

43. Whitfield continues his explanation, with a kind of morbid jubilation: "'It was the meat, the flesh,' the minister said. 'I taken the whole cure to mean that not only the boy's mind but his insides too, the seat of passion and sin, can have the proof that the partner of his sin is dead'" (*H*: 224). The relative distinction established by Claude Lévi-Strauss between the "exo-cannibal" and the "endo-cannibal," especially in the 1974 seminar "Cannibalisme et travestissement rituel" (Cannibalism and Ritual Cross-Dressing) published in *Paroles données* (1984)—with the former incorporating the virtues of its deceased by ingesting the enemy that killed or ate them, and the latter consuming its own dead for similar reasons—suggests that the approach recommended by Reverend Whitfield is destined for failure and could even prove counterproductive. Based on the observations of Lévi-Strauss, the cannibalistic consumption of a close being involves an identification, and hence a coming together, with the ingested being—it is never a means of abandoning it.

44. "That was the fall before the winter from which the people as they became older were to establish time and date events" (*H*: 286).

45. William Mistichelli has also made this observation: "What he learns in loving the cow modifies to an extraordinary degree the severe limitations of his birth. In pursuing her, he is able to triumph over his 'hopeless uncoordination.' [. . .] He grows attentive to the cow's comings and goings, learns to anticipate her needs and show tenderness in meeting them, and discovers joy and ecstasy in her presence" (Mistichelli, Spring 1990: 28).

CHAPTER 9. THE EXACERBATION OF SENSATION

1. In his *Discours sur la nature des animaux* (Discourse on the Nature of Animals), Georges-Louis Leclerc de Buffon considers touch as "the sense most related to thought and knowledge" and points out that "the sense of sight is not reliable, and can be used for knowledge only with the help of the sense of touch" (Buffon, 2003 [1753]: 46).

2. In *The Phenomenology of Perception*, Merleau-Ponty defines the perceiving subject in the following manner:

> For, seen from the inside, perception owes nothing to what we know in other ways about the world, about stimuli as physics describes them and about the sense organs as described by biology. It does not present itself in the first place as an event in the world to which the category of causality, for example, can be applied, but as a re-creation or re-constitution of the world at every moment. In so far as we believe

in the world's past, in the physical world, in "stimuli," in the organism as our books depict it, it is first of all because we have present at this moment to us a perceptual field, a surface in contact with the world, a permanent rootedness in it, and because it ceaselessly assails and beleaguers subjectivity as waves wash round a wreck on the shore. (Merleau-Ponty, 2004: 127)

3. "It was doubtless a continuation of the *instinct*, the inherited constant awareness of gravity, which caused him to look under the bridge for the coin" (*H*: 197; emphasis mine).

4. According to the distinctions made by Aristotle in his treatise *On the Soul*, the idiot can be seen as a kind of elaborate animal endowed with nutritive, locomotive, and sensitive faculties, but entirely devoid of intellect.

5. Here I have borrowed and inversed the distinctions made by Georges Bataille: "the problem of the transition from animal to man, from twilight to conscious life" (Bataille, 1955: 31).

6. André Bleikasten interprets the essential indistinction presiding over Benjy's perception by associating the idiot's psychic system with that of a child still unable to formulate a "self-consciousness"; Faulkner speaks of "the blind self-centeredness of innocence" (Inge, 1999: 123):

The limits of Benjy's language designate the limits of his world. There is no central "I" through whose agency his speech might be meaningfully ordered; in like manner, there is no sense of identity to make his experience his. [. . .] All that is left to Benjy is sensory reflex, emotional response, perception without intellection, and a capacity for the raw intensities of pleasure and pain. He is humanity at its most elemental and most archaic, the zero degree of consciousness.

Benjy's monologue sends us back to the confusions of the presubjective, prelogic, animistic world of infancy. Since there is no distinction between "I" and "non-I," there can be no boundary between inner and outer space and nothing to focalize what Benjy does, perceives, or suffers. Hence the startling eccentricity of all his experiences: sensations, perceptions, and emotions are accorded exactly the same status as objects and occurrences in the outer world. (Bleikasten, 1982: 58–59)

7. Idiots, in Faulkner and elsewhere, have the reputation of eating like pigs: "*Why dont you feed him in the kitchen. It's like eating with a pig*" (*SF*: 70). This leitmotif notably appears in Flannery O'Connor's second novel, *The Violent Bear It Away*, in a scene describing the story's little idiot as he digs into a plate of ravioli in an Italian restaurant: "Bishop had it smeared all over his face. Occasionally he would feed a spoonful into the sugar bowl or touch the tip of his tongue to the dish. [. . .] 'He's like a hog,' he said. 'He eats like a hog and he don't think no more than a hog and when he dies, he'll rot like a hog'" (O'Connor, 1955: 116).

8. Benjy's great proximity to domestic animals, sharing the same instinctive perception of their environment and primal form of existence, brings to mind the idiot Lennie from Steinbeck's *Of Mice and Men*, especially his inordinate taste for warm and gentle little animals such as mice and puppies. He does not know his own strength and cannot adapt to the circumstances, failing to understand that little things such as mice are different from humans and cannot resist his monstrous tenderness. As is the case with Benjy, his sensations are raw and immediate: things are not subsumed into categories of gender and species. In general, the great "abnormal figures" of literature are almost systematically defined in relation to their singular proximity to sensible things and the sensible world.

9. Faulkner maintains the confusion by giving animals names that he elsewhere attributes to humans, such as Nancy, who in *The Sound and the Fury* is a mare whose decomposing carcass in a ditch (it is "undressed" by buzzards) is a fascinating spectacle for the children: "And when Nancy fell in the ditch and Roskus shot her and the buzzards came and undressed her" (*SF*: 33). In "That Evening Sun," Nancy is a young Black woman who occasionally replaces Dilsey in the Compson kitchen. At the beginning of the short story, when the Compson children climb into the ditch (the word appears once again) separating the Black quarters from the white estate to tell her to prepare breakfast, Nancy appears in her doorway wearing no clothes: "we would throw rocks at Nancy's house until she came to the door, leaning her head around it without any clothes on" ("Sun": 290). Nancy has one final avatar or repetition in the character of Nancy Mannigoe in *Requiem for a Nun*; Faulkner affirmed that it is the same person: "She is the same person actually" (*FU*: 79).

10. "The sensible world is 'older' than the universe of thought, because the sensible world is visible and relatively continuous, and because the universe of thought, which is invisible and contains gaps, constitutes at first sight a whole and has its truth only on condition that it be supported on the canonical structures of the sensible world" (Merleau-Ponty, 1968: 12).

11. André Bleikasten has pointed out the hazy affinity that unites the female figure to "la terre immémoriale" (Immemorial Earth): "Literally nowhere, Caddy is metaphorically everywhere. Her presence/absence becomes diffused all over the world, pointing, like so many feminine figures of Faulkner's earlier and later work, to an elemental complicity between Woman and the Immemorial Earth" (Bleikasten, 2016 [1990]: 51). The continuity between nature and femininity is a commonplace, especially in the transcendentalist poems of Ralph Waldo Emerson: I am thinking especially of "Lines to Ellen," in which nature reflects the body of the departed beloved, scattered and torn by death, in the form of a literary blazon. Nature thus becomes the consoling site where the grieving poet can, through the intervention of his senses, reestablish contact with his muse who "diffuses" herself: "Tell me, maiden, dost thou use / Thyself thro' Nature to diffuse?" (Emerson, 2000: 737).

12. Roskus's use of the verb *to know* in reference to Benjy's divinatory instincts is in keeping with my analysis earlier in this chapter of the narrator's terminology in the section recounting Ike Snopes's love in *The Hamlet*.

13. "It was then, and then I saw Darl and he knew. He said he knew without the words like he told me that ma is going to die without words, and I knew he knew because if he had said he knew with the words I would not have believed that he had been there and saw us" (*AILD*: 27).

14. In the river scene from Quentin's monologue, in which he looks back on a particularly intimate and secret moment shared with Caddy, the smell of honeysuckle evokes both the admission of sexual pleasure and the memory of dead Damuddy. This scene, whose narration dispenses with any kind of punctuation and makes wide use of enjambment, can be read as a long visual poem in blank verse: "I had to pant to get any air at all out of that thick gray honeysuckle/yes I hate him I would die for him Ive already died for him I die for him over and over again everytime this goes [. . .] do you remember the day damuddy died when you sat down in the water in your drawers" (*SF*: 151). The instant of death and the instant of pleasure borrow from the same registers, part of the same original mud. The proximity of the admission of pleasure and the memory of the grandmother's death—along with the repetition of the novel's central and primordial image from

childhood—add to the symbolism of young Caddy's soiled underwear. In fact, on the day Damuddy dies, Caddy gets *muddy*, forever stained by her experience of the world of death, which she sees through a window while perched in the branches of the tree (of knowledge), while her brothers stand at the foot of the tree (protected from the revelation that only Caddy faces) contemplating her muddy underwear. The stain that characterizes Caddy from that day forward, and that is inscribed in the grandmother's name (Caddy + mud = Damuddy), symbolically announces the mistake that a few years later will precipitate the destiny of the entire Compson family, namely adultery. The mud that stains Caddy's underwear becomes the symbol for the shame and sacrilege committed (a sense that is present in expressions such as "throwing mud at somebody" or "dragging one's name in the mud").

15. "I become a transparent eyeball; I am nothing; I see all" (Emerson, 2000: 6).

16. "I died last year I told you I had but I didn't know then what I meant I didn't know what I was saying" (*SF*: 123). These are the terms in which Caddy conceives the loss of her virginity when she (supposedly) confides in Quentin.

17. Mrs. Compson's injunction is repeated by Dilsey, who, in spite of her tender protectiveness for Benjy, also believes that it is inappropriate to exhibit the family idiot on solemn occasions (in this case, Caddy's wedding): "*Go on and watch him, Dilsey said. Keep him out the house now.* [. . .] *You go and keep that boy out of sight, Dilsey said. I got all I can tend to*" (*SF*: 37). The precautions taken to conceal the idiot are connected to the popular dictums sprinkled throughout *The Sound and the Fury* (and "The Kingdom of God"), which superstitiously associate the idiot with a bird of ill omen: "*And folks dont like to look at a looney. Taint no luck in it*" (19); "*That boy conjure him*" (32). The bad luck personified by the idiot is deemed to be contagious; according to Roskus, it has spread to the entire home: "Taint no luck on this place" (29).

18. Thanks to the polysemy of the verb "*sentir*" (to sense, to feel, to smell), the French language is especially well equipped to communicate the predominance of olfactory sensations within the idiot's perception.

19. This strategy of withholding information that is crucial to a story—with the conjuring away of the central event (mentioned above on a number of occasions) being an extreme version—will be the subject of a detailed analysis in part 3 of this book.

20. "It is this inextricable that creates the text of the poem and orders the disorder in the world, accumulating it marvelously" (Glissant, 2000: 80).

21. Only taste is missing from this list. It is unsurprisingly reserved for occasions when Benjy brings something up to his mouth.

22. The way in which a form stands out against a background was theorized by gestalt psychology. Perceiving something always involves perceiving a form that stands out against a background.

23. *Twilight* was the first title that Faulkner considered for *The Sound and the Fury*: it is also the only title that appears on the novel's manuscript. It is worth noting that in the novel's first section, the only evocation of twilight prefigures the scene in which Benjy acts aggressively toward his young neighbor: "It was open when I touched it, and I held to it in the twilight. I wasn't crying, and I tried to stop, watching the girls coming along in the twilight. I wasn't crying. [. . .] They came on in the twilight. I wasn't crying, and I held to the gate. They came slow" (*SF*: 52–54). Like moonlight, the twilight in which the contours

of reality fade away can be seen as the preferred territory for transgression: the fence being open, Benjy crosses into forbidden territory.

24. "Tout en chantant sur le mode mineur / L'amour vainqueur et la vie opportune, / Ils n'ont pas l'air de croire à leur bonheur / Et leur chanson se mêle au clair de lune" ("Clair de Lune," Verlaine, 1992 [1869]: 33). "As they go singing in their minor key / Of conquering love and life full of promise, / They haven't the look of believing their words, / And their song now blends with the light of the moon" ("Moonlight," Verlaine, 2019: 41).

25. "[N-----s] say a drowned man's shadow was watching for him in the water all the time" (*SF*: 90).

26. In a 1979 essay entitled "Philosophy and the Form of Fiction," William Gass shows how the rules that govern what form causality takes in a story correspond to necessary choices: "The causal relation itself may be logically necessary or psychologically customary, formal or final, mechanical or purposive. It may be divinely empowered or materially blind. Causality in fiction is usually restricted to the principle that controls the order of constructed events" (Gass, 2000: 23). The dismantling of causality in Benjy's discourse can also be interpreted as being required by the aesthetics of idiocy. Noel Polk shows how this characteristic sidelines any authority ensuring that the story proceeds smoothly: "Readers looking for such narratorial control in the opening paragraphs of *The Sound and the Fury* will not find it. Nothing that happens, nothing seen, heard, or felt is causally related to anything else" (Polk, 1996: 100).

27. Merleau-Ponty speaks of "a veritable touching of the touch, when my right hand touches my left hand while it is palpating things, where the 'touching subject' passes over to the rank of the touched, descends into the things, such that the touch is formed in the midst of the world and as it were in the things" (Merleau-Ponty, 2004: 251).

CHAPTER 10. IDIOCY, ALCOHOL, AND OTHER ILLICIT SUBSTANCES: "A DERANGEMENT OF ALL THE SENSES"

1. This letter is associated with another contemporary letter sent to Paul Demeny; together they are often referred to as the "Lettres du 'voyant'" (Seer Letters).

2. In his essay on *The Sound and the Fury*, François Pitavy develops this idea of a reading-writing. The notion of an intimate relation between the author and the reader of *The Sound and the Fury* had already been developed by Nathalie Sarraute, in the pages she devoted to Faulkner in "The Age of Suspicion" (published in February 1950 in *Modern Times*): "Instead of letting himself be guided by the sign-posts with which everyday custom flatters his laziness and haste, in order to identify the characters, he is obliged to recognise them at once, like the author himself, from the inside, and thanks to indications that are only revealed to him if, having renounced his love of comfort, he is willing to plunge into them as deeply as the author, whose vision he makes his own. Indeed, the whole problem is here: to dispossess the reader and entice him, at all costs, into the author's territory" (Sarraute, 1990: 70–71).

3. This expression is borrowed from Henri Michaux, who had a major role in its subsequent development: "Altered (by what?), I drink in long draughts. Then on the table, not knowing what side to take, is the glass before me. The offensive of things starts, restarts.

The glass wants to drink me. The raisins, the tube of glue, are observing me, or want to observe me" (Michaux, 1966: 72).

4. In his biography of Faulkner, Joseph Blotner describes how Faulkner used bourbon to anesthetize his pain, whatever its nature: "Liquor was for him an analgesic, an anesthetic. Distrusting physicians generally, he would dose himself with whiskey for anything from a sore throat to a bad back" (Blotner, 1974: 227). Alcohol quite often allowed Faulkner to temporarily erase the world surrounding him. His daughter Jill revealed that the completion of a novel was almost systematically followed by a bout of drinking, which could extend multiple days without interruption: "He used drinking as a safety valve. It had to come out some way and almost invariably at the end of a book" (Abadie, 1980: 31). His excesses with alcohol regularly forced Faulkner to accept hospitalization.

5. I would even suggest that a male Faulknerian character who does not drink prompts distrust and suspicion. In *Sanctuary*, Popeye offers the particularity of being a bootlegger who does not drink a drop of alcohol because of his fragile health (*S*: 308); he also happens to be impotent. In *The Sound and the Fury*, while the father's and Uncle Maury's penchant for drink is mentioned on many occasions, Jason Compson (the son) asserts his abstinence from all alcoholic beverages, exposing him to wisecracks and baiting.

6. "'Whooey.' he said. 'Me and Benjy going back to the wedding. Sassprilluh.' T. P. said" (*SF*: 21). Sarsaparilla is a kind of lemonade made from plant extracts, similar to root beer.

CHAPTER 11. THE FURY OF ORIGINS, THE RINGING OF SOUND

1. Ben Wasson reported that Faulkner spoke these words when he gave him the manuscript for *The Sound and the Fury*.

2. "Mistral," published in 1931, and "Wash," published in 1934. Written between the late 1920s and the early 1930s, the short stories "The Big Shot" and "Evangeline" were refused by all of the reviews and magazines to which he submitted them. They were published only in 1979, in the *Uncollected Stories* edited by Joseph Blotner.

3. "I had learned a little about writing from *Soldiers' Pay*—how to approach language, words: not with seriousness so much, as an essayist does, but with a kind of alert respect, as you approach dynamite" ("Intro *SF*, I": 225–26).

4. "*I saw* that peaceful glinting of that branch that was to become the dark, harsh flowing of time. [. . .] *I saw* that they had been sent to the pasture to spend the afternoon to get them away from the house during the grandmother's funeral" ("Intro *SF*, II: 230"; emphasis mine).

5. Quentin's monologue shows how much the older brother is obsessed by Benjy's absurd loss: "we will swap Benjy's pasture for a fine dead sound" (*SF*: 174). Benjy must give up his only heritage so Quentin can destroy himself on the Harvard campus, in the "dead sound" of his drowning, prey to "the first fury of despair" (177).

6. The tribute also extends to *Sanctuary*, in which Lee Goodwin is burned alive in the climactic scene by a frenzied crowd for a crime and rape he did not commit. The scene is narrated from the point of view of his lawyer, Horace Benbow, as he approaches the stake: "then he heard the *sound*, of the fire; the *furious sound* of gasoline" (*S*: 295; emphasis mine). The scene and the chapter come to a close a few lines later: "He couldn't hear the fire, though

it still swirled upward unabated, as though it were living upon itself, and *sound*less: a voice of *fury* like in a dream, roaring silently out of a peaceful void" (296). It is interesting that this echo of the fetish novel comes in the form of an immense fire.

7. "To-morrow, and to-morrow, and to-morrow, / Creeps in this petty pace from day to day, / To the last syllable of recorded time" (*Macbeth* 5.5.19–21).

8. In the incessant play of echoes, this description of Jim Bond is repeated in the evocation of Monk cited below, in which we once again find the sound and fury specific to Benjy Compson and to the novel born from his senses: "they could not hold him, the small furious body (it was naked now) which writhed out of their hands as if it had been greased, and fled with no human sound" ("Monk": 42).

CHAPTER 12. THE AESTHETICS OF IDIOCY: WRITING AND APHASIA

1. Benjy's monologue contains numerous allusions to the hostility and incessant confrontation between Jason and his niece Quentin. Certain chronological inconsistencies bear mentioning. In the narrative present of the first monologue (April 7), Quentin continually threatens to leave: "*If you dont like it, young lady, you'd better get out*, Jason said. *I'm going to*, Quentin said. *Dont you worry*" (*SF*: 69–70). But hasn't Quentin already left? The third monologue (dated April 6) precisely narrates her flight and Jason's pursuit.

2. Repetition of the verb *to start* continues amid an increasing sense of confusion, as though Caddy the child was responding to T. P.'s questions about her own wedding many years later: "'Git on the box and see if they started.' 'They haven't started because the band hasn't come yet.' Caddy said" (*SF*: 38).

3. While this scene is in keeping with other fragments retracing the same event—still the night of Damuddy's death—and repeats its themes (Caddy's attempts to apply the authority her father delegated to her) and leitmotifs (her disobedience, which in this instance is legitimate), the reader can rather easily reestablish the succession of speakers: Dilsey tries to take the children up to their rooms; Caddy protests and looks for allies; Jason refuses her authority but Versh accedes to her whims; Quentin, as he often does, remains silent.

4. This is also true of the verb *to drink*, especially when used in reference to Mr. Compson: "He drank" (*SF*: 43, 44). Mr. Compson's alcoholism can be surmised through the description of a mechanical gesture that is disconnected from its object (its contents). Alcoholism is often less a matter of fluids than the actual gesture of drinking.

5. "'Hush, Benjy.' Caddy said. 'Go away, Charlie. He doesn't like you'" (*SF*: 47).

6. To reassure him and give him the illusion that she is nearby, Caddy lies down next to Benjy, who is no longer allowed to sleep with her, until he falls asleep, until the smooth, bright shapes of sleep appear. She breaks the rules, with Dilsey's approval: "'He be gone in a minute.' Dilsey said. 'I leave the light on in your room'" (*SF*: 44). Still, her good intention is once again based on a lie.

7. "*You cant do no good looking through the gate*, T. P. said. *Miss Caddy done gone long ways away. Done got married and left you. You cant do no good, holding to the gate and crying. She cant hear you.* [. . .] *Aint nothing going to quiet him*, T. P. said. *He think if he down to the gate, Miss Caddy come back. Nonsense*, Mother said" (*SF*: 51).

8. The bawdy joke that Irving Howe identified in the polysemy of the word *balls* takes on its full meaning. Benjy's fright at the spectacle of his nudity—"*I got undressed and I looked at myself, and I began to cry. Hush, Luster said. Looking for them aint going to do no good. They're gone*" (*SF*: 73)—echoes Luster's incidental remarks about the golfers' lost balls: "Maybe we can find one of they balls" (4).

9. In his book chapter "'Monk': The Detective Story and the Human Heart," Edmond Volpe (2004) goes so far as considering this paragraph to be a profession of artistic faith.

10. I have borrowed this expression from François Pitavy: "Trying to say. The expression of a thwarted desire, and the desire to transcend the limitations of the discourse, are present throughout the novel: with the three Compson brothers who each try to say their desire to appropriate a Caddy that escapes them (Jason's hate is the reverse side of this desire), and then with Reverend Shegog, whose *black* sermon tries to say the very Word of God. [. . .] This novel thus has a twin dynamic of desire and writing, with an elusive object as its target" (Pitavy, 2001: 46–47).

11. The expression "stream of consciousness," which in certain cases replaces the notion of interior monologue, is not satisfactory, for it excludes the two other psychological components that play an essential role in constituting the interior monologue, namely the unconscious (the id) and censorship (the superego).

12. In a letter he sent to Dujardin while he was writing *Ulysses*, Joyce admitted being "a sincere admirer of your personal and independent book" (Dujardin, 2001 [1887]: 130).

13. It is important to point out that *Mrs Dalloway*, as well as some monologues from *Ulysses*, adopt the form of free indirect discourse; Mrs. Dalloway and the other characters who temporarily serve as centers of perception in the novel do not express themselves in the first person, except for passages in direct discourse. The notion of interior monologue does not exclude the use of the third person, which "conceals the same I as that of the traditional monologue" (Dujardin, 2001 [1887]: 135).

14. Dujardin presented his novel to his parents in the following manner: "[I]t is quite simply the account of six hours in the life of a young man who is in love with a young woman—six hours in which *nothing*, no adventure happens. [. . .]—the most *ordinary life* possible *analyzed* in the most complete and original way possible" (Dujardin, 2001 [1887]: 125).

15. *Soldiers' Pay* already contained a few stylistic exercises, including the passages describing Margaret Powers's perceptions when the memory of her husband, who died at war, comes rushing back, and the intimacy created by use of the free indirect style: "Dick, Dick. Dead, ugly Dick. Once you were alive and young and passionate and ugly, after a time you were dead, dear Dick" (*SP*: 40).

16. The "Nausicaa" episode begins with a muddle of popular maxims, such as "boys will be boys" or "every little Irishman's house is his castle" (Joyce, 1998 [1922]: 332). On the other end of the novel's referential spectrum is the "Proteus" episode on the beach, which focuses on Stephen Dedalus. The beginning of the episode uses numerous foreign terms including, within the space of a few lines, words or expressions in Italian ("*maestro di color che sanno*"), German ("*nacheinander,*" "*nebeneinander*"), Spanish ("*Los Demiurgos*"), Greek ("*alpha*"), and Latin ("*lex externa*") (37–38). "Proteus" also makes implicit allusions to Aristotelian philosophy.

17. There is a connection between Sōseki's novel and *What Maisie Knew* (1897) by Henry James. The latter novel is a third-person story exclusively focusing on the perceptions and

sentiments of Maisie, a girl bounced from one governess to another, torn between two homes and two divorced parents, each of whom are living their lives. The narrator of *What Maisie Knew* strives to limit the story to the little girl's point of view, and like Sōseki's work the novel's title encapsulates the story. Just as James's novel is literally limited to "what Maisie knew," Sōseki's novel never loses sight of the improbable identity of its "I." Through the filter of a naïve gaze, but in the elaborate language of a well-read adult, the narrator of *What Maisie Knew* retraces the little girl's worries and incomprehension, as well as the strategies she uses to defend her rights, as in this excerpt in which she deliberately adopts the mask of extreme credulity: "Maisie was aware that her answer, though it brought her down to her heels, was vague even to imbecility, and that this was the first time she had appeared to practise with Mrs Wix an intellectual inaptitude to meet her—the infirmity to which she had owed so much success with papa and mamma" (James, 1985 [1897]: 211).

18. In *Toward an Aesthetic of Reception*, Hans Robert Jauss defines the language of everyday reality in opposition to the "poetic language [of the] imaginary world" (Jauss, 1982: 54).

19. Stephen Ross considers Quentin's internal monologue as a chorus of voices that Quentin is continually trying to quiet: "All of Quentin's experiences, as remembered on this last day, take the form of dialogical confrontations. [. . .] On his final day alive the words of others return to haunt his imagination. Quentin mentally objectifies his past as voices, reweaving the texture of his family's life out of their spoken words; people assume the shapes of their disembodied voices, distinguished by what they say or how they talk, not by what they do or how they look" (Ross, 1989: 180). Here the notion of dialogism makes way for polyphony: the omnipresent paternal voice is soon recaptured by the jumbled memory of the mother's constant complaints, Caddy's sensual admissions, and Benjy's bellowing. The peace coveted by Quentin resides in the silence of the voices besieging him—a peace that he will find only in the deafening waters of the Charles River.

20. In its singular neutrality, this speech is nevertheless given to the reader, whose work as a reader precisely involves extracting its meaning. With regard to the scene mentioned above, the reader will deduce Quentin's and Caddy's incomprehension, who see "a party" rather than a wake around the grandmother's body. Between the lines there is also Quentin's propensity to moralize, along with Caddy's determination and extreme sensuality. The unique methods needed to read Faulkner's text will be discussed in the final chapter of this book.

21. Bakhtin asserted in this regard that "poetry needs all of language, all of its aspects and elements, and is not indifferent to any of the nuances of the word in its linguistic determination" (Bakhtin, 1981: 60).

22. Stephen Ross has suggested, with regard to the "incommunicability of subjectivity," that we are all necessarily idiots: "Psychic voice always requires some such suspension of disbelief on the reader's part, for by definition interior discourse cannot be heard in the world. Benjy's inarticulateness objectifies the inevitable distance between all thought and all utterance. His literal verbal silence is emblematic of the more radical silence at the core of every consciousness that would speak itself. All are 'idiots' in the face of the incommunicability of subjectivity" (Ross, 1989: 171).

23. In his book chapter "Concept of Character in Fiction," William H. Gass discusses how empty space and silence "surround every other work of art" through the example of a statue pointing in a direction where there is nothing to see: "On the other side of the novel

lies the void. Think, for instance, of a striding statue; imagine the purposeful inclination of the torso, the alert and penetrating gaze of the head and its eyes, the outstretched arm and pointing finger; everything would appear to direct us toward some goal in front of it. Yet our eye travels only to the finger's end, and not beyond. Though pointing, the finger bids us stay instead, and we journey slowly back along the tension of the arm. In our hearts we know what actually surrounds the statue. The same surrounds every other work of art: empty space and silence" (Gass, 2000 [1970]: 49).

24. "The novel of analysis, as opposed to what I will call the ontological novel, seeks complexity but often finds only complication" (Des Forêts, 1985 [1962]: 24).

25. They rub shoulders with an idiot, the only character in the narrative present who is grounded in the real world in the eleven chapters of *Absalom, Absalom!*

26. Joseph Danan has underscored how the theme of lethargy features prominently in the collapsing intangible barriers separating the ego and the id: "It is the moment when the limit between conscious and unconscious becomes less certain, when the reasonable ego of the waking state gives way, with minimum control, to the fluidity of associations and fantastical shifts" (Danan, 1995: 53). The monologue assumes its loosest form (ellipses are ubiquitous) in chapter 7 of *Les Lauriers sont coupés*, and its freest form when Daniel Prince falls asleep in Leah's arms. In *Ulysses*, the interior monologue finds its most developed and extreme form in the novel's final episode ("Penelope"), which retraces in a single breath the thoughts of Molly Bloom in a long verbal flow barely punctuated by rare indentations (and a final period ending the novel). This interior monologue unfolds as Molly, lying in the dark, waits for sleep to come. The moments when Benjy falls asleep are always central moments in his monologue.

27. I have borrowed this expression from the collection of essays that Maurice Blanchot largely devoted to the poetry of Louis-René des Forêts: "[W]e know that, close to death, we still have to '*keep watch in silence*,' to welcome the secret friendship by which some voice from elsewhere comes to make itself heard. Vain voice? Perhaps. It matters little. What has SPOKEN to us will always speak to us" (Blanchot, 2007: 9).

28. Some critics have listed the words used by Benjy; in his *"The Sound and the Fury": Faulkner and the Lost Cause* (1990), John T. Matthews shows that Benjy's vocabulary consists of approximately five hundred words—essentially verbs and nouns—along with approximately one hundred adjectives and adverbs.

29. Jakobson defines the second type of aphasia through "impairment of the ability to propositionize, or, generally speaking, to combine simpler linguistic entities into more complex units. [. . .] The syntactical rules organizing words into higher units are lost; this loss, called *agrammatism*, causes the degeneration of the sentence into a mere 'word heap.' [. . .] Word order becomes chaotic; the ties of grammatical coordination and subordination, whether concord or government, are dissolved. As might be expected, words endowed with purely grammatical functions, like conjunctions, prepositions, pronouns, and articles, disappear first, giving rise to the so-called 'telegraphic' style, whereas in the case of similarity disorder they are the most resistant" (Jakobson, 1971: 63–64). While its syntactical variety is minimal, and it makes very limited use of subordination, Benjy's language is not agrammatical. Tense agreement is followed, and even though they are rare, logical connections are not totally absent from his syntax. His phrase cannot simply be reduced to a heap of words or a telegraphic style.

30. I discussed the idiot's persistent resistance to polysemy above.

31. Where poet Francis Ponge names and describes apparently trivial objects ("Blackberries," "the oyster," "the cigarette") from multiple perspectives, doing so in minute detail and with a focus on their most imperceptible effects, the idiom of the Faulknerian idiot avoids naming the object; it stops at the details and effects.

32. "Ice. That means how cold it is" (*SF*: 13).

33. In an earlier chapter, I showed how this strategy is repeated in *The Hamlet*, especially in the peep-show scene, where the narrative concentrates on the intense and avid gazes but does not describe the object of their fascination.

34. "Of course you realise that I could be put in the penitentiary for doing what you want" (*AILD*: 246).

35. While waiting for his sister, Vardaman describes the nearby but invisible presence of a cow:

I hear the cow a long time, clopping   on the street. Then she comes into the square. She goes across the square, her head down   clopping   . She lows.

There was nothing in the square before she lowed. (*AILD*: 251)

The "she" of the cow stands in for the absence of Dewey Dell, whose reappearance, in keeping with the text, is described in very similar terms. The term *clopping*, along with repetition of the verb *to low*, can be seen as references to Dewey Dell and the fate the pharmacist has reserved for her. The rape takes place in the interstices of the text.

36. The question Chick asks his mother in *The Town* the day after the death of Eula Varner Snopes—"'Mrs Snopes killed herself last night,' she said. 'I'm going over to Oxford with Uncle Gavin to bring Linda home.' 'Killed herself?' I said. 'How?'" (*T*: 295)—remains hanging until chapter 8 of *The Mansion*, in which he offers, as the narrator, deferred satisfaction for the reader's morbid curiosity. In the excerpt below, Chick puts himself in the shoes of Flem Snopes and tries to imagine what the latter thinks about the event: "my wife went to the beauty parlor for the first time in her life and that night shot herself carefully through the temple so as not to disarrange the new permanent" (*M*: 512).

37. To return for a moment to Eula's disappearance, it is important to recognize that a few impressionistic lines—which appear at the margins of the event they foreshadow and suggest her exit from the scene—feature a great sensitivity that stands in stark contrast to the brutality of her final act. Elegance can therefore be one of the incidental consequences of this strategy of circumvention. The effect produced is not very different from the instances when Benjy describes Uncle Maury opening the sideboard where the bottles are kept, instead of showing him completely tipsy.

CHAPTER 13. THE DISORDERS OF PREDICATION AND THE ORDER OF A WORLD: THE IDIOT IDIOM

1. This principle of incomprehension is defined in the following manner by Mikhail Bakhtin in "Functions of the Rogue, the Clown, and the Fool in the Novel": "The form of 'incomprehension,' which is intentional with the author and ingenuously naïve with his characters, almost always presents itself as an organizing element when it comes to

denouncing pernicious conventions. Once these have been revealed [...] [they] are usually evoked from the point of view of an impartial individual who doesn't understand anything" (Bakhtin, 1978: 309).

2. Jean-Jacques Mayoux believes that "Faulkner was haunted by the representation of the idiot's world, as he was by all extreme states in which consciousness explodes and is eliminated" (Mayoux, 1985: 289).

3. Renaud Barbaras has highlighted how sensation is both a state of the perceiving subject and a content, both an experience and its subject: "All one has to do is avert or close one's eyes in order for an entire section of the spectacle to disappear, to move so that the landscape starts to move: when it presents itself to us as preceding our experience, what is perceived simultaneously appears to be completely dependent on our sensitive subjectivity" (Barbaras, 1994: 4). Barbaras takes up the theme developed by Merleau-Ponty in this regard and applies it to all of the sense organs.

4. "I mean by 'proper' that which cannot be perceived by another sense and about which it is not possible to be deceived, [...] while movement, rest, number, figure, magnitude are called 'common.' For they are proper to none of the senses but are common to all" ("Three Kinds of Perceptible Objects," Aristotle, 2018: 33).

5. The term "apophantic" derives from the Greek *apophainesthai*, which means to show, to manifest, to make appear. In *On Interpretation* (chap. 4), it is the name given by Aristotle to the discourse that can be said to be true or false, as opposed to those referred to as poetic, rhetorical, or aesthetic, which cannot (Aristotle, 1963). An apophantic proposition makes a claim to truth because it has a sense and possesses a referential scope.

6. It bears mentioning that language is aesthetic in the arts. One would not say that Turner's cloud is ochre but rather that this ochre could be a cloud. The failure of apophantic language to establish usual categories in an aesthetic work once again gives pride of place to sensation, which becomes the subject, even though the substance is not clearly identifiable.

7. Zeugma, on which many metonymies and hypallages are built, can be added to this list. Whether it is syntactical or semantic, zeugma puts dissimilar elements on the same level through coordination or juxtaposition, and thereby couples heterogeneous nouns and adjectives. Here is an example: "I could hear the clock and the roof and Caddy" (*SF*: 57).

8. Pierre Fontanier has defined the term as follows: "Comparison involves bringing one object closer to another foreign object, or to itself, in order to illuminate, reinforce, or reveal the idea through relations of suitability or unsuitability: or, if you will, resemblance or difference" (Fontanier, 1993: 377).

9. In all of the comparisons that associate Caddy with the smell of trees, or with leaves or trees in the rain ("Caddy smelled like trees in the rain," *SF*: 9), Caddy remains as elusive (and ultimately versatile) as an olfactory impression. There is a notable exception to this olfactory sketch of Caddy: "Her hair was like fire" (72). This visual comparison is the only allusion—however inconclusive it may be—to Caddy's physical appearance. Caddy is also associated with "smooth, bright shapes," which do not always appear in connection with her but invariably bring to mind the moment when Benjy falls asleep next to her. As mentioned already, his monologue ends with a similar comparison: "Then the dark began to go in smooth, bright shapes, like it always does, even when Caddy says that I have been asleep" (75).

10. "Father took me up. He smelled like rain" (*SF*: 64); "*Quentin smelled like rain, too*" (66); "Versh smelled like rain" (68). In all three cases, the syntax is strictly the same, only the *comparé* changes. However, the adverb *too* in the second example introduces, a few pages later, a comparison of sorts between the comparisons.

11. I have listed about twenty comparisons that are specific to Benjy's discourse; they are accompanied by a certain number of occurrences taken from the words spoken by other characters.

12. This theme is broadly developed in book 1 of *The Hamlet*, entitled "Flem," as well as the short story "Spotted Horses" (1931), in which the mules of Frenchman's Bend are subjected to highly unusual diets so that they appear more healthy than they actually are.

13. This repetition is combined with the phrase "Father was sick there" (*SF*: 34), in which the illness leaves the truth of death indeterminate.

14. It is from a similar perspective that Aurélie Guillain considers the neutrality and absence of affects in Benjy's discourse as the paradoxical expression of a climactic distress: "Benjy's interior monologue speaks of loss and dispossession, but it is not a complaint: his speech stripped of pathos is like a long litotes on the pain that Faulkner wove into the reverse side of his own hyperbolic prose. Benjy's savage prose, recounting the world's brutality without affectation, stands in contrast to the pathetic and grandiloquent excesses that resound in Faulkner's novels" (Guillain, 2003: 57).

15. Nothing attests to the fact that Rosa ever made the avowal; perhaps this allegation is, yet again, just a conjecture made by successive narrators.

16. This phrase, which is both definitive and open through the absence of punctuation at the end of the monologue (for Addie still has things to say), replaces the refrain that marked Darl's earlier monologues: "'She is going to die,' he says" (*AILD*: 28); "'Jewel,' I say, 'do you know that Addie Bundren is going to die? Addie Bundren is going to die?'" (40).

17. It is Dewey Dell who waves the fan in front of her mother's face, but the object is described as moving intentionally and autonomously.

18. Contradicted by this use of adjectives, the worry of approaching buzzards suddenly reappears in Vardaman's desperate attempts to chase them away—"that boy chasing them buzzards all day in the hot sun until he was nigh crazy as the rest of them" (*AILD*: 191)—and through his fear that they could attack the coffin during the night when he lets his guard down: "I went to find where they stay at night" (217, 223, 225). Sometimes in italics and sometimes not, this final phrase echoes like a chorus throughout Vardaman's final monologues.

19. Long avoided through the pronoun *it*, or repetition of the verb *to smell*, which is marked by its neutrality, the smell of Addie's corpse affects those nearby, despite their reluctance to admit what has become of her body during the fire scene: "a thin smell of scorching meat" (*AILD*: 222)—it is the smell of meat.

20. It is first Ellen's sister and then her niece Judith who crystallize the frustrations of Rosa, who "projects" herself in the former and the latter: "projecting upon Judith all the abortive dreams and delusions of her own doomed and frustrated youth" (*AA*: 55–56). Her existence consists of ethereal imaginations that try to overcome her dread that she is "doomed" to never have a life of her own. Just as she covets her sister's husband, and prepares Judith's wedding as if it were her own, she will intrude upon the young girl's

intimacy by anticipation: "Yet this was where she had to go to get the material to make those intimate young girl garments which where to be for her own vicarious bridal" (61).

21. "Writing heroic poetry about the very men from whom her father was hiding" (*AA*: 53).

22. This image repeats, word for word, Benjy's description of Quentin approaching in the night (*SF*: 23), which I discussed above.

CHAPTER 14. TRYING TO READ FAULKNER

1. The first suggestions are rooted in onomastics. André Bleikasten has pointed out that the symbolism of Dewey Dell's first name is "obvious": "With regard to the fairly obvious sexual symbolism of 'Dewey Dell,' it is interesting to note that from the sixteenth to the eighteenth century 'dell' was slang word first for a virgin, then for a prostitute" (Bleikasten, 2016 [1990]: 382). Her name also evokes the expression "dewy eyed," which suggests the naïveté of the ingénue.

2. Dewey Dell makes no allusion to her younger brother Vardaman. This absence of information is a kind of information in itself. At this stage of the story, one can simply conclude that Vardaman is apparently not taking part in picking cotton.

3. At the beginning of act 4, Macbeth summons the witches to give their prophecies: they assure him that despite the vengeance that is brewing (the Dukes of Scotland are about to unite their forces against him), he will remain undefeated as long as Birnan Forest does not draw near the hill where he sits on the throne: "Macbeth shall never vanquished be, until / Great Birnan Wood to high Dunsinane Hill / Shall come against him" (*Macbeth* 4.1.91–93). Certain that this prediction will never come to pass, Macbeth convinces himself that his reign is permanent: "That will never be. / Who can impress the forest, bid the tree / Unfix his earth-bound root?" (4.1.93–95).

4. This is a repetition, in a minor mode, of the scene opposing Quentin and Caddy on the riverside. In fact, Dewey Dell pronounces almost the same words as Quentin, who is concerned about defending his sister's lost honor: "are you going to kill him?" (*AILD*: 27) is the counterpart to "tomorrow Ill kill him" (*SF*: 150). However, Darl clearly does not share the chivalrous values of the eldest Compson brother.

5. Roland Barthes defines "the pleasure of the text" by the extremity of perversion underpinning it: "However, perversion does not suffice to define bliss; it is the extreme of perversion which defines it: an extreme continually shifted, an empty, mobile, unpredictable extreme. This extreme guarantees bliss: an average perversion quickly loads itself up with a play of subordinate finalities" (Barthes, 1998 [1975]: 52).

6. In an article he devoted to Faulkner in his *Histoire de la littérature américaine* (History of American Literature), Pierre-Yves Pétillon observes: "Faulkner casts a very, very long shadow on the American novel" (Pétillon, 2003 [1992]: 56).

7. David Lodge has emphasized this notion of the writing that teaches the kind of reading it requires: "Writing requires reading for its completion, but also teaches the kind of reading it requires" (Lodge, 1977: 9).

8. It is in these terms that Jean Starobinski defined the irresistible fascination exerted by what is hidden: "In dissimulation and absence there is a strange force that compels the spirit

to turn toward the inaccessible and, for the sake of conquest, to sacrifice all it possesses. [. . .] Fascination persuades us, so that we may belong to it, to give up everything, even concern for our own lives. It takes all we have simply by promising everything we want" (Starobinski, 1961: 1).

9. "It is by reason of this masterliness of theirs, this uncompromising idiosyncrasy, that great writers often require us to make heroic efforts in order to read them rightly. They bend us and break us" (Woolf, 1994: 393).

10. Hans Robert Jauss describes literature of entertainment as being akin to "culinary art," which "is characterized by an aesthetics of reception as not demanding any horizontal change, but rather as precisely fulfilling the expectations prescribed by a ruling standard of taste, in that it satisfies the desire for the reproduction of the familiarly beautiful; confirms familiar sentiments; sanctions wishful notions . . ." (Jauss, 1982: 25).

11. The concept of "*différance*" originated with Jacques Derrida in his *L'Écriture et la différence* (1967; *Writing and Difference*). This concept inspired Édouard Glissant's vision of the "deferred" process that governs Faulkner's writing and its reading: "Witnesses pursue—like the hunters chasing the faint trail of old Ben in the Big Woods—this deferred history of the South, which is never given. In Faulkner there appears, for one of the first times and with such great insistence, this thought of the trace, which sends supposedly established truths back to their mutual exclusions. The story told is a trace, one that requires patience and ardor (not to mention art, which can be learned) to identify" (Glissant, 2000: 245). Just as it took time to track the bear in the lush forests of the Delta, patience is needed to clear away the convolutions in Faulkner's writing in order to see what is at play in them.

12. Sartre had already understood this point: "The reader is tempted to look for guide-marks and to re-establish the chronology for himself. [. . .] [However, in doing so] the reader stops, for he realizes he is telling another story. Faulkner did not first conceive this orderly plot so as to reshuffle afterwards like a pack of cards; he could not tell it in any other way" (Sartre, 1987: 265).

13. "Defamiliarization and alienation there certainly is, as the reader struggles to 'make sense' of what is being said: but there is also the sense of play that comes from sharing the punning associations, enjoying the liberty of verbal and mental processes without anchorage and, indeed, without any evident boundaries" (Gray, 1994: 142). The rules of the game change with each new monologue and each new novel: "Essentially, the difference in each section is a matter of code and rhetoric: in the sense that each time the tale is told another language, an alternative model is devised and a different set of relationships occurs between author, narrator, subject and reader" (140).

14. Édouard Glissant has shown how accessing Rowan Oak, Faulkner's estate, is marked by a difficulty and resistance that bring to mind those involved in reading his work:

Our ambivalence turned to panic as the day wore on. It was as though we had to pass a test before we could reach Rowan Oak: as though, in order to enter into the meanings of Faulkner's works, to see them stand before us and cry out in the woods and fields, we had to pass the test of their "difficulty," their resistance, had to force a path into their thick wilderness, into what we could call only their "deferred revelation."

Faulkner's books have always seemed to me to work this way. Deferred revelation is the source of his technique. This has nothing to do with the suspense of a detective novel or with social or psychological clarification; rather, it is an accumulating mystery and a whirling vertigo—gathering momentum rather than being resolved, through deferral and disclosure—and centered in a place to which he felt a need to give meaning. (Glissant, 2000: 9)

15. Similarly, in the chapter devoted to Ike Snopes in *The Hamlet*, the omniscient narrator comments on the idiot's gestures using normative language; in doing so, he offers readers of *The Sound and the Fury* a retrospective user's manual:

He stood looking at his empty palm with quiet amazement, turning the hand over to look at the back, even raising and opening the other hand to look into it. Then—it was an effort almost physical, like childbirth—he connected two ideas, he progressed backward into time and recaptured an image by logical retrogression and fumbled into the shirt pocket again, peering into it, though only for a moment, as if he actually did not expect to find the coin there, though it was doubtless pure instinct which caused him to look down at the dusty planks on which he stood. (*H*: 196-97)

16. "Divorced by him 1911. Married 1920 to a minor movie picture magnate, Hollywood California. Divorced by mutual agreement, Mexico 1925. Vanished in Paris with the German occupation, 1940" ("Appendix": 208).

17. "Deep down—that is, in the reality that is the South—Faulkner acquiesces at the conclusion of the epic by sanctioning the elevation of a class of parvenus, the Snopeses, who conform to the 'Americanization' of the county. In formalist terms, it is in the realist prose of the Snopeses that epic interrogation is extinguished and erased. [. . .] Faulkner's last books are not weak; they are logical in terms of their goal: presenting the quagmire of meticulously calculated profiteering and the extinction of epic tension" (Glissant, 2000: 100).

18. "The repetitive Dixie Cafés or Mac's or Lorraine's" (*M*: 673).

CONCLUSION: FICTION OF ORIGIN AND THE ORIGIN OF FICTION

1. "Transgression has always adopted marvelous forms of expression: poetry and music, dance, tragedy, or painting. The forms art takes have their origin nowhere but in the festival celebration, in all ages the same, and the feast, which is religious, calls for the deployment of all of art's resources" (Bataille, 1955: 38).

2. Idiocy is thus the lifeblood of Faulkner's modernity and perhaps, as asserted by Jean-Yves Jouannais in his writing on idiocy in art, the lifeblood of modernity: "[I]diocy has never been the spectacular dregs or scrap of modernity, but its very motor and spirit" (Jouannais, n.d.). Jouannais points out: "'Idiocy' is quite simply the most relevant term for describing the body and corpus of modernity." Idiocy and the strange forms it engenders are synonymous with what is new and original because they are absolutely free of the constraints that normal humans build for themselves and their art.

3. For example, the omniscient narrator of the story about Ike Snopes discusses the idiot's slow learning, contrasting it with the corruption of his normal fellow citizens: "who is learning fast now, who has learned success and then precaution and secrecy and how to steal and even providence; who has only lust and greed and bloodthirst and a moral conscience to keep him awake at night, yet to acquire" (*H*: 202).

4. From the point of view of Gilles Deleuze and Félix Guattari, in Descartes it is the idiot who says "I" that is behind the cogito: "[I]t is the Idiot who says 'I' and sets up the cogito but who also has the subjective presuppositions or lays out the plane. The idiot is the private thinker, in contrast to the public teacher (the schoolman): the teacher refers constantly to taught concepts (man–rational animal), whereas the private thinker forms a concept with innate forces that everyone possesses on their own account by right ('I think')" (Deleuze and Guattari, 1996 [1994]: 61–62).

BIBLIOGRAPHY

I. WORKS BY WILLIAM FAULKNER

A. Works by William Faulkner cited in chronological order of first publication

Soldiers' Pay, 1997 (1926), New York, Liveright.
Mosquitoes, 1989 (1927), London, Picador.
Flags in the Dust, 1929 (revised and published under the title *Sartoris* in 1974), New York, Vintage Books.
The Sound and the Fury, 1990 (1929), New York, Vintage International.
As I Lay Dying, 1990 (1930), New York, Vintage International.
Sanctuary, 1993 (1931), New York, Vintage International.
Light in August, 1990 (1932), New York, Vintage International.
Pylon, 1968 (1935), New York, New American Library.
Absalom, Absalom!, 1990 (1936), New York, Vintage International.
The Unvanquished, 1991 (1938), New York, Vintage International.
The Wild Palms, 1966 (1939), New York, Vintage Books.
The Hamlet, 1991 (1940), New York, Vintage International.
Go Down, Moses, 1990 (1942), New York, Vintage International.
Intruder in the Dust, 1994 (1948), in *Novels, 1942–1954*, ed. Joseph Blotner and Noel Polk, New York, Library of America.
Knight's Gambit, 1956 (1949), New York, New American Library.
Collected Stories of William Faulkner, 1995 (1950), New York, Vintage International.
Requiem for a Nun, 1994 (1951), in *Novels, 1942–1954*, ed. Joseph Blotner and Noel Polk, New York: Library of America.
A Fable, 1994 (1954), in *Novels, 1942–1954*, ed. Joseph Blotner and Noel Polk, New York: Library of America.
The Town, 1999 (1957), in *Novels, 1957–1962*, ed. Joseph Blotner and Noel Polk, New York, Library of America.
New Orleans Sketches, 1958, ed. Carvel Collins, New York, Random House.
The Mansion, 1999 (1959), in *Novels 1957–1962*, ed. Joseph Blotner and Noel Polk, New York, Library of America.
The Reivers, 1999 (1962), in *Novels 1957–1962*, ed. Joseph Blotner and Noel Polk, New York, Library of America.

Early Prose and Poetry, 1962, ed. Carvel Collins, Boston, Little, Brown.
Uncollected Stories of William Faulkner, 1997 (1979), ed. Joseph Blotner, New York, Vintage International.

B. French translations of William Faulkner's works

Œuvres romanesques I, 1977, trans. Maurice-Edgar Coindreau, Henri Delgove, and René-Noël Raimbault, amended by Michel Gresset, Paris, Bibliothèque de la Pléiade.
Œuvres romanesques II, 1995, trans. Maurice-Edgar Coindreau, René-Noël Raimbault, G. L. Rousselet, and Charles P. Vorce, amended by André Bleikasten, Didier Coupaye, and François Pitavy, Paris, Bibliothèque de la Pléiade, 1995.
Œuvres romanesques III, 2000, trans. Maurice-Edgar Coindreau, René Hilleret, Michel Gresset, René-Noël Raimbault, Didier Coupaye, and Aurélie Guillain, amended by François Pitavy, Michel Gresset, Jacques Pothier, Florence Césari, and Nicole Moulinoux, Paris, Bibliothèque de la Pléiade.

C. Collections and miscellaneous texts

Blotner, Joseph (ed.), 1977, *The Selected Letters of William Faulkner*, New York, Random House.
Brodsky, Louis Daniel, and Robert W. Hamblin (eds.), 1984, *Faulkner: A Comprehensive Guide to the Brodsky Collection*, vol. 2, *The Letters*, Jackson, University Press of Mississippi.
Cowley, Malcolm (ed.), 1984 (1946), *The Portable Faulkner*, New York, Penguin Books.
Fant, Joseph L., and Robert Ashley (eds.), 1964, *Faulkner at West Point*, New York, Random House.
Gwynn, Frederick L., and Joseph L. Blotner (eds.), 1959, *Faulkner in the University: Class Conferences at the University of Virginia, 1957-1958*, Charlottesville, University Press of Virginia.
Inge, M. Thomas (ed.), 1999, *Conversations with William Faulkner*, Jackson, University Press of Mississippi.
Jelliffe, Robert A. (ed.), 1956, *Faulkner at Nagano*, Tokyo, Kenkyusha.
Meriwether, James B., Autumn 1972, "An Introduction for *The Sound and the Fury*," *Southern Review*.
Meriwether, James B. (ed.), Summer 1973, "An Introduction to *The Sound and the Fury*," *Mississippi Quarterly*.
Meriwether, James B., and Michael Millgate (eds.), 1980, *Lion in the Garden: Interviews with William Faulkner, 1926-1962*, Lincoln, University of Nebraska Press.
Watson, James G. (ed.), 2000, *Thinking of Home: William Faulkner's Letters to His Mother and Father, 1918-1925*, New York, W. W. Norton.

II. OTHER WORKS

Abadie, Ann (ed.), 1980, *William Faulkner: A Life on Paper*, Jackson, University Press of Mississippi.
Anderson, Sherwood, 1996 (1919), *Winesburg, Ohio*, London, Penguin Books.

Aristotle, 1963, *Categories and De Interpretatione*, trans. J. L. Ackrill, Oxford, Oxford University Press.
Aristotle, 2018, *On the Soul and Other Psychological Works*, trans. Fred D. Miller Jr., Oxford, Oxford University Press.
Baatsch, Henri-Alexis, 1993, *Henri Michaux: Peinture et poésie*, Paris, Hazan.
Bachelard, Gaston, 1998 (1943), *L'Air et les songes: Essai sur l'imagination du mouvement*, Paris, José Corti.
Bakhtin, Mikhail M., 1978, *Esthétique et théorie du roman*, trans. Daria Olivier, Paris, Gallimard.
Bakhtin, Mikhail M., 1981, *The Dialogic Imagination: Four Essays*, trans. Caryl Emerson and Michael Holquist, Austin, University of Texas Press Slavic Series.
Balzac, Honoré de, 1895, *The Country Doctor*, trans. Ellen Marriage, London, J. M. Dent.
Barbaras, Renaud, 1994, *La Perception: Essai sur le sensible*, Paris, Hatier.
Barker, Deborah E., and Ivo Kamps, Summer 1993, "Much Ado about Nothing: Language and Desire in *The Sound and the Fury*," *Mississippi Quarterly*.
Barthes, Roland, 1998 (1975), *The Pleasure of the Text*, trans. Richard Miller, New York, Hill and Wang.
Bataille, Georges, 1955, *Lascaux; or, The Birth of Art: A Prehistoric Painting*, Geneva, Skira.
Bataille, Georges, 1985, *Visions of Excess: Selected Writings, 1927–1939*, ed. and trans. Allan Stoekl, Minneapolis, University of Minnesota Press.
Bataille, Georges, 2002, *Blue of Noon*, trans. Harry Mathews, London, Marion Boyars.
Bataille, Georges, 2014, *Inner Experience*, trans. Stuart Kendall, Albany, State University of New York Press.
Bergounioux, Pierre, 2002, *Jusqu'à Faulkner*, Paris, Gallimard.
Bettleheim, Bruno, 1967, *The Empty Fortress: Infantile Autism and the Birth of the Self*, New York, Free Press.
Blanchot, Maurice, 1995, *The Work of Fire*, trans. Charlotte Mandell, Stanford, CA, Stanford University Press.
Blanchot, Maurice, 2007, *A Voice from Elsewhere*, trans. Charlotte Mandell, Albany, State University of New York Press.
Blay, Michel (ed.), 2003, *Grand dictionnaire de la philosophie*, Paris, Larousse.
Bleikasten, André, 1976, *The Most Splendid Failure: Faulkner's "The Sound and the Fury,"* Bloomington, Indiana University Press.
Bleikasten, André, 1982, *Parcours de Faulkner*, Strasbourg, Presses Universitaires de Strasbourg.
Bleikasten, André, 2016 (1990), *The Ink of Melancholy: Faulkner's Novels from the "The Sound and the Fury" to "Light in August,"* Bloomington, Indiana University Press.
Bleikasten, André, and Nicole Moulinoux (eds.), 1995, *Douze lectures de "Sanctuaire,"* Rennes, Presses Universitaires de Rennes.
Blotner, Joseph, 1964, *William Faulkner's Library: A Catalogue*, Charlottesville, University Press of Virginia.
Blotner, Joseph, 1974, *Faulkner: A Biography*, New York, Random House.
Brooks, Cleanth, 1963, *William Faulkner: The Yoknapatawpha Country*, New Haven, CT, Yale University Press.
Brooks, Cleanth, 1978, *William Faulkner: Toward Yoknapatawpha and Beyond*, New Haven, CT, Yale University Press.

Broughton, Panthea Reid, Summer 1969, "Masculinity and Menfolk in *The Hamlet*," *Mississippi Quarterly*.

Brown, Arthur A., Summer 1995, "Benjy, the Reader, and Death: At the Fence in *The Sound and the Fury*," *Mississippi Quarterly*.

Brown, Calvin S., 1976, *A Glossary of Faulkner's South*, New Haven, CT, Yale University Press.

Buffon, Georges-Louis Leclerc de, 2003 (1753), *Discours sur la nature des animaux*, Paris, Payot et Rivages.

Canguilhem, Georges, 1966, *Le Normal et le pathologique*, Paris, Presses Universitaires de France.

Canguilhem, Georges, 1980, *La Connaissance de la vie*, Paris, Librairie Philosophique J. Vrin.

Cannone, Belinda, 1998, *Narrations de la vie intérieure*, Paris, Klincksieck.

Carmignani, Paul, Summer 1990, "Olfaction in Faulkner's Fiction," *Mississippi Quarterly*.

Castel, Pierre-Henri, 2003, "Folie," in *Grand dictionnaire de la philosophie*, ed. Michel Blay, Paris, Larousse.

Cazenave, Michel (ed.), 1996, *Encyclopédie des symboles*, Paris, Le Livre de Poche.

Cecil, L. Moffitt, Fall 1970, "A Rhetoric for Benjy," *Southern Literary Journal*.

Chardin, Philippe (ed.), 2004, *Autour du monologue intérieur*, Paris, Séguier.

Clavilier, Michèle, and Danielle Duchefdelaville, 1999, *Commedia dell'arte: Le Jeu masqué*, Grenoble, Presses Universitaires de Grenoble.

Coetzee, John Maxwell, April 7, 2005, "The Making of William Faulkner," *New York Review of Books*.

Cohn, Dorrit, 1978, *Transparent Minds: Narrative Modes for Presenting Consciousness in Fiction*, Princeton, NJ, Princeton University Press.

Coindreau, Maurice-Edgar, 1971, *The Time of William Faulkner: A French View of Modern American Fiction*, trans. George McMillan Reeves, Columbia, University of South Carolina Press.

Conrad, Joseph, 1974 (1898), *Tales of Unrest*, New York, Gordon Press.

Courtine, Jean-Jacques (ed.), 2005, *Histoire du corps*, vol. 1, *De la Renaissance aux Lumières*, Paris, Éditions du Seuil.

Danan, Joseph, 1995, *Le Théâtre de la pensée*, Rouen, Éditions Médianes.

Debord, Guy, 2004, *Panegyric*, trans. James Brook and John McHale, Verso, London.

Deleuze, Gilles, 2003, *Francis Bacon: The Logic of Sensation*, trans. Daniel W. Smith, London, Continuum.

Deleuze, Gilles, 2004 (1994), *Difference and Repetition*, trans. Paul Patton, London, Continuum.

Deleuze, Gilles, and Félix Guattari, 1996 (1994), *What Is Philosophy?*, trans. Hugh Tomlinson and Graham Burchell, New York, Columbia University Press.

Delville, Michel, Fall 1994, "Alienating Language and Darl's Narrative Consciousness in Faulkner's *As I Lay Dying*," *Southern Literary Journal*.

Des Forêts, Louis-René, 1985 (1962), *Voies et détours de la fiction*, Paris, Fata Morgana.

Didi-Huberman, Georges, 1995, *La Ressemblance informe ou le gai savoir visual selon Georges Bataille*, Paris, Éditions Macula.

Dostoevsky, Fyodor, 2003, *The Idiot*, trans. Richard Pevear and Larissa Volokhonsky, New York, Vintage Books.

Dujardin, Édouard, 1990 (1938), *We'll to the Woods No More*, trans. Stuart Gilbert, New York, New Directions.
Dujardin, Édouard, 2001 (1887), *Les Lauriers sont coupés*, Paris, Garnier Flammarion.
Emerson, Ralph Waldo, 2000, *The Essential Writings of Ralph Waldo Emerson*, ed. Brooks Atkinson, New York, Modern Library.
Fitzgerald, Penelope, 1995, *The Blue Flower*, Boston, Houghton Mifflin.
Flaubert, Gustave, 1980, *The Letters of Gustave Flaubert (1830–1857)*, trans. Francis Steegmuller, Cambridge, MA, Belknap Press of Harvard University Press.
Flaubert, Gustave, 1999 (1881), *Bouvard et Pécuchet*, Paris, Le Livre de Poche.
Flaubert, Gustave, 2004, *Madame Bovary*, trans. Margaret Mauldon, Oxford, Oxford University Press.
Flaubert, Gustave, 2005, *Three Tales*, trans. Roger Whitehouse, London, Penguin Books.
Fontanier, Pierre, 1993, *Les Figures du discours*, Paris, Flammarion.
Ford, Madox Ford, 2001 (1915), *The Good Soldier*, Mineola, NY, Dover Publications.
Fowler, Doreen, and Ann J. Abadie (eds.), 1983, *New Directions in Faulkner Studies*, Jackson, University Press of Mississippi.
Frederickson, Michael A., 1966, "A Note on 'The Idiot Boy' as a Probable Source for *The Sound and the Fury*," *Minnesota Review*.
Freedman, William A., Winter 1961–1962, "The Technique of Isolation in *The Sound and the Fury*," *Mississippi Quarterly*.
Freud, Sigmund, 1953, *On Aphasia: A Critical Study*, trans. Erwin Stengel, New York, International Universities Press.
Freud, Sigmund, 2001, *Totem and Taboo*, trans. James Strachey, London, Penguin Books.
Freud, Sigmund, 2004, "Le Fétichisme," in *Œuvres complètes*, vol. 18, *1926–1930*, ed. André Bourguignon, Pierre Cotet, and Jean Laplanche, Paris, Presses Universitaires de France.
Freud, Sigmund, 2006, *Penguin Freud Reader*, ed. Adam Phillips, London, Penguin Books.
Fromilhague, Catherine, 1995, *Les Figures de style*, Paris, Nathan.
Frye, Northrop, 1967, *Fools of Time: Studies in Shakespearean Tragedy*, Toronto, University of Toronto Press.
Furetière, Antoine, 1997, *Les Couleurs*, ed. Cécile Wajsbrot, Cadeilhan, France, Éditions Zulma.
Garnier, Marcel, and Valéry Delamare, 1972, *Dictionnaire des termes techniques de médecine*, Paris, Éditions Maloine.
Gass, William H., 2000 (1970), *Fiction and the Figures of Life*, Boston, David R. Godine.
Genette, Gérard, 1980, *Narrative Discourse: An Essay In Method*, trans. Jane E. Lewin, Ithaca, NY, Cornell University Press.
Gide, André, 2003 (1895), *Paludes*, Paris, Gallimard.
Glissant, Édouard, 2000, *Faulkner, Mississippi*, trans. Barbara Lewis and Thomas C. Spear, Chicago, University of Chicago Press.
Godden, Richard, 2007, *William Faulkner: An Economy of Complex Words*, Princeton, NJ, Princeton University Press, 2007.
Gray, Richard, 1994, *The Life of William Faulkner: A Critical Biography*, Oxford, Blackwell.
Gray, Richard, 1997, *Writing the South: Ideas of an American Region*, Baton Rouge, Louisiana State University Press.
Green, A. Wigfall, and Richard M. Allen, 1999, "First Lectures at a University," in *Conversations with William Faulkner*, ed. M. Thomas Inge, Jackson, University Press of Mississippi.

Green, André, 2002, *Time in Psychoanalysis: Some Contradictory Aspects*, trans. Andrew Weller, London, Free Association Books.
Gresset, Michel, 1982, *Faulkner ou la fascination: Poétique du regard*, Paris, Klincksieck.
Gresset, Michel, and Patrick Samway (eds.), 1983, *Faulkner and Idealism: Perspectives from Paris*, Jackson, University Press of Mississippi.
Guillain, Aurélie, 2003, *Faulkner: Le Roman de la détresse*, Rennes, Presses Universitaires de Rennes.
Guillemin-Flescher, Jacqueline, 1996, "The Linguistic Representation of Perception in Benjy's Monologue," in *Études Faulknériennes I: "Sanctuary,"* ed. Michel Gresset, Rennes, Presses Universitaires de Rennes.
Hamblin, Robert W., and Charles A. Peek (eds.), 1999, *A William Faulkner Encyclopedia*, Westport, CT, Greenwood Press.
Hawthorne, Nathaniel, 1988 (1850), *The Scarlet Letter*, New York, W. W. Norton.
Hönnighausen, Lothar, 1997, *Faulkner: Masks and Metaphors*, Jackson, University Press of Mississippi.
Housman, Alfred Edward, 1994, *The Works of A. E. Housman*, Ware, Herts., England, Wordsworth Editions.
Hugo, Victor, 1997 (1831), *Notre-Dame de Paris*, Paris, Gallimard.
Irwin, John T., 1975, *Doubling and Incest / Repetition and Revenge: A Speculative Reading of Faulkner*, Baltimore, Johns Hopkins University Press.
Iser, Wolfgang, 1974, *The Implied Reader: Patterns of Communication in Prose Fiction from Bunyan to Beckett*, Baltimore, Johns Hopkins University Press.
Jakobson, Roman, 1971, *Studies on Child Language and Aphasia*, The Hague, Mouton.
James, Henry, 1985 (1897), *What Maisie Knew*, London, Penguin Books.
James, Henry, 2001, *Selected Tales*, ed. John Lyon, London, Penguin Books.
James, William, 1890, *The Principles of Psychology*, New York, Henry Holt.
Jauss, Hans Robert, 1982, *Toward an Aesthetic of Reception*, trans. Timothy Bahti, Minneapolis, University of Minnesota Press.
Jehlen, Myra, 1999, "Faulkner and the Unnatural," in *Faulkner and the Natural World*, ed. Donald M. Kartiganer and Ann J. Abadie, Jackson, University Press of Mississippi.
Jouannais, Jean-Yves, 1997, *Artistes sans œuvres. I would prefer not to*, Paris, Hazan.
Jouannais, Jean-Yves, 2003, *L'Idiotie: Art, vie, politique—méthode*, Paris, Beaux Arts.
Jouannais, Jean-Yves, n.d., "L'Idiotie en art, l'anti-Biathanatos," http://labetise.free.fr/biathana.htm.
Joyce, James, 1994 (1916), *A Portrait of the Artist as a Young Man*, Mineola, NY, Dover Publications.
Joyce, James, 1998 (1922), *Ulysses*, Oxford, Oxford University Press.
Kartiganer, Donald M., 1979, *The Fragile Thread: The Meaning of Form in Faulkner's Novels*, Amherst, University of Massachusetts Press.
Kartiganer, Donald M., 1989, "Faulkner's Art of Repetition," in *Faulkner and the Craft of Fiction*, ed. Doreen Fowler and Ann J. Abadie, Jackson, University Press of Mississippi.
Kartiganer, Donald M., and Ann J. Abadie (eds.), 1994, *Faulkner and Psychology*, Jackson, University Press of Mississippi.
Kartiganer, Donald M., and Ann J. Abadie (eds.), 1995, *Faulkner and Ideology*, Jackson, University Press of Mississippi.

Keats, John, 1988, *The Complete Poems*, ed. John Barnard, 3rd ed., London, Penguin Books.
Kierkegaard, Søren, 2009, *"Repetition" and "Philosophical Crumbs,"* trans. M. G. Piety, Oxford, Oxford University Press.
Kreiswirth, Martin, Summer 1981, "Learning as He Wrote: Re-Used Materials in *The Sound and the Fury*," *Mississippi Quarterly*.
Laplanche, Jean, and Jean-Bertrand Pontalis, 2018 (1973), *The Language of Psycho-Analysis*, trans. Donald Nicholson-Smith, Abingdon, Oxon., England, Routledge.
Lencho, Mark, Summer 1988, "Dialect Variation in *The Sound and the Fury*: A Study of Faulkner's Use of Black English," *Mississippi Quarterly*.
Lévi-Strauss, Claude, 1974, "Cannibalisme et travestissement rituel," seminar at the Collège de France.
Lévi-Strauss, Claude, 1984, *Paroles données*, Paris, Plon.
Lodge, David, 1977, *The Modes of Modern Writing: Metaphor, Metonymy, and the Typology of Modern Literature*, London, Edward Arnold.
Lotman, Jurij, 1977, *The Structure of the Artistic Text*, trans. Gail Lenhoff and Ronald Vroon, Ann Arbor, University of Michigan, Department of Slavic Languages and Literature.
Lowry, Malcom, 1984 (1947), *Under the Volcano*, New York, Harper and Row.
Mallarmé, Stéphane, 2006, *Collected Poems and Other Verse*, trans. E. H. and A. M. Blackmore, Oxford, Oxford University Press.
Matthews, John T., 1990, *"The Sound and the Fury": Faulkner and the Lost Cause*, Boston, Twayne Publishers.
Mauron, Véronique, and Claire de Ribaupierre, 2004, *Les Figures de l'idiot*, Paris, Léo Scheer.
Mayoux, Jean-Jacques, 1985, *Vivants piliers: Le Roman anglo-saxon et les symbols*, Paris, Maurice Nadeau.
McCarthy, Melissa, January 6, 2021, "William Hogarth's Satire on False Perspective (1754)," *Public Domain Review*, https://publicdomainreview.org/collection/william-hogarth-satire-on-false-perspective.
McLaughlin, Sara, 1987, "Faulkner's Faux Pas: Referring to Benjamin Compson as an Idiot," *Literature and Psychology*.
Mellard, James M., Summer 1995, "Something New and Hard and Bright: Faulkner, Ideology, and the Construction of Modernism," *Mississippi Quarterly*.
Melville, Herman, 1985, *Billy Budd, Sailor and Other Stories*, ed. Harold Beaver, London, Penguin Books.
Merleau-Ponty, Maurice, 1968, *The Visible and the Invisible*, trans. Alphonso Lingis, Evanston, IL, Northwestern University Press.
Merleau-Ponty, Maurice, 1990, *Phénoménologie de la perception*, Paris, Gallimard.
Merleau-Ponty, Maurice, 1993, *The Merleau-Ponty Aesthetics Reader: Philosophy and Painting*, ed. Galen A. Johnson, Evanston, IL, Northwestern University Press.
Merleau-Ponty, Maurice, 2004, *Maurice Merleau-Ponty: Basic Writings*, ed. Thomas Baldwin, London, Routledge.
Mic, Constant, 1980 (1928), *La Commedia dell'arte ou le théâtre des comédiens italiens des XVIe, XVIIe & XVIIIe siècles*, Paris, Librairie Théâtrale.
Michaux, Henri, 1966, *Les Grandes épreuves de l'esprit et les innombrables petites*, Paris, Gallimard.
Michon, Pierre, 1997, *Trois auteurs*, Lagrasse, France, Verdier.

Mistichelli, William J., Spring 1990, "Perception Is a Sacred Cow: The Narrator and Ike Snopes in William Faulkner's *The Hamlet*," *Faulkner Journal*.

Mortimer, Gail L., 1983, *Faulkner's Rhetoric of Loss: A Study in Perception and Meaning*, Austin, University of Texas Press.

Nietzsche, Friedrich, 1997 (1982), *Daybreak: Thoughts on the Prejudices of Morality*, trans. R. J. Hollingdale, Cambridge, Cambridge University Press.

Nietzsche, Friedrich, 2004 (1986), *Ecce Homo*, trans. R. J. Hollingdale, London, Penguin.

Novak, Phillip, Fall 1996, "Meaning, Mourning, and the Form of Modern Narrative: The Inscription of Loss in Faulkner's *The Sound and the Fury*," *Faulkner Journal*.

O'Connor, Flannery, 1955, *The Violent Bear It Away*, New York, Farrar, Straus and Giroux.

O'Connor, Flannery, 1986 (1971), *The Complete Stories*, New York, Farrar, Straus and Giroux.

O'Connor, Flannery, 1999, *Mystery and Manners: Occasional Prose*, ed. Sally and Robert Fitzgerald, New York, Noonday Press.

Panofsky, Erwin, 2020 (1991), *Perspective as Symbolic Form*, trans. Christopher S. Wood, Brooklyn: Zone Books.

Peavy, Charles D., Spring 1966, "The Eyes of Innocence: Faulkner's 'The Kingdom of God,'" *Papers on Language and Literature*.

Pétillon, Pierre-Yves, 2003 (1992), *Histoire de la littérature américaine, 1939–1989*, Paris, Fayard.

Pitavy, François L., 1983, "Idiocy and Idealism: A Reflection on the Faulknerian Idiot," in *Faulkner and Idealism: Perspectives from Paris*, ed. Michel Gresset and Patrick Samway, Jackson, University Press of Mississippi.

Pitavy, François L., 2001, *Le Bruit et la fureur de William Faulkner*, Paris, Gallimard.

Plato, 1985, *The Sophist*, trans. F. M. Cornford, Princeton, NJ, Princeton University Press.

Polk, Noel (ed.), 1993, *New Essays on "The Sound and the Fury*," Cambridge, Cambridge University Press.

Polk, Noel, 1996, *Children of the Dark House: Text and Context in Faulkner*, Jackson, University Press of Mississippi.

Polk, Noel, Fall 2000–Spring 2001, "Testing Masculinity in the Snopes Trilogy," *Faulkner Journal*.

Pothier, Jacques, 2003, *William Faulkner: Essayer de tout dire*, Paris, Belin.

Powers, Lyall H., 1980, *Faulkner's Yoknapatawpha Comedy*, Ann Arbor, University of Michigan Press.

Prior, Linda T., Summer 1969, "Theme, Imagery, and Structure in *The Hamlet*," *Mississippi Quarterly*.

Proust, Marcel, 1984 (1958), *By Way of Sainte-Beuve*, trans. Sylvia Townsend Warner, London, Hogarth Press.

Radloff, Bernhard, Spring 1986, "The Unity of Time in *The Sound and the Fury*," *Faulkner Journal*.

Rimbaud, Arthur, 1993, *Oeuvre poétique*, Paris, Jean de Bonnot.

Romano, Claude, 2005, *Le Chant de la vie: Phénoménologie de Faulkner*, Paris, Gallimard.

Ross, Stephen M., 1989, *Fiction's Inexhaustible Voice: Speech and Writing in Faulkner*, Athens, University of Georgia Press.

Ross, Stephen M., and Noel Polk, 1996, *Reading Faulkner: "The Sound and the Fury*," Jackson, University Press of Mississippi.

Rosset, Clément, 1986, *Le Réel: Traité de l'idiotie*, Paris, Éditions de Minuit.

Rousseau, Jean-Jacques, 1998, *The Collected Writings of Rousseau*, vol. 7, *Essay on the Origin of Languages and Writings Related to Music*, trans. John T. Scott, Hanover, NH, University Press of New England.
Sacks, Oliver, 1986, *The Man Who Mistook His Wife for a Hat, and Other Clinical Tales*, London, Picador.
Sarraute, Nathalie, 1990, *The Age of Suspicion: Essays on the Novel*, New York, George Braziller.
Sartre, Jean-Paul, 1950, *Baudelaire*, trans. Martin Turnell, New York, New Directions.
Sartre, Jean-Paul, 1963, *Les Mots*, Paris, Gallimard.
Sartre, Jean-Paul, 1981, *The Family Idiot: Gustave Flaubert, 1821–1857*, trans. Carol Cosman, Chicago, University of Chicago Press.
Sartre, Jean-Paul, 1987, "On *The Sound and the Fury*: Time in the Work of Faulkner," in *The Sound and the Fury: A Norton Critical Edition*, by William Faulkner, ed. David Minter, New York, W. W. Norton.
Sartre, Jean-Paul, 1992 (1956), *Being and Nothingness*, trans. Hazel E. Barnes, New York, Washington Square Press.
Saussure, Ferdinand de, 2011, *Course in General Linguistics*, trans. Wade Baskin, New York, Columbia University Press.
Savinel, Christine, October 1995, "L'Informe dans *Sanctuaire*," QWERTY.
Séguin, Edouard, 1997 (1846), *Traitement moral, hygiène et éducation des idiots et des autres enfants arriérés*, Paris, Comité d'Histoire de la Sécurité Sociale.
Senges, Pierre, 2005, *L'Idiot et les hommes de paroles*, Paris, Bayard.
Serres, Michel, 2016 (2008), *The Five Senses: A Philosophy of Mingled Bodies*, trans. Margaret Sankey and Peter Cowley, London, Bloomsbury.
Shakespeare, William, 1971 (1604), *Othello*, Paris, Aubier.
Shakespeare, William, 1988 (1594–1595), *Romeo and Juliet*, in *The Annotated Shakespeare*, ed. A. L. Rowse, New York, Greenwich House.
Shakespeare, William, 1994 (1606), *Macbeth*, ed. Nicholas Brooke, Oxford, Oxford University Press.
Simon, Claude, 1986, *Le Discours de Stockholm*, Paris, Éditions de Minuit.
Sollier, Paul, 1891, *Psychologie de l'idiot et de l'imbécile*, Paris, Félix Alcan.
Sōseki, Natsume, 2002, *I Am a Cat*, trans. Aiko Ito and Graeme Wilson, North Clarendon, VT, Tuttle Publishing.
Starobinski, Jean, 1961, *L'Œil vivant*, Paris, Gallimard.
Starobinski, Jean, 1970, *La Relation critique*, Paris, Gallimard.
Stein, Jean, Spring 1956, "William Faulkner: An Interview," *Paris Review*.
Steinbeck, John, 1940 (1937), *Of Mice and Men*, New York, Triangle Books.
Storhoff, Gary, Spring 1997, "Caddy and the Infinite Loop: The Dynamics of Alcoholism in *The Sound and the Fury*," Faulkner Journal.
Straus, Erwin, 1963, *The Primary World of Senses: A Vindication of Sensory Experience*, trans. Jacob Needleman, Glencoe, IL, Free Press of Glencoe.
Straus, Erwin, 1989, *Du Sens des sens: Contribution à l'étude des fondements de la psychologie*, trans. Georges Tines and Jean-Pierre Legrand, Grenoble, Éditions Jérôme Millon.
Sundquist, Eric J., 1983, *Faulkner: The House Divided*, Baltimore, Johns Hopkins University Press.

Surya, Michel, 2004, *Humanimalités*, Paris, Léo Scheer.
Thoreau, Henry David, 1982 (1854), *Walden*, in *The Portable Thoreau*, ed. Carl Bode, New York, Penguin Books.
Thuillier, Pierre, November 1984, "Espace et perspective au quattrocento," *La Recherche*, no. 160.
Tilley, Winthrop, 1955, "The Idiot Boy in Mississippi: Faulkner's *The Sound and the Fury*," *American Journal of Mental Deficiency*.
Tournier, Michel, 1972 (1967), *Vendredi ou les limbes du Pacifique*, Paris, Gallimard.
Vauchelles, Coralie, 2004, "Dostoïevski, précurseur du internal monologue?," in *Autour du monologue intérieur*, ed. Philippe Chardin, Paris, Séguier.
Verlaine, Paul, 1962, *Œuvres poétiques complètes*, Paris, Gallimard.
Verlaine, Paul, 1992 (1869), *Fêtes galantes*, Paris, Flammarion.
Verlaine, Paul, 2019, *Paul Verlaine: A Bilingual Selection of His Verse*, trans. Samuel N. Rosenberg, University Park, Pennsylvania State University Press.
Vickery, Olga W., 1964, *The Novels of William Faulkner: A Critical Interpretation*, rev. ed., Baton Rouge, Louisiana State University Press.
Voisin, Jules, 1893, *Idiotie: Hérédité et dégénérescence mentale; Psychologie et éducation de l'idiot*, Paris, Félix Alcan.
Volpe, Edmond L., 2004, *A Reader's Guide to William Faulkner: The Short Stories*, Syracuse, NY, Syracuse University Press.
Wagner-Martin, Linda (ed.), 2002, *William Faulkner: Six Decades of Criticism*, East Lansing, Michigan State University Press.
Wasson, Ben, 1983, *Count No 'Count: Flashbacks to Faulkner*, Jackson, University Press of Mississippi.
Welty, Eudora, 2003, *On William Faulkner*, Jackson, University Press of Mississippi.
Winnicott, Donald Woods, 1971, *Playing and Reality*, London, Tavistock Publications.
Woolf, Virginia, 1970 (1942), *The Death of the Moth and Other Essays*, New York, Harcourt Brace Jovanovich.
Woolf, Virginia, 1988, *The Essays of Virginia Woolf*, vol. 3, *1919 to 1924*, ed. Andrew McNeillie, London, Hogarth Press.
Woolf, Virginia, 1994, *The Essays of Virginia Woolf*, vol. 4, *1925 to 1928*, ed. Andrew McNeillie, London, Hogarth Press.
Woolf, Virginia, 1996 (1925), *Mrs Dalloway*, London, Penguin Books.
Wordsworth, William, 1965, *The Poetical Works*, London, Oxford University Press.
Zeitlin, Michael, Fall 1997–Spring 1998, "Returning to Freud and *The Sound and the Fury*," *Faulkner Journal*.
Zola, Émile, 1989 (1878), *Une page d'amour*, Paris, Gallimard.

INDEX

absence, 8–9, 17, 23–25, 33, 35–36, 40, 42, 48, 51–52, 54, 56, 90, 93, 95, 97, 104, 110–12, 116, 118, 129–30, 134–38, 141, 156, 163, 169, 174, 182, 184, 195, 201–2, 216, 221

abstraction, 36, 46–47, 49, 62, 64, 68–70, 86, 95, 128, 134, 142, 165, 167, 175, 179, 181, 196, 199, 201, 221–22

action, 4, 9, 20–21, 33, 42, 77, 89, 100, 111, 134, 169, 187, 211

aesthetics, 12–15, 61, 77, 128, 192–93, 210, 212, 221

affect, 27, 179, 190

analepsis, 26, 125

analogy, 56, 144, 196

anaphora, 157

Anderson, Sherwood, 20

animality, 37, 120, 122, 132–34, 139

animals, 11, 10, 18–19, 23, 26–29, 34, 36–39, 45, 68, 70, 72, 101–2, 105, 109–11, 113–27, 131–33, 140, 147, 158, 162, 172–73, 181, 194–96, 208

animism, 89, 109

anomaly, 4, 8, 18, 22, 27, 29, 33, 87, 125

apathy, 8, 22, 24, 30, 83

aphasia, 161, 166–68, 181–82, 196

approximation, 175

Aristotle, 36–37, 191–93, 257nn4–5

artifice, 36, 43, 50, 57, 73, 98–99, 103–4, 171, 176, 179, 194

association, 56–57, 103, 142–45, 157, 180, 181

ataraxia, 10

Bachelard, Gaston, 84

Bacon, Francis, 39, 41, 97

Bakhtin, Mikhail, 173–75, 212, 254n21, 256n1

Balzac, Honoré de, 8

Barbaras, Renaud, 257n3

Barthes, Roland, 208–9, 259n5

Bass, Saul, 70

Bataille, Georges, 26, 107, 150–51, 209, 219, 222, 261n1

beauty, 15, 24, 74, 120, 184–85, 201, 213, 217, 222

Benbow, Horace (*FD*, *S*), 76–77

Bergounioux, Pierre, 41, 44, 75–76, 213

Blanchot, Maurice, 77, 177, 182–83, 255n27

Bleikasten, André, 6, 15, 45, 90, 97, 107, 158–59, 184, 229n19, 247n6, 248n11, 259n1

Blotner, Joseph, 5, 56, 119, 148, 155, 223n8, 229n21, 230n4, 251n4

blue (color), 15, 23, 83–86, 97, 102, 107, 110, 113, 115, 126

body, 3, 7, 10, 12, 17–18, 22–35, 52, 62, 66, 75, 87, 91–95, 108, 111, 120, 125–26, 128, 131, 134, 136, 141, 144, 147–50, 166–67, 189, 197, 200, 211, 221

Bond, Jim (*AA*), 37, 158, 217

Bookwright (*H*), 116, 126

Brighella, 11

Brooks, Cleanth, 41

Bundren, Addie (*AILD*), 34–36, 62, 78, 178, 184–85, 199–202, 206

Bundren, Anse (*AILD*), 35, 61–62, 199

Bundren, Cash (*AILD*), 10, 26–27, 62, 199, 206

Bundren, Darl (*AILD*), 10, 26–27, 79, 100, 136, 178–79, 186, 196, 199–201, 206, 208
Bundren, Dewey Dell (*AILD*), 96, 184, 185, 199, 205–8
Bundren, Jewel (*AILD*), 26–27, 79, 99, 100, 199, 206
Bundren, Vardaman (*AILD*), 26, 78, 184–85, 196, 199–200

Canguilhem, Georges, 18
Carmignani, Paul, 134
castration, 28, 52–53, 111, 150, 164
causality, 42, 44, 49, 95, 133, 138, 141–43, 181, 191, 211–12
Cecil, L. Moffitt, 45
chaos, 3, 29, 40, 48–49, 75, 78, 88, 94, 102, 149, 158, 160, 166–68, 190, 208, 213
Chardin, Philippe, 173
Charlie (*SF*), 31, 140, 162, 197
childhood, 6, 8, 12, 15, 18, 29, 32, 44, 52–60, 66, 73, 81, 90–91, 101–6, 110–15, 123, 132, 135–38, 140, 156–58, 162, 181, 185, 189, 196, 202–3, 215
chronology, 48, 52, 216
Cinderella, 111
Coetzee, John Maxwell, 6
coherence, 23–24, 30–31, 56, 92, 104, 166
cohesion, 23–24, 30, 92
Coindreau, Maurice-Edgard, 30, 96
Coldfield, Rosa (*AA*), 174, 198, 201
comedy, 11, 26
communication, 32, 39, 43, 132, 172
comparison, 22, 33, 83, 142, 181–82, 193–96, 209
compulsion, 68
concept, 9–10, 14, 33, 57, 61, 63, 95, 116, 130, 133, 179, 182, 220–22
confusion, 3, 25, 30, 37, 44–45, 55–56, 64, 77, 109, 112, 130–38, 141, 146, 162, 168, 175–76, 190, 196, 203, 214
conjunction, 27, 40, 48, 142, 178, 181
Conrad, Joseph, 51, 81, 83–84, 92
consciousness, 12, 14–15, 30, 42–45, 54–57, 61, 65, 73, 75, 110, 114–15, 128–31, 133, 137, 146–50, 158–59, 168, 170–79, 189–90, 196, 200, 202, 204–5, 210–14, 220, 221, 253n11

contiguity, 47–49, 98, 131, 181
coordination, 30, 47, 95
corruption, 12, 22, 34, 119, 162
Cowley, Malcolm, 17, 216
creation, 4–5, 14–15, 20, 26, 43, 50, 60, 77, 114, 123, 130–32, 166–67, 183, 189–90, 194, 219, 221
creature, 10, 25, 29, 51, 75, 83, 100, 118–19, 121, 158

Danan, Joseph, 169–71
deafness, 32, 38, 47, 76, 137, 189
death, 10, 23, 34, 36, 38, 51–53, 57–58, 62–63, 67, 74, 78–79, 102, 107, 113, 115, 121, 125, 136–38, 143, 161, 170, 178, 185–86, 188, 197–200, 204, 206, 211, 214, 219
Debord, Guy, 148
deformity, 23, 27–28, 171
Deleuze, Gilles, 39, 41, 97, 144, 220–21, 261n4
dependence, 37, 49, 56, 74, 114, 181, 191
Derrida, Jacques, 260n11
Des Forêts, Louis-René, 160, 167, 177, 255n24
desire, 27–28, 39–40, 43, 69, 104–5, 110, 114–23, 131, 140, 159, 161–69, 187, 194, 196–98, 207
Didi-Huberman, Georges, 219
difference, 5, 9–11, 14–15, 17–18, 22, 29, 32–33, 37, 47, 52–55, 58–59, 62, 65–66, 71–74, 79, 88, 90–96, 105–6, 114, 132, 139, 148, 161, 172, 178, 183, 190–96, 198, 206, 209, 220
disarticulation, 49–50, 75, 78
disintegration, 26, 28, 75, 78–79, 139, 182
disorder, 29, 47, 49, 52, 106, 138, 141, 168, 176, 181, 205
dispossession, 7, 84, 102, 114, 157
distress, 37, 72, 112
Dostoevsky, Fyodor, 13, 84, 169
Drake, Temple (*S*), 184
drooling, 23, 28, 39, 126
Dujardin, Edouard, 168–70, 173, 253nn12–14

Eliot, T. S., 75
Emerson, Ralph Waldo, 137, 248n11, 249n15
emotion, 46, 105, 155–56, 163, 198, 202, 209, 222

esthesia, 128
experience, 4, 15, 33–34, 45, 51, 56–57, 66, 72, 90, 112, 118, 123, 129, 137, 141–47, 156, 159, 190, 201–3, 208–9, 212, 221
expression, 6, 23, 28, 30–34, 37, 39, 41–42, 46, 59, 63, 71, 83–85, 98, 138, 140, 147, 159, 163–66, 170–72, 186, 189, 195, 199, 204, 216
expressiveness, 39, 90

failure, 15, 10, 18, 28, 33–35, 40, 47, 77–78, 99, 122, 164–67, 187, 201–4, 215, 218
familiarity, 9, 27, 42, 51, 66, 102, 124, 132, 140–44, 146–48, 150, 161, 169, 179–80, 195, 212, 215
family, 5, 22, 28, 32–33, 37, 53, 57–60, 66–68, 72, 76, 90–91, 104, 110–15, 124–25, 130–39, 155–57, 161, 163–64, 178, 184, 188–90, 197, 204, 206, 216
feeling, 14–15, 31, 33, 37, 42, 44, 56–57, 63, 72, 108, 114, 118, 122, 128, 151, 156, 161–62, 209, 215
fetishism, 10, 110–17, 155, 159, 216
Fitzgerald, Penelope, 85
fixation, 110, 121
flabbiness, 17–18, 20–26, 29–30, 84
flaccidity, 22, 30
Flaubert, Gustave, 9, 65, 74–75, 84
flesh, 17, 22–27, 31–32, 35, 52, 59, 95, 100, 125–26, 129, 136, 182, 202–3
flowers, 21–22, 55, 84–87, 90, 101, 110, 113–15, 136, 180, 182
Fontanier, Pierre, 48, 257n8
Ford, Ford Madox, 83
form, 3–4, 7, 10–11, 15, 26, 28, 30–32, 38–42, 47, 49–52, 56, 58–73, 78, 85, 92, 96–97, 100–102, 114–15, 122–24, 127–29, 133, 141–42, 157–58, 161, 166, 169, 171, 175, 178–79, 184, 188–89, 192–93, 202–5, 210–12, 216, 219
fragment, 75, 93–95, 100–103, 108, 129, 136, 167, 168–69, 171, 208
Frazer, James George, 109
Freud, Sigmund, 12, 58–59, 90, 109, 111, 123, 180, 224n15, 241n2, 242n7, 243n16, 245n39, 246n42
Fromilhague, Catherine, 192–94, 196

Frye, Northrop, 51
Furetière, Antoine, 84–85

gait, 23, 27, 29, 78, 215
Gass, William, 250n26, 254n25
gaze, 24–27, 32, 49, 73, 83–98, 102, 107–8, 110, 123, 128, 136, 139, 146, 168, 186, 206, 208, 215, 220, 222
Genette, Gérard, 43, 69
genius, 6, 76, 155–57, 159, 167, 189
Gibson, Dilsey (*SF*), 28–29, 53–54, 57, 72, 98, 102, 109, 112–14, 143–44, 158, 162, 181, 211, 215
Gibson, Luster (*SF*), 23, 29, 32, 37, 46, 48, 54–56, 65, 89–90, 102, 110, 113–15, 141, 211–12
Gibson, Roskus (*SF*), 52, 136–37, 197
Gide, André, 17
Glissant, Edouard, 138, 142, 184, 217–18, 249n20, 260n11, 260n14, 261n17
Glissant, Paul, 144
God, 3–4, 10–13, 17, 20–23, 28, 37, 40, 83, 85, 91, 102, 113–14, 211
Gray, Richard, 213, 260n13
Green, André, 61, 66
Gresset, Michel, 234n3, 243n21
Grinnup, Lonnie ("Hand"), 25, 27, 38, 136
Guillain, Aurélie, 14, 18, 225n3, 226n5, 231n11, 258n14
Guillemin-Flescher, Jacqueline, 47, 64

Harlequin, 11
Hawthorne, Nathaniel, 245n40
health, 10, 17–18, 123, 147
Hera, 121
heterogeneity, 50, 107, 141, 168, 174, 194
hiatus, 66
hierarchy, 45, 49, 58, 144, 170, 176
Hitchcock, Alfred, 70
Hönnighausen, Lothar, 120
Housman, Alfred Edward, 6–7
Houston (*H*), 116, 118, 121–22, 125
hydropsy, 23, 27–28
hypallage, 193
hyperesthesia, 148

iconoclasm, 45, 74, 120, 190
idealism, 12, 21, 125

idiolect, 42, 221
idios, 17, 76
idiosyncrasy, 8, 14, 17, 25, 42, 45, 47, 107, 126, 149, 179, 201, 218
idiotism, 61
ignorance, 11, 22, 24, 51, 172, 190
Ikkemotube, 67
illness, 9–10, 13, 17–19, 22–23, 54, 103, 136, 147, 150, 174, 186, 212
image, 5, 29, 32–33, 49, 52–57, 61, 67, 70–71, 76, 83, 85, 89, 91, 93, 99, 101, 103, 105–6, 112, 114, 121, 129, 135, 137, 140, 156, 162, 168, 170, 179–81, 188, 200
immanence, 4, 33, 85, 221
immediacy, 33, 35, 43, 45, 62, 66, 87, 128, 130–32, 136, 139, 157, 172, 181, 198
immobilism, 128–29
imperviousness, 3, 32–33, 36, 46, 51, 65–66, 84, 115, 136, 163, 176, 184
impossibility, 31, 36, 41, 44, 46, 50, 58, 60, 63, 66, 79, 103, 146, 166, 172–78, 187, 207
inarticulation, 30–32, 37, 40, 58, 126
incest, 60
incompleteness, 7, 29, 87, 168, 175
indeterminacy, 25, 30, 39, 54, 66, 84, 164, 180, 197
infancy, 29, 32, 108, 111, 137, 162, 188, 219–20
infra-language, 40
injustice, 24, 40
innocence, 7, 12, 23, 57, 69, 83, 85, 101, 103–6, 123, 136, 138, 162, 189–90, 220
instability, 50, 77, 100, 102, 222
instinct, 12, 102, 124, 131–32, 140, 144
intellect, 9, 13, 23, 25, 49, 153
intonation, 46
invention, 14, 43–45, 49, 77, 165–66, 170, 173, 183, 189, 219
Io, 121
Irwin, John, 67–68
Iser, Wolfgang, 210, 214
italics, 53, 55–57, 138
Izambard, Georges, 147

Jakobson, Roman, 181–82, 255n29
James, Henry, 93–94, 100, 254n17
Jauss, Hans Robert, 210, 254n18, 260n10
Joe ("Hand"), 25, 29, 32, 37–38
Jouannais, Jean-Yves, 75, 261n2
Joyce, James, 75, 119, 168, 172–73, 253n16, 255n26
justice, 21, 221
juxtaposition, 38, 47–50, 52, 57, 94–95, 165, 168, 180–81, 198

Kartiganer, Donald, 231n12
Keats, John, 121
Kierkegaard, Søren, 72–73
knowledge, 4, 6, 8, 22, 24, 31–35, 39, 42, 45–46, 52, 54, 64–65, 68, 102, 109, 112, 115, 118, 121–26, 128, 130–37, 143, 147, 149, 166, 168–69, 172, 174, 188, 190–91, 194–95, 198, 204, 206, 208, 211
Kreiswirth, Martin, 41–42

Labove (*H*), 118
language, 4, 7, 10–14, 26, 30–47, 49–50, 59–60, 63–65, 86–87, 98, 110, 117, 129–30, 133, 136, 143, 160, 166, 169, 171–79, 181–86, 189–90, 192–96, 198, 200–204, 208, 210, 214, 219–21
Laplanche, Jean, 110, 224n15
Lencho, Mark, 46, 47
Lévi-Strauss, Claude, 246n43
litotes, 74, 185, 197
Littlejohn, Mrs. (*H*), 38, 122–23, 125
Lodge, David, 259n7
loss, 10, 21, 28, 35, 52, 57, 62, 65–67, 72, 101, 103, 106–7, 110–11, 125–26, 134, 151, 161–63, 178, 182, 201, 203, 208–9, 217, 220
Lotman, Jurij, 64
love, 5, 21, 28, 32, 35, 37, 60, 69, 70–71, 76, 102, 116–27, 137, 146, 156, 165, 169, 170, 203–4, 207–8, 221
Lowry, Malcolm, 85, 148
luck, 22, 62, 118, 234n1, 249n17
Lurie, Peter, 14

madness, 9–10, 121, 136, 148, 201
magic, 72, 89, 97, 102, 109, 111–12, 163, 236n4
Mallarmé, Stéphane, 119, 175
Mallison, Charles, 23, 164–65
Matthews, John T., 14, 241n4, 255n28

McCannon, Shreve (*AA*), 59–60, 174, 198
memory, 28, 35, 47, 53, 57–58, 61, 65–66, 70, 95, 101, 104, 115, 129, 135–38, 141, 158, 161, 165, 181, 195, 197, 202, 204, 209, 210
Meriwether, James, 17, 155
Merleau-Ponty, Maurice, 87, 95, 108, 130, 133–34, 144, 235n1, 236n9, 237n18, 246n2, 248n10, 250n27, 257n3
metaphor, 28, 111, 113–14, 128, 158, 181–82, 196, 199, 207
metonymy, 33, 111, 127, 181–82, 193, 196–97, 199–200
Michaux, Henri, 78, 147–49
Michon, Pierre, 219
mind, 5–7, 10, 12–13, 17–18, 23, 26, 28–29, 34, 36, 40–43, 47, 49, 52, 54–56, 62, 66, 69, 74, 76, 78, 90, 93, 100, 105, 107, 112, 117, 124–25, 134, 136, 138, 147–48, 160–61, 165, 167, 170–72, 175, 177, 179, 181, 192, 204, 207, 210, 213, 220, 221
moaning, 28, 32, 37–40, 42, 102, 105, 138, 190, 197–98
modernism, 14, 42, 50, 74–75, 171
modernity, 11, 13, 50, 74–75, 94, 109, 170–71, 179
Monk, Odlethrop ("Monk"), 17, 23–24, 32–33, 164–65
monologue, 4, 13, 27, 34–36, 41–47, 50, 52–54, 57, 62, 64, 77, 95–96, 99–101, 103–6, 112, 131–32, 137, 139, 140–42, 146, 149–50, 160–61, 168–82, 184, 187, 189–91, 193–96, 199–200, 202–6, 209–14, 217–18
monster, 18
movement, 22, 29, 30, 53, 62, 71, 73, 77, 79, 88, 91–93, 95–96, 101–2, 126, 142–45, 155, 167, 170, 181, 190–92, 197, 200, 202, 211, 222
Munch, Edvard, 41
Musset, Alfred de, 84
muteness, 23, 32, 42–43, 172, 220
Myshkin, Prince, 13
myth, 11–12, 49, 58, 71, 114, 120, 155–56

naïveté, 9, 11, 47, 70, 73, 84, 90, 103, 134, 171–73, 184–85, 189, 197
Narcissus, 7, 114

nature, 7, 10–13, 21, 25, 27–29, 32, 39, 48–49, 51, 54, 71–72, 75, 78, 84, 88, 95, 99, 103, 109–10, 114, 116, 119, 125, 129, 131, 134, 137, 143, 146, 148, 157–58, 166, 169, 171–72, 175–77, 184, 186, 191, 194, 198, 214, 218
New Orleans, 17, 20
Nietzsche, Friedrich, 17–18
norm, 10, 13, 17, 22, 24, 31, 46, 49, 73, 97, 132, 138, 157
normalcy, 3, 4, 8, 10, 17–18, 22, 26, 46, 56, 63, 115, 123, 213, 217
Novak, Phillip, 42
Novalis, Friedrich, 85

object, 4, 25–28, 33, 47, 64, 69, 88–90, 95–97, 99, 103, 109, 110–25, 132–33, 137, 142–46, 161, 163–65, 167, 171, 176–77, 180–82, 184, 186, 189, 191–96, 199, 201, 203, 206
O'Connor, Flannery, 15, 209, 225n20, 247n7
ontology, 31, 56, 73, 85, 133, 151, 177, 182–83, 192, 209, 210
organism, 18, 23, 28, 32, 53

pain, 4, 9, 25–27, 32, 34, 43, 68, 107, 147
palingenesis, 73
Panofsky, Erwin, 94, 99
paradox, 30, 41, 43–44, 50, 71, 79, 84–85, 107, 129, 131, 165–68, 171, 176, 190, 200, 203, 213
paraphasia, 180
passion, 24, 34, 53, 73, 118, 121, 167, 208, 222
passivity, 22–23, 44, 76, 90–91, 125, 150
pastoral, 117
perception, 13–15, 17, 25, 30, 34, 45–50, 56, 58, 65, 84–89, 95–98, 100, 104, 107–9, 112, 128–32, 140–41, 143, 146–49, 157, 160, 168, 170–74, 181, 183, 190–91, 193–94, 201–3, 213, 222
periphrasis, 64, 214
perspective, 8, 10–12, 54, 69, 86, 94–98, 100, 102, 133, 171, 189
Pétillon, Pierre-Yves, 209, 259n16
phenomenology, 60, 63, 65, 86–87, 89, 95–96, 108, 130, 133, 143–44, 180, 183, 186, 190, 196, 212, 214
Pitavy, François, 85, 250n2, 253n10

Plato, 133, 220
pleasure principle, 9, 15, 58–59, 90, 114–15, 123, 136, 147–48, 194, 208–10, 213
poetics, 130
poetry, 5, 14–15, 79, 85, 100, 119, 130–31, 142–45, 147–48, 150, 170, 175, 179–83, 194, 210, 214
Polk, Noel, 42–43, 52, 54, 56, 60–61, 138, 212, 228n12, 237n19, 250n26
polysemy, 33
Pontalis, Jean-Bernard, 110, 224n15
prejudice, 47, 137
presence, 12, 21–22, 33, 38–39, 45, 53–54, 62, 64, 91, 95, 104–6, 124–25, 132, 134, 142, 160, 162, 174, 183, 192–93, 197, 209, 220
present, the, 8, 51–58, 107, 135, 178, 206, 213, 220
primitiveness, 11, 29, 34, 43, 49, 88, 97, 108–10, 115, 222
Prior, Linda, 118
Proust, Marcel, 5, 135, 153
psittacism, 63, 65
Ptolemy, 96
punctuation, 46–47, 56, 150, 198, 202

Ratliff (*H*), 34, 38
reaction, 8, 38, 48, 57, 89, 112, 187
reality, 30, 33–36, 47–50, 58, 64–65, 74, 76, 83–89, 92–101, 103, 105, 111, 115, 120, 128, 130, 133–37, 142, 170, 176, 180, 182–83, 189, 191, 210, 213
reason, 4, 10, 13, 21, 49, 75, 96, 116–17, 124, 129, 134, 136, 171, 181, 183, 190, 197
Reba, Miss (*S*), 6
relation, 3–4, 7–8, 13, 22, 33–36, 46, 50, 59, 61, 63–64, 69, 85, 87, 93–94, 97, 102, 109–10, 115, 128–30, 133–37, 143–45, 162, 176, 180, 184, 191, 194–96, 199, 202, 208, 216, 221
remembrance, 30, 47, 55, 57, 73, 104–5, 135, 165
repetition, 6, 11, 18, 24, 28–29, 32, 34, 38–39, 45–46, 54, 58–73, 76, 87–88, 90, 96, 99–100, 102–7, 110, 113–15, 117, 121, 138–40, 157, 161, 163–64, 167, 178, 180–81, 186, 190–91, 194, 197, 199–200, 204–8, 211, 215, 221–22

Rimbaud, Arthur, 146–48
Romano, Claude, 33–34, 49
rootedness, 4, 10–12, 14, 22, 28, 31, 35–37, 49, 53, 72–73, 87, 95, 128–34, 145–46, 155, 164, 169, 181, 186, 189, 193, 201–2, 213
Ross, Stephen, 34, 52, 54, 138, 212, 254n19, 254n22
Rosset, Clément, 13, 35–36, 130, 134, 136
Rousseau, Jean-Jacques, 11, 220, 225n16
rupture, 11, 39, 42, 44, 50, 66, 75, 137, 158, 168, 173, 179, 208

Sacks, Oliver, 65–66
Sarraute, Nathalie, 250n2
Sartre, Jean-Paul, 9, 53, 57, 85, 136, 260n12
Saussure, Ferdinand de, 33, 182
savage, the noble, 11–12, 121
Savinel, Christine, 13, 41
Schnitzler, Arthur, 173
Séguin, Edouard, 8
sensitiveness, 11, 13, 24, 33, 39, 45, 52, 57–58, 69, 103, 105, 109, 113, 116–17, 128–31, 133–41, 143–44, 147–48, 160, 162, 171, 174, 178, 181, 190–91, 193–94, 210, 213
Serres, Michel, 133–35
sexuality, 203
Shakespeare, William, 40, 157, 176, 204, 207, 252n7, 259n3
shape, 4, 18, 22–26, 32, 35, 61, 70, 74, 87, 97, 99, 100, 103, 110, 115–17, 128, 168, 189, 202–3, 215, 219, 221
shapelessness, 22–25, 28, 75, 79, 84, 126, 219
Shegog, Reverend (*SF*), 98
sight, 17, 21, 57, 84, 88, 90, 92, 117, 124, 128, 132, 134, 139, 168, 191–92, 194, 214, 229
signified, 35, 120, 179–80, 193, 214
signifier, 33, 35, 179, 180
silence, 12, 25, 27, 32, 36–41, 43, 62, 70, 100, 103, 105, 123, 126, 134, 136, 143, 147, 158, 168, 173, 175–79, 183–85, 190, 208, 213, 216, 219
Simon, Claude, 176
singularity, 3, 7, 9, 13–15, 17–20, 28–29, 33–34, 36, 41, 45, 48–49, 52, 60, 72–76, 83, 85–88, 90, 92, 94, 98–99, 108, 118–20, 128, 130–31, 134–35, 138, 145–47, 155–56,

158, 161, 172–73, 175–77, 180, 187, 189–91, 199, 205, 209–11, 215, 218–20
skeleton, 22–24
smell, 35, 57, 64, 69, 76, 91, 93, 102–5, 107, 113–14, 117, 126–27, 130, 132, 134–39, 142, 161–62, 180–81, 193–94, 200, 203
Snopes, Eck (*H*), 127
Snopes, Flem (*H*), 117–18
Snopes, Ike (*H*), 11, 24–25, 28, 30, 32, 34, 37–39, 68–70, 73, 83, 92, 110, 114, 116–27, 130–31, 158, 208
Snopes, Lump (*H*), 32, 123–24
Snopes, Mink (*H*), 125–26, 208
Snopeses, 68, 116–17, 124–25
Sollier, Paul, 8
Sōseki, Natsume, 172–73
sound, 32, 34, 37–41, 62, 65, 72, 75, 77, 88, 90, 100, 105, 115, 117, 126, 133–34, 141, 157–58, 174–76, 181, 185–86, 190–91, 197, 203, 214
space, 22, 35, 39–40, 47–53, 55, 61, 70, 86, 93–99, 102, 107–8, 112, 131–32, 135, 137, 140, 142, 156, 159, 185–86, 189, 192, 213, 217
speech, 4, 6, 11–12, 20, 31–32, 34–37, 40, 43–47, 49, 62–63, 65, 124, 157, 160–62, 164, 169, 173–75, 177, 183, 201, 214
stagnation, 37, 61, 73, 107, 129
Starobinski, Jean, 259n8
stasis, 84, 88, 91, 106–7, 115
Stein, Jean, 24, 37, 43–44, 52, 156, 189, 208, 215
Steinbeck, John, 84, 226n6, 227n11, 227n15, 231n10, 247n8
Stevens, Gavin, 23, 27, 29, 164, 185–86
stimulus, 38
Straus, Erwin, 29, 34, 36, 38, 45, 132, 137, 141
stream of consciousness, 43, 141, 168
subordination, 47, 64, 134
substitution, 110–11, 120, 125, 127, 140, 182–83, 186, 211
suicide, 52, 137–38, 174, 185–86
Sutpen, Thomas (*AA*), 37, 58–60, 149, 198
synesthesia, 128, 131, 139, 141–42, 194, 203
syntax, 45–46, 49, 62, 64, 77, 79, 87, 126, 139, 156–57, 168–69, 171, 174, 178, 181–82, 186, 191, 195, 198, 205–8, 211–14, 222

taboo, 114, 123, 125
temporality, 3–4, 8–10, 13–14, 20, 24–27, 31, 37–38, 40, 43, 47–48, 51–58, 61, 66, 68, 70–73, 78, 88–92, 101–2, 106–7, 109, 113, 116–18, 121–22, 129, 135–37, 141, 143–44, 150, 155, 158, 160–64, 166–68, 172, 180, 182, 184–85, 193, 196, 206–13, 215, 217–19, 220
things, 10, 13, 18, 21, 25–26, 28, 33, 35–37, 43–44, 49–50, 57–58, 60, 64–66, 74–75, 79, 85, 87–91, 93, 97, 102, 104, 107, 110–11, 113, 115, 120, 129–36, 138–39, 142, 144–48, 153, 158, 162–67, 169, 175, 178–83, 186, 188–89, 191–93, 198–202, 204–5, 208, 213–16, 220
Thoreau, Henry David, 12, 84
thought, 5, 17, 23–25, 29–30, 34, 42–43, 51, 55, 67, 83–85, 112, 119–20, 127, 130, 133, 142, 147, 149, 158, 168–69, 173, 179, 188, 195, 211, 221
Thuillier, Pierre, 95, 97
Tournier, Michel, 240n41
tragedy, 40, 51, 89, 118, 121, 126, 203
transcendence, 4, 50, 85, 97, 142, 146, 166, 176, 201
transcendentalism, 12, 137
transgression, 10, 114
transitional objects, 48, 93, 111–12, 115
Tull, Vernon (*AILD*), 26, 96

Uncle Bud (*S*), 6
Uncle Maury (*SF*), 52, 55, 103
understanding, 7, 9, 21, 33–34, 38, 44, 48–49, 57, 63, 65, 78, 83, 89, 102, 105, 116, 123, 129, 131–32, 136–37, 139–41, 162, 164, 173, 178–79, 181, 183–86, 189–90, 196, 198, 205, 208, 211–14
unintelligibility, 7, 31–33, 88, 133, 164

Varner, Will (*H*), 38, 116, 118, 185, 208
Varner Snopes, Eula (*H*, *T*), 118, 185–86, 208
Verlaine, Paul, 18, 250n24
Vickery, Olga, 56–57, 115
virginity, 24, 35, 49, 52, 78, 103, 107, 137, 190, 203, 220
vision, 51, 79, 83, 85–102, 106–9, 112, 117, 126–29, 138–39, 150, 157, 161, 163, 172, 190, 201, 203, 210, 214

voice, 4, 14, 24–25, 34–37, 39–47, 51, 58, 65, 74, 107, 133, 143–44, 146, 150, 155, 157, 161, 168–69, 173–77, 179, 182, 186, 202, 215–16, 219
voicelessness, 14, 25, 36, 38, 40
void, 24, 28, 30, 35, 40, 53, 63, 74, 83–85, 93, 95, 101–2, 104–6, 110, 115, 119, 126, 135, 150, 176–79, 183–84, 201, 213
Voisin, Jules, 7
voyeurism, 32, 116, 123, 126

Wasson, Ben, 55, 155
Watson, Jay, 14
Welty, Eudora, 205
whimpering, 30, 37–40
Whitfield, Reverend (*H*), 124–25
Winnicott, Donald Woods, 111–12, 115
Woolf, Virginia, 17, 74–75, 77, 166, 168, 170–72, 210–11, 260n9
words, 7, 11, 14, 17–18, 22, 27, 33–39, 41–46, 48, 53–54, 60–65, 71, 73, 77–78, 87, 90, 95–96, 98, 103–7, 110, 120–22, 130, 133–38, 150, 158, 160–61, 164–65, 167, 170–80, 183, 186–87, 190, 192, 195, 197–202, 204–9, 211, 214–16, 219, 220–22
Wordsworth, William, 7
world, 3–4, 8–11, 13–14, 20, 22, 24, 26, 30–39, 43, 45, 49–50, 52–55, 61, 65, 68–78, 83–89, 91–100, 102, 105, 107–12, 117–19, 128–40, 144–50, 155, 157, 161, 163, 166–78, 182–83, 186, 188–91, 195, 201–4, 206, 208, 210, 213–14, 220–22
writing, 3–6, 9–11, 13–15, 22, 30, 43, 47, 50, 58, 74, 76–79, 96, 99, 119–20, 128–32, 138, 142, 147–48, 150, 153–59, 164–67, 170–71, 179, 184, 186, 188–90, 193, 196, 199–205, 208–14, 216, 218–22

Yoknapatawpha, 6, 14, 41, 60, 122, 157, 202, 220

Zeus, 121
Zola, Emile, 240n37
zoophilia, 123, 233

ABOUT THE AUTHOR

Photo courtesy of the author

Frédérique Spill is a professor of American literature at the University of Picardy–Jules Verne in Amiens, France. She contributed to *Critical Insights: The Sound and the Fury* (Salem Press, 2014) and to *Faulkner at Fifty: Tutors and Tyros* (Cambridge Scholars Publishing, 2014). She coedited *The Wagon Moves: New Essays on "As I Lay Dying,"* published in 2018 (L'Harmattan), as well as the spring 2018 issue of the *Faulkner Journal*. She's part of the editorial board of the *Faulkner Journal*. *The Radiance of Small Things in Ron Rash's Writing* was published by the University of South Carolina Press in 2019. In 2021, she coedited with Randall Wilhelm a special issue of the *Journal of the Short Story in English* devoted to Ron Rash's short fiction. She has also published articles in French and in English on various contemporary American authors.

www.ingramcontent.com/pod-product-compliance
Lightning Source LLC
Chambersburg PA
CBHW021959220426
43663CB00007B/888